FREEDOM AND ORDER

by Anthony Eden

★

FOREIGN AFFAIRS

Mr. Eden in a jeep with Mr. Churchill at Tunis — summer 1942

Freedom and Order

SELECTED SPEECHES 1939-1946

The Right Honourable
ANTHONY EDEN
M.C., M.P.

HOUGHTON MIFFLIN COMPANY BOSTON

The Riverside Press Cambridge

1948

KRAUS REPRINT CO.
New York
1971

First published, 1947
First published in the United States, 1948

L.C. 48-8656*

Reprinted with the permission of the original publisher
KRAUS REPRINT CO.
A U.S. Division of Kraus-Thomson Organization Limited

Printed in Germany

FOREWORD

Our modern world suffers many grievous wounds. At times, as we seek to probe and cure them, their multiplicity is baffling. We seek to diagnose and classify, and as we do so, the essential remedy becomes clearer—to establish a just balance between freedom and order. This is as true of international as of domestic affairs. At home, a way must be found to reconcile the constructive contribution that a Government can make to our national life with the right of each individual freely to develop his or her own personality. For it is only thus that the individual can make the best contribution to the nation.

This faith is, of course, the antithesis of Socialism with its doctrine of State ownership of all the means of production, distribution and exchange, and its modern addendum of the 'tinker's cuss'.[1]

I tried to express this thought when I spoke at Plymouth in the autumn of 1946.

'The essential problem facing the modern world is to reconcile freedom and order. It is no new problem. It has been with mankind ever since civilization began. To each succeeding age it presents itself in a different form, and each generation must find its own solution. Wherever you may look you will see how in essence this problem, the reconciliation of freedom and order, underlies the struggles and the difficulties of statesmen and governments' (page 426).

In the international sphere we are confronted by the conflicting claims, on the one hand of modern scientific and industrial development, and on the other, of national sovereignty. Within these pages the reader will find repeated reference to the influence that scientific development has played in demonstrating how out of date are some of our political conceptions.

The world has become smaller at a great pace; the physical

---

[1] Speaking at the Electrical Trade Unions' Conference at Margate on 7 May 1947, Mr. Emanuel Shinwell is reported to have said: 'We know that the organized workers of the country are our friends—indeed it could not be otherwise—but as for the rest they do not matter a tinker's cuss'.

action has been too rapid for our processes of political thought. Meanwhile, the number of sovereign states has continued to multiply. This, in itself, would not have mattered much if at the same time there had been a growing acceptance by all of them of rules of international behaviour and of a standard of international law. Of this there is as yet no sign. But it is only by the acceptance of these fundamental truths that we can take account of our smaller world. We may all now live on one village street; we may even understand that we do. Yet we behave, so far as international law is concerned, as though Pekin and Edinburgh were still as far apart as they were a century ago.

Political development has failed to keep pace with modern industrial and scientific development, which knows no frontiers, and yet in the political sphere there is no great divide to be crossed, there is no more reason for the nations to refuse a rule of law now than there was for the warring barons to do so in our own country at the conclusion of the Wars of the Roses. Maybe the barons did not much want to accept such a rule, and only exhaustion compelled them; but are the nations of the world to-day in much better case, and is not the threat that overhangs them if they fail infinitely more intimidating than that which menaced rival feudal houses?

There are certain lessons of the two great Wars which all now accept. No nation, however powerful, can immunize itself against war in the modern world. We have therefore no need to discuss these issues that concern the authority of international law against the conviction of some nations that they can do without it. All now understand that unless a world order can be accepted and enforced the consequence is eventually war, from which all nations must accept to suffer.

The world of to-day is unlikely to be content to live under one ideology or one religion, nor is it necessary for the maintenance of peace that it should do so. What the world must do is to accept certain rules of conduct and restraint in international affairs, and to practise and uphold them. It will be argued that this involves some surrender of national sovereignty. I do not consider that surrender is the right term; merger is more appropriate. What is indispensable is that all should be equal before the law, including the police. For nations to accept restraints upon their individual conduct, when the collective international life would thereby be better ordered, is to surrender nothing. It is not a question of whether we should give up some national prerogatives hitherto jealously guarded, but whether we should join with others in entrusting to wider authorities powers which they alone can use for the benefit of all. When the Act of Union was passed between England and Scotland, no doubt there were many who thought that some sovereignty had been surrendered—there may be some who criticize the existence of Great Britain on those grounds to-day, but can it be disputed that this event, though perhaps in advance of contemporary thought, was essentially in step with our own?

Unhappily there is little enough sign that this lesson has been learned on the wider international plane. No real progress with the acceptance of international law or with the merger of sovereignty can be made unless there is a measure of confidence between the great Powers. Good faith between them must be practised and upheld, for it is only thus that a high international moral standard can be established.

These pages will show how constant was our search during those war years for international confidence between the great Powers who were allies upon the battlefield. War brings about a temporary community of interests between nations which can only too easily be lost around the peace table. The consciousness of this was always in my mind as Foreign Secretary during the war years. I strove to use our contacts and our common cause to build the foundations of peace. So it was that we signed the Anglo-Soviet Treaty. So it was that during the war we first discussed, as far back as the Moscow Conference of 1943, the establishment and powers of the United Nations Organization. Our concern then was never lest we should be drawn further into the camp of one great Power or another, but rather to promote confidence within the triangle and to enlarge it as the liberation of Europe made progress. That is why there was never any question in my mind as to whether we should be more friendly with the United States of America, or with the Soviet Union. That was never the issue. The question was rather whether we could grow to understand each other well enough to agree that we would all accept to obey an international order to the authority of which we would contribute our own strength.

I think it right to set down these reflections in the Preface to these speeches because to-day we are wandering far afield from that endeavour. Perhaps the most unhappy feature of the extravagant invective with which one great Power belabours another in these days is that the process increasingly undermines mutual

FOREWORD

confidence and therefore delays that acceptance by the world of international authority, upon which its survival depends. It must be our prayer and our endeavour to make wiser counsels prevail.

In all of this the British Commonwealth of Nations has a lesson to teach the world. It is not arrogant to say that all its peoples base their government on liberty and their way of life on law. It was not just a coincidence that in September 1939 each of the great Dominions freely took its decision to join with us in defence of international good faith. The Dominions, and the Colonies, and all those who owe allegiance to the King, trod voluntarily the dangerous road with us. They did so because, in the words of one of their soldiers, 'it seems there is a job of work to be done'. There is still a job of work to be done. It demands of us the same qualities as were required in the days of the war: courage, determination, and a sense of service. It requires, too, the same faith that our mission has yet to be fulfilled.

ACKNOWLEDGMENTS

I am deeply grateful to Brigadier A. R. W. Low, C.B.E., D.S.O., M.P., for the arrangement of these speeches and for the valuable notes of contemporary events which provide the essential background.

The reports of the speeches delivered in the House of Commons and reprinted here are taken from the 'Official Report' of Parliamentary Debates in the House of Commons.

I take this opportunity to express my thanks to the Controller of H.M. Stationery Office for permission to reproduce them.

A.E.

CONTENTS

CONTENTS

CONTENTS

1939

I

OURSELVES AND OUR AIMS

Mr. Eden returned to England from his unofficial visit to the U.S.A. on 22 December 1938. On landing he said:

"The last thing we want to do is to entangle other countries in our troubles. At the same time it is surely most important that we should have the fullest information as to the outlook of that great democracy across the Atlantic on the world problems of to-day. It is always healthy from time to time to see ourselves as others see us. If that image is not always flattering, so much the healthier for us."

Throughout the winter the international storm clouds gathered thicker and thicker.

On March 15, the German Army marched into Prague, and Bohemia and Moravia were annexed the following day.

On March 21, Memel surrendered to Germany.

On March 31, Britain guaranteed Poland against aggression.

On April 7, Italy invaded Albania.

During the early months of 1939, Mr. Eden spoke several times on the international situation, both in the country and in the House of Commons. He laid particular emphasis on the importance of trying to secure the best possible relations with the Soviet Government of Russia.

Meanwhile his speeches were not confined to Foreign Affairs. In National Service Rallies, Constituency Meetings and other occasions his theme was the British belief that freedom is the basis of all progress.

Speaking at University College, London, on March 16 he urged upon Youth:

"It is no bad inspiration for the work that lies before you to determine what was good enough for your fathers shall not be good enough for you." But such were the times that: "We shall none of us suceed in building a better Britain unless we can first build a safer Britain."

On May 6, Mr. Eden attended the International Rotary Conference at Brighton, and in his speech said:

We live in uncertain, dark and troubled days. Over men and women everywhere, as they go about their daily business, broods a continuing anxiety. No man can tell what the next day may bring forth in menace, shock or international upheaval. In such conditions there is a natural temptation to a mental fatalism. We are apt to content ourselves with momentary shifts and devices.

Yet it is just at such times as these that we need to be most certain of ourselves and of our aims. The more general the confusion, the more urgent the obligation clearly to set before us the conception of life that we wish to see realized at home, and the form of international order that it is our aim to join in establishing abroad. The successive squalls and sudden buffets which are now the staple weather of international affairs should make us look the more closely into ourselves. As Bacon reminded us long since: "Men ought to know that, in the theatre of human life, it is only for God and angels to be spectators." Through the centuries we in this country have evolved a system of government in which we take pride. In the nineteenth century we were sincerely flattered, for we had many imitators. Our Parliamentary system was adopted and adapted in many lands. That transplanting was far from universally successful; the stranger soil was no doubt sometimes unsuited or the climate unfriendly.

These foreign failures, however, though sincerely regretted, have not in any way affected our own faith in our own methods and in our own traditions, as preserved and developed among English speaking peoples. We have now reached the point where it is generally accepted that the art of government consists in striking a just balance between the claims of the individual and those of the State of which he is a citizen. We do not accept in this country that man is nothing more than an instrument destined blindly to serve the purposes of the State, an unthinking cog in a remorseless machine. On the other hand we do recognize that citizenship carries with it certain obligations of service and we accept and conform to the law. Every time that we obey a regulation, every time that we pay a tax we, to that extent, limit our freedom; but we do so, if not voluntarily, at least consciously conforming to the will of the people as a whole. The mechanical devices by which that will finds expression may not yet be perfect. But the intention is there, none the less, and it is the intention that counts. So it is that there can never be compulsion in this country in any sphere, unless it be based on voluntary consent.

The art of statecraft, as we conceive it, is to give to men and women the fullest opportunity to develop personality in a free self-governing community. It is the duty of the State to seek to better the conditions of life so that every individual personality may have a fair chance to live and grow. We are still far from attaining that ideal, no doubt. There is yet no true equality of opportunity. The slums still exist, even though the mansion has become a rarity; and there is much that is unsatisfactory, much that is unjust and harsh in modern England. But we know whither we would go and have even made some progress.

If in this country we lay so much emphasis on the importance of personality it is because we are convinced that freedom to think, to speak, to write, to experiment and to act, is the essential prerequisite of all progress. At long last we have won the essentials and we will not yield them up. On this issue we cannot be meek. The essence of the matter has been admirably expressed in one of Professor Macneile Dixon's Gifford lectures: "Every man desires to be his own architect, and the creator of his own design, the sentimentalist himself among the rest. And the last and greatest insult you can offer to the human race is to regard it as a herd of cattle to be driven to your secluded pasture. You deprive the individual of his last rag of self-respect, the most precious of his possessions, himself. If you treat him as a thing, an inanimate object, which can be pushed hither and thither, if you treat him as one of a drove of oxen, you take away his birthright, and for this loss nothing can compensate him, not all the soothing syrups and honeys of the world."

No one, I think, in the English-speaking world would challenge for an instant the truth of those sentences.

When we turn to the consideration of the international sphere manifold new problems crowd in upon us. Here, too, there are, however, certain fundamentals in the faith of the British people.

We are convinced that with the aids which science has introduced to us, the nations of the world could, if they would, develop a prosperity in excess of anything that the wealthiest peoples enjoy to-day. It is true that the world's goods are not justly proportioned to-day; probably they never will be. It is also true that one nation can by seizing some part or all of the goods of its neighbour temporarily increase its nominal wealth. Yet the advantage thus derived, if advantage be indeed the right word, is as nothing to the benefits that could be gained by other and very different methods. In modern conditions an aggressor State can plunder the whole world and live a beggar. Some seem bent on travelling that road.

It is not merely because we as a people admittedly hold a position of some advantage in the balance of worldly goods, that we have had more than enough of gangster tactics. If we oppose methods of snatch and grab it is because this practice among nations puts a stop to progress in every sphere. Under our eyes the world now remilitarizes itself physically, mentally and materially. We all put on uniform again. This must seem to many of us a melancholy prospect. The dangers to which it points are the same as those to which other periods of rising armaments have led. As a people there is scarcely any material price we would not pay that war might become as antiquated as duelling, to be hung up as "quite out of fashion, like a rusty nail in monumental mockery".

If we feel this, it is not because the British people are decadent or soft, but because they know that war, when it is not unbelievably degrading, is unspeakably stupid. It is inconceivable that they should glory in war for its own sake. Nor have we as a people any quarrel with any other peoples on the earth's surface. Left to themselves, would this not be wellnigh true of the peoples everywhere? This influence is at the same time the one element that gives us a reasonable hope. Against this we have to set certain conceptions of statesmanship. "Everyone admits", wrote Machiavelli, "how praiseworthy it is in princes to keep faith, and to live with integrity, and not with craft. Nevertheless our experience has been that those princes who have done great things have held good faith of little account, and have known how to circumvent the intellect of men by craft, and in the end have overcome those who have placed reliance on their word." Whatever may be thought of the truth or otherwise of Machiavelli's contention as a statement of historical fact, the greater interdependence of the modern world, the constant contacts, the reduction and indeed the virtual elimination of the problems which distance once created, have rendered the conduct of international affairs on such a basis impossible. So it is that our first need now is of a return to good faith between nations. Without it international society, like human society, can only drift into ever-widening confusion.

It is not a question of morality only, but of the plainest practical politics. Whatever success has attended this gospel of Machiavelli, up to date, its scope has now been clearly limited, a warning has been uttered, and precautions have been taken. Let there be no mistake about that. We now know that the world can only keep the peace if its rulers will learn a like language, practise the same philosophy and keep an open faith.

2

IN PARIS—JUNE 1939

May 10. The Prime Minister reported progress in negotiations with Russia and a Debate took place on May 19 in the course of which Mr. Eden stated again that it was his conviction that it would be a gain for peace, to the advantage of Russia and of Europe, that an understanding should be speedily arrived at between France, Russia and Great Britain.

May 12. Anglo-Turkish Agreement announced.

May 18. Military Training Bill passed third reading in the House of Commons.

May 31. Russia expressed herself still unconvinced of Britain's good faith.

On June 15 Mr. Eden spoke at *Les Conférences des Ambassadeurs* in Paris in the Théâtre de Marigny with M. Reynaud in the chair. The next day at the request of the organizers of the Conference he repeated the speech, when M. Herriot took the chair. The speeches were delivered in French.

Monsieur le Ministre, Excellence, Mesdames, Messieurs. Je vous suis très reconnaissant de l'accueil que vous m'avez réservé, et des termes éloquents et amicaux dont s'est servi Monsieur Paul Reynaud pour m'exprimer vos sentiments de bienvenue. C'est pour moi un très réel plaisir de me trouver à Paris. Croyez bien que ce n'est pas là un compliment conventionnel, mais l'expression sincère d'un sentiment que j'ai toujours éprouvé pour votre belle capitale. C'est toujours un plaisir de venir à Paris, non seulement à cause de ce qu'est Paris, mais aussi à cause de ce que Paris représente dans le monde. Et cela n'a jamais été plus vrai qu'aujourd'hui où si peu de pays honorent et pratiquent la courtoisie, la tolérance et la liberté comme vous savez le faire.

Songer à la France c'est se rappeler ces lignes de Shakespeare —lignes que je n'oserai essayer de traduire.

'Age cannot wither her, nor custom stale her infinite variety.'

Je me suis laissé dire que dans vos Conférences, il est d'usage que le conférencier fasse à son public des révélations sensationnelles sur les secrets de son passé. Je veux dire, naturellement, de son passé politique. Permettez-moi de le déplorer, car, malheureusement, mes secrets politiques vous sont déjà connus, ainsi que mes convictions politiques.

Vous savez, par exemple, que j'ai toujours été convaincu qu'une amitié franche et une entente solide entre nos deux pays figurent au premier rang des conditions indispensables du maintien de la paix. Il n'est aucune phase de l'histoire de l'après-guerre qui n'ait, selon moi, vérifié ce grand principe de la politique européenne, et les évènements des dernières années ont achevé d'en confirmer la certitude. Lorsqu'une solide et sincère amitié unit nos deux pays, on peut bâtir sur cette amitié une politique commune qui est capable d'exercer sur les destinées de l'Europe une influence stabilisatrice considérable. Inversement, de nos désaccords n'est jamais résulté et ne résultera jamais rien de bon, ni pour aucun de nous, ni pour la paix. Certes, de ce que nous sommes d'accord, il ne s'ensuit pas nécessairement que nous ayons raison. Et je n'entends pas soutenir que les pensées auxquelles nous nous sommes arrêtés ensemble, que les actions que nous avons décidées ensemble ont toujours été bien inspirées. Une chose en tout cas est certaine, comme tout le monde aujourd'hui s'en rend compte: quand ils sont d'accord, nos deux pays peuvent commettre des erreurs, mais, s'ils ne sont pas d'accord, aucun des deux ne peut poursuivre séparément une politique quelconque de quelque durée. L'amitié qui existe entre nous, Français et Anglais, cette amitié qui grandit tous les jours, procède à la fois de nos volontés et de la nécessité. Le mariage de John Bull et de Marianne est à la fois un mariage de cœur et un mariage de raison. Et c'est pour cela qu'il ne saurait exister de liens plus forts, ni plus sûrs.

Et ici permettez-moi d'ouvrir une courte parenthèse. Si nous voulons que la politique de nos deux pays aboutisse aux résultats que nous espérons, cette politique doit être quelquechose de plus qu'une politique vaguement, ou même fermement défensive. Elle doit être stimulée par la poursuite d'un but commun, dont cette défensive ne saurait être que le moyen et la garantie. Nous aussi, nous devons avoir un programme, que nous ne devons pas craindre de proclamer, de soutenir et, si possible, d'appliquer. Nous devons faire savoir partout, nous devons faire connaître à tous les peuples, le monde que nous voudrions créer, et que c'est un monde où il y a place pour tous.

Mais l'objet de cette conférence est moins ambitieux, et je me contenterai d'esquisser devant vous, avec le détachement qui n'est permis qu'à ceux qui n'ont aucune responsabilité officielle, un panorama de l'Europe de 1939 et de vous décrire rapidement l'attitude de mon pays à l'égard des problèmes actuels.

Nous avons, comme vous, une haine profonde de la guerre. Cette haine de la guerre ne peut en vérité qu'être partagée par tout homme civilisé. La guerre, c'est la destruction, la brutalité, la réaction. Elle inflige d'atroces souffrances à l'esprit, au corps et à l'âme; pour des hommes d'Etat dignes de ce nom, c'est un terrible aveu d'échec ou d'impuissance. Il s'ensuit que la haine de la guerre doit toujours jouer un rôle important dans l'orientation des politiques de nos deux pays. Au cours des années qui viennent de s'écouler, on a essayé à plusieurs reprises de traduire ces sentiments sur le plan des réalités politiques, par exemple en créant la Société des Nations, ou encore en signant, ici, à Paris, le Pacte Briand-Kellogg qui porte le nom de l'un de vos hommes d'Etat les plus éminents. Il faut reconnaître qu'à l'heure actuelle, l'autorité de la Société des Nations est tristement réduite, et que certains actes récents de certains gouvernements constituent une violation flagrante du Pacte de Paris, qui pourtant porte leur signature aussi bien que les nôtres. Pour ma part, je conserve entière la conviction que les principes sur lesquels reposent le Pacte de la Société des Nations et le Pacte de Paris sont justes, et qu'ils sont vraiment indispensables à l'organisation pacifique du monde. Déjà les plus sceptiques sont forcés d'avouer qu'il nous faut y revenir. Un jour le monde comprendra combien est vraie, sur le plan international aussi bien que sur le plan national, la fameuse maxime de Pitt: 'Où finit la loi, commence la tyrannie.'

En attendant, une distinction essentielle s'impose. Les peuples de France et de l'Angleterre sont profondément pacifiques. Ils aiment la paix pour elle-même, et parce qu'ils ont foi dans le progrès humain, lequel ne peut exister sans la paix. Ils détestent donc la guerre. Mais une chose est détester la guerre, autre chose la craindre. Aucune politique fondée sur la peur, aucune politique faisant appel à la peur, n'est une politique qu'un grand peuple puisse adopter sans se condamner à déchoir. Une politique de ce genre n'est pas en tout cas de celles que le peuple britannique envisage en ce moment. Il importe que personne, nulle part, ne nourisse à ce sujet la moindre illusion.

La reine Elizabeth, qui fut un de nos plus grands souverains, fut aussi de ceux qui aimèrent le plus la paix. Mais cet amour de la paix ne l'empêcha pas de faire dire un jour à un monarque étranger: 'L'Angleterre n'a pas besoin d'implorer la paix.'

Certes nous préférerions vivre dans un monde où l'ordre régnerait entre les nations. Tous les peuples, dans tous les pays, préféreraient incontestablement qu'il en fût ainsi. Malheureusement les peuples sont enfermés à l'intérieur des frontières; ils ne peuvent communiquer librement, pas plus qu'ils ne peuvent exprimer librement leur volonté. D'autre part si l'on pouvait mettre sur pied un ordre international, si un accord réglementant les armements était signé, contrôlé, observé, il n'y a aucun doute que nous serions, quant à nous Anglais, tout disposés à contribuer—et à contribuer sans lésiner—à l'œuvre commune. Malheureusement on ne saurait nier que tous les Gouvernements ne partagent pas notre manière de voir. Certains d'entre eux ressemblent aux quêteurs de la 'Chasse au Snark' de Lewis Carroll: 'Ils ramassent l'argent des autres, mais eux, ils ne donnent rien.' Ce procédé est de ceux, surtout quand y ajoute la contrainte, qu'on ne saurait tolérer indéfiniment. C'est pourquoi la quasi-unanimité du peuple britannique a maintenant accepté—on pourrait presque dire: a demandé—qu'un Front de la Paix fût constitué pour résister désormais à tous actes d'aggression. On ne saurait exagérer l'ampleur et l'importance de la révolution qui vient ainsi de s'opérer dans la politique étrangère de la Grande-Bretagne. Elle a été soudaine, mais elle a été totale, à tel point qu'il serait difficile de lui trouver des précédents dans notre longue histoire.

Il est vrai que cette politique avait depuis longtemps dans mon pays des partisans sincères et convaincus, mais ils n'étaient qu'une minorité. L'automne dernier leur nombre s'est sensiblement accru de ceux que les évènements avaient achevé de convaincre, et qui se sont joints à eux pour demander avec insistance qu'on entreprît sans délai l'effort maximum d'organisation et de mobilisation de nos ressources en hommes et en richesses que leur paraissait exiger le salut de la paix. Mais, même alors, et quelque fondé que fut leur jugement, ils ne constituaient pas encore la majorité. L'entrée des Allemands à Prague a accompli d'un seul coup ce qu' aucune des violences ou menaces de violence antérieures n'avait réalisé. Maintenant nous sommes unanimes. Nous sommes tous d'accord, à quelque parti que nous appartenions et quelles qu'aient été nos préventions du passé. Et revenir en arrière est devenu impossible.

La plus grave erreur que pourrait commettre l'étranger serait de sous-estimer la fermeté de la volonté présente du peuple britannique. Emerson a dit de nous: 'Je trouve que l'Anglais est, de tous les hommes, celui qui se tient le plus fermement dans ses souliers.' Telles sont incontestablement les dispositions qui prévalent en ce moment chez nous. Dieu veuille que personne n'en doute.

Les garanties que nous avons donneés en Europe Orientale et Sud-Orientale n'ont pas été données à la légère. Aussi bien ne saurait-il y avoir de témoignages plus clairs de notre résolution que l'effort, vraiment remarquable, que nous sommes en train d'accomplir dans le domaine des armements.

Le programme de réarmement intensif accompli au cours des dernières années a déjà amené notre marine à un degré de puissance considérable. Loin de ralentir, notre effort se poursuit à une cadence sans cesse accélérée. A l'heure actuelle l'Amirauté a en construction plus de 200 navires de guerre représentant un total d'environ 600,000 tonnes. Pour cette année, les dépenses prévues au département de la Marine se montent à £150 millions, soit 26 milliards, 400 millions de francs. C'est la somme la plus considérable qu'un Parlement britannique ait jamais votée en temps de paix pour notre armement naval.

En ce qui concerne l'aviation, la production a maintenant atteint un chiffre très élevé, que le Gouvernement, et à mon avis très justement, ne désire pas rendre public. Vous pourrez cependant avoir une idée du développement de notre puissance aérienne si je vous dis que les effectifs de l'Armée de l'Air qui étaient en 1934 de l'ordre de £30,000 s'élèveront cette année a 118,000.

Enfin dans le domaine de l'Armée de terre, vous savez l'effort que nous sommes en train d'accomplir. Peut-être ne savez-vous pas que les crédits pour l'Armée dépassent cette année de £10 millions (soit près d' 1 milliard 800 millions de francs) les crédits pour la Marine.

Mais sans doute est-ce dans le domaine des effectifs que notre effort militaire prend sa plus grande signification. En quelques semaines, l'armée territoriale a été quasiment doublée. Vous savez, vous Français, combien serait mal inspiré quiconque sous-estimerait la qualité et la valeur de ces volontaires. De plus, nous venons d'instaurer le service militaire obligatoire. Il n'est pas douteux que la nation dans son ensemble approuve cette mesure, comme une contribution à la consolidation de la paix qu'exigeait

25

la gravité de la situation. J'aimerais vous expliquer rapidement les raisons de cette décision que vous me permettrez de qualifier de sensationnelle. Ce n'est pas que nous avions douté de pouvoir lever, sur la base du volontariat, une armée considérable, comme nous l'avons fait il y a vingt-cinq ans. Le peuple britannique—et ceci s'applique à tous les partis—n'a jamais montré un esprit plus élevé de décision et d'abnégation. Mais il est apparu que si nous n'adoptions pas le service militaire obligatiore, certaines nations auraient douté de notre résolution. Et rien n'était plus nécessaire que de dissiper ces doutes. C'est pour cela que nous avons accepté le bouleversement de nos traditions comme nous sommes prêts à accepter tous autres que les circonstances pourraient exiger. Car nous pensons que c'est seulement de cette manière que nous pouvons contribuer le plus efficacement à empêcher la guerre.

Voltaire nous a donné depuis longtemps la réponse—vous vous souvenez des propos de Jacques en *Candide*:

'Il faut bien, disait-il, que les hommes aient un peu corrompu la nature, car ils ne sont point nés loups, ils sont devenus loups. Dieu ne leur a donné ni canon de vingt-quatre, ni baionettes; et ils se sont fait des baionettes et des canons pour se détruire.'

Eh bien, voila où nous en sommes.

Où tout cela nous menera-t-il? Nous savons que dans une lutte de longue durée, les ressources dont nous disposons en fait de richesses, de matières premières et aussi sans doute d'effectifs, doivent nous assurer finalement une grosse supériorité. Mais cette supériorité ne nous suffit pas: nous aimerions mieux ne pas avoir à en faire la preuve. Ce ne sont hélas! partout que bruyants préparatifs de guerre à un rythme de plus en plus accéléré. Il ne faut pas cependant considérer la catastrophe comme inévitable. On a encore le temps de s'arrêter sur la pente fatale, et de comprendre. A coup sûr, personne ne peut plus, maintenant, se méprendre sur la résolution de la France et de l'Angleterre. On commettrait la plus tragique des erreurs, si, en s'obstinant à ne pas vouloir se rendre compte de notre sincérité et de notre détermination, on se lançait dans des aventures de violence qui déclencheraient la guerre générale.

Si, au contraire, on reconnaît enfin que désormais l'aggression ne peut plus être une bonne affaire, alors enfin nous nous trouverons engagés sur la voie d'une paix durable. L'arbitrage, la conciliation, l'établissement d'un ordre international, la limitation et la réduction des armements; telles sont les méthodes du vrai progrès vers la paix. Le monde s'en détourne. Ne pouvons-nous y revenir aujourd'hui, avant qu'il ne soit trop tard?

3

THE INTERNATIONAL SITUATION
IN JULY

During the spring and summer there had been a number of appeals for political unity at home. Mr. Eden called for it himself in a number of his speeches.

At the beginning of July there were reports of demands that Mr. Churchill and Mr. Eden be included in the Cabinet, and part of the Daily Press backed these demands.

Mr. Eden continued to support a campaign in the country to put vigour into the drive for recruits and armaments.

From mid-July onwards, German troops infiltrated into the town of Danzig.

On July 31, in the last Foreign Affairs Debate before the summer adjournment, Mr. Eden spoke on the Far Eastern as well as the European position. The Prime Minister had spoken earlier, defending the Government's foreign policy.

I am happy that it falls to my lot to express the congratulations of all hon. Members to the hon. Member for North Cornwall (Mr. Horabin) on his maiden speech. I am sure that is no mere empty and formal compliment. We all appreciate the modesty and sincerity with which the hon. Member spoke, and we all hope that in the months and years to come we shall have the privilege of hearing him often in our Debates.

This is the first Debate we have had on foreign affairs for a very considerable period, and I think no one in any part of the Committee has taken exception to the Debate taking place. I feel that it has been worth while if only to obtain from my right hon. Friend the Prime Minister the very direct and forthright statement of policy to which we listened. I think that the observations which he made, by their very frankness, particularly in connection with the Russian negotiations, cannot but do good. I shall have a few words to say about Russia in a moment, but I should like now to say that I do not think it was quite fair—and I do not think my right hon. Friend intended to do this—to blame hon. Members in connection with the Russian negotiations, for in truth the rumours that have appeared from day to day were not statements made by any of us, or even to us, but were made in various sections of the Press. However, I think that the terms which my right hon. Friend used with regard to the Russian negotiations and with regard to the Far East will render a definite service in an extremely delicate international situation.

We have been reminded of the delicacy of that situation. It is difficult, anxious and, in my judgment, menacing. There is no improvement and no relaxation of the tension; nor, I think, can any of us expect such a relaxation in the coming weeks. False optimism would be as unjustified to-day as anything in the nature of jitters, which is not existent among the British people. My right hon. Friend has appealed to us that we should not in these delicate conditions say anything to make the existing problems sharper still, and for my part, I need hardly say that I shall do my utmost to respond to that appeal. Indeed, in what I shall say, I shall seek only to put to my right hon. Friend and the Government certain concrete suggestions which in the present international situation have been brought to my mind. If the situation is—as we admit it is—one of unrelieved gravity, that does not mean that there are not actions which the Government could perhaps take which would assist to better it. I will begin with an observation or two about the Far East.

What are the realities of the Far Eastern situation? Amid all the conflicting evidence and the conflicting claims, there is one reality which is surely abundantly plain to all of us, and that is that Japan has failed to conquer China. The end of that war is now even more remote than it was when the war began some two years ago. Indeed, since the fall, last October, of Hankow and Canton, Japan has made no progress, not even in the narrowest military sense of the term "progress". On the contrary, since those events last autumn from all the information which comes to us—I expect the Government will be able to confirm this—the Chinese morale and power of organization have made a most remarkable recovery. In the territory which remains to them, they have not only reorganized their armies, but they are even reconstructing their industry. China has adjusted herself to new conditions in a manner which calls for a warm tribute of admiration from all of us. I cannot help feeling that there are many in Japan who thought in the early days that the war would be profitable and soon over, who must now be deeply regretting their error of judgment. Therefore, I repeat that in the Far Eastern situation the first reality is that Japan can never wholly conquer China.

The second reality is that Japan having failed to complete her military victory, is seeking for some other way to obtain the same or similar results, and in seeking for that way, she is now attempting to bring about the collapse of the Chinese currency. The aim of Japan is to secure the assistance or connivance of this country in that attempt. I was delighted to hear the categoric terms in which my right hon. Friend the Prime Minister dealt with that situation this afternoon. There is very little doubt in my mind that the demand for the silver in Tientsin, which is held by our banks and the French banks in the Concession, and the demand that we should substitute the Japanese currency for the Chinese dollar in use in the Concession, are aimed at trying to weaken the Chinese currency and to obtain by that means the results which Japan has failed to achieve by military action. It is obvious that this country could have no lot or part in such an action. To modify our policy at the dictates of a foreign Power is exactly what my right hon. Friend said he was not prepared to do, and to agree to join in such a movement as that would be gravely injurious to our interests not only in China, but throughout the East, India, Malaya, and everywhere.

There is one question I should like to put to whoever is going to reply to the Debate for the Government. The Prime Minister has made it quite plain that we stand firm in our intention not to assist in any attempt to weaken the Chinese currency. I hope the Government will go a little farther than that and make it plain, perhaps when the Debate is wound up, that not only will we not connive in any attempt to weaken the Chinese currency, but we shall continue the policy on which we have hitherto been engaged of doing all we can to support the Chinese currency itself.

Something has been said about the negotiations which have been going on in Tokyo. I shall not attempt to examine the formula or discuss those negotiations in detail. Frankly, I do not think it particularly helpful to do so while they are taking place. In the end, that formula and any other negotiation will be judged by what has happened, and the first condition, it seems to me, of any improvement in relations between this country and Japan, is the cessation of the anti-British activities which are at present being stimulated by Japan in China. If Japan truly wants our friendship she cannot expect—no country can expect—to have it, while she is engaged in activities of that kind. So far, the conversations have not had that result. The blockade at Tientsin continues and apparently food supplies, even to Hong Kong, are being interfered with.

I am sure that when my right hon. Friend replies he will make it plain, as I think the Prime Minister made it plain just now, if I understood him aright, that any friendship with us depends on the cessation of those activities and a reversal of the present attitude of Japan. If that does not take place we in this country do not lack action that we can take. The United States have shown us what form that action might take. There are some of us who wish that the action which the United States has taken had been taken on our part when the Tientsin blockade began. That is a matter for argument but what is certain is that the Government will receive the support of every section of opinion in this country, if they find it necessary to speak in those plain terms to the Japanese Government.

I turn from that subject to say a word about Russia. I do so with some temerity, because I know of no subject which is more prickly and more productive of controversy in all quarters of the House. But we have not this afternoon to discuss whether we want an agreement with Russia or not. That has been decided some time ago. It is the Government's declared policy that they do wish for such an agreement. My right hon. Friend has reiterated that with considerable vehemence this afternoon and what I desire to concern myself with now is the question of machinery. Accepting the position that we do want this agreement with Russia, is there anything further we can do which will enable us to bring it about? It must be admitted that these negotiations have pursued a somewhat strange course. I was delighted to hear my right hon. Friend speak of the decision to send this military mission—military in the widest sense—to Moscow. I agree that it is an unusual proceeding. I agree also that it is calculated to help to remove mistrust and that is why I, for my part, most warmly welcome it.

These negotiations with Russia are always being forecast either in this country or in Paris as just about to finish but they never seem quite to reach their end. Indeed in this connection I am reminded of La Rochefoucauld's definition of love and ghosts—everybody is always talking about it but nobody has ever seen it. We hope despite that, that we very soon shall see it, in this case. For my part, I wish that two months ago the Government had made up their mind to send the most authoritative mission possible to Moscow and that they had put at the head of that mission some political personality who could negotiate directly with the remarkable man who is head of the Russian Government to-day in everything except name. If that mission could then have been accompanied by military, naval and air advisers so much the better, but where doubts and suspicions have to be allayed—and everybody knows that they exist—personal contact can be more effective than the exchange of diplomatic notes however skilfully drafted. There are times when an hour's talk may be worth a month of writing. I wish that step could have been taken.

I have long believed, as the Committee know, that there are no fundamental divergencies of interest between us and the Russian Government. I am speaking of exterior political circumstances and not at all of our internal politics with which we are not, as I see it, concerned in this connection. There is nowhere on the earth's surface any reason why those interests should conflict, but there is this long legacy of suspicion which, particularly in the case of Russians, is by no means easily removed. In conclusion, on this subject I would ask the Government, since they are now going to send a military mission to Moscow, if there are still political difficulties and if the Government still feel those difficulties to be formidable even now, that they should enlarge this military mission and make it a political mission as well. Why should we not arrange it so that not only will our generals talk to the Russian generals but that there will also be someone who can talk to M. Stalin and see if we cannot finish the whole thing in one week? I know that that is asking much, but I cannot help feeling that a direct approach to the men concerned is more likely to produce results than other methods. I know how difficult it is, but I would beg of the Government, at this time, that they should give consideration to that proposal.

May I say something now about the situation in Danzig? My right hon. Friend said he stood by the declaration which he made the other day. That declaration received the endorsement of every section of this House, and, if I may say so, I thought it could not

3

have been improved by one word or comma. The truth is that there is no Danzig issue in the narrow sense of the term. What does exist is an issue concerned with the future independence of Poland. Germans in Danzig to-day do not undergo any servitude, except that servitude which they care to impose upon themselves. The city is ruled by the Nazis; they have suppressed all other political parties and all other newspapers, they have expelled the Jews, and they do exactly as they like, as regards internal affairs.

As to the actual system which now exists I would like to say this. There have been many critics of the Versailles settlement in respect of Danzig. My right hon. Friend the Chancellor of the Exchequer and I have had, perhaps, rather more to do with the working of that system than anybody else. I have no particular reason to defend the Treaty of Versailles. I have been accused of many misdeeds but nobody has ever said that I drafted that Treaty. But I can say, and I think the Chancellor of the Exchequer will bear me out in this, that that system, though not ideal, is definitely workable, if there be the will to work it. We have to remember that at Versailles the Powers were faced by two conflicting demands which could not be wholly reconciled. Poland wished Danzig to be included in her territory and Germany wished to retain Danzig in her territory.

All through the centuries there has been this problem of Danzig's special position, and it seems to me that the solution which the Powers, when they made the Peace Treaty, sought to work out, was by no means unreasonable. It gave Danzig its own life and it gave Poland its own port. Let us not forget that without that port Poland's life could hardly be maintained. The Fourteen Points of President Wilson, which Germany herself is so fond of acclaiming, recognized Poland's right to a secure outlet to the sea. Therefore I say that there is no narrow Danzig issue. If you like there is the issue of the so-called Corridor. Dr. Goebbels has tried to link it up with Danzig but in point of fact the Corridor has always been Polish in population and if you were to deprive Poland of the Corridor and of the use of Danzig, then, I repeat, that country's life would be placed in jeopardy.

As we watch these manoeuvres is it possible to escape the conclusion that we are being confronted with exactly the same technique as that which was used last year? The object is exactly the same. Nobody can foretell precisely what the tactics will be in the next few weeks. No doubt there will be many moves. We shall be lulled and soothed, we shall be threatened and provoked, but in essence the Nazis' purpose remains the same—to impose upon

Poland this year the fate which they imposed upon Czechoslovakia last year. To counter this, the Government have embarked upon their policy of the Peace-Front and are seeking to build up that front. It is useless to argue now whether that is the right line to take or not. The decision was taken last March after the German troops entered Prague and, for my part, I am convinced that no other policy stands a chance of averting war under present conditions. That has been confirmed by the Foreign Secretary in his recent speech and by my right hon. Friend to-day.

There cannot be any turning back and there will be no turning back. My right hon. Friend's speech made that clear. What then is the best contribution that we can make? I come back to the statement that the purpose of the Government's policy is not to win a war but to avert it. Therefore the best contribution that we can make is to complete this Peace-Front at the earliest possible moment. On that basis we shall be in a position to act, to speak, to negotiate with greater freedom. Once every would-be aggressor in Europe can be compelled to recognize that aggression cannot for the future pay, it may be that then, at last, we shall enter upon the long and difficult road to a lasting peace.

4

THE MOOD OF BRITAIN AT THE END
OF AUGUST 1939

(I) IN THE HOUSE OF COMMONS—AUGUST 24th

Ribbentrop went to Moscow to sign the Non-Aggression Pact
with Russia on August 22. The pact was signed on August 24.

Mr. Eden went to camp on August 13 with the 2nd Bn. The
Rangers (K.R.R.C.) the T.A. battalion of which he was Second-
in-Command, but he was back in the House of Commons when
Parliament was recalled on August 24. The Emergency Powers
Bill passed through both Houses in one day. In the course of a
Debate on the International situation, Mr. Eden said:

It is not my intention to delay the House for more than a few
moments. As I conceive it, this is an occasion upon which we
must each of us try to contribute something to the expression
of that national unity which undoubtedly exists in the country at
this time. We all appreciate the sincerity with which the hon.
Member for Bridgeton (Mr. Maxton) has expressed his point of
view. He is not alone in hating war. That is an issue upon which
we all join. Nor is he alone in believing that the continuance of a
state of war is the continuance of a state of barbarity. Indeed,
man's whole effort in creating civilization has been an effort to
attempt to build up some system of international order which will
make it impossible for us to lapse into a state of barbarism. But
if it is true that it takes two to make a quarrel, it is also true that
it takes two to make a peace. I have tried in vain to see any small

indication of reciprocity, however many concessions we may make, however far we may go along the path to meet the demands. Surely recent experience has shown us that the only result is more demands, more unjust and more ruthless demands, at the expense, not of ourselves, perhaps, as yet, but of other people.

As I conceive it, the House has met to-day not in a mood of demonstration, still less of recrimination, but rather in a mood of sober resolution. The Prime Minister's declaration has, I believe, voiced the feelings of the people of this country. The situation with which we are faced is, in my judgment, as grave and as perilous as any that this country has faced at any time in its history. I say that deliberately. Everywhere in the world where peoples are still free they are at this moment asking the question—Does this mean war? I believe that at the moment the gravest danger of war lies in the belief of the German people, a belief which has been fostered by every means of a powerful propaganda machine, that whatever action the German Government may take against Poland will not result in war with this country and France. I believe, also, that in signing this Pact with Russia the German Government have made the gravest miscalculation. They appear from their own declarations in their own Press to believe that as a consequence of that Pact we should go back on our pledge to Poland. That is unthinkable; and the Prime Minister has made that plain. Indeed, the leaders of the German people would appear to know little of our history if they are unaware of the fact that the greater the odds and the greater the difficulties which the British people have to face, the stronger becomes their determination to stand by those to whom they have pledged their word.

The Prime Minister said that he did not want to take any action in a military sense which might be regarded as provocative. I think we shall all endorse that but I would add this. I do not believe that the chief danger of war lies in that. I believe that the chief danger of war still lies in the German refusal to believe that we are in earnest in what we say, and, therefore, I say that if any action can be taken in a military sense, such action would only add to the deterrent value of the statements which have been made. There are many things that could be done. I think there is another danger, and not having the responsibility of office I do not see why I should not state it. It is possible that there are at this moment many people in Germany who believe that in the event of hostilities with Poland they may in a few short weeks or months obtain their military objectives in the East, and that, having done that, they appear to believe that we should take no further interest in the matter. If there are any who really think that, they are making the greatest error in history. Having given our pledge and repeated it, there can be no turning back.

Before the House adjourned we had a foreign affairs Debate in the course of which I ventured to forecast that it would not be very long before the Danzig issue was broadened to include the issue of the Corridor and other large areas of Poland. And so it has been. The methods which have been employed are exactly the same as those which were employed against Czechoslovakia last year. Step by step and stage by stage the subjugation of Poland has been the object, and if that process is continued, if we do not join with others to resist it now, who can doubt that there will be yet another victim next year? While it is fearful to have to contemplate the use of force, I am convinced that the attitude of a large and overwhelming majority of the House endorses that determination as the only means by which at this late hour we may save Poland, and also save our children from what some of us went through in the years gone by.

(II) A BROADCAST TO U.S.A., AUGUST 30

August 24. President Roosevelt appealed to the King of Italy to maintain the peace and a day later he sent two appeals to Hitler.
August 28. France closed the German frontier.
On August 30, Mr. Eden broadcast to the U.S.A. and said:

I deeply appreciate the compliment paid to me by this invitation to broadcast to the people of the United States this evening. At the same time you will, I feel sure, all understand me when I say that the task has its difficulties. Certainly none but the rashest and most impulsive of mortals would try to forecast the international future at this time. I, at least, do not propose to make any such attempt, nor is the moment one at which it is possible to essay any reasoned appreciation of the foreign policies of the Powers principally concerned in the present international crisis. Not one of us would be willing to increase, by even a careless word, the risks of a European conflict: its deep shadow is all too near to-night.

But if I cannot speak to you of foreign principalities and powers I can speak to you of England. I propose, therefore, to use this opportunity to put before you what I believe to be the British point of view in these critical days.

Would that you, who are listening to me, could now pay a visit to us in these British Isles. Some of you, I know, have done so in more settled and happier times, and we have been very glad to welcome you. But if you were to come now, your dominant impression would, I feel sure, be one of surprise at the normality and calm which characterize our national life to-day. There is no excitement, no hysteria, no demonstration; the national spirit is essentially one of sober resolution. This even temper is due neither to fatalism nor to any lack of imagination, but to a much simpler reason: the British people has made up its mind. The days of false optimism or of wishful thinking are gone. At long last the issue has become clarified to all, and it is being squarely faced. There is no hesitation anywhere.

And what is the issue which confronts Europe to-day? It is not merely a question of the future of Danzig or as to whether this great Power or that is to rule the Polish Corridor. We are not here concerned with some recent phase in the age-long conflict betwixt Teuton and Slav. Something much bigger than this is at stake for us all. Whether Europe is to be ruled by the threat of force, whether free peoples are to be called upon one by one to stand and deliver, or whether aggression is at length to be checked and respect for international engagements restored. These are the true issues, of which the threat to Poland is only the immediate expression.

In the last resort all civilization depends on the maintenance of certain standards of international conduct. At this moment it is the doctrine of force that is in conflict with these standards. But if the doctrine of force were once abandoned, so that the world was no longer haunted by the daily fear of war, who can doubt that all outstanding questions would become possible to solve? Surely the possibilities of international economic progress would then become wellnigh immeasurable? Whatever the differences in respect of the conduct of our foreign policy in the past I should like to emphasize that the Prime Minister and the Foreign Secretary have the support of each one of us, and indeed of the whole country, in their determination to fulfil our engagements and in their desire to build a constructive peace, if once the method and menace of force is removed.

Thus it is that we are all of us convinced that the issues by which we are confronted can admit of no patchwork compromise. We are in an era of fateful decision. For us no solution of the present situation can be acceptable unless it decisively strengthens the peace-front, unless it manifests beyond cavil that this time the attempt to extract concessions by force has failed. This time the conception of good faith in international dealings, of respect for the rights of peoples, be they small or great, is going to prevail. We pray that the victory will be peaceful, but whether peaceful or not, the challenge will be met.

For too long Europe has lived under the threat of recurrent crises. That situation has now become intolerable. The British people could not accept a compromise solution which merely postponed until six months hence another world crisis of a similar character. Nothing is to be gained that way.

In the meanwhile it becomes daily more evident that in its negotiation of the German-Soviet Pact the German Government has been guilty of an extraordinary psychological error. It is now clear that the German Government thought that the conclusion of this Agreement would create such dismay in the hearts of the nations composing the peace-front that their whole attitude to the German demands upon Poland would be radically modified. The Western Powers, it was considered, would be so thunderstruck that they would at once go back upon their pledge to Poland. There could not have been a more extravagant miscalculation.

It is true that the Western Powers were taken completely by surprise, but those who have been thunderstruck have not been the Powers of the peace-front who had given their pledge to Poland but the friends and political allies of the Nazi Government, whose whole political philosophy has thus been thrown into confusion. How is it possible for even the most gullible any longer to pretend that the present regime in Germany is a bulwark against Communism when the German Foreign Secretary within the last few days has himself been warmly clasping the chief protagonist of this alleged menace by the hand?

But whatever we may think of these abrupt changes in international policy, they cannot affect the main issue so far as the commitments of this country towards Poland are concerned. Our obligations will of course be honoured. They will be honoured not only because our pledged word has been given, but also because it is now universally understood that something of much greater significance is at stake than the determination of one frontier, or even the freedom of one people, however brave. The world has to choose between order and anarchy. For too long it has staggered from crisis to crisis under the constant threat of armed force. We cannot live for ever at the pistol point. The love of the British people for peace is as great as ever, but they are no less determined that this time peace shall be based on the denial of force, and a respect for the pledged word. Only when good faith between Governments has thus been restored can the nations again enjoy security, only then can mankind look forward with confidence to a future of happiness and hope.

5

WAR—A UNITED PEOPLE

August 25. The Anglo-Polish Treaty of Mutual Assistance was signed in London.

September 1. Germany invaded Poland.

September 3. Britain and France declared war on Germany. The Cabinet resigned and in Mr. Chamberlain's new Cabinet Mr. Eden rejoined the Government after eighteen months' absence, as Secretary of State for the Dominions with access to the War Cabinet. Mr. Churchill returned to the Admiralty and became a member of the War Cabinet.

Australia

On September 2, Mr. R. G. Menzies, Prime Minister, said:

"There is unity in the Empire ranks—one King, one Flag, one Cause."

On September 3, he announced with the support of the Labour Party and the Country Party, that a state of war existed between Australia and the German Reich.

New Zealand

On September 3, the New Zealand Government declared that New Zealand was at war with Germany. No formal declaration was made.

On September 6, Mr. Savage, the Prime Minister, said:

"With gratitude for the past and confidence for the future, we range ourselves without fear beside Britain. Where she goes, we go; where she stands, we stand."

Union of South Africa

On September 4, General Hertzog, the Prime Minister, introduced a motion in favour of neutrality. General Smuts moved an amendment rejecting neutrality and declaring for the severance of relations with the German Reich. General Smuts' amendment was accepted by 80 votes to 67.

On September 5, General Smuts became Prime Minister.

On September 6, the Union declared war on Germany.

Canada

The Canadian Parliament was not sitting on September 3. True to his promise, Mr. Mackenzie King, the Prime Minister, delayed formal declaration of war until Parliament reassembled.

On September 10, Canada declared war on Germany.

On September 11, it was announced that the British Expeditionary Force had arrived in France and on the same evening Mr. Eden broadcast to a United Empire.

Aweek has passed since this country found itself at war with Nazi rule in Germany, and to-day we are a united people more closely knit one to another in our common resolve than at any time in our history. More united, if that were possible, and certainly no less determined than when, some twenty-five years ago, we pledged ourselves to fight in a good cause. For such a cause we are fighting with one heart and mind to-day.

How has this come about? What is it that has levelled the internal barriers—the party and political barriers—and brought our people to be of one mind?

First, we have a good conscience. The White Paper which the Government recently made public and which disclosed the story of the ten days that preceded the outbreak of war has made it clear beyond a doubt that the Government not only strove to keep the peace, but took great risks for peace.

And yet there was this difference between the days which preceded the outbreak of war in 1914 and the period through which we have just passed. It has sometimes been said that if before the last great war we had made our position more plain and clear, peace would have been saved. I am not concerned this evening to argue whether that was a right or a wrong view. To-day one fact stands out and it is this, that before war broke out we did all that

41

words could do to make our attitude unequivocably clear to Germany's rulers so that—and here I use the Prime Minister's own words—there should be no "tragic ambiguity". Neither this German Government nor any German Government in the future will ever have justification for saying that there was doubt as to the action which we must take. Our position was put before the world for all to see long before the German Government decided to submit its fate to the dread arbitrament of war.

You may remember the famous story of the Roman Envoys who went to Carthage before the first Punic War. Confronted by the Carthaginian Senate their spokesman said: "I have here two gifts, peace and war, take which you choose."

No such grim alternative was given to Herr Hitler. Every inducement was offered him to enter the way of peaceful negotiation. The Polish Government had accepted this principle of negotiation. Herr Hitler deliberately and with set purpose made negotiation impossible. Instead he chose to embark upon a war of naked aggression, and this country and France have in consequence fulfilled their undertaking to Poland, an undertaking with which you are all familiar, an undertaking into which we had entered with full publicity before the world as long ago as last April.

The German Chancellor carried cynical dissimulation so far as finally to invade Poland because Poland had failed to accept peace proposals which she had never even received from the German Government. There has never been a more flagrant mockery of international good faith.

We have always desired to live and let live. We considered that there was no dispute that could not be resolved by peaceful means if once the threat of force were removed, and other nations have shared our point of view. Poland was always ready to negotiate, as Czechoslovakia was ready to negotiate a year ago. Herr Hitler has preferred force. He has made the choice; he must suffer the decision. For us now there will be no turning back. We have no quarrel with the German people, but there can be no lasting peace until Nazism and all it stands for, in oppression, cruelty and broken faith, is banished from the earth. This is an issue that admits of no compromise.

First, then, our conscience is clear.

But secondly, our memory is long. Herr Hitler has claimed that his sole aim was to remedy the injustices of the Treaty of Versailles, which he contended was the root of all evil. This it was, we are told, which had forced him to build his colossal armaments, to march his legions into Austria, to imprison its Chancellor, to absorb Austria into the German Reich. This it was that compelled him to break faith with the British and French Governments, and despite his pledge, so recently and so solemnly reaffirmed, to invade and subdue Czechoslovakia and to attempt to reduce her people to the status of hewers of wood and drawers of water. This it was that left Herr Hitler—we are assured—with no alternative but to turn against Poland with whom some five years ago he had solemnly signed a pact which was to run for ten years. And a pact, you will recall, which laid down that the status of Danzig and the Polish Corridor would, by consent of both Poland and Germany, remain unchanged until 1944.

Faced with such a catalogue of broken vows and discarded pledges, how is it possible to escape the conclusion that the Treaty of Versailles was not a grievance to redress, but a pretext for the use of force?

Five times in the last eighty years the rulers of Germany have embarked with only the slightest pretext upon a war of aggression. Against peaceful Denmark in 1864, against Austria in 1866, against France in 1870, against the whole world in 1914 to 1918, and now against France, Poland and Great Britain in 1939.

With such a record her present rulers, had they been honest and sincere, might well have thought that they should accept to negotiate with nations who wanted nothing more than to live at peace with Germany, and who, as the documents which have been published show, excluded no subjects from peaceful discussion.

Herr Hitler and his Nazi associates would have none of it. Flouting all the lessons of history, ignoring or deriding even their own country's experience of British character, they preferred yet once more the path of lawlessness, the path of misery and of bloodshed, the path of anarchy and want. Let the Nazi leaders ask themselves now to what destiny they are leading the German people.

Our conscience then is clear. Our memory is long, and thirdly, our determination is unshaken.

This war has broken out in circumstances which have no parallel. Herr Hitler is invading Poland with the help of overwhelming numbers and the merciless use of the air arm, while he acts on the defensive in the west. These methods are leading to strange illusions among the Nazi leaders which had best be dispelled at once. Let there be no mistake about this. Our determination to see this war through to the end is unshaken. We must make it clear to the Nazi leaders and if we can to the German people that this country

43

—as the Prime Minister said—has not gone to war about the fate of a far-away city in a foreign land. We have decided to fight to show that aggression does not pay, and the German people must realize that this country means to go on fighting until that goal is reached. It is already evident that the Nazi Government seeks to delude its people into thinking that a quick victory won in Poland will be followed by the indifference or the capitulation of the western democracies. That is not the truth. The people of this country are ready to fight a very long war to the bitter end if that must be to rid the world of Hitlerism and all that Hitlerism implies.

In the meanwhile, let the Nazi leaders take heed and let us all take encouragement from what has been happening in the British Commonwealth of Nations during the last few days.

One by one the free peoples of that great association have been accepting the risks and responsibilities which the United Kingdom has taken upon itself. Canada, Australia, New Zealand, South Africa, each in turn has given the answer to the challenge, each in turn has made the cause its own.

And not only these great Dominions, but India also. The Colonies, too, have offered their aid. From all quarters of the globe have come messages of loyalty to the Sovereign and offers of help. Once more, Britain stands armed and resolved with her sister nations at her side.

For some of us the challenge has come a second time in our generation. There must be no second mistake. Out of the welter of suffering to be endured we must fashion a new world that is something better than a stale reflection of the old, bled white.

It had been better could we have set ourselves to the task in a world of peace. Herr Hitler has decided otherwise. Nazism, however, is but a passing phase. Like all systems built upon force it cannot endure—in the long roll of history it will count but as a spasm of acute pain. The suffering will be bitter, the devastation wide. But what really matters is what follows after. Can we do better this time? Can we finally rid Europe of barriers of casts and creed and prejudice? Can frontiers and faiths, language and commerce serve to unite nations and not divide them? Can we create a true unity in Europe? Can we set before it a common aim of service, can we inspire it with common ideals of freedom, toleration and mercy? This is what must be. While the Nazi system exists it cannot be, and so the Nazi system and all that it implies must be swept away.

WAR—A UNITED PEOPLE

By Herr Hitler's own decision our new civilization must be built through a world at war. We would have wished it otherwise. But our new civilization will be built just the same, for some forces are bigger than men, and in that new civilization will be found liberty and opportunity and hope for all.

6

RECONSTRUCTION AT HOME

September 17. Russia invaded Poland. Warsaw surrendered on September 27, the partition having been announced on September 22 by Russia and Germany.

October 6. Hitler, in a speech to the Reichstag made his "last peace offer" to the Allies.

October 24. Ribbentrop stated that: "Germany, when she wins, will save the world by destroying the British Commonwealth of Nations."

October 25. Mr. Eden broadcast a welcome to the Dominion Cabinet Ministers who had come to London to confer with H.M. Government in the United Kingdom on the best ways of co-ordinating the contribution of each country to the common cause. In the course of this broadcast, Mr. Eden said:

"Attempts have been made in the past to establish an international system which, by its very nature, should outlaw war and make possible free co-operation between the nations in search of a common prosperity and a common civilization.

Some of these attempts have failed, others have succeeded, and of all the successes perhaps the outstanding example is afforded by the British Commonwealth of Nations. Here we have a number of equal states, each the master of its own destiny, yet conscious of the mutual advantage to be derived from constant co-operation and consultation upon the problems which face them all."

After a conference in London, Mr. Eden accompanied the Dominions Ministers on a tour of the British and French Armies in France.

During the Debate on the Address in reply to His Majesty the King's speech after the opening of the 1939–40 session of Parliament, the Labour Party moved an amendment in the following terms:

"But regret the absence of any proposals for organizing to the full our human and material resources in the national interest for the effective prosecution of the war, for the provision and maintenance of an adequate standard of life for all, and for the solution, on the basis of social justice, of the problems which will arise on the return to peace."

After a full debate on this Amendment on December 5 and 6, which was opened by Mr. Arthur Greenwood, Mr. Herbert Morrison summed up for the Opposition and Mr. Eden, still Secretary of State for the Dominions, replied for the Government. In the Division which followed, 125 voted for the amendment and 303 for the Government.

Mr. Eden summed up as follows:

The right hon. Gentleman the Member for South Hackney (Mr. H. Morrison) has given us a characteristic speech, and an extremely fluent one. I do not think that hon. Members on this side of the House will complain greatly of the manner in which his criticism was presented. Once or twice as I listened to him it seemed to me that he contradicted himself a little. He admitted that there has been an improvement in world conditions, and in particular in the social conditions of this country, since the late war. With becoming modesty, he took credit for that state of affairs upon himself and his colleagues in the Socialist Party, for he said they had managed to drive reluctant Governments to good deeds which, but for the inspiration of the Opposition, they never would have thought of. It is just conceivable—but the right hon. Gentleman will forgive me if I say it is highly improbable—that the historian of the future will endorse that diagnosis. If that be accurate, it was hardly fair that in the same breath he charged us with paying attention to criticisms in our actual conduct of the war. It was apparently only right to listen to suggestions or to give heed to criticisms when they came from the benches opposite. As I listened to the right hon. Gentleman, I felt sure that he thought there was one easy remedy for all these ills, and that was to substitute himself and his hon. Friends on the benches opposite for those who occupy these benches. [HON. MEMBERS: "Hear hear."]

I am not in the least surprised that that sentiment should be so heartily endorsed by hon. Members opposite, and they will perhaps not complain that the majority of the House for the moment do not take that view. Therefore, in consequence, our discussion of that aspect of the matter is a somewhat barren one. . . .

The right hon. Member for Wakefield (Mr. Greenwood), when moving the Amendment yesterday, told us that the war would shake many strongly held views. I fear that this war will do very much more than that. The war will bring about changes which may be fundamental and revolutionary in the economic and social life of this country. On that we are all agreed. In fact, every war has done so, and since the rise of industry in the modern sense of the term the upheaval has been all the greater. We saw this after the Crimea, a minor war for this nation as compared with the one that we are fighting now. It brought about a complete reform of the War Office, but, fortunately, we can do that now without a war. It brought about other changes. It brought about the beginning of our medical system, and the beginning of the nursing system in this country. Again, the Boer War disclosed the poor standard of health of the recruits; it brought home to all concerned the standard of health at that time. The physical standard which was then disclosed resulted in the beginning of the school medical service. So it was in the last war.

The reason why we quote the last war is not to draw comparisons in the sense of saying that because the position is better than it was in the last war it is good enough. That is not the point. The point is to remind hon. Members of the many changes brought about in the course of war and, as a result of war, in the actual operation of government. In the course of the last war the Council of Industry was set up; there was no Ministry of Health and no Ministry of Labour. It is hard to believe that the Minister of Labour, whose genial presence is rarely absent from this bench, was then engaged on an even more contentious occupation. Nor had we a Trades Union Congress. [*Interruption.*] Perhaps hon. Members opposite will not dispute that the last war brought about changes in the organization of industry. Not a single industry before the war was organized as an industry to act as a unit. The war brought that about. I am mentioning these examples to show that changes are inevitable and that in this war, as it proceeds, changes will be brought about in our economic, national, and social structure. When we are asked to forecast exactly what these changes will be, no Government is able to do that.

RECONSTRUCTION AT HOME

The truth is that war presents an audit of the nation; it exposes weaknesses ruthlessly and brutally, and this war is going to do that too. These weaknesses will call for changes. But there is one contrast which I think hon. Members will already have noticed, in which we can take comfort, and that is the improvement in our social services, of which the right hon. Gentleman rightly spoke. Anybody who knew the average battalion of the new armies in the last war, say K.1 and K.2, and compares the physique of the men then with the physique of the average Territorial battalion of to-day, cannot help being impressed by the change that has taken place. I have had it from an officer whom I respect very greatly, and who has had exceptional opportunities for judging, that in his view the German Army of to-day is physically, as well as in other respects, below the standard of the Germany Army of 1914. That may be true, but the opposite is true of our own, and I think it is an example which we can take to show that under our Parliamentary Government we can achieve results which are better than those achieved by the dragooning methods of Germany. It is said that it is never wise to underrate your enemy's strength. There is an old Turkish proverb which says: "If your enemy be an ant, imagine that he is an elephant." For the purposes of·war, that is not a bad proverb.

The Amendment urges us to organize to the full our human and material resources. If we are to do that, there are three factors which we must call into play. We have to use the most advanced technical knowledge. For that, we are not ill-placed. We have the Department of Scientific and Industrial Research and the Medical Research Council, but despite their help we can be quite sure that the war will set us many new technical problems and that further research and co-ordination will be necessary. The second factor is the machinery of government. However much we know, an efficient use of that knowledge is vital. There, too, will anybody doubt that the war is going to bring changes? It will make reforms necessary. We have a Civil Service which is unsurpassed and unrivalled in the world, but some of the methods which are in use to-day date from the time when the tasks of government were almost exclusively tasks of regulation and when there was little need for the flexibility and initiative that are called for to-day. There again as this war proceeds there will be a call for a new technique and new methods, as there was during the last war, and I ask the House to believe that the Government are not by any means blind to these considerations.

RECONSTRUCTION AT HOME

The third factor which I thought the right hon. Gentleman should have stressed a little more is the rights of the individual, and here I think we need to keep on our guard. It will be true to say that by more vigorous and more ruthless methods, by entirely disregarding individual rights, you could organize the State more successfully and more rapidly and thoroughly than by our own methods, in which we try to take some account of individual rights and positions. You have to choose whether it is better to dragoon or to try co-operation. We believe in the latter. Let me give an example to the House—the way in which this country has now accepted compulsory national service, the way in which it has accepted the heavy burdens put upon it financially, and yet at the same time has maintained, through the Opposition and through other means, an active and indeed a healthy criticism. That combination is exactly an example of how order and freedom can be reconciled. It seems to me that the problem which any self-governing people has to solve in war is how to achieve the maximum efficiency from collective service without endangering the essential rights of the individual.

The Amendment refers to the standard of life and the right hon. Member for South Hackney also referred to that. The Government entirely agree that to cut down standards does not make for greater efficiency, and it is neither the desire nor the intention of the Government to cut down standards. As regards social reforms, about which the right hon. Gentleman asked, there is no closed mind on these benches to that issue. But it is fair and reasonable to say that we shall have to judge, as matters develop and as hostilities develop, on the basis of the conditions in which we find ourselves.

The hon. Member for Jarrow (Miss Wilkinson) made a remarkable speech earlier in the evening, and I want to answer one of her questions. She asked, quite rightly, whether the Government were considering how to handle the question of nutrition, especially for the children, during the war period; our warships, she said, kept the seas clear, but were we making the best use of the products brought to us? I can tell the hon. Lady that my right hon. Friend the Minister of Health and the Secretary of State for Scotland are already in communication with leading authorities—Sir John Orr and others—on the subject of nutrition, for the precise purpose of trying to see how best we can ensure good results in respect of nutrition during the war period. I can tell the hon. Lady that the Government recognize the immense importance of this subject. In

50

all those respects we are in agreement, but where I have to part company with the hon. Lady, and with many hon. Members opposite, is in this: We cannot at a time like this—and I do not think hon. Members opposite would ask us—attempt to justify an increase of any non-essential nature, when we have to use all our resources for victory; at a time, I would ask the House to remember, when our French Ally is undergoing very severe restrictions as a result of the war.

The right hon. Gentleman the Member for Wakefield, in the Debate yesterday, said that the Prime Minister's view, according to his own submission only a week ago, was that we must wait until the war is over before we can even begin to think about the future. As a matter of fact, my right hon. Friend did not say anything of the sort. I think he would be justified in saying, like a character in one of George Eliot's books: "Don't you go a-swallering my words and bringing them up again as if they were none the worse for the process." The words were very much the worse for the process. What my right hon. Friend said was that he was not prepared at this moment to put forward detailed plans. He did not say that the Government were not thinking about the subject; he did not say that because, in fact, they are. That is the very opposite of what the right hon. Gentleman the Member for Wakefield said was true. We do not say at this time that the moment may not come in the course of the war itself when we may think it right to put forward detailed plans of economic reconstruction. That may happen. What we cannot do at the outset of the war is to bind ourselves to detailed plans now and promise to lay them in the immediate future. I think the whole House will appreciate the reasonableness of that attitude. We welcome the fact that there should be discussion now of these problems of post-war reconstruction.

My hon. Friend the Member for Walsall (Sir G. Schuster), in a speech which deserved an infinitely larger House to listen to it, put forward some very important ideas on the subject of world economic co-operation. He made one suggestion. He said that it would be very helpful to some hon. Members if they could put some of their ideas to the Government's economic advisers and to Lord Stamp, in particular. My hon. Friend said that he did not wish to argue with Lord Stamp or to ask him to state his point of view, but that if Members could so express themselves to Lord Stamp, it would be helpful. I can tell my hon. Friend that the Government will gladly consider whether something of that kind can be worked out. Therefore, in the economic sphere there is not much division between us. We have, for instance, in the Anglo-French Economic Agreement, which the right hon. Gentleman opposite rightly quoted, an example which may lead to very important results in the future. No one can tell yet—the thing is only at a beginning —but it is one example of those developments in war-time which may have important results.

May I now say a word or two about another aspect of our present war effort? Much as I agree with the suggestions which have been made in the Debate about how we are to make our post-war effort, it seems to me to be essential that we should remember that, before we can do any of these things or hope to do them, we have to win the victory, and that the task is going to be a formidable one. Hitler himself is not a phenomenon; he is a symptom; he is the Prussian spirit of military domination come up again. National-Socialism was originally conceived in militarism, and it believes only in force. From the beginning, it has organized its people for war. It is the most barren creed that was ever put before mankind. Therefore, if it is allowed to triumph, there will be no future for civilization, no future for our debates, no future for our suggestions, and no future for the suggestions that have been made by hon. Members opposite. It is that realization, I believe, which has brought unity to our own people, and, what is even more remarkable, has brought complete unity of effort to all the peoples of the British Commonwealth.

In the five minutes before I close my speech, I would like to say a word or two about that effort, for even now it is not perhaps altogether understood here. You may take one of the smallest of the lands that form part of the British Empire, Newfoundland, and you will find that from there already some hundreds of men are on their way to join the Royal Navy here and to play their part as in the last war. Take another country: small in white population, Southern Rhodesia, a self-governing Colony, has already sent numbers of trained white men for military service outside the Colony, and has hundreds of others ready or in training. In addition, Southern Rhodesia has also offered us three squadrons for the Air Force, and one of them is now in service in another part of Africa. Go from there to the greater Dominions. The Union of South Africa is making ready. We are assured of her full cooperation within the limits laid down by General Smuts, her Prime Minister. Her air patrols are helping us now on the seas round the South African coasts, and recently they were successful in intercepting a German ship.

RECONSTRUCTION AT HOME

Turn to the naval sphere generally. Each one of the Dominions has made the whole of its naval resources available to work in co-operation with the Admiralty. For some, it has meant leaving their own home waters and being several thousands of miles away from their own countries. I know that my right hon. Friend the First Lord of the Admiralty would be the first to pay a tribute to what that co-operation has meant. On land, we shall see very soon soldiers from Canada, Australia and New Zealand in those fields of war in which they won imperishable fame some twenty-five years ago. If we turn to the air, hon. Members of this House who are in the Air Force will know that a large part of our Air Force to-day consists of personnel from the Dominions. Over and above that, the new Dominions air training scheme is going to bring to our help not hundreds but thousands of Dominion pilots and air crews as the scheme develops.

All those examples mean something which we should try to understand. What is the cause of this movement? It is not merely loyalty and sentiment. It is not even only the desire to overthrow Hitler, laudable as that is. It is based, as I believe, on a positive faith, and that positive faith is in Parliamentary government by a free community. In that spirit, which, I assure the House, I find daily in the work that I have to do now, lies our certainty of ultimately winning this conflict. In the future, it may be, the machinery of Parliament will change; it is certain that the personalities will change. But that spirit is what must live on, and it is that spirit which will ensure a better and braver world for the generations to come.

1940

7

A SURVEY OF THE WAR

On December 18, the first wave of Canadian troops arrived in the U.K., the second followed on December 30: both were met by Mr. Eden, in company with Mr. Vincent Massey, the Canadian High Commissioner.

On January 13, Mr. Eden visited the Australian Army in England.

On February 8, Mr. Eden left London for the Middle East; he returned on February 19. Whilst he was in Egypt he welcomed the Australian and New Zealand troops who arrived at Suez on February 12, and he visited the Australian troops who had already arrived in Palestine. He inspected Indian troops in camp at Mena just outside Cairo.

On February 24, Hitler speaking at Munich, referred to "Democratic Mummies".

On February 29, Mr. Eden addressed his first large war-time meeting in the country—in the Philharmonic Hall, at Liverpool.

I have never forgotten how, nearly three years ago, in what was then an acutely difficult international situation, you here in Liverpool gave me a message of encouragement which immensely heartened me in my task. We are here members of all parties and all faiths to discuss with a freedom we are proud to enjoy our joint effort in a common cause.

In these opening months, the main theatre of war has been at sea. In that sphere our Navy and our merchantmen have performed feats of courage and of endurance that will find their place in history. You, here in Liverpool, have every reason to appreciate the splendid quality of these men who sail the seas, for so many of your own sons and brothers are to be numbered among them. They are indeed a gallant company. Nor must we forget the invaluable help given to them at sea by the airmen of the Coastal Command.

But with this exception the autumn and winter has been a period of relative inactivity in Western Europe. This respite has proved most valuable to us for our preparations, since the aggressor in any war is almost inevitably a lap ahead of those who take up his challenge. But the gain of time, valuable as it has been to us, affords no ground whatever for complacency. Indeed, it may even be dangerous if it is not constantly borne in mind that it is victory in the last phase of war which means the defeat of the enemy. These first six months have been of great assistance in helping us to forge our weapons. Once forged, those weapons have to be used. You will recall the passage in *Pilgrim's Progress* where Christian and Hopeful say:

"We will need to cry to the strong for strength," and the Shepherd's reply:

"Aye, and you will have need to use it, when you have it, too."

What is the nature of the challenge that we are facing? The German war aim has been clearly defined by Goebbels and von Ribbentrop as the destruction of Great Britain. Goebbels, indeed, was even more explicit when he told us that Germany had never before had such splendid prospects as now to achieve a dominating position in the world. And that, of course, is the true Hitlerian objective, world domination. Vienna, Prague, Warsaw: the fate of Austria, Bohemia and Moravia; the sufferings of Poland; these things are but milestones on the path of Nazi ambition whose goal is world dominion.

We were reluctant to believe it; perhaps too reluctant. But it is now surely clear to all that from the very first such was the scope and scale of Hitler's insatiate ambition. To compass his aims all means are legitimate. This he has made plain enough in *Mein Kampf*. The most sacred promises can be given one day and broken the next. That is part of Hitler's stock-in-trade. He can speak to you with every appearance of ardent sincerity. I can recall a conversation which I myself had with him in which, while inveighing against the alleged iniquities of the Treaty of Versailles, he stated emphatically that, in contrast to Versailles,

Locarno was a freely negotiated treaty upon which he would never go back. I believed him. Within a year he had torn the Treaty of Locarno to shreds. No one who had been through that experience could easily believe Hitler a second time.

Hitler has continued his faith-breaker's progress. It has all been deliberate, carefully planned with one end in view, to subjugate Europe and dominate the world. To achieve that purpose, no scruple, no pledged word, no sufferings inflicted upon any peoples small or great could be allowed to weigh for one instant in the balance. That is the true Hitlerian doctrine. .

And if you ask how is it that the German people can be so easily deceived, how they can follow a leadership, at once so false and so unscrupulous, the answer is given you by Hitler himself in *Mein Kampf* in his contemptuous reference to his own people:

"The majority are lazy and timid," he writes. "The mass of our nation, that great, stupid flock of easily driven sheep" who "believe and obey because they are too stupid to understand."

At the moment there is not one of us who is not watching with deep concern the gallant struggle of a small nation—Finland— against desperate odds. Not Russia only but Germany also, bears a terrible responsibility for what is happening in Finland at this hour. Hitler and Ribbentrop, these men and their policies alone made Stalin's aggression possible. Stalin is the aggressor in Finland, Hitler the abettor. It seems strange to think now how many hours I used to spend listening to the present German Foreign Secretary when he was Ambassador in London, when he used to expound to me, as indeed he did also in public, many times, the dangers and horrors of Bolshevism. He was never tired of expatiating on this theme. Soviet Russia, this untouchable with whom Nazi Germany could not sit down at a conference table, this leprous thing, this cancer. Many a time the British people were taken to task because we, it was alleged, did not understand the extent of our peril. We did not appreciate, we were told, the realities of the European situation. Only Hitler could do that. He, alone, we were assured, stood as a bulwark between Britain and Red Russia. But for the Hitlerian St. George the Red Dragon would have swallowed us long since. So ran the German fable with its many variations. And what has happened now? The Red Dragon has taken the Hitlerian St. George for a ride. It may be that one day in the not so distant future the German Foreign Minister may have need to recall his own warnings.

In recent months it has been my privilege at the Dominions

Office to work in close contact with His Majesty's Governments overseas. When Germany launched her unprovoked aggression against Poland she made many miscalculations. Perhaps the gravest of all was her confident belief, so frequently expressed, that at the outbreak of war the British Empire would crumble into ruin. At the first critical hour, the Nazi propagandists confidently foretold, this flimsy structure would fall to pieces. They could not understand that in our greater freedom lay our greater strength. How should they understand, these men who have extinguished the last spark of freedom in their own land? These Nazi prophets of evil have been utterly confounded by the event. It would be impossible for me to find words in which to pay adequate tribute to the ready willingness with which collaboration has been given to us on every hand. The nations of the Empire have been spontaneous and whole-hearted in their response. This afternoon I want to give you some brief account of what the co-operation of the overseas Dominions already means.

If I were to attempt to describe to you what that effort means by detailing to you the help which is being given in every sphere by each of the Dominions, my story would repeat itself in a record of the mobilization of their resources in finance, production and man-power which would be impressive indeed. But it is not even in such a record that the true significance of the action of the British Commonwealth is to be found. The contribution of each part is great, even splendid, but it is in its cumulative effect, in the unity of each and all that its true strength lies. We are indeed participating in one great joint endeavour, ourselves and our kinsmen and partners in the Dominions side by side, straining every nerve for victory.

At sea, from the declaration of war the naval forces of the Dominions have co-operated closely with our own. Canada's navy and air force stand guard upon her Atlantic and Pacific seaboards. Her ships have helped to convoy her soldiers on their long journey to Europe. Ships of the Royal Australian Navy are at this moment giving invaluable help in seas remote from their own shores. There could be no more characteristic gesture of generosity than this. As for New Zealand, the cheers for the victors at the battle of the River Plate still ring in our ears. *Achilles* is, as you know, a ship of the New Zealand Division of the Royal Navy. Behind her six-inch guns, as they exchanged salvo for salvo with the eleven-inch guns of her foe, were New Zealanders, sharing with *Ajax* and *Exeter* the hazards and the honours of that glorious action.

A SURVEY OF THE WAR

It was a happy coincidence that on the day when the men of the *Ajax* and the *Exeter* were being acclaimed in London, the people of New Zealand were thronging to welcome the men of the *Achilles* at Auckland. Such events as these bring home to us all that in truth the seas unite.

Now let me turn to the Army. Some of you may perhaps have seen men of the Canadian Active Service Force who are already training in our midst. If you have seen them, you can have no doubt that they will worthily uphold Canada's splendid military tradition. From Australia and New Zealand have come the first detachments of their overseas forces and they in their turn have reached their stations in Egypt and in Palestine. I have been fortunate enough to have seen these men. You can take it from me that in spirit and in stature they cannot be beaten.

Now as to the air. As you know, there is a large percentage of pilots from overseas in our existing air force. In addition, Canadian, Australian and New Zealand squadrons are now operating from bases in this country. But over and above all this is the great conception of the Empire Air Training scheme. On Canadian soil there is now taking shape a far-reaching plan for the training of men for the Air Forces of the British Commonwealth which may well prove to be the decisive factor in the war. As a result of this great effort, men from this country, from Australia and from New Zealand will be trained side by side with Canadians on the aerodromes of Canada. These will be in addition to the pilots who will be training under the same plan in Australia and New Zealand also. From this vast scheme as it develops there will flow a continuous stream of pilots, observers and gun crews to be numbered not in their thousands but in their tens of thousands every year.

The Union of South Africa, and the self-governing Colony of Southern Rhodesia, are staunch partners in the south of the great African continent. There, in the last war, the campaigns in the German colonies cost us dearly in men and material. This time we may be thankful to be spared a strain on our resources such as those Colonial campaigns imposed. Nevertheless, we have from that great statesman, General Smuts, the promise that if, as the war develops, our Colonial Dependencies in Africa should be threatened, the forces of South Africa will be beside us in their defence. Those forces are being expanded, trained and equipped so that if the time comes, we shall know again, as we knew in the last war, the dour courage of the South African, English-speaking and Afrikaner alike. An air unit from Southern Rhodesia is already

60

on duty in Kenya, and in no less than seven of our African Colonial Dependencies Rhodesians are to-day performing invaluable military service. The Cape of Good Hope still plays its historic part on the sea routes of the world, and so we find there at the naval base of Simonstown the Royal Navy co-operating with the forces of South Africa for the protection of our common interests in these waters. It was a notable instance of co-operation in maritime warfare when, flying southwards from the Cape, a reconnaissance flight of the South African Air Force recently intercepted a fugitive German vessel and put an end to her career on the high seas.

In addition, plans are in the making for personnel to be trained for the Royal Air Force in Southern Rhodesia, and also in the Union, side by side with the young men for the South African Air Force.

There is one further contribution that must not be overlooked —that of Newfoundland, our oldest Colony. From that island six hundred men have already come to join the Royal Navy, and a thousand more will follow. In addition, two thousand loggers are already here in response to an appeal to help us. Finally, recruiting for the Royal Artillery has recently been started in the Island and I am delighted to be able to tell you that the response has already been excellent.

In this survey which I have given you I have dealt exclusively with co-operation in the military sphere. Behind all this endeavour in each one of the Dominions are men and women doing their part in the spheres of production, in the fields and in the factories alike, turning out those supplies of food, raw materials and munitions on which our war effort essentially depends. This vast effort is swinging into its stride, already it is gathering momentum.

Let me try to describe to you three scenes, each in their special setting an expression of the war effort of the Empire. The first is a grey morning at a Western port. A number of our ships of war are in line ahead, their convoy duty over. Slowly the giant liners steam in, their decks packed with cheering soldiers. They are there in their thousands. As the transports pass a band on one of the warships strikes up "Oh, Canada", and a momentary hush falls over the waters. The first contingent of the Canadian Active Service Force is here.

The second picture is in sharp contrast. Many thousands of miles away, in a different clime, under a warm sun, transports slowly stream into Suez. Once more the decks are packed with soldiers in their thousands. This time from "down under". Australia and New Zealand have taken their place too in the common effort.

The third picture is of no display of military might, but its message is scarcely less plain spoken. During the flights which I made recently in the course of my visit to the Middle East, we landed to refuel on one occasion upon an aerodrome in a very remote spot. There was scarcely more than a handful of people present, none of them Europeans. The only other machines on the ground at the time were two single seater fighters of a British make. We went up to them and spoke to the two young pilots, one of them turned out to be a Scot from Lanarkshire and the other a South African from Johannesburg. From the opposite ends of the world these two men had come as volunteers to serve the same cause, and here on this remote aerodrome we met for a few minutes' conversation before each flying our separate ways, we northward, they back to the east from which they had come.

There seemed to me to be a message in this chance meeting. What is it that has brought these men, Canadians, Australians, New Zealanders, South Africans, across the world? What is it that has moved them to leave their homes, their work, their factory or farm in their tens of thousands and offer man's proudest gift, his service as a volunteer? It is something more than sentiment, deep as no doubt that sentiment is. It is something stronger even than the ties of kinship, strong as those ties are. It is because, as one of them put it himself, in the simplest but most expressive terms: "It seems there is a job of work to be done." Just so. Though separated by thousands of miles of ocean, these men, who might very well have been excused had they failed to appreciate the extent of the peril that pressed in the first instance upon us, saw clearly from the first. They understood the issue, and it is this clear perception, the vision of the men beyond the seas who see truly, that should give us courage now. The truth is that if there is to be any hope for the future of the human race, then the Nazi system and all it stands for must go. An end must be put to this era of broken faith; political perjury must be shown to have had its day. Until this is established beyond question, until Hitlerism and the international gangsterdom for which it stands is finally destroyed, there can be neither security for the present nor hope for the future.

Any truce, any patchwork compromise that ignored these stark realities would confront us with greater dangers in a few months' or at most in a few years' time. It might then be too late, and for a free people the servitude of Nazidom is worse than death. We were reluctant, very reluctant, to take up this struggle. Now that we are in it we shall see it through to the end, whatever the cost. Any other course would be to lose the present and to betray the future.

After this war the task of statesmanship will be hard, more exacting even than in 1918, but there will be elements of hope and cheer. First and foremost there is the close collaboration of the nations of the British Commonwealth. Next there is our ever more intimate unity with our French Allies. A unity which must be carried through in its entirety into the post-war years, for this time our co-operation must come to stay. Many of us indeed believe that it is capable of further development, and that in the economic and financial as well as in the strictly political sphere Anglo-French co-operation offers a most hopeful augury for the future.

Along these paths, though the way may be hard, progress is possible, but any compromise with those whose only faith is in brute force, whose methods are in themselves a denial of civilization, could only plunge us back into the dark ages.

And so we can go forward, conscious of the severity of our task, but strong in the knowledge that we do not stand alone. We are one of a team with the overseas Dominions, Canada and Australia, New Zealand and South Africa, with Newfoundland and Southern Rhodesia, the Empire of India and the Colonies, with France and her Empire, with Poland whose spirit is unquenched despite her suffering, with the Czech people who have for so long endured so much. For nothing in the world would we change our team for theirs. Together we are a team, and we can take as our watchword that message from a soldier "down under". "It seems there is a job of work to be done." With God's help and yours, it will be done.

8

THE TWO IMPERIALISMS

March 11. Mr. Sumner Welles, President Roosevelt's special
envoy, reached London after having visited in turn, Rome,
Berlin, and Paris.
March 18. Hitler and Mussolini met at the Brenner Pass.
April 9. The Germans occupied Denmark and landed in Norway.
April 15. British troops landed in Norway.
On April 17, Mr. Eden addressed a meeting at the Constitu-
tional Club, London.

This war is not a clash between rival dynasties. Its basic causes
are not economic; nor is it even a struggle to decide the balance of power. Nazidom's record of broken faith has established long since that there can be no negotiations with a Nazi
Government. But even this is not the whole and heart of the problem.
The German Government's conception of the world's future is not
compatible with ours; nor is there room for both. For Nazism,
humanity consists of one race that rules—the German race, and a
number of other races, all and always inferior. We are convinced, on
the other hand, that there can be no hope for mankind unless
peoples, small as well as great, are free each to develop their own
civilizations in security and at peace. It is therefore fundamentals
that are at stake. No more vital issues have ever been fought out in
any war in history.

The German conception of dominion and the modern British
conception of imperialism present as sharp an antithesis as man-

kind has ever known. The German conception is based upon subjection and repression, ours upon equality and development. Hitler has expressed his thought clearly. In his own words, the type of peace that he envisages is one, to quote *Mein Kampf,* "that would be guaranteed by the triumphant sword of the people endowed with the power to master the world". In contrast to this thesis we have but to recall the words in which the Imperial Conference Resolution of 1926 described the British Commonwealth: "Free institutions are its life-blood. Free co-operation is its instrument."

While nations with widely divergent systems of internal government can make shift to live together after a fashion provided their conceptions of international conduct are approximately the same, there is no room on this earth for the practice of two fundamentally antagonistic conceptions of world order. Either the German doctrine of submission or our own doctrine of equality must prevail.

At this moment both methods can be seen in practice and they are worth some analysis on our part. It is a mistake to imagine that Hitler is some fantastic nightmare being, the like of whom has not been seen before and will not be seen again. Hitler is not a phenomenon, he is a symptom. He is not something distinct from the German nation, he is the direct expression of a great part of it. His plans are inherited from Bismarck and Nietzsche and other earlier exponents of the German faith in brute force. His methods are a caricature of those methods, but at the same time not an extravagant one.

Germany has not fought her aggressive wars for economic gain, nor was she interested in the fate of Sudeten Germans when she demanded Sudetenland eighteen months ago. These things were the pretext. The aim is to make Germany infinitely the most powerful nation in the world, and by the ruthless use of that power to compel Europe to submit to German rule and the world to yield to German authority. It would be a mistake to underestimate the conviction with which this faith is held. These Nazis believe that it is for the good of Germany that the world should be ruled and run by Nazis. And what is good for Germans must be good enough for the world. If others cannot understand this crude and simple proposition they must be beaten until they do. Not even the most credulous optimist can now have any hope that Nazi Germans will ever understand that any point of view than theirs can be tolerated, for of course if they did they would not be Nazis.

If any proof were wanted of this unhappy truth it is only necessary to observe the methods by which Germany popularizes her rule in the alien lands she has conquered. The rights of small peoples are not merely set aside or neglected, they are extinguished. For Bohemia and Moravia, for Poland, for the Northern lands, for any country that falls under German dominion there is no future whatever but that of the slave state. They must be assimilated to Germany; they must form part of Nazidom in mind, body, and estate; they can have no other life, no thought of their own, no creed, no conscience. No more graphic illustration of the Nazi mentality can be found than in an official announcement which was published in a captured Polish city a short while ago. I quote four articles from it.

"1. The Polish inhabitants of both sexes are obliged to make way before the representatives of German authority in so far as the latter can be recognized through their uniforms or through armlets on their sleeves. The streets belong to the conquerors and not to the conquered.

"2. The Polish inhabitants of male sex are obliged to show their respect to all leading personalities of the State, the Party and the Military Forces by uncovering their heads."

The next might be regarded by some as the first act of clemency in the German occupation of Poland. It reads as follows:

"3. The Poles are forbidden to employ the German form of greeting by raising the right hand and exclaiming 'Heil Hitler'."

The fourth article reads:

"4. In the shops and at the market stands all representatives of German authority, members of their families and all German nationals must be served first, before the conquered."

And after other regulations in the same temper, this document concludes:

"... Poles who have not yet grasped that they are the conquered while we are the conquerors and who will not comply with the above decree, will be punished with all the severity of the law."

There is one other contrast I would like to bring before your mind. We heard much some eighteen months ago of the alleged persecution of the German minority in Czechoslovakia and yet, no one has ever denied that this German minority always enjoyed the use of its own schools and language, while in the heart of Prague itself a great German university flourished. To-day in the whole of Bohemia and Moravia the Czech language is suppressed, and the only university that survives is this same German university in Prague.

And such are the conditions that exist over the large part of

Europe that is to-day under German rule. The peace that broods is only too often, not only spiritually and morally but even physically also, the peace of death. Under Nazi rule there can be no other peace.

For ourselves, just as our conception of world order is the exact opposite of the Nazi, so is our practice in the British Commonwealth the antithesis of theirs. Let us for a moment examine the working of that Commonwealth, for I share the view so well expressed by the Prime Minister of Canada, Mr. Mackenzie King, that "the experiment in ordered relationships between free countries, which we call the British Commonwealth of Nations, has, we may venture to hope, value for other countries as well as for our own".

Let us start by refuting some of the most vulgar fallacies about the nature of the British Empire. First, the fallacy that we own a quarter of the globe. This is absolutely, even ludicrously, untrue. No part of the Empire owns any other part. Equally wide of the mark is the fallacy that Great Britain rules over the whole of the British Commonwealth. Britain no more rules over Canada than Canada rules over Britain. Australia no more rules over New Zealand than New Zealand over Australia. The equality of each and all of the self-governing Dominions is complete and absolute. In other parts of the Empire varying degrees of self-government exist. This brings us to the third fallacy, that the government of one people by another is necessarily a hammer and anvil process. Article 22 of the Covenant of the League of Nations reads as follows:

"There are territories which are inhabited by peoples not yet able to stand by themselves under the strenuous conditions of the modern world. The well-being and development of such peoples form a sacred trust of civilization."

This is the spirit in which we seek to discharge our task.

We do not own any of the Empire; we do not govern the greater part of the Empire. In those areas for whose government we are responsible we are fulfilling a trust.

Admittedly, these truths are not easily grasped by those who have made no study of the history of our Imperial development. I remember once seeking to explain Dominion status to a distinguished foreign statesman who, after I had finished, electrified a luncheon-table of foreigners by the emphatic assertion: "Moi, je veux être Dominion."

To what is due this evolution of the British Commonwealth, unique as it is in history? In part, without doubt, to the fact that we are an island people, with splendid natural frontiers within which we have been able to develop in liberty and continuity. This spirit of liberty and continuity has found full expression in our Empire. Let us admit frankly, too, that we owe something to our friends in the United States who taught us a rude lesson and taught it us betimes.

Philip Francis well summed up the experience of the American War of Independence when he wrote:

"Since I have been obliged to study the book of wisdom, I have dismissed logic out of my library. The fate of nations must not be tried by forms."

Thus it is that we have abandoned forms and formalism. Our whole system is based upon growth, change, development. At this moment, in a critical hour for the world, we see what that development has meant in the willing co-operation which has been brought to us from each of the self-governing Dominions. But the magnificent things which the Dominions are doing are only a proof of what they are, and it is their essential nature which I would emphasize to-day. They are entirely self-governing. Their policies—social, economic, military and cultural—are in no way dependent on the Mother Country. Yet they unite with the Mother Country to form a living whole. The Dominions are a living refutation of the Nazi thesis that liberty is synonymous with decadence and that a system based upon freedom cannot last. In truth a system based upon freedom is the only one which can last.

In speaking of the voluntary co-operation of the great Dominions we must not overlook how splendid and spontaneous has also been the offer of help from India and from all parts of the Colonial Empire. This has taken many and varied forms from princely gifts to humble offerings. One of the most delightful messages of which I have heard was from the colony of Nigeria, where a native community asked the Governor to write to the Secretary of State for the Colonies and exhort "*it* to remember King Alfred and the spider".

This overwhelming and spontaneous loyalty is our secret weapon. It is a thing which the Nazis cannot begin to understand. They fail to realize that a democracy is never weaker than it appears, and a dictatorship never stronger than it appears. They have seized on every free expression of opinion and have taken it as a sign of decay. They have failed to understand that what may seem to be a source of weakness can prove in times of crisis a source of unbounded strength.

68

THE TWO IMPERIALISMS

I have attempted in the space of a few minutes to hold up German and British Imperialism side by side. Can any two conceptions of life be more different? The contrast between French and German Imperialism is fully as sharp. We and the French are at this moment engaged on a gigantic work of co-operation, destined to endure far beyond the war which has called it into being. Exactly where this co-operation will lead us none can tell; but this much is certain—our two Empires will draw continually closer together. The concord between them which has already been proclaimed and established will become steadily firmer. That is only possible because these two systems, with their many superficial divergencies, are built on the same solid foundation of freedom and spontaneous growth. Between the British Commonwealth and the German Reich there is no such basic similarity. Here the difference is not superficial and relative; it is fundamental and absolute. It is as absolute as the difference between plant and stone. If we fail to recognize this tremendous fact we cannot begin to perceive the real nature of the war we are fighting or the issues which depend upon its outcome. In some neutral countries which are not at all enamoured of our enemy, the belief persists that this is merely a war of interests. One imperialism against another imperialism. One profiteer against another profiteer. Profit is its only basis and self-interest its only motive. No. Many wars have been fought in the past on that basis and with that motive, but this is not one of them. This is much more than a conflict of interests. It is a conflict of worlds. The whole story of civilization waits upon its issue.

Let us look into the future for a moment. What would happen to Europe and the world if the Nazis were to triumph? They have boasted that the Third Reich will last a thousand years. If it did, there would be a thousand years of repression, a thousand years' blight. But who could believe that the Nazis would last a thousand years, even if they were to triumph now? A system which is entirely rigid can never last. You cannot stifle change. Change is perhaps the one thing in the universe which is constant. By trying to thwart it, you only drive it underground. It becomes fitful and eruptive instead of ordered and continuous. Should the Nazis triumph now, I believe the history of the next centuries would be one of violence and bitterness, of revolutions and counter-revolutions. The repercussions of the hatred they have stirred up would be lasting and terrible.

Now let us glance at the other future, the future that lies in the hands of the Allies. Ours is a more modest but surely a much more realistic conception. We do not attempt to look a thousand years ahead. We do not seek to stifle development, but merely to guide it. That is our claim. The world's destiny is inscrutable; we cannot determine it, but we can help to direct it in vigilance and with humility.

Our reluctance to declare our war aims has been taken by some as an indication that we are without constructive purpose. Neutral observers, relatively favourable to our cause, have advanced the argument that our Imperialism is only preferable to that of the Germans in that it is satisfied and therefore peaceable, whilst theirs is unsatisfied and therefore violent. We are fighting, they say, to preserve the *status quo*. Nothing could be farther from the truth. Ours is not a static principle. It is dynamic. We are not fighting to preserve the *status quo*. We are fighting to preserve the possibility of progress. Our refusal to predict the details of the future arises from soberness of judgment, not from barrenness of ideas.

Already the British Empire has shown itself, by its example of toleration and wise government, to be a civilizing and humanizing influence over the whole world. It has been an instrument for raising the standard of life among backward races. It has been a great spiritual force, creating better feeling and understanding between nations. The duty of the British Commonwealth in the future will be to work side by side with the French Empire in order to guard and multiply these blessings.

Such, then, is our task. Both during and after the war it will be one of great difficulty. We must remain alive to its magnitude; we must not fall into an attitude of complacency. We say that ultimate victory in the war is certain. It is only certain if we make it so. The British Commonwealth has shown itself strong and united in time of trial, but we must not take its strength and its unity for granted. We must remember with pride and profound gratitude the splendid efforts of our brothers, separated by thousands of miles of ocean, to whom the war might well have seemed not half so real as it seems to us here in its very shadow. And this recognition must be a spur to us in our own efforts.

Looking beyond the war, we say that the future is ours. It is only ours if we make it so. We must sweep away the cobwebs of that placid ignorance which regards British Imperialism as a disreputable relic of a shady past. It is no such thing. It is a bridge to the next age. It is a source of comradeship and an opportunity of service. We must recognize it as such. In that recognition the future is indeed ours, not as rulers, but rather as servants of Empire.

9

LOCAL DEFENCE VOLUNTEERS

May 1. In Norway the last British troops left Aandalsnes in Central Norway, but operations continued throughout the month round Narvik. Mr. Eden made a speech at the Cordwainers' Dinner in the City of London, giving a warning against underestimating the enemy.

May 7. A two-day Debate began in the House of Commons, at the end of which, Mr. Neville Chamberlain decided to offer his resignation.

May 10. Germany invaded Holland and Belgium using airborne troops. The B.E.F. and French forces moved forward into Belgium as planned.

Mr. Neville Chamberlain resigned and Mr. Churchill was appointed Prime Minister. In the new Government, Mr. Eden became Secretary of State for War at the age of forty-two.

May 13. Queen Wilhelmina left Holland.

On May 14, Mr. Eden broadcast as Secretary of State for War, announcing the raising of the Local Defence Volunteers and calling for men to join:

I want to speak to you to-night about the form of warfare which the Germans have been employing so extensively against Holland and Belgium—namely the dropping of troops by parachute behind the main defensive lines. Let me say at once that the danger to us from this particular menace, though it undoubtedly exists, should not be exaggerated. We have made preparations to meet it already.

LOCAL DEFENCE VOLUNTEERS

Let me now describe to you the system under which these parachute raids are carried out. The troops arrive by aeroplane; but let it be remembered that any such aeroplane seeking to penetrate here, would have to do so in the teeth of the anti-aircraft defences of this country. If such penetration is effected, the parachutists are then dropped—it may be by day, it may be by night. These troops are especially armed, equipped, and some of them have undergone specialized training. Their function is to seize important points such as aerodromes, power stations, villages, railway junctions and telephone exchanges—either for the purpose of destroying them at once, or of holding them until the arrival of reinforcements. The purpose of the parachute attack is to disorganize and confuse, as a preparation for the landing of troops by aircraft.

The success of such an attack depends on speed. Consequently the measures to defeat such an attack must be prompt and rapid. It is upon this basis that our plans have been laid. You will not expect me to tell you, nor the enemy, what our plans are; but we are confident that they will be effective. However, in order to leave nothing to chance, and to supplement from sources as yet untapped, the means of defence already arranged, we are going to ask you to help us, in a manner which I know will be welcome to thousands of you.

Since the war began, the Government have received countless inquiries from all over the Kingdom from men of all ages who are for one reason or another not at present engaged in military service, and who wish to do something for the defence of their country. Well, now is your opportunity.

We want large numbers of such men in Great Britain, who are British subjects, between the ages of seventeen and sixty-five—seventeen and sixty-five—to come forward now and offer their services in order to make assurance doubly sure. The name of the new Force which is now to be raised will be "The Local Defence Volunteers"—Local Defence Volunteers. This name describes its duties in three words. It must be understood that this is, so to speak, a spare-time job, so there will be no need for any volunteer to abandon his present occupation.

Part-time members of existing civil defence organizations should ask their officers' advice before registering under the scheme. Men who will ultimately become due for calling up under the National Service (Armed Forces) Act may join temporarily and will be released to join the Army when they are required to serve.

Now a word to those who propose to volunteer. When on duty

72

you will form part of the armed forces, and your period of service will be for the duration of the war. You will not be paid, but you will receive uniform and will be armed. You will be entrusted with certain vital duties for which reasonable fitness and a knowledge of firearms is necessary. These duties will not require you to live away from your homes.

In order to volunteer, what you have to do is to give in your name at your local police station; and then, as and when we want you, we will let you know. This appeal is directed chiefly to those who live in country parishes, in small towns, in villages and in less densely inhabited suburban areas. I must warn you that for certain military reasons there will be some localities where the numbers required will be small, and others where your services will not be required at all.

Here, then, is the opportunity for which so many of you have been waiting. Your loyal help, added to the arrangements which already exist, will make and keep our country safe.

10

THE BATTLE OF THE PORTS

May 16. The B.E.F. was in position along the River Dyle.

May 17. General Gamelin's last Order of the Day.

May 21. M. Reynaud tells the French Senate that "the country is in danger".

May 24. Boulogne evacuated. Calais—sharp fighting begins.

May 26. Mr. Roosevelt, in the course of a broadcast talk, mentions "the futility, the impossibility of isolationism".

May 27. British troops captured Narvik in Norway. Calais falls.

May 28. King Leopold offers to surrender.

May 29. Dunkirk—mass evacuation begins.

June 3. All resistance had ceased at Dunkirk.

On June 2, the Secretary of State for War broadcast an account of the "Battle of the Ports" in the Home Service of the B.B.C.

I n the Battle of the Ports which has been raging during the past three weeks, Germany has made great strategic gains. The loss to us in equipment and in material has been heavy; but there is now another side to this picture. The bulk of the British Expeditionary Force has been saved; and quite apart from what the French have done for their own forces, we have been able to bring tens of thousands of our French Allies off with us from Dunkirk. Nor is the effort ended. Four days ago not one of us would have dared to hope that the isolated Allied Armies could have fought their way through the bottle-neck to the coast.

It is the spirit of the B.E.F. that has won through. These men

74

have marched hundreds of miles; they have fought countless actions with an enemy that hemmed them in and pressed upon them from three sides. The German High Command proudly announced that they were surrounded. They have fought their way out. How have they achieved the seemingly impossible?

Man for man, the British troops have proved themselves superior to the Germans wherever they have met them. All accounts show that the B.E.F. took a toll of the enemy greatly in excess of that suffered by themselves. On at least two occasions—at Arras and on the Ypres-Comines Canal—the losses suffered by the German Army were enormous. So it is that at the last the German strategy was foiled, and that despite the surrender of the Belgian Army, our own troops and our French Allies with them have fought their way through.

Let me now state the sequence of events.

At the call of the King of the Belgians, the British Expeditionary Force advanced into Belgium, and took up its position on the River Dyle. The advance lasted several days. Through events it could not control, our Army had to come back in less than half that time. It did so with little confusion and with few losses. Seventy-five miles forward, a fight at the end of the advance, and seventy-five miles back, fighting all the way; all in the space of ten days. That was the first phase of the Battle of the Ports, and it was brilliantly executed. I have a report of one division which did not lose a single straggler on that 150-mile march.

And here is a quotation from an account of an eye-witness of our troops under fire: "No display of drill at Olympia could be smarter than the work of men of our Forces that I saw. The feeling of confidence was magnificent."

And so the B.E.F. found itself back on the Scheldt with its strength in men and material almost intact. But meanwhile the German mechanized columns were pouring through the gap to the south, advancing across our lines of communication, biting ever deeper into our back areas. Desperate efforts were made to stem the tide. Units who had been sent to France to supply some of the much needed labour behind the lines were thrown into the fight and acquitted themselves splendidly. Others were sent to hold the Channel Ports in an effort to keep open communications with the British Expeditionary Force.

The story of the Battle for Boulogne has already been told. At Calais a small Allied Force put up a magnificent resistance. In spite of repeated attacks by the enemy and of continuous air and artillery bombardment, the garrison held out for several days. A summons to surrender was rejected by the British Commander. His troops fought on, to the end. We now know, from certain information which we have received, that this gallant defence drew off powerful German mechanized forces which must otherwise have been free to attack the flank of the B.E.F., at that time dangerously exposed.

While these events were taking place near our own shores, the Expeditionary Force was fighting for its life in its retreat on Dunkirk. Mechanized forces already encircled its western flank, and the collapse of the Belgian Army left open a wide gap between its eastern flank and the sea. There was no time to be lost. Divisions were moved rapidly to hold the flanks and heavy fighting took place while the enemy tried desperately to cut off the Allied Armies from the only base which was left to them. Some troops marched thirty-five miles in twenty-four hours. British brigades on the flanks stood firm. Despite the enormously extended frontage they have now to defend (at one one time the Expeditionary Force of nine divisions was holding a front of eighty miles) they held on, and they fought back. On the west, British troops defended the narrowing gap to the sea. Day after day the battle continued. At the end of it they had fought themselves to a standstill, but they held their ground, and by doing so they enabled the remainder of the Expeditionary Force to get clear.

On the east, Corps Artillery, coming into action against the enemy massing for attack, inflicted such heavy casualties that the attack never developed.

The stories of individual exploits at this time are legion: an anti-tank gunner who knocked out seven tanks; a subaltern who, after knocking out hostile tanks, swam a canal to bring back marked maps and other booty. But the triumph is not the triumph of individuals, however gallant; it is the triumph of an army. There is no braver epic in all our annals.

Here, then, is the story of the Battle of the Ports. From the moment of the collapse of the Belgian Army, there was only one course left to the Allied armies—to hold a line round Dunkirk, the only port that remained, and to embark as many men as possible before their rearguards were overwhelmed. Thanks to the magnificent and untiring co-operation of the Allied Navies and Air Forces, we have been able to embark and save more than four-fifths of that B.E.F. which the Germans claimed to have surrounded. The Army's debt to the Royal Navy, to the Merchant Navy and to the Royal Air Force can never be forgotten. We have been compelled to destroy much valuable material. We have suffered casualties. Once again, our Ally has to bear the invasion of the sacred soil of France. But the Germans, in spite of the huge losses which we know them to have suffered, have failed in their main object: to surround and annihilate the Allied Armies in the north.

The British Expeditionary Force still exists, not as a handful of fugitives, but as a body of seasoned veterans. We have had great losses in equipment. But our men have gained immeasurably in experience of warfare and in self-confidence. The vital weapon of any army is its spirit. Ours has been tried and tempered in the furnace. It has not been found wanting. It is this refusal to accept defeat that is the guarantee of final victory.

Our duty in this country is plain. We must make good our losses and we must win this war. To do that we must profit by the lessons of this battle. Brave hearts alone cannot stand up against steel. We need more planes, more tanks, more guns. The people of this country must work as never before. We must show the same qualities, the same discipline, and the same self-sacrifice at home as the British Expeditionary Force have shown in the field.

The nation honours with proud reverence those who fell that their comrades might win through. The innumerable actions, the countless deeds of valour of the last week, cannot all be recorded now. Each will have its place in history. Soldiers, sailors, airmen, who gave their lives to help—theirs is an immortal memory. Their spirit must be our banner, their sacrifice our spur.

II

THE DEFENCE OF THE HOME COUNTRY

June 10. British troops from Narvik returned to Britain.
June 11. Italy at war with France and Britain.
June 14. Germans entered Paris.
June 16. Marshal Pétain succeeded M. Reynaud.
June 17. France asked Germany for Armistice terms.
June 18. German forces reached Swiss frontier. Hitler met Mussolini.
June 22. Italians bombed Alexandria.
June 26. The Secretary of State for War broadcast on the defence of the home country.

The time is approaching when the enemy, having overrun all the outlying forts of liberty, will launch his assault on the main citadel, our own land. He has already delivered bombing attacks at night. No doubt these attacks will be continued. Possibly other forms of attack will be attempted also.

I am convinced that these can be repulsed. We shall, moreover, subject the enemy in his own country to constant and heavy attack from the air. We are confident that the enemy will be beaten off. And I will tell you why.

Your character is the first reason for my complete confidence. We know that you will never flinch. We have learned from the tragic fate of the French nation that civilization cannot be preserved by material means alone. We have seen that ramparts of concrete are not enough. It is only by the dedication of the human

78

spirit and the human will the length and breadth of the land that complete and final victory can be won.

These are dangerous days; days when the fibre of our race will be put to a hard test. But we also know in our hearts, that they are days of great opportunity such as come to few generations.

It is our privilege as an Empire, fighting together, to preserve, to restore, and, in the end, to extend the frontiers of freedom, and the presence of troops in these islands from every part of the Commonwealth is a stirring sign of the deep unity of purpose which inspires all its peoples. Their troops here are evidence of that.

The world has nowhere to look but to us for the salvation of the precious heritage of civilization which must inevitably pass from Europe unless we, like our brothers from overseas, show the invincible will to defend it. Those over whom the iron wheels of the conqueror have passed, those whom the conqueror now begins to threaten, alike base their hopes on our victory. We shall not fail them.

In this great adventure, each has his part to play. Those of you who are not in the Forces have already been told what to do in the case of attack. May I underline one point in the official advice you have received? That point is: stay where you are. Refugees on roads or railways hamstring those upon whom your defence depends. They are the outward and visible signs that the enemy has succeeded in creating the conditions on which he counts for military success.

The mass of refugees helped to lose the battle of France; they will not lose the battle of Britain. If you "stay put" you will find that the physical and material effects of air raids are by no means equal to their noise. Their bark, in fact, is more impressive than their bite. The enemy deliberately augments the noise to create alarm. He attaches devices to his bombs to magnify their noise, but these devices don't kill anybody and don't destroy anything. He thinks that we are a people who can be frightened out of our wits by these theatrical effects. We will show him that he is wrong.

I say these things to you because a brave and disciplined civilian population is the essential foundation of Home Defence. But the enemy will soon learn that it is not in the nature of our people to sit placidly and be bombed without retort. My confidence in the result of this conflict rests not only on the British character. We have an exceedingly powerful Air Force which will give the enemy a very bad time. Already, though operating at great disadvantages, it has inflicted severe losses upon him. It has often had to fight far from its bases, or from extemporized bases. So far it has never met the enemy without the numerical odds being in the enemy's favour. But remember what happened on the only occasion when it was operating from its own bases at home, and when the numerical odds were not utterly fantastic. During the evacuation from Dunkirk the R.A.F. are known to have destroyed as many as seventy German aircraft in one day. Our airmen can hope to do even better than this when fighting in their own skies.

But I must add one word of warning. If some of the enemy planes get through, as they will, or if the sky above your head happens to contain no British aircraft, don't ask angrily what the R.A.F. are doing. They will be bringing down enemy planes a hundred miles away or more who would otherwise be attacking you. They will be preventing damage to those things by which and through which we and our defences will live—docks, factories, ships or aerodromes.

We have great numbers of machines and we are getting more every day; but we shall always have to use them where they can most harm the enemy. And don't forget our guns, with which this country is now well provided, nor our balloon barrage which caught a couple of raiders the other night. I can't promise you that you will not be bombed; but I can and do promise you that the lot of the invader will become increasingly unenviable.

You have doubtless read that we are now a fortress. So we are, until the time comes to sally forth from the fortress to the attack. Remember that it is not sufficient merely to defeat the attack on these islands. I have told you why I believe that the air offensive of the enemy will be broken even though it may cause us loss, anxiety and distress. I will now tell you why I believe that every other form of offensive will end in defeat for the enemy.

The Prime Minister said last week that we had a million and a quarter men under arms in this country, without including the 500,000 Local Defence Volunteers. Since he spoke, these forces have been increased by the arrival of Australian and New Zealand contingents and by the return of large numbers of British, Canadian and Allied troops from France. Many of these men have met the enemy. They are confident that they can beat him.

Never before have we had a greater number of soldiers in this island. We are confident that we can throw a sufficient force against any enemy who lands on our shores, attack him and defeat him. If he is able to run the gauntlet of the Fleet and the Air Force, or descend upon our land from the air, we shall be attacking the enemy on our own soil, for our own homes, with all our forces under our own command, unhampered by the necessity of sending supplies and reinforcements overseas.

We do not underestimate the enemy; but for once *he* will be operating under the disadvantages which *we* have always experienced in our continental wars; and in addition he will have to supply his forces overseas without possessing the command of the sea. I can, therefore, speak to you to-night in a spirit of reasoned confidence.

I know that we have to face hard and anxious times, but I also know that our strength and spirit are sufficient for any trial. At times like these there are bound to be faint-hearted people. Never listen to them. Remember also that apart from our own strength, we are receiving great help from the United States of America. The United States, with the strong support of public opinion in that country, are sending us supplies of arms and munitions. By so doing they are rendering us a service of which we are in need, for a cause which they have fully understood.

Let me make it quite clear that we are obtaining these munitions not in a mere hope that they will enable us to delay a conquest of our island, but because we are firmly convinced that they will enable us to win the war. It is not only we who are being besieged— Germany too is beleaguered. For she and her ally Italy remain cut off from supplies of many things without which a long prosecution of war is impossible. Our stranglehold is still round their necks, and our Navy can and will keep it there.

I want to impress upon you once more that no battle can, of course, be won by standing on the defensive or even by successful counter-attack alone. When the time comes, as assuredly it will, to carry the war against the enemy, wherever he may be found, you can be certain that we shall do so with all our might. Already, in other parts of the world, we are achieving success in offensive operations. It is this offensive spirit which so clearly animates our forces in the Middle East. It augurs well for the future.

We can have no doubt of the issue, you and I. This is a conflict between two ways of life which admits of no compromise. It is the age-long struggle between good and evil. It is not enough merely to preserve Christian civilization, now in such deadly peril and placed for a time on the defensive. Real and complete victory will come because the British peoples are inspired by burning faith in their own high ideals and by a determination to set them up again in places where for the time being those ideals have been beaten down.

If the challenge is formidable the opportunity is without parallel. This is a struggle for the future of man, for the eternal freedom of his mind and soul.

12

A SURVEY OF OUR POSITION—
AUGUST 1940

June 29. Roumania having accepted Russian terms, Russian troops occupied Bessarabia and Bukovina.

July 3. Britain assumed control over ships of the French Fleet lying in British waters and after an ultimatum disabled the French warships at Oran.

July 8. Marshal Pétain's Government broke off diplomatic relations with Britain.

July 12. Britain agreed to close the Burma Road to armament traffic for three months.

July 23. Mr. Eden announced in the House of Commons that it was proposed to submit for His Majesty's approval an Order in Council giving the Local Defence Volunteers the title "Home Guard".

August 4. Mr. Churchill warned the country that the danger of invasion is still great.

August 12. The German Air Force launched determined attacks on England. The R.A.F. repulsed the attacks and destroyed 217 German aircraft between August 12 and 16.

On August 14, the Secretary of State for War surveyed the war position in a broadcast after the nine o'clock news:

I n less than a month's time we shall have been at war for a year, and those who thought of this as a short war may be beginning to revise their opinions.

A SURVEY OF OUR POSITION

Of course this is no new story. In August 1914 the Germans were assured by their rulers that they would be home by Christmas. This time German propaganda has promised friend and foe alike that the summer of 1940 will see the end of the war.

We think otherwise. We disagree both as to the time and the manner in which the war will end. For us the real war, in which the British Empire will put forward the whole of its strength, has hardly begun. For us the real war will begin when we take the offensive and strike home at the enemy. That is the way wars are won, and that is what we mean to do.

But first let us look back for a moment. Much has happened since last I spoke to you some six weeks ago. I spoke then at a dark and menacing moment in our history. The great evacuation operation at Dunkirk early in June had saved nearly the whole of the British Expeditionary Force. The spirit of that force was unbroken, but it was a force which had been compelled, through no fault of its own, to leave in enemy hands most of its equipment and transport. Therefore, a tremendous task had to be tackled, and tackled immediately.

First of all, over two hundred thousand men had to be sorted out into their original units, infantry, gunners, sappers, tank units, just as they had come up out of the sea.

For several days trains left our south-eastern ports every few minutes, packed with troops and carrying them to their sorting stations all over the country. We owe our railways a debt of gratitude for what they accomplished during those hazardous days.

Then each unit had to be brought up to strength. Some of them had lost heavily, especially in officers and non-commissioned officers. Fresh drafts, however, were immediately forthcoming.

When these had been absorbed, each regiment or unit had to be moved to its appointed position in the combined defence scheme organized for the immediate protection of our island against invasion. All these moves were speedily completed.

But even that is not the whole account that has to be given. These units had to be re-equipped. For two months and more the re-issue of arms and equipment of every kind has been going on at top speed.

Thanks to the sustained and devoted effort of our armament and munitions workers, output has been accelerated and continuously increased from day to day.

To these divisions of the B.E.F. we had of course to add many divisions of the Army which have not yet had experience abroad.

84

Some of these have had a monotonous duty to perform. They were handicapped during the winter months by hard weather conditions and shortage of equipment; but their spirit remained steadfast, and their material difficulties are now being overcome.

But—and this is what I want to emphasize—we had not only to provide for the present; we had to build for the future. If the Army was to play its full part in the struggle that lay ahead, we had clearly to do more than re-equip the B.E.F. and reinforce them with the existing divisions at home.

For that reason we have greatly accelerated the rate of intake into the Army in the last three months. The previous pace has been multiplied many times.

Since May we have called up for actual training half a million men.

The other day I visited a large contingent of the more recently joined of these recruits, to see the progress of their training. I must say I was astonished. After only four or five weeks they are drilling and moving like veterans.

Their one thought seems to be to fit themselves for active service in the shortest possible period of time. Never have I seen a more striking example of the spirit of the true soldier.

But our native Home Forces do not stand alone. We have Canadian, Australian and New Zealand troops with us, and everybody knows what that means in vigorous fighting strength.

We have a contingent of French troops of the Army of all Free Frenchmen. We have Polish troops, Czechs, Norwegians, Belgians, and Dutch, all eager for our first great counter-attack; because that is what a successful defence of our island must prove to be.

Both in men and in material our reserves, too, are mounting day by day.

And here I should like in particular to say a word about the Home Guard, now over a million and a half strong. When I made my first appeal I knew you well enough to realize that the response would be immediate. I knew, too, that, with our national talent for local organization in our towns and villages, a formidable army would spring into life. But my expectations have been far exceeded.

Difficulties, and these were bound to be many, have been overcome, by cheerful willing service and we have to-day a force which in our estimation is admirably adapted for its particular task.

These results have impressed me greatly, but what has impressed me infinitely more than any of them is the wonderful spirit of this magnificent body of volunteers which has sprung into existence, a spirit which cannot fail to act as an inspiration to the whole Army.

To-day the Royal Navy commands the seas, and the Royal Air Force have shown themselves more than a match for their opponents, whether in attack or defence. The exploits of both these services have been most gallant; a splendid epic in our history.

Meanwhile, the Field Army at home has watched with admiration their deeds and those of all three services in the lands of the Middle East. Now, maybe one day soon it will be the turn of the Army at home. If so, every soldier will welcome the challenge. The second phase of the Battle of Britain appears to be opening. We make no boast, but we feel a quiet confidence.

This is a world war and not a European war in the sense that the result of this war will decide the future course of the world, whether it is to relapse into savagery or whether it is to go forward on the path of free and ordered progress. I would like, therefore, to make this suggestion:

When you open your atlas, as you doubtless often do, to study the progress of the war, do not open it at the map of Europe but at the map of the world. The map of Europe is misleading, because it does not tell the whole truth. It merely tells a flattering tale to Germany. It consists very largely of Germany itself and various "German occupied" or "German controlled" countries. All that can be seen of British power and British effort is comprised within two islands, looking rather small and inconspicuous, somewhere up in the left-hand top corner of the map.

The general effect from the German point of view is most impressive—awe-inspiring. In fact, for us to hold out a moment longer seems to Dr. Goebbels and his satellites nothing more or less than a piece of foolish British obstinacy.

Well, we have our own opinion as to our capability to hold out; and not merely hold out, but strike out. Let us turn back a page or two of the atlas and look at the map of the world. Straight away a very different face of things is seen, and Europe assumes its proper proportions.

Europe then becomes a very much smaller place and the oceans are seen to be very large. The Seven Seas come into the picture, covering twice as much of the earth's surface as all the continents put together; and that is where Britannia has a word to say, the last word. Over these oceans come the immense resources which help to forge our engines of war, and beyond these oceans are the other members of the British Commonwealth, who are body and soul with us in this struggle, and many others too who ardently desire our victory and are giving us material help to secure it.

Given this picture as correct, there are two questions often asked here and elsewhere by our sympathizers.

How are the British going to win the war and what are their plans when the war is won?

An answer can be given without revealing any military secrets to the enemy. Modern wars require the command of world resources, and in order to have these resources at your command sea-power is the first essential.

It has been proved before and it will be proved again that sea-power is a stronger weapon than land-power, which is limited in scope. The Germans know this well, but they hoped in this war to overcome the difficulty by mastery of the air.

There are those in Germany who contend that overwhelming air-power without sea-power is a possible means of achieving victory, but vastly superior sea-power with rapidly growing air-power is a much more likely means. That is our position, and that is one of the reasons why the chances of victory are more in our favour than in Germany's.

Superior power at sea which we possess, and in the air, which we are determined to reach, combined with an ever-increasing army, will secure our victory. The proper use of this power for striking the enemy in each of these spheres is the way that we shall win the war.

And when the time comes for us to strike, where will Hitler's Fifth Column be found? Where will he find friends in Poland, Czechoslovakia, Norway, Denmark, Holland, Belgium, France, Austria?

Like ghosts arising from the dead with arms in their hands the nations that he has ravished for a season will turn upon him. Then we shall not be alone. Then the Foreign Legions, now forming in our midst, small in numbers but great in heart, will be swollen into a multitude of men demanding their freedom and going out sword in hand to recover it. For a short season we fight alone and we are proud to fight alone until the forces of freedom are marshalled in their tens of thousands.

And now, what of the future? Hitler's plans in so far as he has revealed them are fairly clear. A Europe under his control is described as his new order for Europe. It is certainly not new. There is nothing new about tyranny.

It was practised in every country in the world till men became civilized enough to prefer individual liberty. Nor can it properly be called order. For a minority to attempt to hold down in permanent subjection the vast majority is a direct invitation to disorder: and Hitler in the foreign lands he rules to-day can establish no order save the rule of force.

We, too, want a new order, but an order of a very different kind, a really new order throughout the world in partnership with other nations, nations free to direct their lives, free to make their choice. We know that all the nations now forced to yield to German pressure desire our victory, so that they may freely make that choice.

We are determined that the world shall not be the same after this war as it was before. There must be no war-weariness or peace-weariness this time. There must be no wishful thinking about the future. There must be no third war in our time or in our children's time.

We have to fashion a new world where our ideals will prevail and where we shall have and keep the force to see that they do prevail. No half-measures, no buying-off of implacable enemies, but a full measure of peace, peace between free nations based upon principles in which we have confidence because we know that they are right.

We are standing alone against the greatest tyranny in history to win the kind of peace we believe in for ourselves and for others, and we mean to have it. The world is going to go forward, not back. That is our firm determination, and by God's help we shall achieve it.

1941

13

THE MEDITERRANEAN AND THE
MIDDLE EAST

Mr. Eden remained at the War Office until December 23, 1940 when, at the request of the Prime Minister, he returned to the Foreign Office after an absence of nearly three years.

During the late summer and autumn, he had, in conjunction with the C.I.G.S., the late Field Marshal Sir John Dill, recommended the transfer of strong land and air forces from the U.K. to the Middle East. In October he paid his second war-time visit to that theatre. In the ensuing weeks he had several conferences with General Wavell; he visited General O'Connor's Headquarters in the Western Desert in company with General Wilson, and also flew with General Wavell to Khartoum for a conference with Field Marshal Smuts, before returning to the United Kingdom.

October 28. Italy invaded Greece.

November 4. British troops landed in Crete.

November 9. General Wavell's offensive started in the Western Desert.

January 22. Tobruk was captured.

February 8. Benghazi was captured.

In February 1941, accompanied by the C.I.G.S., Mr. Eden returned for a third time to the Middle East, on this occasion as Foreign Secretary. On February 22 they went to Athens; and on February 26 they arrived in Turkey where they met General Inönü, the President, M. Sarajoglu, the Foreign Minister, the Chief of Staff, and Sir Stafford Cripps who had flown down from Moscow in a plane provided by the Soviet Government. Full agreement with Turkey was announced on February 28.

March 1. German troops entered Bulgaria.

March 2. The Regent of Yugoslavia, Prince Paul, went to Berchtesgaden.

March 3. First detachment of British troops arrived in Greece.

March 25. Yugoslavia signed the Three-Power Pact (Italy, Germany and Yugoslavia).

March 27. Coup d'état in Yugoslavia.

March 31. German troops counter-attacked our outposts at El Agheila.

April 1. Mr. Eden and the C.I.G.S. again went to Athens, whence the C.I.G.S. flew to Belgrade.

April 6. German troops invaded Greece and Yugoslavia.

April 11. German troops invested Tobruk.

April 28. Main body of British troops had completed the evacuation from Greece.

May 2. War flared up in Iraq due to action by Rashid Ali. British troops intervened.

On May 6, Mr. Eden spoke in a Debate in the House of Commons.[1]

---

[1] It has emerged from the documents captured after the German surrender in 1945, and put before the Nuremberg Court, that Hitler first ordered preparations to be made for the occupation of Greece on 12 November 1940. In a further order dated 13 December 1940, he directed that the invasion of Greece was to start as soon as the weather was advantageous.

How far the German occupation of Greece was in Hitler's mind a necessary precaution to the invasion of Russia, may never be proved. However this may be, there is no doubt that the Yugoslav *coup d'état* caused a diversion of German land and air forces and a modification of the build-up against Russia which had already begun. It is hard to believe that the instigators of the Yugoslav *coup d'état* would have taken action without the known support of British diplomacy and the presence of British arms in Greece.

Documents show that on 6 September, 1940, General Jodl signed a directive about the cover plan for the increase of troops on the Eastern front, and that on November 12, the same day as the order for preparations to be made to invade Greece, Hitler wrote that the political task to determine Russia's attitude had begun. The first plan for the invasion of Russia (operation Barbarossa) was issued on November 16. D-Day for Barbarossa was not finally fixed until May 1, when Greece had been completely cleared of British troops, though it appears that a date much earlier than June 22 was originally intended.

I beg to move:
"That this House approves the policy of His Majesty's Government in sending help to Greece and declares its confidence that our operations in the Middle East and in all other theatres of war will be pursued by the Government with the utmost vigour."

It was my hope to-day to give the House as full and as clear an account as I could of the events of the last two or three months, particularly in their relation to hostilities in the Middle East; but I find myself in a position of some little difficulty in trying to do this. We are not alone: others listen in to every word that is said in these Debates; and there is much that I would like to tell which, perforce, I am unable to tell at the present time, for I have so to phrase my remarks that, while I give the House and the world as much information as lies in my power, I do not assist the enemy in any way in his activities. I am reminded of a notice which will be familiar to a great many Members of this House, which used to be written up in the railway carriages in France and in most restaurants, wherever one went in the last war: "*Taisez-vous, méfiez-vous, les oreilles ennemies vous écoutent.*"

MR. THORNE (Plaistow): Translate.

MR. EDEN: I was going to do so. I might translate it as: "Shut up, watch your step; there are Huns about." I would adopt that guiding principle in what I am about to tell the House. I would bring the memory of the House back to the early days of February and what then seemed to the Government to be the German plan for the early spring campaign. The Germans had then assembled a large number of divisions in Roumania, and they were beginning a process of infiltration into Bulgaria; German civilians were taking up positions on Bulgarian aerodromes. It seemed quite clear to us then that the object of all this was, step by step, to overrun the Balkans; and, having occupied Roumania, by methods we know of, to establish themselves in Bulgaria; thereby to encircle Yugoslavia, to subjugate Greece, to immobilize Turkey; and, from that position, attained, if possible, without firing a single shot, to deliver their main blow from secured bases at our position in the Eastern Mediterranean. That, it seemed to us at the beginning of February, was the German intention. I said: "Without firing a single shot." I did so deliberately, because it was obviously a part of the German plan to secure the natural resources of the

Balkans and to keep their communications intact, in order to further their next stage of attacking against our positions in the Eastern Mediterranean. There was, no doubt, a subsidiary purpose in this plan, to bring help to their Italian ally, whose war was not going any too well in Albania. Hitler has described how well the Italians did. He congratulates them on weakening Greece—45,000,000 weakening 7,000,000. I do not suppose that ever a more insulting tribute has been paid to any ally. As we watched that Greek campaign in Albania, supported by our Air Force, but against the heaviest odds in men and material, we must have thought of a paraphrase of my right hon. Friend's words: never was so much surrendered by so many to so few.

Now, I come to February 8, which was the date on which our Forces entered Benghazi—a brilliant exploit, which brought valuable gain. But, with the supreme effort entailed by that advance, the armoured troops who had so large a share in it had to rest and refit. Their vehicles, the House will recall, had not only been engaged in a continuous advance for two months but had, many of them, been engaged in action for a much longer time with hardly a rest. So there was no prospect of prolonging the advance with those armoured vehicles beyond the point reached at Benghazi, and any prolonged advance by those formations into Tripoli was out of the question. I mention that, because I would like to tell the House also that the previous plan had been to stop after the capture of Tobruk and make the Western flank there, but so brilliant had been the success, and so great had been the disorganization of the enemy, that it was rightly decided to seek to realize rapidly a further brilliant advance. Another consideration of which the House will be aware when considering a further advance was that the harbour at Benghazi was then unusable. Its preparation must have taken some time; and, meanwhile, any further advance would have had to be based on the small harbour at Tobruk, which, although good, is small, while our main base would, of course, have been back in the Delta. I mention this point, although of course, there were others, including air and naval problems, upon which I will not dwell.

On that date, February 8, there reached His Majesty's Government a Note from the Greek Government. That Note confirmed the determination of the Greek Government to resist German aggression. It told us that Greece had united her fate with ours, and would fight until final victory. It asked us to consider what help we could give, and the conditions upon which we could give it. But I must make this clear. This Note from the Greek Government was no cry for help. The Greeks have never cried for help. It was a statement of the Greek position, and a request that we should state ours. In the face of those conditions the Government decided to maintain the position at which they had previously arrived, to halt the desert advance at Benghazi, and to prepare forces to go to the help of Greece. That decision was, of course, a decision of the Government and of their chief military advisers. If Greece was to be helped in the conditions then existing, it was obvious that that help must be made ready and brought to bear very rapidly. Many problems required discussion and solution— diplomatic and military problems: the position of Yugoslavia, Greece's northern neighbour; the necessity for keeping Turkey informed of our plans. It seemed to the Government, in doing that, that the wisest step to take was to attempt direct negotiations in an endeavour to solve these questions. So they entrusted the Chief of the Imperial General Staff and myself with the task, and we were sent out as envoys on this mission. Perhaps the House will allow me to say that neither of us ever had the least doubt of the odds against the full success of our mission. We knew perfectly well that the German plans were far advanced, we knew how great was their material power, but I still think we should have been to blame, if we had not made the attempt.

May I make one other observation before I come to what followed, because it is pertinent to an understanding of the whole position? When, last summer, the French Government sued for an armistice, we were left, in the Middle East, in a position of the utmost difficulty and gravity. Let the House remember that the three main armies in the Middle East were French armies—the army in Syria, the army in Tunis, and, on a smaller scale but strategically most important, the French forces in Jibuti. With the armistice and the collapse of French resistance, our Forces were left to meet the situation without the help of any of those armies, and our Forces were relatively small. What was worse, they had many serious shortages of equipment, and I am revealing no secret if I say that in the late summer of last year the Government here at home were deeply exercised by the situation in the Middle East. After General Wavell had come home for consultation, my right hon. Friend the Prime Minister and the Government took the decision to take great risks to reinforce that army. We then sent out armoured units, men and material and aircraft, and it was this equipment and these weapons which enabled General Wilson and General O'Connor, in their desert advance, to secure such brilliant successes. I have no doubt the decision was justified, but it is only fair that the House should appreciate that it was taken at the gravest risks, in the light of the then state of our equipment here. Since then, we have maintained a continuous stream of men and materials to the Middle East, and the country has contributed to making that stream possible by submitting to restrictions of imports here.

That is not the whole story. By the Anglo-French Agreement with Turkey we were, jointly, under an obligation to provide Turkey with certain important war materials, and this country had given, as long ago as April 1939, a guarantee to Greece. Therefore, with the collapse of France the fulfilment of those obligations— the equipment of Turkey, and the guarantee to Greece—fell exclusively on our own shoulders. That is the background against which, I think, the House should view the problem with which we were confronted.

Now as regards our mission. After certain unhelpful eccentricities of weather, we arrived in Cairo several days behind schedule. But that fact imposed no delay, because we found when we got there, that the three Commanders-in-Chief were in complete agreement with the policy advocated in London, the policy, that is, of sending help to Greece, or, to put it more accurately, of supplementing the help already sent to Greece, by the despatch of land forces. We found, moreover, that the land formations to be sent had already been decided upon in principle, and that preparations were in hand for their concentration, and, if all was agreed, for their despatch. I would not think it necessary to mention that, except that there have been certain malicious reports of disagreements between, I believe, the C.I.G.S. and myself and the Commanders-in-Chief out there. The C.I.G.S. has asked me to associate him with the statements which I make that there is not a word of truth in any of these reports. I cannot help thinking, as many of us may have felt on reading them, that perhaps Goebbels might be left to do his work for himself. I would like to pay my tribute to the way in which these three Commanders-in-Chief—the Commander-in-Chief Middle East, General Wavell, the Commander-in-Chief Mediterranean and the Air Officer Commander-in-Chief who were all present at our conversations and all in agreement—shouldered these new responsibilities, realizing perfectly well what they must entail for them. I should add that it was considered that the Forces to be left in Cyrenaica would be sufficient to meet any threat that could be expected to develop there.

After a very brief interval we decided therefore, all of us, to go at once to Athens. I say "all of us", but I ought to exclude the Commander-in-Chief in the Mediterranean, Admiral Cunningham, who had, at that moment, one of his occasional appointments with an elusive enemy. He was, of course, represented. We went to Athens to see the representatives of the Greek Government. That, I think, probably would be about February 22. The moment we landed at the aerodrome I received a message saying that the King and the Prime Minister wished to see me alone before the actual meeting began. When I saw them they told me this: They made it once more abundantly clear that Greece was determined to resist German aggression as she had resisted Italian aggression. The Prime Minister added that, whatever the hope of repulsing the enemy, Greece would defend her national territory, even if she could count only on her own forces.

I should like to say at this point how deeply impressed we all were by the courage and loyalty shown by the Greek leaders with whom we had to work, at every stage of these discussions and of the later events as well. These men had laboured long and earnestly to build up the prosperity of a small country that had never menaced anyone. I know something of what it meant to them to appreciate that, having beaten one aggressor, now an even more formidable bully was approaching to destroy their country. Yet knowing that, neither the King, nor the Government, nor the people ever flinched or faltered. Nothing perhaps is more characteristic of their spirit than that, as they greeted our troops on their arrival with flowers, so they greeted those who left, at the end of the fighting, with flowers.

At these discussions we told the Greek Government our views of the German plans, and we told them what forces could be made available by our Commanders-in-Chief in the Middle East. Then the Chiefs of Staff and the Commanders-in-Chief of the two armies considered what were the possibilities of holding a line, with our forces and with such forces as the Greeks could make available. They were fully aware, of course, of the risk, politically, and they knew the risks being run particularly in respect of the air, but they came to the conclusion that the establishment of Anglo-Greek forces on the Haliakmon Line afforded a reasonable fighting chance of holding the German advance. The decision as to the line to take was reached very quickly and in complete agreement between the military experts of the two countries. There were two other alternatives, with which many Members of this House will be familiar. One was the frontier line, strongly defended, known as the Metaxas Line, and the other was the line of the Struma, also a very strong natural position; but in view of the uncertainty about Greece's northern neighbours, it was decided by the military commanders—and, I think there can be no question, rightly decided—that the short line of Haliakmon was the line to attempt to hold.

I submit to the House, with this Motion, that that decision was, politically and militarily, the right decision. Wolfe has said: "War is an option of difficulties."

War is certainly an option of difficulties until our strength in every arm, in every theatre, is so great that it makes the odds all even. May I recall to the House the conditions in which Greece came into the war? I am not sure that the House is familiar with the circumstances. In the early morning, at three o'clock, the Italian Minister called on General Metaxas and presented him with an ultimatum, which, he said, would come into force at six. The ultimatum contained this clause—that Italy demanded certain bases in Greece. General Metaxas said: "What bases?" The Italian Minister said that he did not know. Those were the cynical conditions in which the first attack on Greece was made, before even the ultimatum expired, and those were the conditions in which our guarantee first came into effect. So that was the position, politically. We had given Greece an unsolicited guarantee. The Greek Army had fought most gallantly and had, with the help of the Royal Air Force, flung back the Italian invader. The Greek Government had made it plain that they would resist German aggression.

In this war we are fighting, not for gains, but for causes; and Greece is the embodiment of those causes. I believe that had we not gone to her help, we could not have raised our heads again. It so happened at that time that we had the advantage of consulting, in Cairo, that most wise statesman and tried warrior, General Smuts. I asked him if he would be kind enough to come to Cairo while we were there, and with characteristic generosity he did so, and we were able to consult him on the situation. He has authorized me to say—and indeed his speeches have since made plain—that he too was in complete agreement with the decision arrived at. From Greece there have been no repining and no recriminations. Greece knows now that she has to live through an unhappy interlude until she regains her freedom. It is our duty to ensure, by every means in our power, that that interlude shall be as short as possible.

On the military side, there are one or two observations that I would like to make. Hitler has had to fight his way through two countries—Yugoslavia and Greece—through which he hoped to march unchallenged. Both in supplies and in communications, from the Danube to the Peloponnese, problems and difficulties have been created for him from which he hoped to escape by subjugating these countries without a shot being fired. The other day I sent, at the request of an hon. Member of this House, who was cheered by this House, a message to the Greek Government congratulating them on the valour and actions of their troops, and I have received a reply to this which, I think, I ought to give to the House:

"I thank you for your cordial message. Please assure the House of Commons and the British people that their eulogies of the Greek Army will touch the hearts of our whole nation. We will never forget the loyal and courageous help which the British and Imperial troops gave to our soldiers in the defence of their native land. Our Allies showed themselves worthy to rank with the ancient heroes of Thermopylae and wrote new pages of gold in the glorious book of British history. I desire once again to assure you that we will continue the struggle by the side of our great Ally, the noble peoples of the British Commonwealth, until victory is won and the triumph of the ideals of liberty, morality and international justice is achieved."

I think you will agree that the generous spirit of that message was the spirit which has animated the Greek nation throughout its ordeal.

I now turn to another aspect of our problem. It was clearly of the utmost importance to know what policy was going to be pursued by Greece's northern neighbour, Yugoslavia. Of course, we had been attempting to do that for a long time through the ordinary diplomatic channels. When we arrived out there we did all we could to probe this subject to the bottom. We got plenty of assurances that a German attack on Yugoslavia would be resisted, but that was not enough. What we needed was a common plan, so that if the attack developed, we would have the best chance of resisting it together. We made every effort to secure it, and every effort failed, until the moment of the *coup d'état*. We did have one brief Staff contact, but that did not lead to any real progress. But that is not quite all. During these conversations we were given to understand over and over again that the Yugoslav army was mobilizing, and when we expressed our anxiety that they would be too late, the reply always came: "But we are mobilizing, so that, if the worst comes to the worst, we shall be ready." In fact, however, that mobilization was not proceeding fast enough, and it was not, again, until the *coup d'état* took place that the new Government of General Simovitch made a real, immediate effort, an urgent effort, to get the armies ready. It was then too late, too late with the best will in the world, to mobilize the armies and to concentrate them where they had to be if they were to give us the support and help we needed. So it was that despite all the gallantry of the Yugoslav army, which has been as splendid in this war as it was in the last, despite all that, the Yugoslav armies could not stop and did not stop the German drive right through southern Serbia to the Monastir Gap. Perhaps it is idle and unprofitable to speculate, but had the Government that preceded the *coup d'état* in Yugoslavia as clearly understood their country's true interest as did the Government of General Simovitch, then the whole story might have been different. But none of these things can detract from the courage of the decision which the Yugoslav people eventually took. We have pledged ourselves to redeem Yugoslavia's independence, and that pledge will be honoured.

Now I come to another country. While we were in the Middle East, as it is so inaccurately called, we had, of course, frequent opportunities for conversations with Turkish statesmen. A glance at the map will show the House how Turkey's strategic position differs from that of Greece or of Yugoslavia. The contacts we had with these Turkish Ministers enabled us to lay before them the Balkan situation as we saw it, and to discuss it with them on a firm basis of mutual confidence. The Turkish Government were informed, as an ally, of our plans in connection with Greece, and they were naturally cognisant of the development of the situation in Yugoslavia. I must tell the House that I was, throughout these conversations, deeply impressed by the loyal friendship shown by the Turkish statesmen whom we had occasion to meet and by their determination and the determination of their people to stand firm against any menace to their sovereignty or any encroachment on their rights and interests. Since the beginning of this war Turkey has rendered great service to our cause by her policy of independence. The importance of her role as a bulwark against fresh aggression in the Middle East is obvious, and I am sure that loyalty to their alliance with this country is, as ever, the basis of the Turkish Government's foreign policy.

Meanwhile, trouble has been created in another country which is of great concern to Turkey and ourselves—Iraq. Unconstitutional action by Rashid Ali has already led once to his fall from power. When later he seized power again His Majesty's Government saw no reason why this or any other event in Iraq should deprive them of their clear Treaty rights. They accordingly informed the Iraqi Government of their intention to land troops at Basra and to open up lines of communication through Iraq in accordance with the terms of their Treaty. Nothing can excuse the action of the Iraqi military leaders in first accepting and then challenging our clear Treaty rights. This country has a record of which it has no need to be ashamed in its dealings with Arab people, and, above all, with Iraq. It is we who assured the independence of modern Iraq, and it is we who have assisted her and in every respect have kept our word. I do not propose now to describe in detail the events of the last few days, but only to make plain to the world our present position. We are very grateful for the offer of good offices by the Turkish and Egyptian Governments. Our position is as follows: the first requisite is the withdrawal of troops from Habbaniyah and the cessation of hostilities against His Majesty's Forces in Iraq. When this has been done and fighting between Allied nations has in consequence ceased, His Majesty's Government are prepared to discuss the fulfilment of their Treaty rights, which His Majesty's Government must make it plain that they are in all circumstances determined to maintain.

May I say this one word of friendly counsel to all our Arab friends? No people have more reason to fear an Axis victory than those who dwell in Arab lands. Many of their most distinguished leaders have already realized this. For a long time past Italian papers have recurrently been full of the day which they are heralding when they hope to see a British defeat. Why? Because on that day, if their hopes are fulfilled, it is Italy which will control the Arab lands of Northern Africa and elsewhere. Every Arab must know what that will mean. In all recent history there has been no rule more cruel or ruthless than that imposed by Italy on the Arabs in Tripoli and Libya. If anybody doubts it, let him read an interesting neutral book written by a Dane who knew the Arab world well—*Desert Encounter*. He will find there a record of that rule and of the literal decimation of the Arab population. What of the other partner? Hitler said the day before yesterday that he was an interested spectator in the Balkans—a spectator whose rule is based on military might and the Gestapo. Arabs in any land must know that the approach of Axis rule means the end of their liberties, which they have jealously guarded and which, in alliance with us, are safe to-day.

Let me try to sum up. Now and for some time to come the dominant note must be for ships and munitions of war and for more ships and for more munitions of war. Every move in the diplomatic field is conditioned by our military strength. To-day with no country, does Germany or Italy show in any way the least respect for engagements; the only sanction is force. No effort now must be spared to reduce disparity, for it is thus that we shall come to victories in diplomacy just as much as on the battlefield. The United States to-day are helping us greatly in many spheres and in many ways. The more fully, the more rapidly, the more certainly that help can reach the battlefields in Asia, Africa and Europe, the shorter will be the duration of the war.

MR. BENJAMIN SMITH (Rotherhithe): We had better do a bit ourselves.

MR. EDEN: I was presupposing the maximum effort by ourselves and by the United States of America. That is why I welcome the immense step forward taken by the United States in deciding to send their ships to the Red Sea.

Germany to-day enjoys material advantages; she enjoys also the advantage of fighting on inner lines. But there is another side to this story, and I will mention just one incident, in conclusion, to illustrate it to the House. A little while ago two prisoners, British soldiers who had been captured in northern France, were transferred to a prison camp in East Prussia. From that camp they escaped, and they travelled all through Poland, across Hungary, through Yugoslavia, and through Greece to Athens. They could speak no word of any language but their own. They are at this moment, I believe, with their units in the Western Desert. That clearly was not only a fine feat by the men themselves, but it was only made possible because in each one of those countries there are thousands, nay, millions, of people longing for an opportunity to help a British victory. Hitler, though he may rule the lives of these people, cannot rule their hearts. So, it seems to me, no one tyrant can rule over all Europe for longer than a brief span. It must be our privilege, backed by the help we are receiving from the United States, to win for the nations of Europe the right to live their own lives in peace and tranquillity, secure at last from the haunting dread that shadows our own time.

14

REPLY TO HITLER'S NEW ORDER

On February 6, Mr. J. G. Winant was appointed U.S.A. Ambassador to the Court of St. James. He arrived in London on March 1. In welcoming him on May 14, Mr. Eden said of him: "He cares much for his work, little for party politics, not at all for himself. Humanity is the key to Mr. Winant's life work."

On March 11, President Roosevelt signed the Lease-Lend Bill.

By the end of April, U.S. Navy patrols were operating 2,000 miles out into the Atlantic, and were shadowing Axis raiders in the Atlantic.

May 12. Hess landed by parachute in Scotland.

May 15. Mr. Eden announced that French airports in Syria were being used by German aircraft and warned Vichy.

May 20. Germans launched airborne assault on Crete.

May 27. The *Bismarck* was sunk. H.M.S. *Hood* had been lost on May 24.

May 30. Rashid Ali fled as British troops closed in on Baghdad, and the next day the rebels asked for an armistice.

June 1. Fifteen thousand British troops had been evacuated from Crete where organized resistance had now ceased.

June 2. Hitler and Mussolini met at the Brenner Pass.

On May 29, Mr. Eden delivered a speech at the Mansion House. He concentrated his remarks mainly on the future of Europe after the war, but at the beginning he referred to the desire amongst many Arabs for a greater degree of Arab unity. This speech, in which Mr. Eden showed that the Government took a parallel line to President Roosevelt on the future of Europe, created an excellent impression in the U.S.A. where non-interventionists had been asserting that the aim of Great Britain was to put the British Empire back where it was, entirely for the benefit of the investing classes and "Imperialists".

REPLY TO HITLER'S NEW ORDER

My Lord Mayor, your Excellencies, my Lords, Ladies and Gentlemen.

This meeting is a symbol of the spirit of London. You, my Lord Mayor, have invited this distinguished audience in defiance of the worst the enemy can do to this historic Mansion House. Though bombed and battered, this city, which is at once the heart and capital of the Empire, is stronger in spirit than ever in its history. It is thus the prototype of our other great cities which the enemy has wantonly attacked. He can shatter their bricks and mortar, he only steels their courage. No one driving through your streets to-day could fail to feel the indomitable spirit of this City of London.

My first words must be to welcome the great message broadcast a few hours ago by the President of the United States, in which he described with incomparable breadth of vision the scope of the struggle in which we are engaged. That speech is a momentous world event. By his words the President has given resolute expression to the fixed determination of the most powerful nation on earth. He defined the settled policy of his country in terms which are as vigorously encouraging to us as they must be disheartening to our enemy. To give effect to this policy the President has decreed a state of unlimited national emergency in the United States. For our part, we have listened with hearts full of thankfulness to the President's determination that the cause of freedom can and will prevail.

"We do not accept, and will not permit, this Nazi shape of things to come." In these historic words the President expresses the determination of all freedom-loving countries.

Perhaps the keynote of the President's speech lies in his repeated declaration that the national existence of free nations must ultimately depend upon the freedom of the seas. This freedom has been maintained in the past by the British and American Navies and both countries have fought on many occasions to preserve it. Freedom to trade, he has declared, is essential to the economic life of America.

This applies with equal force to the British Empire, for without the ability of the ships of the world to sail freely on their lawful occasions no modern nation can hope to maintain its commercial or political freedom. The President has pointed the way for the free nations of the world. He has done more, he has accomplished a great act of faith and statesmanship.

REPLY TO HITLER'S NEW ORDER

This is an anniversary occasion. This afternoon, while our thoughts are with our forces now engaged on the battlefields of the Eastern theatre, our recollection naturally goes back to the solemn events of a year ago. It is the anniversary, within a few days, of the bombing of Rotterdam and, within a day, of the surrender of the Belgian Army.

That was a time of grave and most painful anxiety for the position of the Allied armies. I should like to pay tribute to each one of our Allies, who are all of them fighting gallantly this battle for freedom in circumstances which vary but are always harsh and often cruel. But our thoughts to-day turn, in particular, to those Allies of the anniversary I have mentioned. We recall with pride and gratitude the staunch and dogged loyalty of the Dutch, who have revived their ancient tradition of opposition to an alien invader. The Belgians are also in our thoughts, grouped round King Leopold, who maintains with unbroken dignity his position as a prisoner of war. They recreate the spirit of resistance which inspired the whole Belgian nation in a previous ordeal. We must pay our tribute to a small but courageous people—the Luxemburgers, who, though few in numbers, manfully uphold the ideals of democracy and of independence. All honour, too, to those Frenchmen who refused to accept what they considered a dishonourable armistice and left their hearths and homes in order to maintain the struggle at our side under their gallant leader General de Gaulle. I am convinced that they carry with them the hopes and prayers of the great mass of the French people, to whom the subservience of the Vichy Government to Germany is bitterly abhorrent. In our hearts we must never fail to differentiate France from Vichy.

Before turning to the broad world scene that to-day confronts us I should like to speak for a moment about the position in Iraq. Reports from that country are encouraging. The pretensions of Rashid Ali to speak for the Iraqi people have been proved false. Since his return to Iraq a few days ago the Regent has received innumerable messages of loyalty and support from all over the country. Many of Rashid Ali's followers have already fled. I hope, therefore, that very soon we shall have rid Iraq of this self-constituted dictator who has brought much unnecessary suffering on his fellow-countrymen. Then we shall be able to establish a basis for sincere and cordial co-operation with the Iraqi people in accordance with our treaty and mutual interests. That is all that we ask. We have no designs of any kind against the independence of Iraq.

REPLY TO HITLER'S NEW ORDER

This country has a long tradition of friendship with the Arabs, a friendship that has been proved by deeds, not words alone. We have countless well-wishers amongst them, as they have many friends here. Some days ago I said in the House of Commons that His Majesty's Government had great sympathy with Syrian aspirations for independence. I should like to repeat that now. But I would go further. The Arab world has made great strides since the settlement reached at the end of the last war, and many Arab thinkers desire for the Arab peoples a greater degree of unity than they now enjoy. In reaching out towards this unity they hope for our support. No such appeal from our friends should go unanswered. It seems to me both natural and right that the cultural and economic ties between the Arab countries, yes, and the political ties, too, should be strengthened. His Majesty's Government, for their part, will give their full support to any scheme that commands general approval.

In Europe, since last May, Hitler has won many victories. His arms have been carried in triumph across many lands. He has had some defeats, and one of these may in the long run prove of more enduring consequence than all his victories. The air battle of Britain in August and September of last year was at least a turning-point in the war.

But it would be foolish to belittle Hitler's conquest of the greater part of the continent of Europe; it is a remarkable and ruthless military achievement. From northern Norway to the southern mainland of Greece, from the western shore of Brittany to the eastern marshes of Poland, this one man rules over scores of millions of conquered peoples, either directly or through his creatures, be they Nazis or Quislings.

It is this man and his satellites, all except the Deputy Führer now otherwise engaged, who control the lives and liberties of all who dwell in these vast territories. In all these lands, once free, no man or woman can by any legal means read in a newspaper, hear on the wireless or harbour a thought of which the Führer does not approve.

There has never been anything so brutally thorough in all history. Hitlerism imposes servitude not only on the body, but on the mind and even on the spirit. It is serfdom made absolute. It is tyranny imposed by a military machine of immense power; it is tyranny directed by an utterly ruthless despotism.

Yet this vast and sinister fabric will not endure. For this many reasons could no doubt be given. I will be content with two. First, because as this Nazi despotism is utterly ruthless, so is it boundless in its ambition. It threatens every land in Europe that it has not overrun. It has crossed into Africa and into Asia, where Hitler seeks to dupe Arabs into slavery on the Euphrates by exactly the same methods that he employs on the Tiber or by the waters of Vichy. The Nazi menace must continue its march to every country and to every continent. None will be safe anywhere until this system is smashed. It is the universal realization of this truth that will first set a term to Hitler's power.

Here I come to the second reason why Nazi tyranny cannot endure, because no system that is built upon hate can survive, and the Nazi is hated in every land he rules. He is the alien and the oppressor. Wherever Germany's vast armies of occupation are stationed, the men of those armies know that the peoples whom they hold in subjection by their presence pray for their defeat and flight. The Nazi uniform is the emblem of servitude in all these lands. So it is that the Nazi is building up against himself a flood of hate unparalleled in force and volume. When the dam bursts it will sweep Hitler and his gang away, the Gestapo, the Quislings and the satellites, and much else besides. Every German in his heart must know and fear this. He has good reason to do so. The reckoning will indeed be wide and fierce.

So it is that Nazism seeks to pretend to itself that there might be some permanence in the thraldom it imposes. And so it is that Hitler has found it necessary to give some decent covering to the naked policy of terror and robbery on which he has embarked in Europe. He has for this purpose invented what he calls the "New Order". Hitler pretends that this New Order is to bring prosperity and happiness to those countries which had been robbed by him of their liberty and their means of livelihood.

But what is the reality behind Hitler's high-sounding announcement? It is not easy to find much which is definite in Germany's New Economic Order, except the plan by which the more important industries are to be mainly concentrated within Germany herself.

Meanwhile, the satellite and tributary nations are to be compelled to confine themselves to agriculture and to other kinds of production which suit German convenience. Currency devices will fix the terms of exchange between Germany's industrial products and the output of the other States, so as to maintain a standard of life in Germany much above that of her neighbours. Meanwhile, all foreign commerce would become a German monopoly. As part

REPLY TO HITLER'S NEW ORDER

of the New Order citizens of tributary States will doubtless be forbidden to learn engineering or any other modern industrial arts.
The permanent destruction of all local universities and technical
schools will inevitably follow. In this way intellectual darkness
must aggravate low physical standards, and the national revivals
which Hitler fears so much would be indefinitely postponed.

All this could only be the prelude to an extention of the war,
which would carry to other continents the imperialist exploitation
which had already devoured Europe. Such is the "New Order".
It should surely be impossible even for Dr. Goebbels to make
attractive to its victims a system of imperialist exploitation verging
upon slavery.

Inspired by their theory of the master race, the Germans plan
to be the new aristocracy in the territories under their domination,
while the unfortunate inhabitants of non-German origin are to
become the mere slaves of their German overlords. This vision of
the conqueror's rights and of the treatment to be meted out to the
conquered has been long in Hitler's mind. It was clearly laid down
in *Mein Kampf*.

The process of national destruction of conquered peoples is in
operation wherever the German armies march. *Mein Kampf* shows
clearly that it is not merely for the Germans a phase of military
operations to be abandoned with the cessation of hostilities. It is
much more than this. It is a fixed and deliberate policy of subjugation. The first step in the "New Order" for Europe is the creating
of slaves.

But to-day it is not my main purpose to expose the hollowness
—indeed the wickedness—of Hitler's "New Order".

Hitler has destroyed the bases of political and social co-operation
throughout Europe and he is destroying her economic structure.
The future of Europe will depend upon how moral and material
construction is brought about throughout the world.

While all our efforts are concentrated on winning the war, His
Majesty's Government have naturally been giving careful thought
to this all-important matter, which has been equally in the mind
of the President of the United States of America.

We have found in President Roosevelt's message to Congress in
January 1941 the keynote of our own purposes. On that occasion
the President said: "In the future days which we seek to make
secure we look forward to a world founded upon four essential
human freedoms. The first is freedom of speech and expression—
everywhere in the world. The second is freedom of every person

to worship God in his own way—everywhere in the world. The third is freedom from want, which, translated into world terms, means economic understandings which will secure to every nation a healthy peace-time life for its inhabitants—everywhere in the world. The fourth is freedom from fear, which, translated into world terms, means a world-wide reduction of armaments to such a point and in such a thorough fashion that no nation will be in a position to commit an act of physical aggression against any neighbour—anywhere in the world. That is no vision of a distant millennium. It is a definite basis for a kind of world attainable in our own time and generation. That kind of world is the very antithesis of the so-called 'New Order' of tyranny which the dictators seek to create with the crash of a bomb. To that new order we oppose the greater conception—the 'moral order'."

On this occasion I will not attempt to elaborate our views about the President's first and second freedoms—freedom of speech and thought, and the freedom to worship God—save to say that we realize that these freedoms are fundamental to human development and to democratic responsibility.

Nor do I to-day intend to discuss the political questions involved in giving real effect to President Roosevelt's "freedom from fear". I will only say that, as I hope to show this afternoon, as His Majesty's Government intend to strive in co-operation with others to relieve the post-war world from the fear of want, so will they seek to ensure that the world is freed from fear.

To-day I wish to put before you certain practical ways in which "freedom from want" may be applied to Europe.

We have declared that social security must be the first object of our domestic policy after the war. And social security will be our policy abroad not less than at home. It will be our wish to work with others to prevent the starvation of the post-armistice period, the currency disorders throughout Europe, and the wide fluctuations of employment, markets and prices which were the cause of so much misery in the twenty years between the two wars. We shall seek to achieve this in ways which will interfere as little as possible with the proper liberty of each country over its own economic fortunes.

The countries of the British Empire and their Allies, with the United States and South America, alone are in a position to carry out such a policy. For, irrespective of the nature of the political settlement, continental Europe will end this war starved and bankrupt of all the foods and raw materials which she was accustomed to obtain from the rest of the world. She will have no means, un-aided, of breaking the vicious circle. She can export few goods until she has, first of all, received the necessary raw materials. Wasteful war-time cultivations in many lands will leave agriculture almost as weak as industry. Thus Europe will face the vast problem of general demobilization with a general lack of the necessary means to put men to work.

Let no one suppose, however, that we for our part intend to return to the chaos of the old world. To do so would bankrupt us no less than others. When peace comes we shall make such relaxations of our war-time financial arrangements as will permit the revival of international trade on the widest possible basis. We shall hope to see the development of a system of international exchange in which the trading of goods and services will be the central feature. I echo Mr. Hull's admirable summing up in his recent declaration, when he said: "Institutions and arrangements of international finance must be so set up that they lend aid to the essential enterprises and continuous development of all countries and permit payments through processes of trade consonant with the welfare of all countries."

However, to meet the problems of the immediate post-war period action in other directions will also be required. The liberated countries, and maybe others, too, will require an initial pool of resources to carry them through the transitional period.

To organize the transition to peaceful activities will need the collaboration of the United States, of ourselves, and of all free countries which have not themselves suffered the ravages of war. The Dominions and ourselves can make our contribution to this because the British Empire will actually possess overseas enormous stocks of food and materials, which we are accumulating so as to ease the problems of the overseas producers during the war, and of reconstructed Europe after the war. The Prime Minister has already made clear the importance he attaches to this.

What has Germany to offer on her side? Absolutely nothing. An official of the Reich Economics Ministry, in a moment of hard realism, published last autumn a statement that the present German rationing system must continue for at least one year after the restoration of peace, and perhaps for several. The huge latent demand for food, clothing and other articles of prime necessity which cannot be satisfied under war conditions will, he went on to say, again become active after the signature, but the production of such commodities will not for a long while exceed war-time output.

All this is not only true but obvious. But if peace brings disappointment and such conditions continue beyond the disciplined period of war, social security can hardly survive.

No one can suppose that the economic reorganization of Europe after the Allied victory will be an easy task. But we shall not shirk our opportunity and our responsibility to bear our share of the burdens. The peaceful brotherhood of nations, with due liberty to each to develop its own balanced economic life and its characteristic culture, will be the common object. But it is the transition to this end which presents the problem. It is the establishment of an international economic system, capable of translating the technical possibilities of production into actual plenty, and maintaining the whole population in a continuous fruitful activity, which is difficult. The world cannot expect to solve the economic riddle easily or completely. But the free nations of America, the Dominions and ourselves alone possess a command of the material means, and, what is perhaps more important, these nations clearly have the will and the intention to evolve a post-war order which seeks no selfish national advantage: an order where each member of the family shall realize its own character and perfect its own gifts in liberty of conscience and person. We have learnt the lesson of the interregnum between the two wars. We know that no escape can be found from the curse which has been lying on Europe except by creating and preserving economic health in every country.

Under a system of free economic co-operation Germany must play a part. But here I draw a firm distinction. We must never forget that Germany is the worst master Europe has yet known. Five times in the last century she has violated the peace. She must never be in a position to play that role again. Our political and military terms of peace will be designed to prevent a repetition of Germany's misdeeds.

We cannot now foresee when the end will come. But it is in the nature of a machine so rigid as the German to break suddenly and with little warning. When it comes, the need of succour to the European peoples will be urgent. Shipping will be short and local organization in Europe in a state of collapse. It is, therefore, important to begin in good time the discussion of priorities and of allocations. Our friends and Allies now represented in London will tell us what their liberated countries will need most urgently, in order that we may all co-operate and be ready for prompt action.

In speaking of the reconstruction of Europe I do not overlook the fact that its settlement may affect and be affected by developments elsewhere, such as, for example, in the Far East. After the unhappy struggle now in progress between Japan and China, there will obviously be problems of similar magnitude to be faced in that part of the world, in the solution of which all countries concerned will, we hope, play their part.

The right economic outcome after the war requires on our part no exceptional unselfishness, but will require constructive imagination. It is obvious that we have no motive of self-interest prompting us to the economic exploitation either of Germany or of the rest of Europe. This is not what we want nor what we could perform. The lasting settlement and internal peace of the continent as a whole is our only aim. The fact that at the bottom of his heart every combatant knows this is the ultimate source of our strength. To every neutral satellite or conquered country it is obvious that our victory is, for the most fundamental and unalterable reasons, to their plain advantage. But that victory stands also for something greater still. Only our victory can restore, both to Europe and to the world, that freedom which is our heritage from centuries of Christian civilization, and that security which alone can make possible the betterment of man's lot upon the earth.

In the tasks that lie ahead may there be given to our statesmen the vision to see, the faith to act, and the courage to persevere.

15

THE GERMAN INVASION OF RUSSIA

June 8. British and Free French troops invaded Syria. After the capture of Beirut an armistice was signed on June 15.

June 11. Reports of heavy concentrations of German troops on the Russian frontier. Sir Stafford Cripps, the Ambassador in Moscow, returned to London.

June 12. Allied declaration of unity signed at St. James's Palace, London.

June 14. All German and Italian money frozen in U.S.A.

June 18. Turkey signed a friendship pact with Germany without prejudice to Turkey's existing obligations to Britain.

June 22. Germany attacked Russia at 4 a.m. The Prime Minister offered Russia whatever help we can give.

June 24. President Roosevelt promised to help Russia.

On June 24, in the House of Commons, the Foreign Secretary opened the Debate on the German Invasion of Russia.

The Prime Minister, on Sunday night, told the world after his own unrivalled fashion of the decisions at which His Majesty's Government had arrived as a consequence of the German invasion of Soviet Russia. To-day, I would wish to give the House a brief account of the diplomatic events which preceded that giant act of aggression and of the developments which have followed upon it. The House and the country will, I think, desire to take a severely practical view of these matters. We keep our eye on the target; that target is Hitler's Germany. Let us pay him the compliment of understanding that he too keeps his eye on the target, and that target is the British Empire, which he still rightly regards as the chief obstacle in his path to world dominion. The invasion of Soviet Russia is not an end, but a means. Through his attack upon Russia Hitler hopes to break the military power of that vast State and thus to free himself from any contemporary or subsequent Eastern anxiety when he turns to his duel with our own land. We are back to the German policy on Russia set out in *Mein Kampf*, and despite the sudden revulsions of Hitler's diplomacy, he has in truth never strayed far from it. Let mankind never for a moment forget that the dominating theme of that turgid revelation of boundless ambition is world dominion. All treaties, all pacts, all agreements are for Hitler but the chloroform to new aggression.

In the difficult and dangerous political and diplomatic situation which exists to-day, it would clearly serve no useful purpose to enter into a prolonged analysis of the vicissitudes of Anglo-Soviet relations. But I would recall this fact, which seems to me a cardinal truth in assessing them. In 1935 we agreed in Moscow with the Soviet Government a statement which declared among other things that there was no conflict of interest between the two Governments on any of the main issues of international policy. I have always believed that those words expressed a plain statement of fact, and that the relations of our two countries would benefit from their mutual acceptance. And though since 1935 the relations of our two countries have undergone many a modification, they remain as true to-day as when they were agreed upon between us. The political systems of our two countries are antipathetic, our ways of life are widely divergent but this cannot and must not for a moment obscure the realities of the political issue which confronts us to-day. Germany has perpetrated upon Russia an act of studied and deliberate aggression. Two years ago Germany and Russia signed a pact of non-aggression. At no time since the signature of that pact has Germany complained of its performance. At the hour when Germany, without warning, struck her blow, no representations had been made and no discussions of any kind were in progress.

Here I would ask the House to let me deal for a moment with the latest of the false statements of the German Foreign Secretary, Herr von Ribbentrop. I must quote what he said:

"While German troops were concentrating on Bulgarian and Roumanian territory against the increasing landings of British troops in Greece, the Soviet Union tried, now already in a clear agreement with England, to stab Germany in the back by firstly supporting Yugoslavia openly politically, and in secret militarily, by trying secondly to influence Turkey, by giving her a covering guarantee, to adopt an aggressive attitude against Bulgaria and Germany."

Those are Hitler's charges, and in face of that I must make it plain that much as we in His Majesty's Government and this House would have welcomed an agreement with the Soviet Union in order to maintain the solidarity of the Balkan peoples before they were overrun by Germany, an opportunity for such an agreement unfortunately never presented itself. There was never any sort or kind of agreement with the Soviet Union in this matter, and I will tell the House the reason. At every phase in recent history the development of Anglo-Soviet relations was always retarded by the attention paid by the Soviet Union to the observance of their pact with Germany. Time and again we reviewed the possibility of clearing the path of Anglo-Soviet co-operation of any obstacles which we could, but on every occasion, every time investigation was made, whether the matters were trade or whether they were political, it became clear to us that the Soviet Government were not prepared to negotiate in view of their anxiety not to introduce any embarrassment into their relations with Germany.

What was our attitude? Our attitude was equally clear. We on our side never had any intention to conclude any arrangement with the Union of Soviet Socialist Republics except on a basis of mutual interest and satisfaction, in fact, on a basis of reciprocity. In the light of the Soviet Union's pact with Germany no such basis existed. I explain that to the House in order that they may see how completely devoid of any foundation, in fact, is Ribbentrop's statement, published to the world.

There is another aspect of the matter on which I would give the House some information. My right hon. Friend the Prime Minister has told the world how, some time ago, he warned the head of the Russian State of the peril which he, rightly, saw was impending. That is not quite all. Some time before the events of the last few days we at the Foreign Office were already convinced from the information at our disposal that Hitler, true to his usual technique, was going to attack Russia from behind the smoke screen of his non-aggression pact. With my right hon. Friend's consent, I accordingly asked the Soviet Ambassador to come and see me, and I told him of the information at our disposal, and of the danger which, I was convinced, confronted his country. I gave him, at his request, details of that information as we thought we were bound to do. Even at that late hour the Soviet Government were careful to avoid any expression of opinion which might seem to throw doubt on their own observance of their engagement with Germany. [An Hon. Member: "When was that?"] It was some weeks ago. I think it is fair that these things should be said now.

It was this assessment of impending events that caused me to ask His Majesty's Ambassador at Moscow to return to this country for consultation. I felt that his experience and his advice would be invaluable to us at such a time, and so it has proved. The House and the country are deeply indebted to my hon. and learned Friend the Member for East Bristol (Sir S. Cripps)—if I may give him for a moment his Parliamentary rather than his diplomatic description—for work done under conditions of the utmost difficulty. For the reasons I have given, he was unable to conclude any of those pacts or agreements which were once so dear to the diplomatist's heart, although, to-day, they enjoy but a brief butterfly life. Yet it is clear that, by his influence and by his example, my hon. and learned Friend has shown to the Soviet Union the fundamental desire of His Majesty's Government to maintain our relations upon a normal footing. When he returns to his post, he will be able, with his marked ability, to advise and direct the help which it is the declared intention of His Majesty's Government to give to the Soviet Union at the present time.

As the outcome of the events of the last few days, conversations have, of course, been proceeding between the Russian Government and ourselves. The House will appreciate that I am not able to reveal the full results of those discussions, but I can tell the House that I have now heard from His Excellency the Soviet Ambassador that his Government have accepted our offer to send military and economic missions to Russia to co-ordinate our efforts in what is now, beyond doubt, a common task—the defeat of Germany. The Soviet Government have made it plain to us that in the period of military collaboration which now lies ahead, help will be upon a mutual and a reciprocal basis. His Majesty's Government accept and endorse that view.

Mr. Garro Jones (Aberdeen, North): May I ask my right hon. Friend a question? I am sure the House would wish to know at this stage whether application has also been made to send an air mission to Russia at the same time.

Mr. Eden: My hon. Friend will, perhaps, appreciate that I use the word "military", the significance of which I think must be

THE GERMAN INVASION OF RUSSIA

clear to everybody. This latest demonstration of German perfidy, the attack on the Soviet Union, in defiance of solemn and repeated pledges, has given mankind the final proof, if further proof were needed, of the world-wide scope of the Nazi lust for power. Hitler has shown himself, once again, a cynical traitor to his own pledged word. A pact one day, an aggression the next. Soothing words in the winter, bombs and tanks in the spring. Those are the methods by which he seeks to subdue all nations, great and small, in the pursuit of world dominion. No Nazi posturing can now deceive the world. All must realize that whatever their system of government, wherever their geographical position, the great and immediate danger to their security is the existence in the world of the Nazi system. Whatever other consideration may be in balance, that is the greatest.

This country has probably fewer Communists than any nation in Europe. We have always hated the creed, but that is not the issue. Russia has been invaded, wantonly, treacherously, without warning. Not even the Germans have seriously pretended provocation. The Russians to-day are fighting for their soil. They are fighting the man who seeks to dominate the world. This is also our sole task. Confronted with his latest aggression, it is our determination not to relax but to intensify our efforts. Napoleon, if I remember aright, once said: "I have always marched with four millions or five millions of men." We are marching to-day, after Hitler's last act of aggression, with the opinions of hundreds of millions of men. There is one reference I would ask the House to let me make. At a time like this our thoughts go out with heartfelt sympathy to our Polish ally. Once again, their soil is a battlefield. Once again their people suffer for no fault of their own. The Polish people have had a hard history. By their courage in a time of unparalleled ordeal, they have earned and they will redeem their freedom. That remains our pledge.

Turkey has declared her neutrality in this conflict. From the date of the signature of our Treaty of Mutual Assistance in October 1939 our relations with Turkey have been on a very special basis. Turkey is our friend and ally. The Turkish Government have kept us fully informed of the progress of their recent negotiations with the German Government. The conclusion of that agreement, therefore, came as no surprise to His Majesty's Government. But I make no mystery of the matter; we should naturally have preferred that no such treaty had been concluded. None the less the preamble of the treaty expressly safeguards the existing contractual engagements of each party. The Turkish Government have repeatedly made it plain to us that, first and foremost among these engagements stands the Anglo-Turkish Treaty, and they have specifically assured our Ambassador since the conclusion of the Agreement with Germany, and once again within the last twenty-four hours, that our Treaty stands intact.

I must say a word on the events on the northern flank of the new war. The Finnish Minister asked to see me yesterday, and he gave me a message from his Government. He assured me that Finland's attitude was, and would continue to be, a purely defensive one in the present conflict. There was, he told me, no change in the diplomatic relations between the Soviet Government and Finland. It was the hope of his Government that his country would not become involved in the conflict. I told Mr. Grippenberg that I had taken note of his assurance, and that I was quite confident that the course which his Government had announced their desire to follow was the right and only course for Finland.

I cannot conclude this brief survey of the events of the last few days and hours without referring to, and offering on behalf of all Members of this House, a word of hearty welcome to His Excellency the United States Ambassador who has returned to our shores. He has come back to us, as I can testify from conversations with him, refreshed by his brief sojourn in his own country, re-inspired by his contacts with his President and his countrymen, and stimulated by what he has seen of the immense effort being made in the United States. The past few days, indeed the past few hours, have brought fresh indications, fresh assurances, of the continued and increasing support of our American friends, support both material and moral, the volume of which will overwhelm Nazi resistance and crush Nazi power. The House will, I hope, have read the declaration by Mr. Sumner Welles which appears in the Press this morning. On behalf of the Government we heartily endorse his statement that any defence against Hitlerism, from whatever source, will hasten the eventual downfall of the present German leaders. Mr. Winant has brought us, too, the renewed expression of the determination of his great country to aid us in the tasks to which we as a nation are dedicated. The one aim, the one irrevocable purpose to which the Prime Minister only two nights ago pledged us once again, is the destruction of Hitler and the Nazi regime. In that task we shall not falter until the final victory is won.

16

HITLER'S PEACE OFFENSIVE

June 25. The Prime Minister revealed in a Secret Session of the House of Commons that in the previous twelve months, 4,600,000 tons of Allied shipping had been lost.

June 27. Sir Stafford Cripps arrived in Moscow with a Military Mission.

June 28. Fierce battles raged round Minsk in Russia.

July 1. General Wavell left the Middle East for India. General Auchinleck became C.-in-C. Middle East.

On July 5, Mr. Eden addressed a large outdoor demonstration at Elland Road Football Ground, Leeds, giving a survey of the war, in the course of which he warned the nation of post-war problems as follows:

"During the last war we looked on war between civilized nations as such a barbarous anachronism that we called it a war to end war. In this we erred.

"If we have learnt one lesson from the last twenty years it is that the forces of evil can only be held at bay by strong and resolute men and nations prepared to undertake the responsibility and the burden of protecting the frontier of freedom.

"It is idle to think that we shall enter into some golden age. Experience has taught us the stern realities of the world in which we live, and that the foundations of peace are constant vigilance and sufficient armed strength to strike and overwhelm any possible aggressors. A new order will not grow and will not endure unless it is justly framed, strongly ordered, and firmly maintained. It must be no scrap of paper to be torn to shreds, while those charged with its observance stand aside indifferent or preoccupied."

July 7. U.S.A. troops occupied Iceland and Greenland.

HITLER'S PEACE OFFENSIVE

July 8. A Russian Military Mission arrived in London.

July 12. "Cease Fire" in Syria: the armistice was signed on July 15.

July 25. Britain and U.S.A. froze all Japanese assets and instituted a trade blockade.

July 28. Finland now fighting with Germany against the U.S.S.R. broke off diplomatic relations with Britain and the U.S.A.

On July 29, Mr. Eden addressed the Foreign Press Association at the Savoy Hotel after lunch:

We are met in the midst of big-scale events, and their development is by no means wholly unfavourable to us. Four great communities are moving ever closer together in their determination to withstand the common menace of Hitler and of any who work for him.

The U.S.S.R., China, the United States of America and the British Empire are surely pretty formidable obstacles to aggression.

It may be this sense of events to come which is causing a new note to creep into Hitler propaganda, covertly for the present, but, we may be sure, more openly later on.

Hitler has broken countless promises. He has betrayed in turn every nation to which he has given pledges. There are in this room Allied statesmen who are living witnesses to his perfidy.

But now, for the first time, there is a change. Now he is trying desperately to keep a promise. It is a promise that he has made to the German people; a promise that the war shall end this year in a victorious German peace. In an attempt to fulfil it Hitler has embarked upon his Russian campaign.

He seeks two objectives in these vast Russian spaces. First, to smash speedily Russia's military power; second, in the pose of the champion of anti-Communism, to offer a German peace to the world.

Hitler's time-table for the first objective is plainly already out of joint. The Russians are putting up a magnificent resistance, which clearly exceeds the German calculations and many other calculations also.

This does not mean that his second objective has been abandoned. Another kind of German blitz will soon be hurled at us—a peace blitz, by means of which Hitler hopes to keep his promise to the German people. For if Hitler cannot secure a German peace this year—and he cannot—he will offer a compromise peace, and plan to try again later. Others, he hopes, will be less watchful and less ready to take up arms again.

I have recently made it plain, on behalf of His Majesty's Government, in a speech at Leeds only a few weeks ago, that we are not prepared to negotiate with Hitler at any time on any subject.

Let me now explain our position a little further.

A peace with Hitler is a contradiction in terms. There can be no peace with such a man, there can only be a truce, an uneasy truce which will give him time to overhaul and oil his war machine, a truce which will give the German people a breathing-space before he and they resume the war.

Hitler will never abandon war, he will only interrupt it as a matter of tactics, or of military necessity.

Of course all this will be carefully disguised from the world and from the German people.

We must not underrate the attractions of the mirage which will dazzle our eyes. The business will be cleverly staged.

The offer of a compromise peace will be a monument of moderation and sweet reasonableness—and hypocrisy.

It will promise many things to many peoples, perhaps even liberation to some of the occupied countries, maybe restoration of France to her place as a great Power, recognition—indeed perhaps a guarantee—of the British Empire.

Such an offer in itself should suffice to warn us, for few indeed are the nations that have survived a Hitler guarantee of their integrity. His enmity is less dangerous than his friendship.

Germany, we shall be told, will be ready as a good neighbour and a good European to co-operate in the restoration of trade.

This is a man who conducts his diplomacy with two sets of weapons, guns and olive branches. The olive branches served for many years to mask the guns when it suited Hitler's purpose. They deceived many and they brought us to deadly danger. They will soon be in evidence again.

But what would be the value of any promises given by such a man? Would Norway believe him? Would Holland? Would Belgium? Would Poland? Would Yugoslavia? Would Greece? Would Czechoslovakia? Would Russia? Each and all of them have had a taste of Hitler's promises and broken faith.

Above all, would this country believe him, knowing as she does that she always and inevitably stands in his way, barring the road to world domination?

The stark truth is that any peace or truce with Hitler would last just as long as Hitler chose for the execution of his own plans. Such a truce would bring no security to the world, no return of confidence, no opportunity of reconstruction. It would be a denial of everything that we have fought and striven for for nearly two years. Just consider the conditions that would exist under a Hitler truce.

Every nation would have to remain at its war stations so as not to be caught unawares by a sudden attack launched without warning. We could never demobilize, we could never relax our war preparations and our war restrictions, the fortifications round our coasts could not be removed, our factories would have to continue to manufacture munitions of war to keep up with those which Hitler would be piling up in secret for his next war—his next bid for world domination.

Our Air Force would have to go on patrolling the skies by day and by night; our Navy would have to remain cleared for action.

So long as Hitler and his men rule in Germany, so long as Germany's military power is unbroken, we and Europe, and indeed the world, can only expect lies, deceit, and plots, culminating inevitably in another and more terrible war than the present one. For Hitler is the embodiment of war. The only peace he can endure is a peace of annihilation, a peace of universal conquest, in fact a victorious German peace, a peace that is death for freedom everywhere.

Let us recall this.

Hitler is not a rare and transient phenomenon in German history. He is a symptom. He is the expression of the present German will and temper which has shown itself over and over again in German history. It is his mission in life to give the German people war. It is all he has to give them.

And so long as he is in power the German people will continue to expect war. They will begin again to prepare for war. They will wish and work for war. You cannot get figs from thistles and you cannot get peace from one of the greatest war-makers the world has seen.

If we are to have peace in our lifetime the German people must learn to unlearn all that they have been taught, not only by Hitler but by his predecessors, for the last hundred years by so many of their philosophers and teachers, the disciples of blood and iron.

They can never even start to do this until Hitler, the great war-maker, has been exposed as a fraud and deposed as a failure.

Therefore we state in advance: we are not interested in any peace terms that Hitler and his Government may put forward.

We are determined upon the destruction of Hitler, his regime and all it stands for. For we know that until this is achieved no foundation will exist upon which lasting peace can be built.

How then do we conceive the future of Germany?

It seems to me that, when this war is won, the nations will have a two-fold task with which to deal.

In the military sphere it is our bounden duty to ensure that Germany is not again in another twenty years in a position to plunge the world into the misery and horror of total war. It would be criminal to neglect any precaution to ensure this. It would be unforgivable to run risks in this sphere, after the lessons that we have been taught with so much pain and so much suffering. Our conditions of peace for Germany will therefore be designed to prevent a repetition of Germany's misdeeds.

But while these military measures must be taken, it is not part of our purpose to cause Germany, or any other country, to collapse economically. I say that, not out of any love of Germany, but because a starving and a bankrupt Germany in the midst of Europe would poison all of us who are her neighbours. That is not sentiment, it is common sense.

Let us look for a moment at the future that is beginning to shape itself before our eyes.

Germany will be defeated. Yes. But what then?

Europe, after this war, will be in a state of exhaustion, short of materials necessary for reconstruction, torn by hatreds, confused and doubtful of the road to follow.

Then there will be a great task to be undertaken. And as we believe the United States of America will help us—is indeed helping us—to defeat Germany, so we hope that they will work with us in keeping, through the generations, the peace we shall have won.

We have suffered bitter disillusionment between the two wars. We had believed perhaps too easily that a peace system that would recommend itself to the good sense of all peoples could be planned and debated in the Council Room without other effort and without harder sacrifice on our part.

We have learnt that that is not so: that the price of peace is constant vigilance, readiness, courage; and we must never forget that lesson.

HITLER'S PEACE OFFENSIVE

The sacrifices of peace-time, necessary to guard against the ever-recurring danger of war, are hard, but they may be hardening and salutary. They will, for some time to come, be inevitable.

But while keeping watch and ward, it will be our duty to start at once upon the fashioning of the world in such a shape that the causes of rivalry and hatred may be gradually removed and, we pray, eventually eradicated. Only in proportion as we can be sure that this healing influence is having its effect shall we be able to relax our vigilance.

We are already beginning to formulate our own ideas on the shape of things to come. And in one sense we are truly fortunate. Here in London are the Governments of many Allied Powers.

They form an invaluable nucleus for the work we have to do. We are already meeting and discussing our problems, though not always publicly. We have had one public meeting at St. James's to register our united purpose. I hope that we may shortly be able to hold another in which we can begin our examination of the problems that the "Cease Fire" will bring in its train.

If we can look forward, in all this work, to the sympathy and co-operation of the United States of America and indeed the American continent as a whole, then we can feel that we are building on a solid foundation, and we can go ahead in the firm faith that, however dark the outlook, our task can and will one day be achieved.

17

COVENTRY—30 AUGUST 1941

1940
November 14. All-night raid on Coventry. 554 people were killed and 865 seriously injured. Two days later Mr. Eden visited Coventry, part of which city he at that time represented in Parliament.

1941
July 30. Russo-Polish pact signed in London, in which Russia recognized the pre-1939 Polish boundaries and agreed to help organize 200,000 Poles to form an Allied Army against Germany.

August 2. R.A.F. started new bomber offensive by raids on Berlin, Hamburg and Kiel.

August 7. Russian aircraft made their first attack on Berlin.

August 11. General mobilization in Japan.

August 12. Germans claimed they were encircling Odessa.

August 14. The Atlantic Charter signed by President Roosevelt and Mr. Churchill.

August 25. British and Russian forces invaded Iran following an unsatisfactory reply to a request for the expulsion of German agents. British and Russian troops met on September 1.

On August 30, Mr. Eden addressed a meeting at Coventry, where he said:

This city of Coventry has a long proud history. Nothing in all its record can equal the example Coventry has set for the last twelve months. This city will ever be in men's minds the symbol of the Battle of Britain. Here the shock of total air war first made itself felt. Here you were the first to suffer the unmitigated fury of the worst a Nazi blitz could do. The spirit in which you met that challenge has been an inspiration to those cities which were called upon to meet a like attack. You here never for an instant lost the will to win. It is this determination that will prove decisive, for here in Britain in the factories of hundreds of our great industrial towns the issue is being fought out.

We shall win the battle for mere survival. We have yet to fight the battle for victory. Production is still the key to victory. The output of war material of the Allied and associated Powers, including the contribution of the United States, still falls far short of our needs. And those needs will grow, as the tide of war sweeps wider until it engulfs the world. Our success will be measured by our ability to provide ourselves and our allies with the materials they need at the time they need them. To ensure this we must have larger quantities of supplies than the enemy needs since he works upon interior lines. Every ounce of industrial effort of which the resources of the British Empire and the United States are together capable could be used twice over. With Soviet Russia fighting as our Ally the resources in manpower of the nations linked against Hitler are enormously increased. But these Russian forces are fighting with magnificent courage in a struggle of unparalleled intensity on a front of two thousand miles. They are using up huge quantities of munitions. We have now all of us a greater call to meet. Together we must help to supply Russia's needs as well as ours. Here is a call to duty in which we cannot fail.

The problem is not only how much but when. Time is the master. Every day that is spent without the freedom-loving countries having developed their full strength is an additional day of war and suffering for mankind. All effort short of total effort means that some of our strength is dissipated and thus we prolong the world's agony.

Look back at the great battles of the war. Look at the Battle of Poland, the Battle of France, the Battle of Britain, the Battle of Greece. All these are part of history. Through them all runs like a refrain the word "machines". To be short of materials in war is the most costly method of waging war, not only in life but in material. Had we and our French and Belgian Allies possessed in France last summer the armoured units and the air support that the German armies enjoyed, Germany might to-day be fighting a war on land on two fronts. As it was we ourselves could contribute insufficient of the latter and scarcely any of the former. And in the events that followed we ourselves lost 1,000 guns which 2,000 tanks and 2,000 planes could perhaps have saved. To be richly supplied in equipment is the best economy in war. Our losses in equipment in France left us here last year with an almost empty cupboard. You worked unsparingly to fill it. And then out of our still perilously scant resources we sent to General Wavell in the autumn the tanks and guns and aeroplanes of which he and his commanders and his men made such brilliant use last winter.

Even more important than the quantity of the equipment is its quality. I have myself seen old vehicles in the Western Desert which have stood up magnificently to the strains and stresses of modern war in dust and grit and sand. We cannot ourselves be content until our men command in every arm weapons which in design and execution are fully a match for the best the enemy can do.

And if our men have the equipment you may be sure that they will make good use of it. The superiority that our airmen have gained over the enemy airmen is no accident. You have provided the planes. They have done the rest. Given fair odds the army will do the same.

In war courage counts for much. Skill counts for much and experience too. But there is another quality which counts also, imagination. When men are together on the battlefield each man knows that he depends upon his neighbour and that his neighbour depends upon him. Thus is born a spirit of comradeship, a sense of confidence, upon which the life of armies depends. It is not so easy in the factory or in the office to understand that the lives of others are hanging on one's own efforts. It is not so easy to remember that an item of production may affect a flow of munitions with decisive consequences on the battlefield. It is not so easy to keep in the mind's eye, for instance, the picture of Russian troops, millions upon millions of them, each with his own life, his own hopes, his own family, fighting week after week, giving everything for a country which is his own and a cause which is ours as well as his. Yet this is the true picture. This is the time for each one of us, whether engaged in production or in the management of production, to think of his own job, to examine his own heart and conscience, to ensure that at least he is doing all that a man can do to support and sustain the cause which is common to us all, to give to those who are fighting our battles the weapons which alone will bring victory.

All over the world we need your weapons. In Russia, in the Far

East, in Libya, over Germany, and only this last week we have had to meet by action another attempt by the enemy to widen the area of war. German intrigue threatened to involve Iran.

The problem created by German activities in Iran is not a new one. As long ago as last January I warned the Iranian Government of the danger which the existence and composition of this large German colony must create. Germans have a special technique when living in foreign lands. They are appointed; organized and drilled for a wide variety of fifth-column activities. This war has shown in Norway, in Holland, in France, and in countless other countries how effective these German agents can be. The Iranian Government argued in reply to our representations that we exaggerated the number of Germans and exaggerated the peril. But whether those Germans in Iran were to be numbered by hundreds or thousands, no one with a knowledge of the workings of the Nazi system could doubt the true purpose of their presence in Iran. Nobody has disputed that amongst these Germans were many young men of military age, physically and mentally well fitted to take their place in the ranks of Germany's fighting forces, yet the German Government encouraged them to linger in Iran. No one is going to suppose that they were there for the good of their health alone. Nor could we forget that earlier in this year much of the German activity which preceded Rashid Ali's abortive rebellion in Iraq was organized by German agents acting from Iran. After the collapse of Rashid Ali many of his partisans fled to Iran. Until recently they were still there and at large, in communication with Nazi diplomatic circles in the Iranian capital.

Knowing full well of this state of affairs, two courses were open to us. We could have pretended not to see what was daily more apparent. We could have turned a blind eye to these German activities and allowed these Nazi agents to go on with their fell work until the moment came when it suited them to stage a *coup d'état* or by some other means to strike at us and at our friends. Or alternatively we could put the position squarely to the Iranian Government and ask them to deal with the activities in their midst which must in the final resort menace Iran as much as us. We chose the latter course. We represented what we knew to be the true facts to the Iranian Government and we asked them to deal themselves with the danger. We made these representations many times in Teheran, and I spoke myself to the Iranian Minister in London. We did indeed practise the Iranian proverb "Patience is from God, and haste is from the Devil". We met with no adequate response. Pretexts, excuses, insignificant concessions were all that we obtained.

The months went by and Nazi activity increased in intensity, until in the last few weeks it became apparent to ourselves and to our Russian allies that we must not scotch this Nazi snake but kill it before it struck at us with all its venom in its own time. Unfortunately despite every plea and every warning, the Government of Iran, perhaps as the outcome of German intimidation, could not bring itself to take the necessary action and send these Germans home. As a consequence we and our Russian allies were compelled to act. We have acted, our troops and Soviet troops crossed the frontier. Happily there was from the first little fighting. The Iranian Government and people, I am confident, understood in their hearts the motive of our action. They appear as a result to have offered only token resistance, and now even that token resistance has ceased. Indeed the latest reports which reached me before I left the Foreign Office this morning show that everywhere the inhabitants are very friendly to our troops. Everyone in the British Empire will rejoice at this. There have been within these last few days diplomatic exchanges between London, Moscow and Teheran. The Soviet Government and ourselves are in full agreement and the Iranian Government will soon know what are the conditions we must impose. They are not extravagant and they are of course only temporary.

Meanwhile let me make plain once again our general attitude. We have no territorial claims against Iran. We covet no square inch of Iranian territory. We have no design nor have our Russian allies any design to annex any part of the areas which our forces have now occupied. His Majesty's Government and the Soviet Government have repeatedly assured the Iranian Government of their determination to respect the political independence and the territorial integrity of Iran. We have repeated that pledge to the Government of our ally Turkey and to the Governments of neighbouring States. That pledge stands. We shall, as soon as military conditions permit, withdraw our forces from Iranian territory. Neither we nor the Soviet Government wish to seize any part of Iran.

Indeed I have hopes that out of the troubled events of the last few weeks may grow a closer and more intimate friendship between the Allies and Iran. There is nothing that we should like better. We know how great a contribution Iran has made to the culture of the world. We know, too, that a strong and independent Iran is an essential element in the stability of the Middle East. We covet neither Iranian lands nor her wealth. We are not going to repeat the mistakes of past policies in this respect. The collaboration of friends and not an occupation by enemies is the goal we seek in Iran. In this respect our policy and that of Germany are in sharp contrast. Iran is to-day short of food, because in earlier years she sent that food to Germany. The Germans are locusts and devour the lands over which they sweep. Now our troops have entered the country. The food will follow after them, not only for our armies, but for the people of Iran. All that we can do to ease their lot will be done. Let us hope that in the future we can work together. The British Empire and Russia are making their contributions to create the prosperity of Iran, and the Nazi locusts are trapped or away on the wing to their German homeland.

It is no part of my intention to attempt a broad survey of international relations this afternoon. Recently, however, the Soviet Government have taken two steps which have been of exceptional value for the consolidation of international relations. Since we have, as a result of the close diplomatic relations which now exist between us and the Soviet Government, ourselves been to some extent concerned in these events, I should like to make a comment or two upon them. The Soviet Government have made an agreement with Poland which restores relations between the two countries and provides for the formation of a Polish army on Russian soil. The Soviet Government have also made jointly with ourselves a declaration to Turkey in which they say that they are prepared scrupulously to observe the territorial integrity of the Turkish Republic and to render Turkey every help and assistance in the event of her being attacked by any European power.

These two acts by the Soviet Government have been warmly welcomed by us because both countries concerned, Poland and Turkey, stand in a special relationship to ourselves. We have treaties of mutual assistance with both. Poland is our gallant ally on the battlefield. In virtue of their geographical position and their own national qualities Poland and Turkey will both be called upon to play an important role in international affairs after the war.

When President Roosevelt and the Prime Minister met in the Atlantic it was more than the meeting of two great men. It was more than the coming together of two great peoples, the United States of America and the British Commonwealth. It was more than another nail for the coffin which is being prepared for Nazism.

COVENTRY

It was a declaration that we, too, have our plans for peace as well as our strategy for war. Europe—yes, and Germany—know now the choice which lies before them—Hitler's New Order—or ours.

Speaking recently I said that our policy towards Germany after the war must have a two-fold purpose. On the one hand, Germany must be placed in conditions in which it will be impossible for her again to re-arm and to resume the struggle for domination over peace-loving nations. We have had enough of that from Germany. On the other hand, it is equally important that she should not become a source of poison to her neighbours and to the world by economic collapse.

To-day I would go a step farther. These two fundamental principles must govern not only our relations with Germany after the war, but all international relations. This is the plain meaning of the Roosevelt-Churchill Declaration. No nation must ever be in a position to wage aggressive war against her neighbours. And, secondly, economic relations must be so regulated that no nation can in future be starved out of its proper economic position by autarchic methods of trade arbitrarily imposed. For autarchy, whether in political affairs or in economic affairs, means anarchy.

I hope no one here thinks that these are matters which can be safely left to others to look after, for they concern vitally every one of us here. For there can be no individual security for any of us, security from want, from unemployment, from a decline in the standard of living, unless we have international security. And there can be no international security unless there is also economic security, not only in this country but in other countries, for from want and unemployment come war and upheaval. International security and economic security are in fact inseparable and indivisible. And finally, we can have neither international security nor economic security unless every one of us, in this country as in all other free countries, remains alive and vigilant to the demands of peace.

Our enemies were not slow to draw a comparison between the eight points of the Atlantic Charter and the fourteen points which President Wilson enunciated twenty-five years ago. They have lost no time in reminding us how the high idealism of 1917 degenerated through the disillusionment of the post-war years until Europe was engulfed in a second and more bestial German war. For this warning we are grateful to them. They have reminded us that idealism, if it is to prove more than a dream, must guard itself against the German character. There must be no sixth German war. We may

130

be grateful, too, that we have been reminded of certain fallacies into which we might be prone, perhaps, to fall again ourselves.

Those of us who have lived through two wars, who have seen victory give way to disillusionment and doubt, must always ask ourselves how it happened. By now we know a good deal of the history of the past twenty-five years. We have formed our own opinions of the political or economic tides which swept Europe once again to war. But there is one element in the tragedy to which, I think, we have scarcely given sufficient attention. It is this.

We thought, in 1918, that when the war was over we would sit back and all would be well. We know better now. We know that we must be as alert and watchful to win the peace as we need to be vigorous and persistent to win the war. In this work that lies ahead I hope that the younger men, particularly those who have taken an active part in this war, will play their full part. We shall have need of them if the mistakes of the past are not to be repeated in the future.

Let me then sum up. The contrast with fifteen months ago is indeed one to give us courage. At that time few of us would have dared to hope for so marked a change in our fortunes. But we should commit a crime if on this account we were content to speak comfortable words to each other. A call for immense effort lies ahead, especially in the field of production. It is in that sphere that the struggle will be finally decided. War is a cruel arbitrament. Sacrifices are being asked of each one of you in Coventry to-day. I am asking of you further efforts, further sacrifices. There is no choice. For there is only the choice between victory and defeat, between freedom and slavery. For us that is the choice between life and death. Sacrifice there must be. We can do no more than determine that in so far as the issue lies with us, the sacrifice shall not be in vain. We have to-day good grounds for hoping that it may be so, and that out of this welter of human suffering we shall come in the end to a world, not perhaps more comfortable, but to a happier world, for us and for all men.

18

AN INTERNATIONAL AND WAR SURVEY
—OCTOBER 1941

September 3. Official British estimate of German aircraft lost since 3 September 1939 (excluding those lost in the campaign against U.S.S.R.)—8,020 aircraft. British losses in the same period—3,089 aircraft.

September 16. The Shah of Persia abdicated in favour of his son.

September 21. Kiev evacuated by Russian troops.

October 10. Russians admitted an exceedingly grave threat to Moscow.

October 17. Tojo became Prime Minister of Japan.

On October 25, Mr. Eden spoke at Bellevue, Manchester, on the international and war situation:

No Government in the history of our country has had to deal with more momentous events than those which have taken place since the present Prime Minister took office in May last year.

Let us think back for a moment over that dramatic sequence—the German break-through in France, Dunkirk, the defeat of the French armies, the surrender of the French Government, with the result that we were left to maintain the fight alone against our German and Italian enemies here and on all the African fronts.

Last summer was for those of us who knew how weak was then our military strength at home and overseas a period of unparalleled anxiety.

Under the inspired leadership of the Prime Minister the British people rose magnificently to the occasion. Production was speeded up. At great peril to our position at home tanks, guns and aeroplanes were sent on the long voyage round the Cape to the Middle East, just in time to enable us to hold our position there. Then came General Wavell's brilliant series of victories against superior numbers and superior armaments in Libya and in Abyssinia.

Meanwhile, the Battle of Britain had been fought and through the gallantry of the Royal Air Force Germany suffered her first defeat.

Then with the spring came the challenge in the Balkans. Greece, which so magnificently withstood and defeated Mussolini's armies, was threatened by attack from Germany, whose onslaught was made possible by the treacherous connivance of Bulgaria.

That action will not be forgotten when the hour of final reckoning comes. We gave Greece all the aid in our power as we were unquestionably right to do, and bound to do.

Yugoslavia threw out a government that would have surrendered to Germany and, though ill-prepared for the challenge, fought with brilliant courage.

Her people are fighting still. In their mountains and valleys tens of thousands of these brave men are fighting as a guerrilla army the divisions Hitler has been compelled to move against them.

There can be no question now that this Yugoslav decision to resist, our aid for Greece, and Greece's brave defence upset the time-table of Hitler's plans and delayed his pre-arranged attack upon Russia for at least six most important weeks. What would those six weeks of campaigning weather be worth to Hitler now?

Then came the evacuation from Greece and the battle for Crete which, by the destruction it wrought in the enemy's air force, gave us time to scotch the German attempt to establish themselves in Syria, gave us time also to free Iraq from Raschid Ali's usurping government.

During all these months the Battle of the Atlantic continued, as it continues still, with unabated vigour. Immeasurable is the debt we owe to the men of the Royal Navy and the Merchant Marine. Meanwhile at home Hitler sought by battering our cities to weaken the spirit of our people. He failed, his blows only strengthened the will to resist, the determination to win through to final victory.

Then, in June of this year, Hitler launched his attack upon

Russia. True to form, without parley, without pretext, he broke his pledged word and attacked the nation with which within a year he had signed a pact of friendship.

Each one of us has felt the deepest admiration for the heroic resistance which the Russian people, their armies and their air force are offering to the invader.

If you are watching every phase of this struggle, so is the Government; if you are deeply moved so are we. It is given to us to be human too. We know only too well that the Russians are bearing now a burden that was ours a year ago. You may be sure that the Government has done and will do everything within its power to give help to Russia.

And here I would say again that I have never liked the phrase: "All help to Russia." That is not the issue. It is not a question of aid to any one country, but of aid to the common cause. Russia's cause is our cause, her battle our battle.

Lord Beaverbrook gave to the House of Lords on Thursday a full account of the Conference in Moscow. He told how we were able to promise Stalin practically all the raw materials for which he asked, aluminium, copper, lead, zinc, rubber; we had also undertaken to send steel, phosphates, machine-tools, he said that we had given tanks to such an extent to Russia that we must now have an immense increase in output at home; finally we were sending aircraft complete with equipment and ready to fight.

That is the plain truth, and Lord Beaverbrook has told all that can be told of the despatch of our supplies without giving information to the enemy which he would no doubt be glad to have.

Broadly speaking, our purpose is to seek with American help to make up to Russia by our supplies what she has lost through the German occupation of a part of her industrial territory. That is an immensely formidable task, not only in production but in shipping.

The geographical difficulties are many. We shall overcome them. The production effort required will be enormous. You, I feel sure, will make it.

It is in relation to this task that the problem of Persia assumes such importance. The Germans had established in that country a number of their own nationals under the guise of specious occupations but in reality as potential Fifth Columnists, ready to strike when the moment was opportune and actively intriguing against us and against the true interests of Persia.

Over and over again we sought to make the ex-Shah and the former Persian Government understand their peril.

They would not heed our warnings and so we took action.

Mercifully with very few casualties, our losses were under a hundred all told, our troops, together with those of our Russian ally, advanced into Persia and compelled the acceptance of our terms—terms which were in truth as much in the interest of Persia as of ourselves. Now to-day that German colony is rounded up, the women and children have been sent home and those of military age are in our hands.

I am now glad to be able to give you an encouraging report of recent developments in Persia. The new Government has co-operated loyally with us and with our Russian allies and has embarked on an enlightened programme of internal reforms designed to benefit all classes and to put an end to the corruption and tyranny which were typical of the last years of the ex-Shah's regime. The new Shah has shown his sympathy for democratic principles and is encouraging his Government's efforts to reform. These efforts are of course receiving our full support.

You will remember that some weeks ago British and Soviet troops were sent to Teheran, in order to put an end to the obstruction and trickery by which the German Minister was attempting to delay the handing over of German nationals for internment. He was trying too to hinder his own most desirable expulsion. Happily this object was achieved some time ago and, as the result of the whole-hearted help given by the new Persian Government, we and our Soviet allies have felt able to withdraw our troops from Teheran. They have now all left the neighbourhood of the capital.

We have also suggested to the Persian Government that they should sign a treaty of alliance with the Soviet Government and ourselves. They have already accepted this proposal in principle. I hope soon to be able to announce the conclusion of an alliance which should do much to ensure stability in this area which is so vital both to our Soviet allies and to ourselves.

These welcome developments in Persia have enabled us to open up a route of supplies to Russia which has the inestimable advantage of being available at all seasons of the year. Arrangements to increase the capacity of the railway and the volume of traffic that the roads can carry are already being made.

From the Caucasus through Persia, Iraq, Syria, Palestine and Egypt to the Western Desert, there is now one unbroken Allied front. To that front reinforcements and supplies have been speeding continuously during the summer and before, supplies, not only from this country but from India and other parts of the Empire and from the United States of America.

Our position in the Middle East has in truth been immensely strengthened since this time a year ago. The whole scene has been transformed. In lands where we were anxiously considering at what point the enemy, much stronger in numbers and in war material, might strike us next, we are now building up reserves ready to meet any challenge that may be brought against us.

The Afghan Government, with whom I am happy to say our relations have always been excellent, have agreed to a joint Anglo-Soviet request that all non-official Germans and Italians should be expelled from their country.

The problem presented by the German colony in Afghanistan was on a totally different scale from that which ultimately gave rise to Allied action in Persia. Unlike the ex-Shah's Government in Teheran, the Afghan Government always kept a watchful eye on Axis nationals and saw to it that the German colony remained within reasonable limits.

Nevertheless, the presence of a number of able and unscrupulous Germans in departments of the Afghan Government and in control of various important industrial projects constituted a potential menace to British and Soviet interests which the Afghan Government were quick to appreciate.

They had no desire to see their country used as a base for intrigue or operations against their neighbours and only wished to preserve their full and genuine neutrality. Their decision to expel the Germans and Italians from Afghanistan thus provides further evidence of their goodwill.

At a time like this when the minds of each one of us are with the Russian armies on their battle fronts, it is natural that some of you should be tempted to ask the question: Will the Foreign Secretary tell us when and where we are going to strike? or at least that we shall strike?

That is the one point on which it is not in my power to enlighten you. But this I can tell you: from the first hour of the German attack on Russia the War Cabinet and the Government as a whole have concentrated every effort in their power upon the task of giving their utmost help to Russia. There has been neither hesitation nor reserve.

It is right and natural that any who feel moved to do so should make any suggestions that come to their minds to stimulate, encourage or even drive us. No Government should object to that, nor to constructive criticism either. We would much rather be barked at than that there should be supine indifference. But as to the decisions which must be taken after all the evidence is weighed, those decisions must be the responsibility of the War Cabinet, and of the War Cabinet alone.

So long as we enjoy the confidence of Parliament and the country, we will continue to carry out that responsibility to the full limit of our strength, undismayed, I hope, by dangers and unprovoked by clamour.

This may be an uncomfortable saying at a time like this, but any other course would be pure folly. We shall take no action to gain a transient popular favour, we will dare any action where we believe the hazards to be justified. The Government indeed have but one purpose, which is yours and Stalin's too: how best to encompass Hitler's defeat. We will not be deterred from that task for one instant even for the luxury of answering our critics.

War is a long-term business. The issue will not be settled by any sudden brilliant improvisation. Not one of my colleagues in the War Cabinet would pretend that in these fourteen storm-tossed months we have made no mistakes. Such a claim would be ludicrous, but we do think that our effort, and above all the efforts of our Prime Minister, have merited a measure of your confidence, and I am sure that such confidence will be given to us in the anxious days that no doubt lie ahead.

All those who serve in public life must expect to have charges levelled against them; that is all part of the business. But I must confess that I never expected to live to hear the suggestion that our own Prime Minister was backward in action. He has been accused of many things, but never of that before, and it is indeed the most ludicrous of all charges to any who know the man and the true spirit of his leadership.

Let us now examine in contrast those with whom we do battle. The man Hitler is a genius—an evil genius. He has a genius for probing the weak spots in a man's armour. He knows, none better than he, how to play upon man's fears, upon his ambition, upon his greed.

Hitler knows the weakness of man, but perhaps he underrates his strength. He understands the cowardice of man, perhaps he does not know his courage. He knows how venal man can be, he doesn't know how noble man can be.

AN INTERNATIONAL AND WAR SURVEY

This is the lesson Hitler is learning in the Europe which he is seeking to subdue to his tyranny.

The cruel and ruthless executions in Norway, in France, Czechoslovakia, Poland, Yugoslavia, in Greece and the other lands where Hitler seeks to impose his tyranny, are a sign of weakness not of strength. These acts of barbarity will not be forgotten. To seize hostages and execute them for acts of violence committed by others is murder. The enslaved peoples will not forget these deeds. Nemesis will overtake these modern Huns.

The free peoples of Europe will never accept Hitler's rule based on the firing squad and these lands he has opened up to his New Order of tyranny and pillage will never freely work for him.

One day I believe it will be said of him, not that he conquered France, not that he enslaved Greece, not that he tormented Europe.

It will be said of him: This man despised, but could not debase mankind.

We are all agreed that there can never be any peace nor any negotiation between us and Hitler. This man's New Order, that modernized version of Prussian militarism, is the antithesis of the faith of all free men. By lying, by treachery and deceit, Hitler has climbed to power. With such a man there can be no truce nor compromise. It is his destruction or ours.

I have in my hands the manifesto recently issued by you, my Lord Mayor, and by the Mayors of Salford and Stretford. It is headed "Towards a Christian Britain".

In this manifesto you write:

"For civilization depends upon sincerity of purpose in politics, in business, and in home life. If we build on any other foundation we build on shifting sands, and the security we long for will never be achieved."

This is the fundamental truth that underlies our struggle. Hitler can never understand it, Mussolini could never understand it. In the contest of perjured faith, it is indeed a close race between these two guilty men. Yet it is the world you describe which we are determined to create. The same spirit, I have no doubt, animates all peoples of the British Empire, our Allies, and the people of the United States.

If we are to build better when the menace represented by Hitler and Mussolini is destroyed, we must not be afraid to admit the mistakes of the past.

Recently Mr. Sumner Welles, Under-Secretary of State in the United States, has reviewed with admirable courage and clarity

138

some of the mistakes of which, in his opinion, his own and other countries have been guilty in the past.

We must recognize that in the last twenty years we have taken a number of wrong turnings in economics and politics alike. To review and consider these mistakes among ourselves is essential if we are to shape our future policy aright. These are the problems which are being considered and studied now by the Government.

I firmly believe that in international economics the good-neighbour policy is the best policy. But it is from the aspect of duty rather than self-interest that I ask you to give this matter a few moments' thought now.

No democratic world will work as it should work until we recognize that we can only enjoy any right so long as we are prepared to discharge its equivalent duty. This applies just as much to states in their dealing with one another as to individuals within the states. Here then is another cause why Hitler and Mussolini and all they stand for must be utterly destroyed.

We are aware of the weight and the burden of the sacrifices we shall have to accept after the war. But we have made up our minds to shoulder our international responsibilities courageously and conscientiously, and to answer, for our part, the call which Mr. Welles himself has made to the citizens of the United States. I look forward with confidence to an association with the United States of incalculable value not only to ourselves, but to the whole world besides. Herein lies, surely, the greatest hope for the future.

Greater men than Hitler have tried and failed to dominate the world of their time. In their failure they left behind them records of achievement. Much of what they did survived in so far as they did not attempt to crush the human spirit but gave it a new outlook and a new impulse. But Hitler's doctrine of total war carrying with it the practice of total domination implies the crushing of the human spirit.

That doctrine can only survive by the force on which it depends. When that force has been broken and the nations are free to choose the way they will live and govern themselves and order their relations with their neighbours, the world will repudiate with thanksgiving the sum total of the teaching and practice of Hitler.

Hitlerism and the teaching of German thinkers which has led to and been embodied in Hitlerism must be swept from the fair face of the world where God has planted men to practise their duty towards their neighbour.

That is our task.

1942

19

VISIT TO RUSSIA—WINTER 1941–2

Throughout October and up to the end of November the German Army, despite enormous losses, pushed on eastwards and on November 22, captured Rostov-on-Don. The Russians recaptured Rostov on November 29, carried on their advance westwards, and on December 30, secured a foothold in the Crimea. On November 6 Stalin estimated the German losses since June at four and a half million men, and he expressed a hope that Britain would be able to create a second front in the west.

Other war events

1941
November 18. General Sir Alan Brooke succeeded Sir John Dill as C.I.G.S. The Eighth Army launched a full-scale attack in the Western Desert.

December 7. Pearl Harbour attacked. Japanese invade Thailand, Malaya and the Philippines.

December 8. Britain and U.S.A. declared war on Japan.

December 10. H.M.S. *Prince of Wales* and H.M.S. *Repulse* sunk.

December 11. Germany and Italy declared war on U.S.A.

December 21. Hitler took over personal command of German Army.

December 22. Mr. Churchill with Chiefs of Staff in Washington. He went on to Ottawa after Christmas.

December 24. The Eighth Army entered Benghazi.

1942
January 1. A Grand Alliance signed against the Axis by twenty-six nations.

On January 4, Mr. Eden broadcast about his visit to Russia.

VISIT TO RUSSIA

Leaving Scapa in mid-December he had sailed the northern route to Murmansk in H.M.S. *Kent*. He spent a week in Moscow with Marshal Stalin and Mr. Molotov, and, after a visit to the Russian front, he arrived back in England on December 30.

I am just back from a long journey. I am glad to be home but I am even more glad that I went. It's not the first time I have made the journey to Russia. Nearly seven years ago I was in Moscow. We were not at war then. The sky was not even overcast, but the clouds of war were beginning to gather on the distant horizon. You could just discern them. That was why I was in Moscow in 1935 talking with Mr. Stalin. I believed then, as I believe now, that there was no real conflict of interest between the Soviet Union and this country. We both said so in our communiqué at the time. I believed then, as I believe now, that, despite the many obvious differences, our overriding purpose was the same. We both wished to maintain the peace. Well, we lost that peace, but we are determined not to lose this war or the peace that will follow it. And so I was glad of a chance to go again to Moscow to speak again with Mr. Stalin.

The Royal Navy carried us to our destination in North Russia with swift, quiet efficiency. They were wonderful hosts, but it was not an easy journey. We drove through heavy winter seas and at one time (so they told us) we had tons of ice on board. I confess I was glad when we had rounded the North Cape and were sailing along the Murmansk coast. It was snowing hard in the dim half-light of the Arctic noon, where the sun never rises above the horizon in the winter months, when we landed on Soviet soil. A detachment of Russian soldiers was drawn up on the shore. They were a grand type of man, dressed in their warm sheepskin coats, a much more practical uniform, I can tell you, than the ersatz clothing and the sweepings of Goebbels' jumble sale in which Hitler's armies have to retreat through the Russian snows. These Russian soldiers were flanked by officers carrying the Union Jack and the Hammer and Sickle. The yellow ochre of the uniforms, the bright splashes of colour of the two flags against the snow-covered hills, the uncanny twilight at midday, the silence of falling snow, all these formed a most impressive setting for our first landing on Soviet soil. But it was friendly. Indeed the courtesy and friendliness of this greeting was typical of our welcome at every stage of our journey.

Flying conditions were very bad, so we travelled to Moscow by train. One stretch of our journey was over a section of the railway which Goebbels has often told you has been cut by enemy action. I can tell you from practical experience that Goebbels is wrong. The railway is intact, undamaged, and working smoothly and well. It was on this journey that we first understood the meaning of a Russian winter. An occasional stop gave us a chance to stretch our legs and to freeze our moustaches in a temperature of 58 degrees of frost. To keep an engine running in such a temperature is a problem all to itself. To keep a human body alive, if you do not know just how to set about it, is not too easy either. All this and much more the Germans are learning in the Russian winter.

Our Ambassador in Moscow, Sir Stafford Cripps, came some way north from the city to meet us. Mr. Maisky, the Soviet Ambassador in London, was the best of travelling companions. They both gave our delegation most valuable help in every phase of our work.

Mr. Molotov and other representatives of the Soviet Government met us on our arrival late at night in Moscow, the city Hitler had hoped to capture long ago. The next day we began our series of talks with Mr. Stalin and Mr. Molotov in the Kremlin. These talks went further than any political or military discussions that have taken place at any time between our two countries since the last war.

They fell naturally into two parts. In the first we dealt with the conduct of the war. You won't expect me to tell you a great deal about that. Events will speak for themselves, I hope. But this assurance I can give you, that when our communiqué speaks of our identity of views on all questions relating to the conduct of the war, those words are not mere diplomatic jargon, they tell you the literal and absolute truth. I have no doubt in my mind that this part of our work alone would have more than justified the journey. But, personally, I attach as much importance to the discussions which we had upon the organization of peace and security after the war. We talked over what must be done to prevent any German aggression in the future. We talked over the conditions of the peace, and the machinery for keeping it. Obviously the Soviet Government and ourselves alone could take no final decisions at our meetings. Intimate consultation with the Governments of the Dominions, with the United States and with our other allies, will be necessary in the months that lie ahead. We must move forward together, but it is all to the good that a start has been made in the discussion of these questions between ourselves and the Soviet Government.

Wherever I went in Russia I found the note was one of confidence and resolution—not a confidence based on any light-hearted underestimate of the enemy. The Russians know very well how formidable is the German military machine, but they believe that they have now the measure of their foe. They are determined that he shall pay to the uttermost for the destruction of the towns and the villages, the farms and the factories of the Soviet Union. The method Hitler chose for his attack, the sudden unheralded swoop upon a people with whom he had signed a pact of friendship only nine months before—that method gave him, no doubt, valuable military advantages to begin with. But politically it was stark lunacy. Hitler united all Russia by that one act. He made the war a crusade—a crusade to rid the Soviet Union of the last German. In all the territory that Hitler has overrun, there is not one Russian Quisling. All through the summer and autumn Soviet forces were engaged in a fighting retreat. They defended every farm and field, so as to wear down their enemy. Now the tide' has turned. Russian counter-attacks have developed into counter-offensives. The Germans now will have to bear the bitterness and cruelty of the Russian winter. Whatever lies Hitler may tell, his armies were not prepared for that.

The spirit of these Russian troops is magnificent. Their morale is higher than ever. They are striking at the retreating Germans without mercy and without respite. I saw a little of this myself. We drove along the Moscow-Leningrad road to Klin and some miles beyond. There were plenty of signs of fighting by the roadside— shell-torn trees, derelict guns and shattered homes. We saw something, too, of the scorched-earth policy. Most of the houses in these parts are built of wood, the chimneys only being of brick, so that, when the houses have been burnt, gaunt brick fingers point solitary to the sky; scorched earth in a frozen land. The effect is even more awful than total destruction would be.

It is difficult for those familiar with the Western Front of the last war to picture the giant distances. So when you look at a map of the Russian front it is a good habit to have beside you one of England on the same scale.

The German Army has been driven back fast and far. For instance, we reached Klin at noon on a Friday. On the Monday fighting had still been going on in the town, and though we drove perhaps six or seven miles beyond it, I don't think that we were at any time within twenty miles of the nearest Germans. Hitler has always liked a war of movement. He is getting it now. We saw what had evidently been the scene of pretty tough fighting some few miles north of Klin. Russian and German tanks were knocked out by the roadside. In a ditch were frozen German corpses. On the way back we saw a small group of German prisoners who had been captured the day before. I talked to some of them myself. They were young, not much more than boys, although three of them were N.C.O.s, ill-clad and suffering bitterly from the cold. They were not a bit like the soldiers of a victorious army. They were just half a dozen more of Hitler's unhappy victims. I had a look at their clothing, and they were quite ready to talk about it. Their overcoats were thinner and lighter than the service overcoat worn by the British troops in this country. The tunics too were thin and of poor material. The boots were an imitation of the Russian top boot but not so stout or so warm. Even the tunic buttons were cheap and shoddy, and the whole turn-out had an ersatz appearance. They had no gloves and only thin cardigans and they kept trying to pull the sleeves down over their frozen fingers. I asked whether their clothing was typical of that issued to the Germany Army on the Russian front. They said that it was, and from what I heard later I am sure they were telling the truth. But there is one exception I must make. Hitler's own personal S.S. troops are privileged, and have distinctly better equipment. Remember that the worst of the Russian winter has still to come. You will understand then that there is reason for this Russian confidence; reason indeed for anxious heavy hearts in Germany.

And now one word about supplies for the Russian armies. The output of tanks and aeroplanes was of course affected by the first rush of the German advance. But the figures of Russian output are now climbing again, to an extent which astounded me. Our help too, I am glad to say, is coming along steadily. British material has been tried in battle, and has proved itself. Good accounts were given of our aircraft, and the Hurricanes are especially popular. Our tanks, too, have done most valuable service at a critical time. The output of British and American factories is being put to splendid use on the Russian battlefields. You need have no shadow of doubt about that.

The experience of my visit, the talks that I had with Mr. Stalin and Mr. Molotov, have convinced me that closer political collaboration between us can and will be realized. We can't ignore the difficulties. We have to get rid of a legacy of suspicion on both sides. There is the contrast in forms of government. But I will never accept that this need divide us.

What matters in foreign affairs is not the form of internal government of any nation but its international behaviour. The trouble with Hitler, for instance, was not that he was a Nazi at home. The trouble with him was that he would not stay at home. He was and is a ruthless aggressor with an insatiable appetite for world dominion. He cannot tolerate free and independent nations, and no free nation will be secure so long as he lives and the German military power is unbroken.

Contrast this with Russia's attitude and our own. The Soviet Union is determined upon the utter defeat of Germany; so are we. The Soviet Union is determined to do all that is in its power to ensure that Germany cannot launch further wars upon the world; so are we. Out of the untold human suffering of the present war the Soviet Union wishes to gain a lasting peace for all its peoples; so do we. For these common objects we must work together to win the war and to win the peace. With the experience of our Moscow talks fresh in my mind, I am convinced that we can do both.

20

SOUTH WALES AND THE WAR

January 30. General Rommel reoccupied Benghazi.

January 31. British troops withdrew to Singapore from the Malayan mainland.

February 12. Scharnhorst, Gneisenau and *Prinz Eugen* dashed through the Channel.

February 15. Fall of Singapore.

February 19–22. Government changes including appointment of Sir Stafford Cripps as Lord Privy Seal and Leader of the House of Commons.

February 20. The Japanese landed in Timor.

March 6. Japanese captured Batavia.

March 8. Japanese landed in New Guinea.

March 9. Rangoon evacuated.

March 10. Mr. Eden reported to the House of Commons on the atrocities committed by the Japanese on prisoners and civilians in Hong Kong.

March 12. Mr. Oliver Lyttleton became Minister of Production.

March 22. Sir Stafford Cripps arrived in India on his special mission.

March 25. Japanese occupied the Andaman Islands.

March 26. The Prime Minister stated that the Battle of the Atlantic had worsened.

March 28. "Zeebrugge" raid on St. Nazaire.

On March 29, Mr. Eden went to Merthyr Tydfil and addressed a large gathering:

SOUTH WALES AND THE WAR

To reach you to-day I have driven through your beautiful Welsh valleys. To do this is to understand why it is that his home casts a spell over a Welshman which he is never able to throw off. I can understand why it is that Welshmen, wherever they may be, cling to the language of their fathers and to the tastes and traditions of their homeland. The sons of Wales are scattered far and wide, across oceans and beyond mountain ranges. But wherever they may be, their hearts are never very far from home. And when they get the chance they come back to the valleys that bred them.

Your land is always lovely, and I suppose that it is never more beautiful than now, when the spring is beginning and the snow has left the mountains and the warm sun is filling the valleys. Spring. When we think of spring in these troubled days we not only think of warmth and life. We think of war, and of death. And when I think of spring my mind goes back to a journey I took some little time ago, to another land a long way away from this valley, a land where men and women are fired with the same love and devotion to their country that the men and women of Wales feel for the Principality. It was not spring, when I was in Russia. It was icy winter.

Let us consider for a moment how stupendous has been this Russian achievement. Confronted suddenly with the whole military might of Germany, these Russian soldiers fought back across their land in a stubborn and organized retreat. At every step they took their toll of the German armies. And then just when Hitler was boasting that in a few days he would be in Moscow, the Russian counter-offensive was launched. There have been few more remarkable achievements in the military history of the world. We must measure it not in terms of strategy alone, but in terms of individual, human effort when we pay our tribute to the courage and endurance which could suffer so much in retreat for so long; and then at the very moment when the enemy thought that resistance was finally broken, fight back and fight back triumphantly.

Hitler last summer boasted that the Russians would be pleading for peace in a few weeks. When this did not happen Hitler in the autumn announced that the Soviet leaders would be fleeing for their lives from Moscow within a few hours, and that the Russian capital would be his in a few days. When this did not happen Hitler, who had boasted that his campaign would be over long before the winter, declared that his advance would continue in

149

spite of it. All this has gone awry. Hitler's much-vaunted intuition has led him into gigantic mistakes. Millions of young Germans have paid for these mistakes with their lives and with maimed, frost-bitten limbs.

While these great events were shaping the future of the world, we also played our part. Russia told us of her needs in the materials of war. She gave us a list of her imperative requirements. We promised to send these materials and we have fulfilled our promise. Nor have the quantities been small. I am not going to present the enemy with the details of the numbers and types of weapons and materials we have been sending. Hitler would be very glad indeed to know how many ships, tanks, aeroplanes, guns and vehicles, how much ammunition and what other armaments we have been sending in an unceasing stream. Hitler would no doubt be interested to read the tonnage figures of the raw materials which have been pouring into the Soviet Union. He would no doubt very much like to know the quantities of strategic metals, explosives, chemicals, industrial equipment, foodstuffs, army uniforms and equipment, medical and surgical supplies, we have been despatching. I cannot give these details. But when I was in Russia at Christmas time, I was able to see for myself that our tanks and aircraft and other munitions had reached the front, and I was told at first hand what value the Russian armies attached to their performance.

You will readily imagine that the arrangements for seeing that all these materials are packed and shipped in good order and in accordance with a regular plan, have involved the setting up of a special organization. We have to see that the munitions go forward from the factories and depots, to the loading ports. We have to see that the ships are available to take them, and that the cargoes are carefully stowed and secured against the icy blasts and stormy weather which are invariably the lot of those who sail the Atlantic and Arctic Oceans in the winter months. And here I would like to pay my tribute to the workers in the factories and men and women in the depots and stations, to the railway men and the dockers, the seamen and shipping staffs, every one of whom has worked with enthusiasm to carry out this great task. All this has taken a little time to organize, to plan, and to keep going at a healthy and rhythmic speed. Much of the machinery has had to be provided at short notice, and nearly all the work has had to be done under the pressure of great urgency. When the full story comes to be given, I foretell that we shall have no reason to reproach ourselves with what we have achieved.

SOUTH WALES AND THE WAR

And it is good to read the reports that are now coming in of the excellent work which our Hurricanes are doing in the hands of the Russian fighter pilots on many sectors of the Eastern Front. They have contributed in no small way to the air defence of Moscow. They have taken part in the defence of Leningrad and have helped to save that heroic city from the added stress and strain of bombardment from the air. Russian pilots, who are most capable and experienced airmen, have destroyed many German aircraft in their British planes, and are loud in their praise of their performance, even in the most exacting conditions of arctic winter. We have received, too, favourable reports of the performance of British tanks on the Russian front. But when we give thanks to those who have helped with this work, pride of place must always go to the Royal Navy and the men of the Merchant Marine. Week after week, through the heavy seas of those northern latitudes, where all the exposed portions of the ships are often coated thick with ice, where the temperature is so low that to touch metal is to have skin torn from one's hands as though one had grasped a red-hot poker, where the Germans are desperately eager to intercept, with all their available sea-power and air-power, the flow of supplies, our sailors and our ships have kept the seas and delivered the goods. That is a truly great achievement.

Let us recall that in another way the Royal Navy has played its part in this winter campaign in Russia. For over two and a half years it has imposed a blockade on Germany. It has reduced the wool, the cotton, the leather and other goods which would otherwise have poured into Germany. The Royal Navy has in fact played its part in taking the warm clothes off the backs of those millions of German soldiers whom Hitler exposes to the bitter cold of Russian winter.

Meanwhile much work has been done in forging another link between Russia and the United Nations. A route has been opened through Persia, which country we now welcome as an Allied Power. This route is being developed ahead of schedule. In January we carried over it double the amount of material carried last November; by May we hope to double the figures of January. A warm tribute is due to those who are carrying through this work at such speed against many difficulties.

The story of our sea-power in this war can never be adequately told. Because our ships are for the most part out of sight over the horizon, they should never be out of mind. After France surrendered and until the United States came into the war, the Royal

Navy alone faced the united naval power of the Axis, keeping the seas open for our merchant ships and denying the seas to the enemy. Let me provoke your imagination by half a dozen examples of the Navy's work. From the beginning of the war until the end of last year, one battle cruiser had covered 137,000 miles; one cruiser had steamed no less than 196,000 miles; one little destroyer had during that time logged 172,000 miles; one aircraft carrier 180,000 miles; one submarine had covered 26,000 miles in five months. Always a ceaseless vigil, always searching for the enemy, always on the alert for attack from submarine or aircraft.

In every home in Britain the Royal Navy is not only admired, but beloved. No matter how far from the sea we can travel in this small island, that sentiment is deep and strong. Nothing can shake it, and reason supports that instinct. We cannot maintain this conflict unless we and our allies maintain our sea-power; we cannot win it until we have destroyed the enemy's sea-power. Meanwhile the strength of our Air Force continues to grow and the R.A.F. plays its part by day and by night on every front.

But to say this is not to ignore the growing importance of the part the Army has to play. In pre-war days the Army was our most neglected service. And after Dunkirk, less than two years ago, our equipment cupboard was literally bare. Our Army had no sufficient store of modern weapons with which to train and to fight. Yet it had to meet a challenge in a dozen fields: here at home, where the defence of the citadel was truly vital, in Libya, in the Sudan, in Somaliland, in Abyssinia, in Greece and Crete, in Syria, in Iraq, in Persia. In all these lands the men of the British Commonwealth had to fight and did fight with splendid gallantry with limited resources and often against great odds. All this within the space of little more than a year. Now a new challenge confronts them in the Far East.

We are in the sternest period of the war. In Europe the Allies and the Axis and the Axis powers make ready for what may be the decisive struggle. In such conditions smooth sayings are utterly out of place. It is a time for harsh and unremitting endeavour. We have become accustomed to tell ourselves that victory is certain; victory is only certain for those who deserve it. In many respects the period which we have now to fight through will prove more difficult than even the summer of 1940 when, after the French collapse, we stood alone. Our effort now must at least equal our effort then. The national drive and energy must be keyed up to the same pitch. The effort is admittedly harder to make. After Dun-

kirk every man and woman could feel and see the danger. To-day
the battle is not beating so nearly about our heads. There is no
air battle of Britain, there is no night bombing. During the long
months from the defeat of Poland to the attack on France and the
Low Countries, Hitler sought to break the French morale by
tedium. In a large measure he succeeded. By the same methods
he may be now trying to encourage the British people to relax
their efforts. He cannot be allowed to succeed, even for a day.

I know well the sense of frustration which at times we all have
to fight against. I cannot discuss with you what our future operational plans may be, for there are others who would overhear us.
But we must not let ourselves be frustrated. It is well, no doubt, to
be aware of our shortcomings. But it is well sometimes to have regard for what we ourselves have done. We have suffered great
reverses, but there are solid achievements too. Complacency is a
bad thing. But pride, self-respect, those are not bad things. When
the history of our time comes to be written, one event will not be
overlooked: that we in this small island, together with our faithful
partners in the British Empire, stood alone when all else failed.
We hoped, when all mankind despaired. Our example it was which
shone like a flame, and will shine for generations of men to come,
because we fought on alone before we had powerful allies to help
us. There is nothing in this of which we need feel ashamed. We
have a tendency towards self-depreciation. That is all right in
moderation. But you can have too much of it. And when you have
too much of it, it is dangerous. We are told sometimes of slackness
among workers, of greed and incompetence among managements.
No doubt there are black sheep. Believe me, they are a minority,
even a small minority. The people of this country, whatever their
class, whatever their calling, are out to win this war. We will give,
all of us, all we have to that. If we feel that the national effort is
still not enough, then let us, each one of us, search his own heart
or conscience and leave his neighbour's conscience to his neighbour's care. If we do that, we shall not fail. Production for war
presents many and changing problems. In war-time you cannot be
certain of continuity of supplies. In this island we have to work
upon materials that are brought here from all over the world.
They are subject to the hazards of war, and sometimes they must
fall to the hazards of war. But when the material does come to
hand, we must get to work not with less but with more zeal because of any delay there may have been.

But I have not come to South Wales to exhort you to further

efforts. I know what South Wales is doing for the war effort. I know that it is magnificent. I know that you will go on to the end without fear or faltering. We should take as our motto in the coming months of the war, which may well prove the decisive months, the lines from Burns:

Wha does the utmost that he can,
Will whyles do mair.

The stage of war compasses the earth. It is so vast that the human mind can scarcely comprehend it. Yet each one of us must never allow himself for an instant to forget that by his example, by his courage, by his resolution, he personally has a part to play in the decision of this titanic struggle.

This is a total war in every sense of the term. Everything that we have built up in the centuries of our island's history is at stake. We know what would be the price of defeat. We have no illusions as to the fate that would befall us. We know what has happened in Greece, we know how the people of Greece—men, women and children—have been left, to die of hunger in the streets. We know what the people of Poland, of Norway, of Belgium, of all the conquered territories have had to endure. Not very long ago it was my duty to tell the House of Commons about Hong Kong. It was not a pleasant duty. While I could believe that it might be untrue, while I could believe that it might be exaggerated, I did not want to tell the story. But when it was clear that it was the truth—beyond any possibility of doubt—then the nation had a right to know the truth. Hong Kong is far away from here. Poland, Norway, Belgium, Greece, Holland—they all seem far away. But what has happened there, that would happen here—if we were defeated. Yes, the fate of a conquered country is a harsh and ghastly one. We are determined that it shall be a passing one—and that the sun of peace and liberty and happiness shall shine once again on those poor suffering lands. And it shall shine here too. We at home have to do better. There can be no return to what was bad in the old days. Some things were bad.

Here, in these Welsh valleys, the people suffered between the two wars. Here, in Merthyr, you knew poverty, you knew unemployment, you knew the bitter feeling of despair which comes from the knowledge that one is not wanted. We cannot go back to that. Your sons, who are fighting, must not come back to that. This time, by a truer unity, a wiser foresight and a greater vigour, we must make a more worthy use of the victory over the enemy. This time victory must mean not only the triumph of our arms, but the dawn of better conditions for every section of our people. It will not be easy, I cannot promise you an easy life, when the war is over. No one can promise that—for any of us. It may well be that life for all of us, when the war is over, will be hard. But we need not be afraid of that. We may even welcome that.

But we must see to it that life is good, that, if it be hard, it is still worth living. We must see to it that each one of us has his part to play when the war is over. We must see to it that there are no unwanted men in Wales—or anywhere else in our land. It is in that faith and that hope that we must strive for victory. In that faith we must work—and work together—when the victory is won.

21

THE SCOTTISH WAR EFFORT

April 16. The George Cross was awarded to Malta.

April 20. M. Laval, in a broadcast speech, bitterly attacked Britain.

April 22. Commando troops raided French coast near Boulogne.

May 5. Japanese troops having captured Lashio at the western end of the Burma Road, entered China from the west.

Corregidor, the last U.S.A. stronghold in the Philippines, surrendered to the Japanese.

May 7. French naval and military commanders in Madagascar surrendered to British troops.

On May 8, Mr. Eden made the following speech at Edinburgh:

Scotland was in the front line from the start of the war. She felt the first blow of the battle of the Atlantic (the *Athenia* was a Glasgow ship), and the first German aircraft struck down on the mainland fell not far from the place where I am now speaking. There is no need to explain to a Scottish audience how you and your kin are still in every front line at home and abroad. From the Battle of France to the latest Commando raid, and unceasingly on the sea and in the air, the famous fighting names have never been lacking.

Scottish homes, too, have endured the devastation of war, but Scottish workers are producing the arms for our return blows. In mines, shipyards and factories, men and women are giving their skill ungrudgingly by day and by night, and on the land farmers have broken in more than half a million acres to feed a people at war.

The personnel of civil defence, hospitals and the other emergency services have played their gallant part. Even those who have not encountered the full blows of enemy assaults have by their constant practice and vigilance rendered these assaults more difficult. The importance of the operations which have recently been taking place in Madagascar is self-evident. Diego Suarez is one of the finest harbours on the Indian Ocean. It has been developed as a naval base, and in Axis hands would constitute a very serious menace not only to South Africa and British possessions in East Africa, but also to our communications with Australia, New Zealand, India and the Middle East. Axis raiders would be able to prey on the supply lines to the Far East, the Middle East and Russia.

Prevention is better than cure. The Japanese of course, had their eyes on Madagascar. We knew that. The United Nations could not take the risk of leaving the island open to them. We therefore decided to act and forestall the enemy.

With the full approval and support of the Government of the United States, British forces landed in the early morning of May 4. The operation has been wholly successful. Diego Suarez is already in our hands, and available for the use of the ever-growing forces of the United Nations.

His Majesty's Government and the United States Government are agreed that the territory of Madagascar remains French and will continue to be part of the French Empire. In this, as in other aspects of policy towards France, we and the United States Government have been and are in complete accord. In particular we have been agreed with the policy of the United States Government to maintain contact with the Vichy Government.

Vichy forces in Madagascar received orders to resist and they obeyed. It was repugnant to us to be forced by them to shed French blood. Operations were not actually begun until a demand for the surrender of Diego Suarez had been rejected by the local governor.

How different is Vichy's attitude towards the Axis. The Vichy Government considered it honourable to allow Japan to use Indo-China as a base for operations against the United Nations. Would any shreds of French sovereignty remain there if the Japanese were successful in this war? Do any remain now?

The Vichy Government considered it honourable to give facilities to the Germans in Syria for operations against us. Yet when British and Free French forces entered Syria to save it from the

THE SCOTTISH WAR EFFORT

Axis the Vichy Government ordered the local forces to oppose every resistance. They have done the same in Madagascar.

What would Clemenceau, Foch and Joffre and the other great Frenchmen of the past think of Vichy's present attitude? What do the people of France themselves think? We know what they think. We know that all true Frenchmen loathe and despise the policy of the men of Vichy. They understand that the salvation of France depends on an Allied victory. The denial of Diego Suarez to Japan brings that victory nearer and so Frenchmen in their hearts will approve what we have done.

Last week Hitler made a speech. It contained cold comfort for the German people and their motley band of associates. Hitler is usually profuse in promises; he was more cautious this time. The German people are suffering from the effects of our nightly bombardments. They are harassed by the thought that the weight of the attack will steadily increase. They are quite right to be troubled by these things.

Lübeck has already suffered more than Coventry, and the blows will become heavier as the months pass. Yet in his speech Hitler gave no promise of protection against Allied attacks from the air. He could only threaten reprisals.

Perhaps next time he speaks he will quote Goering's assurance given to the German workmen during the first week of the war: "I will see to it that the enemy can drop no bombs." Or perhaps Goering would repeat that statement now in Lübeck, in Rostock, in Cologne, in the score or more of other German cities, that have been attacked or are to be attacked in their turn.

But Hitler did make some promises. He promised to remove the last vestige of personal rights and legal process in Germany itself. Hitler has made himself the supreme judge. He has set himself above the law, and his powers will be exercised by the ruthless gang of thugs around him who wield ever-increasing power. Hitler has now destroyed the law as he is destroying other cherished institutions of European civilization.

Hitler also threw a backward glance to what he called his "numerous offers" of understanding with England. He still seems to be under the delusion that there are people in this country who would be prepared to make peace with him. This wishful thinking is not unknown in Germany. We have witnessed the phenomenon before.

Almost a year ago another Nazi, Hitler's Deputy, one Hess, descended somewhat unexpectedly upon this fair country of Scotland from the air. Perhaps he was under the same delusion as Hitler.

When will these leaders of Germany understand that the millions of people in this country and in the British Empire, and indeed throughout the United Nations, are unanimously determined to have no truck of any kind with Hitler or the Nazi regime? Our people are not dulled by propaganda, they are not hypnotized by a myth. They have made their resolve as free men and women, which is something no doubt that Hitler cannot understand. They have counted the cost, and they are willing to pay it in order to re-establish in the world the basis of a free civilization and that respect for international engagements without which there can be no lasting peace.

Except for a few wretched Quislings all the peoples of Europe whose lands have been temporarily overrun by the German armies have the same faith. They continue stubbornly to resist the Nazi and Fascist oppressors with such means as they can command. The German people and Hitler's satellite rulers, Mussolini, Antonescu and others should be in no doubt as to the light in which they are regarded by free men all over the world. The longer the German people continues to support and to tolerate the regime which is leading them to destruction the heavier grows their own direct responsibility for the damage that they are doing to the world.

Therefore, if any section of the German people really wants to see a return to a German State which is based on respect for law and for the rights of the individual, they must understand that no one will believe them until they have taken active steps to rid themselves of their present regime.

Meanwhile Hitler's speech has sounded the death knell of the much-vaunted New Order. The New Order is dead. It was never really alive. The New Order was not like spring, it was never more than winter, whose icy grasp clamped down death and hunger and disease upon Europe. The New Order will fade away and be forgotten of men.

But this does not mean that we suppose that after the war everything will be the same. Nor that we would wish it so. We shall not awake from this nightmare and find that there is waiting for us the old world that we knew. I don't think that many of us would want that world exactly as it was even if we could have it. Certainly I would not want it. We had plenty of good intentions then. Our intentions were excellent. I do not suppose that forty million

1 1

THE SCOTTISH WAR EFFORT

people, in the whole history of mankind, have ever had such good intentions.

We wanted peace. We wanted kindliness. We wanted comfort and prosperity. We wanted, very badly, to be healthy, wealthy, and wise. That was what we wanted.

What we got was something very different. We got unemployment. We got, in a world teeming with riches, an almost complete breakdown of international trade. We got war. Our good intentions were not enough. Good intentions never *are* enough; unless they are matched with intelligence and vigilance and, beyond everything, unless they are matched by will.

I am speaking to you as Foreign Secretary. And when, as Foreign Secretary, I think of the world after the war I am thinking, primarily, of how we shall be able to keep the peace. For me that is the fundamental problem. But it is the fundamental problem for all of us. For without peace, without stability in international relationships, without active co-operation between the peoples of the world, without the removal of the constant threat of war, there is no hope for us anywhere. Without peace we cannot rid ourselves of the recurring scourge of unemployment.

Without peace we must look forward to ever-falling standards of living, to ever-increasing social stress.

When I speak of peace I do not mean simply the absence of war. When Germany and Japan are defeated, whether it be this year, or next, or whenever it may be, the war will come to its end. But that will not mean peace, in the sense in which I am using the word. It is only then, when the war is over, that we shall *begin* to make peace.

When the war comes to an end we shall be faced with the problem, but we shall not have solved it. That will be for the future, and for the long future. We cannot win peace in a day. We cannot win peace in the months of a conference. We cannot win it even in a peace treaty, however careful our draftsmanship.

These are the bones, the skeleton of peace. Only human will and perseverance can give them flesh and blood. We can only build up peace over long years of effort, of vigilance, above all of determination, of will. We did not make peace last time. How shall we make it now?

First of all I would say, and it is not a hard saying, that we must make sacrifices for peace. It is one of the laws of life, and we need not be afraid of it, that you do not get something for nothing. Everything has to be paid for somehow, at some time. We have learned that, if we have learned nothing else, in the past twenty-five

160

years. And the first thing that we have to do is to understand, as we did not understand before, that we have a direct and inescapable responsibility for peace at all times. That is a responsibility which is not ours alone. We share it with the other nations of the world. We have continually to revise our understanding of geography.

Before ever this war began the world was shrinking before our eyes. The war has accelerated that process. The world after the war will be a still smaller place. There will be no room for isolation, no room for selfish policies, or unneighbourly policies. There will be but one village street from Edinburgh to Chungking.

But because we are a great people our own responsibility is great. We must never neglect our own British interests. But we cannot afford to disinterest ourselves from the interests of other nations. There can be no isolation for the British Empire, ever again. We must assume the burden of leadership. It is a burden which others will share with us. But a great part of the burden is for us.

How are we to discharge this responsibility of leadership which will be ours? First of all, we must give visible proof that we accept the responsibility. We must show not only that we are willing to bear our share in the enforcement of peace. We must show that we have the force and the will to do it.

I am not suggesting another armaments race. I am suggesting that never again shall we so neglect our armaments that we frighten our friends and delight our enemies. I am suggesting that never again shall our weakness give a free hand to the gangsters of Europe and Asia and betray all of those who, like ourselves, seek to work out their own lives in freedom and in peace. And these are, never forget, the overwhelming majority of mankind.

We must show that we can act as well as preach. That will mean sacrifice. But the sacrifice will be light by comparison with the reward. And unless we are prepared for that sacrifice nothing, neither fuller employment nor fuller economic opportunity nor better education nor better housing, nothing will be assured to us.

Peace is more than frontiers and peace treaties. There must be force and will as well. But peace is more than force. And you will never have peace on this earth unless you have an economic system in which men and women who are willing to work are able to work and find the reward of their labours.

I said just now that there could be no social advancement without peace. But it is equally true that you will not get peace without social improvement. If there are three million unemployed here, and countless millions of unemployed in Europe and America and

Asia, you will not get peace. If there is unemployment and mal-nutrition and animal standards of life, and poverty that can be remedied is not remedied, in any part of the world, you will jeopardize peace.

There is first a fundamental need. The United Nations together must possess sufficient force to provide the police to prevent high-way robbery and the success of gangster methods. We have to aim at a state of affairs in which the four great world powers repre-sented by the British Commonwealth of nations, the United States of America, the U.S.S.R. and China will together sustain this peace system. In peace they will look for aid from other peace-loving countries, just as they do now in war. But upon them must fall the main burden for the maintenance of peace and the main responsi-bility for the economic reconstructions of the world after the war.

What is true of our foreign relations is also true of our Colonial Empire. You cannot run a large Colonial Empire well unless you are determined to do so, and unless you are proud to make the necessary sacrifices to carry through the task.

In that period between the two wars, in which our intentions were so excellent and our purpose was so woefully weak, we almost became shy of the fact that we were entrusted with a vast Empire. That must never happen again. I use the word entrusted advisedly. Our purpose in developing our Colonial Empire must not be to gain commercial advantage for ourselves nor to exploit transient material opportunities. Still less should we seek to uproot native habits of life. It must be our privilege to develop our Colonial Empire, to raise the standard of life of the many races dwelling in it, to gain their confidence, their trust, their free collaboration in the work we have both to do. This means that men and women must be ready to give up their working lives to this service. This same Colonial Empire has given us the lives and work of many of its sons and daughters during the war. We pledge ourselves not to fail them in the period after the war.

I have not concealed from you the formidable nature of the problems that the future holds. But I would not have you believe on that account that I am a pessimist for the post-war period. We have heard much of Hitler's strength through joy movement, and we don't think much of that. But I am no advocate of a strength through misery movement. We can find our own happiness in our own way by the dedication of our working lives to the cause for which we have taken up arms, the sanctity of the pledged word, and freedom and opportunity for our fellow-men.

22

THE ANGLO-SOVIET TREATY—
26 MAY 1942

Throughout the late winter and spring, the Red Army continued its advance westwards and on February 24 won a great victory in the Staraya Russa area. In May, after a lull in the battle, the Germans attacked again.

On May 26, in London, Mr. Eden signed the Anglo-Soviet Treaty on behalf of Great Britain. Mr. Molotov signed for U.S.S.R., and left for Washington next day.

On behalf of His Majesty's Government in the United Kingdom, I welcome you, Monsieur Molotov, as Foreign Secretary of the Union of Soviet Socialist Republics. We are met in a world at war, when our two countries are together at grips with the common enemy. Under the impact of war we have found that understanding which escaped us in the uneasy years of peace.

The Treaty which we have just signed engages us to continue the struggle together until the victory be won. On behalf of my colleagues I give you the pledge that there will be no wavering in this endeavour on the part of the Government or people of these islands.

Such, then, is the first chapter of our task, the overthrow of Hitler and the destruction of all that his regime stands for. But there is a second chapter also to our treaty. One day the war will end; one day the common enemy will be defeated and there will be peace again. We must see to it that this time peace endures. In the treaty which we have signed we pledge ourselves to work together for this purpose. Never before in the history of our two countries has our association been so close, or our mutual pledge for the future so complete. This is surely a happy augury.

There is nothing exclusive in our agreement. We are seeking peace and security not only for our two countries, but for all the United Nations. But understanding between us is one of the foundations of peace, not for us alone, but for the world.

We have signed our treaty, and part of the work is behind us. I would like to say now, Monsieur Molotov, how much we have valued the statesmanship and insight which you have shown in our negotiations. I would like, too, to thank Monsieur Maisky, your Ambassador, who has done so much in his years here to build a bridge between our two countries.

Part of the work is behind us, but the greater part yet lies ahead. There is the war to win; there is the peace to build. Neither of these tasks is for ourselves alone. You yourself, Monsieur Molotov, are leaving our shores for the United States. Upon the co-operation of the Soviet Union, the United States of America and the British Commonwealth the future of mankind will largely depend.

We thank you for your work with us here and we wish you well upon your journey.

23

WELCOME TO THE U.S. FORCES IN
THE U.K.

May 26. Rommel attacked in Libya.
May 30. First 1,000-bomber raid by R.A.F. on Cologne.
June 18. Mr. Churchill in Washington.
June 20. Tobruk fell to Germans.
July 1. Sebastopol fell to Germans.
July 2. Fighting in the desert west of El Alamein.
July 19. Russians evacuated Voroshilovgrad.
July 24. Germans captured Rostov.
August 9. Germans claimed to have reached Caucasian foothills.
August 19. Dieppe raid by the Canadian forces.
In August Mr. Churchill, having visited Moscow, returned via
Egypt. General Alexander succeeded General Auchinleck as
Commander-in-Chief, Middle East. General Montgomery was
given command of the Eighth Army on the death of General
Gott.
Mr. Eden attended the Guildhall Lunch on September 2 given
by the Lord Mayor to welcome the United States Forces and in his
speech said:

T he idea of this luncheon was something of an inspiration on
your part. It marks the City's welcome to United States
forces. It marks, too, the City's confidence in the future of
Anglo-American relations.
The date is aptly chosen. We are met together here on the eve

of the day when, three years ago, we declared war on Germany. Our life, and much more than our life, depended upon that decision.

Perhaps you will allow me to make one or two brief reflections upon that event, reflections inspired by this unique Anglo-American occasion. The decision to go to war was freely taken by a united nation. It was endorsed without hesitation by each of the great Dominions of the British Commonwealth. Acting entirely of their own will, they joined us in word and deed.

When men and women all over the world are moved to act in such accord, there must be a deep-seated reason for it. And the reason is a very simple one. We acted to keep faith with a written undertaking to our ally Poland, which had been freely given and accepted.

This was the exact opposite of the doctrine of a scrap of paper which the Germans have made their own. Hitler is an apt pupil in perfidy. He has outclassed all his predecessors in crime. We must give the devil his due. His German political ancestors must turn in their graves with envy sometimes when they see how much he has outclassed them in the methods they taught him.

For us, and I know for you, there can be no compromise with such treachery, because to keep faith is the only basis for international relations as it is for all human relations. Once a nation abandons this elementary standard of conduct it has entered on the slippery slope that leads to its downfall. Ideals then become distorted and all sense of values becomes obscured. Fanaticism is not enough to bury the sense of guilt; indeed in the very effort to bury it, crime is heaped upon crime, until we get the appalling panorama of German crime we see in Europe to-day.

Whatever be our shortcomings as a nation we have a deep respect for law, for the sanctity of treaties and for decency in our relations with our fellow-men. It is not hypocritical to say these things and to be proud of them: they are true. If ever they cease to be true we shall be on the path of our decline. So long as they are true we can hold up our heads and be proud of the British Commonwealth. You can only have faith in somebody who keeps faith with you and with others. And so our American guests will understand us when we proclaim from the housetops our faith in our nation on this day of all others when our nation kept faith.

You, the soldiers of the United States, have come three thousand miles over a perilous sea to join with us in the cause of the United Nations, united to overthrow the most shameless and the most inhuman tyranny the world has ever seen, and united to put in its place a world where men can live freely and work freely. Our two nations have been working out their destinies at a distance of three thousand miles from one another. But that distance, though it has produced certain diversities in outlook, has not changed the basic ideals which we share in common. Twice in a generation we have come together in a common cause; yet we find no need to explain to one another the meaning of that common cause.

The United States of America and the united members of the British Commonwealth understand full well that our cause must triumph, and that its triumph must be as total as the war which is waged for it is total war. Great causes have the merit of being simple causes; they demand no casuistry to explain them. The contortions of a Goebbels are fortunately not necessary for the spokesmen of the United Nations.

Great causes need only one thing to make them great: they need faith, deep, burning faith. They need roots in the past, strength in the present and faith in the future.

The cause that we and you are serving to-day is the cause that we and you have served in the past. The men who expounded that cause in the past in your country and in ours spoke the same kind of language as the men who are expounding that cause to-day. The same authentic ring repeats itself in our histories. If we remain true to the faith that has been in us it will repeat itself in the future.

We belong to an older nation in time than you do, but a nation only grows old when it loses the power in each generation to pass on to its youth the spirit which kept it alive and vigorous. In that sense of the word a nation need never grow old; but unless it believes fervently and actively in the part it must play in the world, unless it believes that it can and will play that part, its history is closed. From the moment that we cease to believe that we have a real mission in the world, one that we will fight and die for, one that we will work for with everything that is in us after the fighting is over, we shall find ourselves slipping back into the same state that produced this war. And that will surely happen if we promise ourselves and our people that victory in this war is going by itself to produce a new world.

The new world is going to demand a much greater sense of responsibility, a greater readiness to face realities, with plain speech and honest action.

We here believe as deeply in the future of the British Commonwealth as you, I know, believe in the future of the United States.

WELCOME TO THE U.S. FORCES IN THE U.K.

We also believe that our futures must be worked out together in the closest possible partnership and understanding. Together we have a mighty part to play now and in the days that are coming.

Our soldiers and your soldiers are the forerunners in the cause that we are all serving. It is they who will mark the return of liberty to the European continent. Each one of them must think of himself as commanding an outpost in that cause, a crusader for the faith.

It is good that the United States Army should be here amongst us. The more Americans and British meet, and the more informally they meet, the better. They will get on all right. I am not bothered about that. They will get on all the better if their relations are not fussed over and analysed too much.

My Lord Mayor, you have brought us, British and Americans, together this afternoon here in this City of London, which has nobly played its part in the cause of the United Nations, this City of London, which is not without its scars. No hall in the world is richer than this in the tradition of peace, friendship and goodwill. There could be no more appropriate meeting place. By your hospitality you have helped Englishmen and Americans to meet. You have given Londoners the chance to welcome their American guests. For this, and still more for the thought that prompted you to a wise and generous action, we your guests, say most sincerely "thank you".

24

SCOTTISH UNIONIST CONFERENCE—1942

September 2. The German troops reached the Volga and, at the end of September, Hitler made his most boastful speech in Berlin.

In Egypt, Rommel's last attempt to reach the Nile, which began on September 1, failed and his troops, hotly pursued by the Eighth Army, began withdrawing on September 4. Throughout September and the early part of October, the Eighth Army trained, rested and regrouped.

October 23. The Battle of El Alamein began.

October 21. General Smuts addressed both Houses of Parliament.

On October 30, Mr. Eden addressed the Scottish Unionist Conference at Glasgow. In the course of his address he said:

A few days ago we were listening to the tribute which Field-Marshal Smuts paid to the people of this country. It was a great tribute, paid by a great man. In that speech of his, General Smuts (perhaps I may be permitted to call him by the title which is so familiar to us) applied his penetrating vision to the course of the war, and to those problems which will follow the war. He illumined all these great matters; he put them in their true perspective. To listen to him was to understand once again that history is not a series of isolated and disjointed incidents, but a continuous process. For nations, like human beings, are fashioned and moulded by their past.

You cannot wholly escape from the past. You can improve upon it. Certainly you must improve upon it.

Sometimes nations act as though they would make a complete break with the past, taking no account of its teachings and traditions. That is not our way. Our own national characteristics are deeply rooted in the past, so deeply rooted that they are a determining influence upon our future. The British people have shown an aptitude for grafting the present on to the past. That is not an idle boast. We have shown this aptitude in times of calm and in times of stress.

During most of our lifetime we have been spectators of far-reaching changes, or actors in them. All this vast world upheaval is not just a passing tremor on the face of the waters; it is something more than that. During our life-time we have witnessed immense and violent and, historically speaking, sudden changes—economic, scientific, yes, and political. We have seen a vast and almost miraculous development in the technique of production. We have seen a sudden and dramatic acceleration in the speed of communications. We have seen, in our own country as well as outside of it, the spread of education and the application of the machinery of democracy to the people as a whole—it was only in 1918, after all, that we had adult suffrage in this country.

These are facts; they are not matters of opinion or matters of prejudice. And it is only if we recognize the facts that we shall be able to master them, to control them.

It has fallen to us, in our generation, to ride the storm. It has fallen to us to make order out of chaos and to build upon the past a greater future. This is a heroic task. But it is also the kind of task which, by temperament, by experience, by tradition, our people are especially qualified to perform.

We have a long road to travel, and a hard one. Make no mistake about that. Nothing is more dangerous than to suppose that victory will bring relaxation.

Our first task is to determine what sort of society we are working for at home, and what is to be the relation of that society towards the world at large. The two problems are inseparable. We shan't get the kind of ordered society at home that we want unless we accept very far-reaching responsibilities to the world at large. We shan't establish our position in the world unless we show that we are making the best of our own inheritance. Home affairs and foreign affairs are parts of a whole. You cannot separate them.

Although party politics have been put aside for the duration of the war with the agreement of all the main parties, that does not mean that the members of those parties should put aside the habit of political thinking. We are here to-day as members of the Conservative Party. That is as it should be. The Conservative Party has played a great part in the history of our country. Of course we believe that we still have a great part to play. But we are here also as British citizens, who are working with our fellow-citizens, of every kind of political belief, to win this war and to build upon our victory an enduring peace.

As a people we have always prided ourselves upon our practical approach to the problems of the day. That is wise. But sometimes we have been over-content to let events catch up with us and then to grapple with them as they arose.

Looking back over the years between the two wars, who can doubt that we placed too much confidence in improvised methods. We thought we could always deal with problems as they arose. We kept hoping, like Mr. Micawber, that something would turn up; we steadfastly refused to make long-term commitments; in the end we lost control. Events took charge of us; we were hurtled, how unwillingly we can remember, down the road to war.

We are fighting this war to secure, for ourselves and for the world, a free and ordered society. Freedom and order must go hand in hand; the whole basis of British political thought has been to keep a just balance between the two.

Government is made by man for man. This is a truth which has never been disputed by civilized peoples.

25

RECONSTRUCTION IN INTERNATIONAL AFFAIRS

NOVEMBER–DECEMBER 1942

RUSSIA

With counter-attacks on other parts of the long front and firm resistance in the Stalingrad area, the Red Army halted the German advance and fought back. By December 15 they had encircled the German force which had penetrated into part of Stalingrad. As the New Year dawned the Red Army began its victorious advance along the whole front.

NORTH AFRICA

November 7. British and American forces under General Eisenhower landed in North-West Africa.

In Egypt, the Eighth Army's victory was won and Rommel's forces were in full retreat by the second week in November.

By the end of the year the Eighth Army had reconquered Libya.

In North-West Africa, General Giraud assumed command of all French forces on November 14; Dakar was handed over to the Allies on December 6. Algeria, Morocco and part of Tunisia were under Allied control, but the Germans were strengthening their hold on Bizerta, Tunis, and southern Tunisia.

FAR EAST AND BURMA

The Americans won a great naval victory in the Solomons against the Japanese Fleet.

In Eastern India, British and Indian troops began advancing into Burma.

172

INTERNATIONAL AFFAIRS

AT HOME
November 22. Mr. Eden became Leader of the House of Commons, and Mr. Herbert Morrison a member of the War Cabinet.

December 1. Sir William Beveridge's Report on Social Insurance was made public.

His Majesty the King opened the Fourth War Session of Parliament on November 11. In the course of his speech His Majesty said:

"The declaration of the United Nations endorsing the principles of the Atlantic Charter provides a foundation on which international society can be rebuilt after the war. As a first step, my Government have entered into consultation with the Governments of the United Nations in preparation of the urgent needs which will arise when the victims of oppression regain their freedom. . . ."

On the ninth day of the Debate on the Address, Mr. Pethick Lawrence moved an amendment to the Address:

"Urging the necessity of your Majesty's Advisers reaching practical conclusions in co-operation with the United Nations to fulfill those undertakings, and taking the necessary legislative and administrative action to implement without delay the pledges given to your Majesty's subjects in the U.K."

The Debate on this Amendment was taken on 1 and 2 December. Mr. Arthur Greenwood, who had been the Minister in charge of Reconstruction problems and had left the Government in February 1942, spoke first. Sir William Jowitt who had succeeded Mr. Arthur Greenwood, spoke later on in the first day and gave a full review of the problems that faced the Government, particularly in the sphere of domestic policy.

Mr. Eden wound up the Debate on the second day adding a short survey of post-war problems in the international sphere.

I have been fortunate enough to hear most of the speeches during the past two days, and I think there is a general feeling in all parts of the House that this Debate has been both timely and useful. Indeed, in many respects I regret that we could not have had still more time for it, for I know that many hon. Members still have contributions to make; but I console myself with the reflection that it is unlikely to be the last Debate which we shall

173

have on reconstruction. Before I pass on to deal with some of the points raised in this Debate, I think I must make at least a brief reference to the speech of the hon. Member for Westhoughton (Mr. Rhys Davies). I feel with him, and of course every Member of the House feels with him, a hatred of war. But that is not his unique and privileged position. Many of us have seen war, perhaps more than he has, and perhaps hated it at least as much as he does. Where, perhaps, his mind seems to stop is that it does not draw any conclusion. If we were all to follow his attitude, not only could he not have made the speech he has made, which would have been unfortunate in a free Assembly, but, still more, this country would be exactly in the position which, say, Poland occupies at present. I have been receiving in the last few days, as others probably have, representations about the state of the Jews in Poland and the appalling things that have been happening there. If we all adopted the hon. Gentleman's attitude, there is nothing to stop exactly the same thing happening here. It is impossible to adopt an attitude like that.

MR. JOHN WILMOT (Kennington): The Poles did not adopt it.

MR. EDEN: They certainly did not. In listening to the Debate and to the many constructive suggestions which have come from all parts of the House, my dominating impression was of the immensity of the task which is going to confront us at home and abroad. I was glad that the hon. Member for Abertillery (Mr. Daggar) deprecated false optimism. Of course, he is right. It is natural enough that he should feel and speak as he did, and as the hon. Member for Houghton-le-Spring (Mr. Stewart) did, about the areas which suffered so much in the period between the two wars. Our task this time is going to be more difficult in some respects than it was after the last war. The wreckage is greater, and the business is not over yet. The duration is still uncertain. Yet we have to turn to these tasks, and I think the hon. Member for Nuneaton (Mr. Bowles) was a little unfair to my right hon. and learned Friend when he complained of chapter headings. It is a true statement. Much of the work at present is chapter headings. In the first instance it must be. But perhaps my right hon. and learned Friend's speech is not the last word to be said on the subject. It is the first time that any statement has been made on the subject at all. I was deeply astonished to hear the hon. Member complain of Tory Ministerial week-end speeches. We all have bad habits, and I think week-end speeches are a very bad habit. But I think my Labour colleagues indulge in them much more freely than I do. But the hon. Member made a more serious charge than that. He spoke of a report which had reached him as to the Prime Minister's attitude to legislation about the post-war period, and asked me a question which I want to answer. He said: "It is being stated that the Prime Minister is taking a stand at this stage against legislation concerning post-war reconstruction. Is that so?" The answer, quite definitely, is that it is not so, and if my hon. Friend will consider the position for a moment, he will realize that a number of the statements which my right hon. and learned Friend made yesterday in fact foreshadowed legislation. Legislation will be necessary and will be introduced. So the hon. Member can certainly give his friends who raised the point that assurance on the Prime Minister's behalf. We admit that this programme will need to be more substantial. We ask the House to accept it as a first account.

I wish to deal with a subject that has been referred to by many hon. Friends, my hon. Friend the Member for East Aberdeen (Mr. Boothby) and my hon. Friend the Member for South Dorset (Viscount Hinchingbrooke) among others, on the subject of the immediate post-war situation in Europe, how we are going to deal with it and what we propose to do in the way of relief. One or two hon. Members seemed to think that we were relying on other countries to make all the running in the matter. I might perhaps, therefore, give a word of explanation. The Prime Minister said long ago in the dark days of 1940, a time of which the hon. Member for Bodmin (Mrs. Wright) reminded us in an admirable speech, that it was our intention to arrange in advance for the speedy entrance of food into the occupied countries as soon as they had genuinely regained their freedom, and that we would do our best to encourage building up reserves of food all over the world for this purpose. Since that statement was made our own position has undergone a pretty fundamental change. So far as the reserves of food and raw materials are concerned, our own situation is that they have been very largely used up. Inevitably the primary responsibility for this building up of stocks must be with the Dominions and with the United States who have the necessary food available. That does not mean to say that we are not working out these plans with them. We are. Perhaps the House saw a recent statement of the President of the United States authorizing the extension of Lease-Lend to areas occupied by United States forces wherever they were. That is of the utmost importance for the future progress of our plans. Then came the announcement that Governor Lehman was to be appointed to undertake the organizing of the work of American participation in the relief activities which are co-ordinated by the United Nations.

DR. HADEN GUEST (Islington, North): Has Governor Lehman any responsibility to the committee of Allied representatives in London?

MR. EDEN: As I understand it, he will organize the United States share of the relief which has been co-ordinated by the United Nations. To that extent I think that my hon. Friend is right in his assumption. This is an enormous task, but I can tell the House that this country, despite its difficulties and its fewer resources, is determined to do what it can within its power to help in the immediate relief of post-war Europe, even though at some expense of sacrifice to ourselves, because we understand perfectly well that the immediate alleviation of this problem is essential to the recovery of Europe and to our own recovery as well.

May I refer to what my hon. Friend said about the administration of the relieved countries? He drew a comparison between the thorough German method and our own which he feared was not so good. We are at work on these things, and I think the House will admit that the planning, for instance, of the North African operation, even in these details, was fully complete. But there is a distinction, which the House must not forget, between the German method, which is the method adopted by an invading army, in occupied countries and our position when we shall arrive as liberators and when the governments and local authorities of those countries will, I trust, be given the task of setting order in their own areas. The last thing I desire is that the impression should get abroad that we want to arrive in Europe to impose our methods and our will on the countries which have suffered so long from Germany, so though my hon. Friend may be assured that we think of these things, we have to approach them with some thought for the sensibilities of the countries which have suffered so much.

Next, if the House will allow me, I should like to say something about our foreign policy now, and about the trends of that policy so far as it is possible to judge it in the midst of the storms of war. In the first place, may I submit that foreign policy is a continuous process, going on all the time, and that what we do now in the midst of war determines the future much more than what our dreams about an ideal future may happen to be. Here and there there is a tendency to suggest that foreign policy is in abeyance in war-time. If anybody would spend a day at the Foreign Office he would learn that that is not so. In fact the manner in which and the extent to which we succeed or fail to succeed in co-operating with our Allies now will, to a very large extent, determine the course of post-war foreign policy. I have served at the Foreign Office in what was called peace, but was much more like undeclared war, and have also served in a period of war, and I have been impressed by the extent to which, since hostilities have broken out, the Powers fighting together have been able to integrate their foreign policy. It is a depressing thought, but it seems to need an alliance in war to bring about those results which might have prevented the war could they have been realized in peace. But there it is, and our aims must be to ensure that this realization which we can achieve now in war is continued in peace, and it is not going to be easy, because we shall get the inevitable reaction.

The moment the armistice is signed and hostilities are over there will be a desire to let up, a desire to cut our responsibilities, and yet whether we are able to maintain peace or not afterwards will depend on whether we can carry through this co-operation which we have now established with other great Powers, in particular with the United States of America, with Soviet Russia and with China. I was glad to hear one or two of my hon. Friends utter a note of warning about the need for this sustained effort after the Armistice. I believe that is where we, as Members of this House, will have a responsibility and an opportunity. There will be an immense temptation for everybody to relax and to say: "Everything is over," and naturally we shall feel infinitely more cheerful; but in passing over into the period of Armistice and peace we must sustain the effort we are making now. We have got to do it or we shall find we have lost the greater part of what we have been fighting for.

I have spoken of four great Powers, ourselves, Russia, the United States of America, and China, but I must make it plain that I do not visualize a world in which those four Powers try to clamp down some form of big-Power dictatorship over everybody else. What will happen when the fighting is over is that these great Powers, and particularly ourselves, the United States and Russia, will have a virtual monopoly of armed strength, and that armed strength must be used in the name of the United Nations to prevent a repetition of aggression. But other Powers, be they great, be they small, provided they are willing to play their part, will, I trust, be secured in the enjoyment of that independence for which they have fought and suffered so long. Indeed, it is essential that the independence of these other countries should be restored if we are to create a free international society in Europe. And so I say that in any world system that is to operate all States will have to play their part.

Now I should like to say a few words about our own position in all this, and then a few words about each of our great Allies. About ourselves first. Our foreign policy is to a large extent dictated by our geographical position. Whether we like it or not, we are part of Europe. Whether we like it or not, we are also the centre of a great Imperial Commonwealth, and so we are, in that sense, a world Power too.

Our duty is to act as a bridge, and there is nobody who can play that part but us—nobody else. It is to us that the nations of Europe will look, and I believe are looking now, for a message as to our attitude after the war. That is the question they are asking. What is our message to them? I would like to try, in half a dozen sentences, to give that message and to see whether the House approves of it. There are two alternatives, broadly speaking, open to us. We can say, in effect, to Europe: "Europe is the concern of Europeans. We wish our friends well. Good luck to you; but, when Hitler crashes it will be for you to work out your destiny as best you can." I hope we shall not give that answer. If we give that answer, we abdicate our responsibilities and we are, as I believe, writing a charter for future German aggression. I would like our answer to be different. I would like our answer to be: "Whatever we can do to help you to re-establish your ruined economies we will do. The first need of Europe will be to build up an enduring system of defence against the possibility of renewed German aggression. We are prepared to make our contribution to that system and we are prepared to do this because we understand full well that peace and security in Europe are part of our own peace and security; and never again shall we turn our backs on Europe." That, I hope, is our message to Europe.

If the peoples are to be free and have a chance to devote themselves, as the overwhelming majority of them wish to devote themselves, to the arts of peace, there must be common action between us of the British Commonwealth, the United States and Russia. What hope is there that we can achieve such co-operation? I believe there is much hope. I may not have been optimistic in what I have told the House so far, but here, I think, there are grounds for hope. I make reference to two speeches which have been made, one by an American statesman and the other by a Russian statesman and will see how they fit in with our own policy. Mr. Sumner Welles, speaking the other day, used these words:

"Peace—freedom from fear—cannot be assured until the nations of the world, particularly the Great Powers, and that includes the United States, recognize that the threat of war anywhere throughout the globe threatens their own security, and until they are jointly willing to exercise the police powers necessary to prevent such threats from materializing into armed conflict."

Then he went on:

"Another essential is the reaching of agreement between the United Nations before the armistice is signed, upon those international adjustments which we believe to be desirable and necessary for the maintenance of a peaceful and prosperous world for the future."

Then he went on—and I think this is of interest to us in this House—to issue a double warning; to warn against extreme isolationism in the United States and to warn against an attempt, from purely idealistic motives, to try to impose American standards on all the peoples of the earth. I regard that speech as an epitome of good sense. I believe that it indicates and represents the great bulk of American opinion at this time. It represents its firm resolve to fulfil a leading role after the war and thus to accept world-wide responsibilities for maintaining peace. As regards the second part of what he said, about the desirability of preparing for the armistice in advance; there, too, we are in full agreement. The difficulties are many and obvious. No one can tell, in the shifting sand of war, in what circumstances or where, or even between what countries, the final shots will be fired; and yet the attempt must be made, and we are ready to join in making them.

Now I turn to the other great country, to Russia. As the House knows, I have for a long time held the view that there was no reason why there should be any conflict of interest between the Soviet Government and ourselves. I believe that policy is firmly based on history. In each of the great world conflicts there have been—the Napoleonic wars, the last great war and the present war —we and Russia have found ourselves on the same side, and each time after it is over we have drifted apart. Then we do not come together again until the next crisis.

MR. MAXTON (Glasgow, Bridgeton): Did the right hon. Gentleman say "drifted apart"?

MR. EDEN: Yes, or lurched apart, or tore ourselves apart.

MR. MAXTON: Actually in historical fact you attacked Russia.

INTERNATIONAL AFFAIRS

MR. EDEN: I was dealing with more than one instance. I do not think that would be the complete historical fact; something happened before we attacked Russia. I do not think there is much object in entering into all that. It does not in any sense conflict with my general thesis, the truth of which I know the hon. Gentleman accepts. I say that is why I attach such importance to the Anglo-Soviet Treaty which we signed here in London this year because that pledges us to twenty years of co-operation after the war. That is perhaps my only difference with my hon. and gallant Friend the Member for Penryn and Falmouth (Major Petherick) when earlier to-day he asked us not to make long-term commitments. This is a long-term commitment which I believe has its roots in history. Mr. Stalin called it the other day an historical turning point. We believe that to be true. Nor, let me add, do we accept that political differences—here I am treading on more delicate ground, to which Mr. Stalin also referred in his recent speech—should or need make co-operation impossible. There are some in this country, not very many, I believe, who think that the existence of a Communist regime in Russia makes co-operation between our two countries in the long run impossible. I do not agree with them any more than I agree with those who think it is necessary to hold the Communist faith in order to co-operate with the Soviet Union in the field of international politics. [*Interruption.*] It has not been my experience. In this connection Mr. Stalin himself recently made some observations which I should like to quote to the House. He said:

"It would be ridiculous to deny the existence of differences in the ideology and structures in the States which form the Anglo-Soviet-American coalition. But does this circumstance exclude the possibility of co-ordinated action by this coalition against the common enemy who threatens them with enslavement? Definitely it does not."

That also is the view of His Majesty's Government. When Mr. Stalin contemplates, as he clearly does in that speech, the extension of this Three Power co-operation into the period of peace, I would say bluntly that on the maintenance of that co-operation lies the best chance of building a new and better international society after the war.

One passage about China. We and the United States are at this moment engaged in negotiations with the Chinese Government, as a result of which we hope by agreement to bring to an end the period of special rights of extra-territoriality and enter into a period of agreement on equal terms. Among the more absurd and fantastic of the Japanese claims for the domination of Asia are those thinly veiled under that most extraordinary phrase: "The Greater East Asia Co-prosperity Sphere." That title sounds for all the world like a prospectus for a bogus company. That is just about what it is. China knows what a complete mockery all that is. Chiang Kai-Shek has lately given his view of what the position of China will be. He has disclaimed any wish on China's part to assume the mantle of an unworthy Japan. He declares that China feels that she has responsibilities, not rights.

Our general object is to form a world system for ensuring the peaceful development of all peoples; but there is an essential preliminary to all this which we must never forget. It is to restrict, let us hope for all time, the aggressive power of Germany and Japan. I make no mention of Italy, because I do not regard that as a major problem. My right hon. Friend the Prime Minister has said all that needs to be said about that for the present moment. I want to say one word about the greater—I do not know about the greater, but at any rate the nearer, of the two outlaw States, Germany. During the last seventy years—these are unpleasant historical facts which we have to face—successive German Governments have consciously and consistently pursued a policy of world domination. This policy and the philosophy that is behind it is the first threat to enduring peace, and it will be the first and imperative duty of the United Nations on the morrow of their victory to elaborate such a settlement as will make it impossible for Germany again to dominate her neighbours by force of arms. That lies at the root of the business, and it would be sheer folly to allow some non-Nazi German Government to be set up, and then, so to speak, to trust to luck. The rooting out of the old false gods will be a long and strenuous business, but it must be accomplished. [An HON. MEMBER: "It will mean Socialism here."] It means, I hope, that whatever political idea is practised in this country, we shall be free of this nightmare.

Some Members may want to know what machinery I visualize. There are certain international services which have gone on during the war which have not died, and which may render great service after the war. There are the international health services and economic services and the work done by the International Labour Organization. We shall need that work more than ever after the war. The I.L.O. has struggled manfully, and with considerable success, to remove certain of the evils which are among

the root causes of war: low standards of living, insecurity, and unemployment. Unless we can cure those evils, no peace structure
can be enduring. The I.L.O. must be strengthened and developed.
I should like to see it become the main instrument giving effect to
Article 5 of the Atlantic Charter. Somebody may say: "How is all
this to be done? What is the machinery to give effect to it?" I
would reply that, although the machinery is important, it is, unfortunately, less important than certain other ingredients which are
essential to the maintenance of peace. The old League of Nations
failed, not because its machinery was faulty but because there was
not the representation or the force or the drive behind it.

To my mind, there are three indispensable attributes—and I
think these come near the definition which my hon. Friend gave
early in the Debate—for any international organization if it is to
have a chance to achieve its purpose. First, it must be fully representative of the powers that mean to keep the peace. The old League
was not. Second, the Powers themselves must have the unity and
the determination to arrive at agreed and positive decisions. And
the third, and perhaps the most important of all, is that they should
have the force behind them to give effect to their decision.

Let us take heed a little from the lessons of the past, and let us try
to learn them. I believe that out of this organization of the United
Nations, based in the first instance on understanding between ourselves, the United States and Russia, a great opportunity opens to
us. After the last war there was, quite naturally, a sudden reaction
against militarism in all its forms and hatred of war such as the hon.
Member for Westhoughton gave expression to a little while ago,
with the result that nations were reluctant to contemplate the use of
force even to keep the peace. After this war we must, in my submission, be ready to make our military contribution to the United
Nations to enable them to keep the peace. I repeat, the task is going to be a heavy one, but there is an opportunity—a great opportunity. Also, one's hopes, perhaps the main hope, lie in the factor
to which we are not always sensible in these islands—the unparalleled suffering which has been caused by the German and
Japanese hordes. Coventry, Rotterdam, Chungking, Warsaw, Belgrade, Stalingrad—all these events are more eloquent declarations
of unity than the words any statesman can use. The Americans
who have died in the Solomons and in North Africa, by their
deaths have pledged their country to work together after the war
more deeply than any speech can do. So I say that the simple
lesson is that, however great the effort, we have to make our co-

operation in peace as true and as effective as it now is in these war years. There has never been a more skilful and complete co-operation than the co-operation in North Africa. Are we really to admit we can only achieve this in battle? It is inconceivable. It can be done, and it must be done. Please God, we do not forget these lessons in the years that lie ahead.

1943

26

VISIT TO NORTH AMERICA—SPRING
1943

January 1. The Russians developed an offensive along the Black Sea coast and as the month proceeded they regained ground lost in the Caucasus.

January 14. Casablanca meeting between President Roosevelt and Mr. Churchill. Mr. Churchill then visited Turkey, Middle East and British troops in Tripoli.

January 18. Siege of Leningrad raised.

January 23. Tripoli captured by Eighth Army. During the month, the Germans having strengthened their hold on Bizerta, Tunis, and southern Tunisia, launched a counter-offensive against the First Army, which was halted by mid-February.

January 31. Battle of Stalingrad ended with the capture of Field-Marshal Paulus and the German troops under his command.

February 7. The Russian advance reached Azov, and the main road to Kharkov.

February 16. Kharkov captured by the Russians.

March 21. Mr. Churchill broadcast on post-war policy announcing a four-year plan.

March 23. Eighth Army pierced the Mareth Line and on April 7 had pierced the Wadi Akarit position.

U.S.A.

Mr. Eden arrived in Washington on March 12 to confer with the United States Government on the following problems: operational matters; political co-operation between the United States and Great Britain in connection with military operations; and other questions resulting out of the war. He had conversations with President Roosevelt and during part of his visit he stayed at the White House. In addition to seeing the Secretary of State, he also saw General Marshall and many political leaders including Mr. Hoover, Mr. Wendell Willkie and Mr. La Guardia.

On his return to London, speaking in the House of Commons with reference to the nature of the relations between Great Britain and the United States, he said:

"Perhaps I may be allowed here one observation on the nature of our relations generally with the Government and people of the United States. I think it is a mistake to attempt to base those relations mainly upon sentiment. We might not always like each other very much. I think it is also a mistake to try to base them on common origin, or common parentage, or even common language, because there will be occasions when we differ one from the other. But I think it is desirable to base them on their true foundation, which is a common interest in the maintenance of world peace and in preventing a repetition of these catastrophic world conflicts every twenty years. If we keep to that foundation, we shall be in less danger of the ups and downs which we have sometimes seen in Anglo-American relations. I believe that definition to be profoundly true, and I believe it to be well understood on both sides of the Atlantic at the present time."

(I) *AT ANNAPOLIS, MARYLAND—March 26.*

On March 26, accompanied by Lord Halifax, Mr. Eden addressed the Maryland Legislature. His speech was relayed to all the State Legislatures in the United States who had met in special session for the purpose. Mr. Eden made his speech standing under the picture of his ancestor, Sir Robert Eden. At the end of the speech, the Maryland Legislature, passed the following resolution:

"Be it resolved by the House of Delegates of Maryland, in solemn assembly gathered, that it hereby formally registers for itself and for the citizens of Maryland whom it represents, its deep respect for the impressive battle given by our valiant Brittanic Ally in her mortal conflict with the Axis Powers, a respect firmly based upon the known qualities of the British people, their unconquerable resolution in the cause which they and we deem to be right, their refusal to admit thoughts of defeat even in their darkest hours, their phenomenal energy, their astonishing self-discipline, their noble effort to cling to the paths of honour despite the indecencies of the enemy; in a word, upon all those traits by which a people comes to be known as great and to be admired accordingly.

"Be it further resolved that rather than commend the example to the people of Maryland as has been done so often and so warmly in the past, the House of Delegates takes this occasion to express to the people of Britain through her Foreign Minister the highest compliment of which it feels capable, the sincere desire to emulate their greatness.

"And be it further resolved that these Resolutions be spread upon the journal and that the Speaker through his Excellency Governor O'Connor deliver a copy of these Resolutions to Mr. Eden in person."

F irst let me say that I feel at home here.
From my earliest years I have been steeped in the atmosphere of Maryland. It is a keen personal pleasure to stand in Annapolis on the spot where Robert Eden once stood. A few miles away, in the City Hall at Baltimore, now hang the pictures of the Calvert family from whom I am proud to be descended. They are friendly faces, which I recognize from my childhood days, when they looked down on me from the walls of my father's house. I am even prouder of the fact that one of the Calverts, the third Lord Baltimore, was the prime mover in the great Act of 1649, by which the early settlers were assured of full freedom to worship God according to their conscience. That was nearly three hundred years ago, but our times have given a new significance to that event.

Four and a half years have passed since I last stood on American soil. They are years that have changed the face of the world, and brought much suffering to the human race. Some of us in Europe thought we saw the catastrophe approaching, and felt the chill of the coming storm, while many, both of my countrymen and yours, were still clinging to the precarious hope of peace. This was no doubt excusable enough. There is always a strong temptation for countries to try to preserve their own peace of mind by turning a deaf ear to the first warnings of danger from abroad.

We know now how vain were these hopes and efforts. So far as we were concerned, Hitler finally destroyed any possibility of illusion by his repeated violation of treaties, by his open repudiation of any rule but that of force. It was plain beyond argument that not Poland, not Europe itself, would satisfy his mad ambitions. His purpose was the conquest and domination of the world. Thus for the second time within a generation we are at war to redeem our pledged word.

The decision to take up the challenge was a decision of a united people at home. It was endorsed at once by the Parliaments and peoples of the great overseas Dominions—Canada, Australia, New Zealand and South Africa, and by all parts of the British Empire. From that day in early September 1939, there has been no turning back, there will be no turning back until victory is won.

We are not yet at the climax of the struggle, and I must repeat the warning I uttered when I first arrived here a fortnight ago. We have yet far to travel before the final triumph over our enemies in the West and in the East. In the interval there will be strains and stresses, setbacks and disappointments. But if we nerve ourselves to meet these; if we work to the utmost of our strength, the result is not in doubt.

In a struggle of this nature it is clearly desirable that those upon whom the responsibility rests in each of the allied belligerent States should meet in personal conference as often as they can. There is in truth no substitute for such meetings. Men who do not know each other well cannot exchange views by despatch or cable to best advantage. This is true even when two countries are represented by such exceptional Ambassadors as Mr. Winant and Lord Halifax. I was therefore happy to accept the invitation of your Government to pay this visit to the United States. Nothing could have exceeded the kindness and hospitality that has been shown to me by everyone, by the President, by Mr. Hull, by the Members of Congress and by all with whom I have been privileged to work. We have done much work together, and we are both well pleased at the result.

For myself, I can only say this. In my life it has fallen to my lot on many occasions to visit foreign capitals, and I am sure that never in my experience has a journey been more worth while.

You will not expect, I trust, sudden and sensational developments. For there will be none. But there has been a meeting of minds between us about the present and the future that will, we are sure, bear fruit.

During my brief visit it has been my good fortune to spend some days in visits to your Army and Navy. I can assure you in all sincerity that I have never known a more inspiring experience. It is at once evident that your methods and organization are thoroughly well planned, but there is much more to it than this. Wherever I went, from the Deep South to the neighbourhood of Washington, I found the same virile spirit of dauntless determination. Your young men are truly splendid. You have every cause to be proud of them, and they to be proud of the country and the cause they serve. It was an honour to meet and speak with them.

Let me now for a moment look back to our experience in this war and see if we may gain from it guidance for the future. I have said that we declared war to defend the sanctity of treaties, and we have tried in the ebb and flow of battle to keep this high purpose clear and constant before our eyes. There have been some dark moments, the darkest probably being those of Dunkirk and the weeks that followed. Then for the first time in our remembered history we as a people faced national extinction. Every horror seemed possible. We walked through the fire. Yet that ordeal strengthened us and brought us a new spirit of fellowship and of endurance and of simple living, which I pray may remain with us long after the peril is passed. We gained then, I believe, a new sense of what our national life could be. Nor shall we ever forget your sympathy and your active help in the days when it needed an act of faith to believe even in our survival.

One incident in particular will be vivid in my recollection to my dying day. It had been my duty as Secretary of State for War at that time to call upon the nation to enrol in a new force, the Local Defence Volunteers, since renamed by the Prime Minister the Home Guard. The men responded in numbers far exceeding our calculation. They were eager to drill and to fight; but we had no weapons for them. We had not equipment enough for the divisions of our regular army saved from Dunkirk. Our industry, though working as it had never worked before, could not meet this demand. It was then that you made your first great gesture. In a brief span you sent us more than a million rifles, guns, machine-guns and other weapons from your arsenals to arm our volunteers. I can recall to-day the anxiety with which we watched the voyage of those ships, and the relief with which we signalled each consignment safely brought to port by the gallant men of the Royal Navy and the Merchant Marine. Those weapons might well have meant the difference between life and death for us. Such acts of generosity and faith mean more in the history of two nations than all the speeches of statesmen or the labours of diplomacy.

VISIT TO NORTH AMERICA

In that year when we stood alone against Germany and Italy we had to take great risks. The collapse of France, with her overseas Empire, had laid bare our strategic positions, not only in Europe but over the whole of that area loosely called the Middle East, and in the Far East also. As a result, perilously weak as we were at home, we had to take armed divisions from our undermanned citadel of Britain and send them round the Cape to reinforce our threatened defences. Even so, we tried to keep faith with our friends.

We had given our pledge to the people of Greece, and the world will not forget their epic resistance. We, for our part, did all in our power to help them. We failed, but that was not a failure of which we shall ever feel ashamed.

It was in this same spirit that, on behalf of our Chinese allies, we reopened the Burma Road in 1941. Let China not misdoubt us. We shall not forget how for years she resisted aggression singlehanded. The Japanese brought against her all the terrors of mechanized war, and she had little with which to oppose them. They burnt her cities. They tore from her large tracts of territory. They forced her armies inch by inch into the interior. But never for a moment did her resolution falter. Never has there been a thought of parley, and China no longer stands alone. The day will come when the Burma Road will once again be open. It will carry to China an ever-increasing volume of supply; which the efforts of your country and mine are turning out daily from the assembly lines.

As I have explained, with the fall of France we lost our reserves of material which had been transported there. If we were to rearm our trained divisions and to expand our forces and equip them, our own production could not suffice.

It was in such an hour that Lend-Lease was born, that great conception by which once again the mighty resources of the New World were called in "to redress the balance of the Old". In that hour we knew, finally and beyond a doubt, that we were not alone in the cause for which we stood.

Lend-Lease began as a one-way traffic. It brought American tanks and guns and aircraft to the battlefields of North Africa and for the defence of Britain. It brought American ships to strengthen the Atlantic lifeline. It brought American supplies of every kind, wherever they could be carried and the need was greatest.

To-day the picture is changing. Lend-Lease has become the machinery for pooling the war effort of the United Nations, the material equivalent of the combined strategic planning of our armies and navies. It is no longer a one-way traffic. Each nation gives to the others what it can send and what they need. The United States will remain the greatest arsenal of democracy, but Britain in her turn is sending supplies to Russia, to her other Allies, to the American forces abroad and even to the United States itself. But if we are glad to take our part in this common effort, we are none the less grateful for what we have received.

Life is hard for many people in Britain to-day. Shortages, discomforts, privations even, have been accepted by our people in a spirit of which they have a right to be proud. Yet we have still to ensure that they have a minimum of rations required for total war. We have to supply our fighting men with weapons to wage war to best advantage. We could not do these things without the food produced by your farms and industries and exported to us by your ships.

You have been generous to those of our people who have come among you. To-day we in our turn are happy to welcome your sons, brothers, husbands, and your daughters too, in our cities and our homes. We are learning from them how alike are our peoples on both sides of the ocean in the things that matter most. London, scarred and seared and blacked-out though it is, yet presents an inspiring sight to-day. The youth of the world is there, united in the common garb of war. Your young men and ours rub shoulders with each other and with the young men of the nations united against a common enemy. There they achieve in a short span that national sympathy and understanding which years of diplomatic exchanges could never give.

On five continents and seven seas, soldiers and sailors of the United Nations are living and fighting side by side. May they cherish in peace the friendship that they learnt in war. May our young airmen who have renewed an old comradeship of the air, carry that spirit with them on errands of peace. Upon them and their like, upon their friendship with one another, rests both the burden and the hope of mankind. Where our generation failed, I pray that theirs may succeed. It may be our last chance; it may be in very truth "the last best hope of earth".

In the period between the two wars, the intentions of the peace-loving nations were excellent, but their practice was weak. If there is one lesson we should have learnt from the distresses of those years, it is surely this: that we cannot shut our windows and draw our curtains, and be careless of what is happening next door or on the other side of the street. No nation can close its frontiers and hope to live secure. We cannot have prosperity in one country and misery in its neighbour, peace in one hemisphere and war in the other. And if we try to have these things, we shall be back on the old road to world war. We shall never find security or progress within heavily defended national fortresses. We shall only find them by the greatest possible measure of co-operation. The United Nations, and in particular the United States, the British Commonwealth, China and the Soviet Union, must act together in war and in peace.

The greatest of all peace aims is to ensure that never again shall unscrupulous leaders be able to carry their peoples into war and bring tragedy on the world. We shall accordingly take steps for the physical prevention of this danger by the enforced disarmament of these gangster nations. We must ensure that this protection of peace-loving peoples is maintained in full effectiveness for whatever period may be necessary. We must therefore be ready to protect and maintain whatever settlement we devise. And one thing, I am sure, is above all essential. Never again must the civilized world be ready to tolerate unilateral infraction of treaties. For that would be to sap the whole foundation of the secure international life, which it is our principal purpose to restore.

We must prosecute the war to a final victory. We must determine together to take steps to ensure that neither Germany nor Italy nor Japan can commit a like aggression again. We can do this if we will. If we do, we will fulfil the first condition of peace.

And I take this opportunity once again to make plain for my country that we have no secret engagements with any other country, nor do we seek as a result of this conflict to extend our boundaries or increase our possessions.

We in the British Commonwealth have grown up in the thought of co-operation. Some parts of the Commonwealth—the self-governing Dominions—enjoy complete independence, while others are moving towards this goal. Our enemies have looked to this war, as they looked to the last Great War, to sound the death knell of this great association. Nothing in the world is more unlikely. The Commonwealth is a voluntary union; its bonds are the will of peoples and races with a common past and a common purpose to travel the same way. Theirs is no static society, shrinking from change or fearful of the future. On the contrary the British Commonwealth is capable of continuing development. We have sought to learn by our mistakes, and you were the first to teach us how.

The British Empire is the first in history to evolve the idea of self-governing Dominions. That is an entirely new conception in the world. We believe that it can help us to reach our common aim, man's freedom and self-government under the rule of law. It is in this spirit that we shall administer our trust for the peoples in our Empire, whom it is our duty and our pledge to lead to full membership of our community of nations.

I maintain that these principles of our Commonwealth are not of limited application. They are inseparable from the kind of world for which we are fighting, the kind of world we hope to see. That hope is to-day gathering strength, in North Africa, the Pacific, China, through enslaved Europe and on the wide plains of Russia.

To-day more than ever war is one and indivisible. The enemies of your country are our enemies. A danger to us is a threat to you, as it is a threat to China and to Russia. Let there be no mistake; we shall not rest upon our arms until every one of our enemies has unconditionally surrendered. We, no less than you, and our partner China, have a score to settle with the Japanese; nor shall we cease fighting until that evil growth in the Pacific has been cut back. We shall be with you in this to the end.

When the defence of one is the defence of all, security and peace have no frontiers. Our common safety demands that overwhelming force be brought to bear against the aggressor wherever he may be. And what applies to war applies, even more, to the peace that is to come. I can say with confidence that to-day the men and women of Britain are alive to the fact that they live in one world with their neighbours. Only within an international system which is backed with sufficient force, can the enterprise and liberty of the individual find protection.

After the last war, the lack of power behind the international system led to the triumph of the dictators. This has more often been said than understood or heeded. On one side we have the idea of a narrow and covetous nationalism which destroys the life of its own people first, and then the life of its neighbours. On the other, we have the idea of a close-knit framework of free nations—"free" as we in Britain and you here understand the word. We believe that it is only within such a framework as this that the individual can rise to the full height of his powers and call his soul his own. And we believe that it has been the world's failure to create such a framework which has twice led to war in our time.

This at least is certain: if we do not find the common ground on which to build this time, we shall not have deserved victory. Any new international authority that we may agree to set up can only succeed if it is backed by sufficient strength. It will not be enough for one country, or even two, to display the qualities necessary to protect the peace. The work will take all that America and Britain, Russia and China, and the United Nations can offer.

Your country is justly proud of the wide vision and the boldness and youthful vigour with which it thinks and acts. You will not find my countrymen bound by any narrower horizon. In the common performance of this task you will find the peoples of our Commonwealth, for I am sure that in this I can speak for them all, full and worthy partners. You will find in them a toughness, a resolution, an unsuspected fund of energy, a vitality of spirit, such as have more than once surprised the world. Our joint task will be hard. But for our part we are proud of the company with which we march. No one flag, no one government, no one language unite the peoples of our great alliance. We have one passport, freedom; one objective, victory, total and unmistakable; and one purpose, a just and lasting peace.

(II) *OTTAWA—1 APRIL 1943*

After leaving the United States, Mr. Eden went to Ottawa for consultations with the Canadian Government.

On April 1, he addressed both Houses of the Canadian Parliament in the Canadian House of Commons.

I am deeply grateful to you, Mr. Speaker, and to the Canadian Parliament for the compliment which you have paid to me in inviting me to speak to you here from the floor of the House.

I understand of course that the compliment is paid not only to me personally but to our own House of Commons at home of which it happens that I am for the time being leader. I feel sure that all my colleagues in the House of Commons at Westminster would wish me to express to you their warmest thanks and gratitude for this truly thoughtful gesture. There is no compliment that could appeal more to the heart of any House of Commons man. Sir, this procedure and these surroundings are familiar to me though I confess that your house is at once more spacious and more generously fitted than our own and less battered. As you are probably aware our own Chamber in Westminster has been destroyed and we now meet in what was formerly "Another Place". Nonetheless I can assure you that the spirit of the House of Commons lives on undismayed in its present more august setting. To think of Canada in these times is to think of her armed forces by land, sea and air. Let me then speak first of these. I have been lucky enough to see much of the Canadian forces from the earliest days of the war. As Secretary of State for the Dominions in the opening months of the conflict it was my privilege to welcome the first contingents of your army to reach the shores of the old country. I shall never forget that scene. It was a beautiful winter morning at a famous port which I suppose must still remain anonymous.

I was a spectator of the scene from the flagship of the Commander-in-Chief of the Home Fleet. As the great armada of liners swung into sight under the escort of the Royal Navy cheering Canadian troops lined the decks. I suppose that seldom in human history have so many great transports and so many powerful ships of war been assembled at one time. That was Canada making her contribution in the hour of need. And that was only the beginning. Many contingents of your army followed the forerunners. When in April 1940 a few brief weeks before the collapse of France the Prime Minister, Mr. Winston Churchill, formed his government he asked me to take over the War Office and once again I had the opportunity of meeting the officers and men of the Canadian forces. Those were the dark days of 1940 when the presence of your troops was at once a safeguard to our threatened citadel and an inspiration to our own effort. Since those days the Canadian Army in Britain has had to endure a long period of training and of waiting. They have sustained this ordeal with a patience and sense of discipline that has won the admiration of us all. Save for the attack at Dieppe carried through with that brilliant daring the world has come to associate with the Canadian Army, the lot of your fellow-countrymen in Britain has been one of waiting for the hour that will come. In all sincerity I can say to you that as the months and years have passed the affection of the British people for their Canadian guests and comrades has grown until we have come to regard them not as visiting kinsfolk but as our very own men whom we respect and admire.

We know that one day their distinguished commander, General McNaughton, will lead these men to victory. Now let me speak of the undying achievements of the Royal Canadian Air Force made possible by the well-planned execution of the Commonwealth air training scheme. It so happens that as Dominions Secretary I also witnessed the first conception and early expansion of that scheme. I don't think that any of us then realized the extent to which its development might influence the whole course of the war even though its potentialities did inspire us to do all we could to ensure the success of its early beginnings. If Canada had done nothing else in this war her predominant share in this Commonwealth air training scheme would ensure her an enduring place in the roll of fame. As we cast our minds back to those early days of the war one recollection above all others dominates the minds of all my countrymen. We can never forget that when we went to war to redeem our pledged word you stood with us. Four self-governing Dominions of the British crown then took their stand in partnership with us. That event is part of recorded history.

It is an event of which the British Commonwealth will always be supremely proud. That close association in the hour of danger was the outward expression of the inner meaning of the British Commonwealth. Let us for a moment consider its significance. It meant that a number of self-governing communities scattered throughout the world realized, as clearly as we who were closer to the danger, the peril that beset mankind. Understanding full well that the threat to one was a threat to all they rallied unanimously in defence of a common cause. That event was all the more remarkable when we reflect that the citizens of the Commonwealth are not all of one common stock.

Here in Canada are millions of French descent, whilst in South Africa the majority is of Dutch origin. Moreover, India and the colonial territories have also, from the first day, taken their place at our side. When therefore all is measured there has been no more striking, no more inspiring episode in human history than this free and spontaneous action by all the peoples of the British Empire. Since those days we have battled through stern times together. We have known dark days and brighter hopes. To-day, when we survey the scene of world war, we are conscious of the support of many and powerful friends so that if we hold together and persist until the end the decision is not in doubt. In recent months encouraging reports have reached us from many theatres of war. We are entitled to rejoice at them, but there would be an element of danger in this were we for one instant to relax our efforts. The better news must not tempt us to underrate our enemies' strength; it must nerve us to greater effort. And so, Mr. Speaker, it is our duty to concentrate with all our strength upon the first task in hand, which is the utter defeat of our enemies. It is well that we should take thought and counsel together as to the future problems that may beset us. It would be bad if we were to allow such necessary preparation to dim for an instant our clear vision of the work at hand and our determination to see it through. Even as I speak, at this hour the Battle of the Atlantic is raging. It is yet undecided. In the struggle that has ebbed and flowed throughout these months and years the Royal Canadian Navy has played a glorious part. The epic of the convoys is never ending. We must still regard the U-boat as our greatest menace. It is the ceaseless task of our navies to protect our lifelines and to fight a way through for our convoys. The enemy is clearly staking heavily upon his U-boat offensive.

We must not only continue but intensify our efforts against this desperate challenge. You may be confident that we shall do so. And now, Sir, having made these provisos let me speak a little of the future. As the war progresses we see the conception of the United Nations gradually taking shape. I believe it is better that this development should come about in this gradual way. Co-operation which is born of stern necessity and forged by experience has the best chance to survive into the years of peace. It is better to build as we go along, to test and develop rather than to devise all at once some elaborate structure into which we should seek to fit the component parts as best we may. In this sphere of international endeavour the British Commonwealth has its specific contribution to make. It has been our practice to allow and encourage co-operation to grow. We have neither rigid rules nor precise formulae between us but we have the spirit of understanding and we know the road that we would travel.

If we can infuse this same spirit into the sphere of international relations we shall have made an essential contribution to a peace that can endure.

Il y a une chose que j'aimerais vous faire savoir à propos de notre peuple britannique et c'est qu'après trois années de guerre ce peuple ne montre aucun signe de faiblesse. Les britanniques sont unis dans une détermination tenace pour mener ce conflit à bonne fin jusqu'au bout, car ils ont pour eux la fortitude, le courage et l'énergie. La diffamation d'avant guerre de leurs ennemis qui les taxaient d'être un peuple épuisé et fini a été réfutée avec une vigueur achevée incomparable dans l'histoire. Avant tout le peuple britannique a un esprit très jeune et vous pouvez compter sur eux de l'est à l'ouest jusqu' à la fin de la guerre, jusqu' à la paix victorieuse. Bien des nations ont souffert douloureusement dans cette guerre. Pour la France l'épreuve fut surtout dur et amer. Toute ma vie j'ai cru à la grandeur de la France: ma foi dans son avenir est aujourd'hui inébranlable. Pour notre part nous n'avons qu'un désir, c'est celui de voir l'union rétablie parmi tous les français qui ont juré de se battre contre l'ennemi commun. Nous serons toujours prêts à leur prêter "main forte" pour en arriver à cette fin, car c'est le premier pas vers la régénération de la France et le commencement d'un nouveau chapitre dans sa glorieuse histoire.

When we consider the unhappy years between the two wars we should do so in the determination to learn the lessons of our failure. I have had myself some experience as has your Prime Minister and other Canadian statesmen of the attempts which have been made to keep the peace by international machinery. One lesson is predominant in my mind.

The League of Nations suffered no doubt from a number of human failings and shortcomings. But what above all it lacked was a sufficiently wide international authority to express its decisions with conviction and an adequate force to see them executed. So it was that the gangster nations, Germany, Italy and Japan could test their strength and work their will. We must never be in that position again. It is essential that when this war is over the United Nations should maintain sufficient force to ensure that neither Germany nor Italy nor Japan can ever again plunge the world into war. The experience through which I have lived is similar to that which many of you have known. I have taken part, as you have done, as a soldier in one war which we had hoped was a war to end wars. I now watch my son preparing to take part in a second war. It is our duty to see that this cruel and inhuman lot is not also the heritage of our children's children. For my part I therefore say definitely that I am not prepared to take risks again with either Germany, Italy or Japan. I have no faith in the promises of their statesmen nor in the smooth assurances of their apologists. There is only one security for mankind in respect of all of them, to ensure that they are totally disarmed and in no position ever to try their strength again. Then indeed peace may have its chance. After the bitter lessons which we have learned we must insist upon the fullest precautions. To say these things is not to show a lack of humanity but to clarify our thought on issues upon which the future life of the world will depend. It is no easy task to co-ordinate the action of the United Nations in war, nor will it be simple in peace, but if the basis which I am propounding is accepted, as I am sure it is by us all, then the task can be achieved.

I have myself been greatly encouraged by the conversations which I have had upon these matters a year ago in Moscow and more recently in Washington. They have been an inspiration to me. Admittedly there will be differences and divergencies amongst us. They are not insurmountable because at heart we want the same things—international security so that all of our peoples may live and develop their lives in freedom and at peace. For this task we shall need not only a close understanding between the British Commonwealth and the United States, Russia and China, but the full co-operation of all the United Nations. Together we can win the war and win the peace. Nothing less should content us. It is our duty to hand on to our children a world in which freedom can live and man command his soul; free from the constant dread which has shadowed our own time. To that task we have set our hands and will dedicate our lives. Let us give this pledge this afternoon. We will neither falter nor fail till we have redeemed our word and opened to future generations a peace and promise that we have never known.

27

CONSERVATIVE PARTY CONFERENCE

APRIL–MAY 1943

Early in April it was announced by General Blamey that the Japanese were massing 200,000 men to the north of Australia. American troops landed in the Aleutian Islands on May 17.

April 7. The Eighth Army in Tunisia joined hands with the American forces advancing from Gafsa and by April 21 had captured Enfidaville. By April 8, the First Army was within twenty-seven miles of Tunis. On May 6 the final offensive was launched on the First Army front; Tunis and Bizerta were captured the next day and all organized resistance in Africa ceased on May 12.

April 26. U.S.S.R. broke off diplomatic relations with the Polish Government.

On May 11, Mr. Churchill, accompanied by Service Chiefs, arrived in Washington for conferences which lasted until May 27. In the Prime Minister's absence, Mr. Eden addressed the Conservative Party Conference in London on May 20.

I come to speak to you this morning in a role which should surely evoke the sympathy of each one of you, to understudy a man who cannot be understudied. As such I crave your indulgence.

I have no doubt the Prime Minister's journey to the United States will, like his previous travels, bring lasting gain to the Allied cause. But it is certainly a grave misfortune for this Conference. Indeed, I can see only one advantage in the Prime Minister's absence, that we shall thus be more at ease to celebrate his virtues. Mr. Churchill has led us through a period of unsurpassed peril in our national affairs. In him the British people have found the expression of their will to resist and the inspiration to wage war until victory be won. Of his many talents I would to-day name only one, for it has sustained our cause against the hardest blows a ruthless enemy can inflict. His buoyant and infectious courage which no anxiety can weaken and no defeat can daunt. He is the greatest Englishman of our time. I am glad that this Conference has sent to the Prime Minister a message of unshaken confidence and heartfelt good wishes to thank him for what he has done and to hearten him for the tasks that lie ahead.

We are met at a time in our national affairs when it is proper to rejoice. Since last the Party were met together in conference we have as a people been through stern and challenging times. There have indeed been moments when only faith in our cause sustained us. There was precious little other help lying about. We went to war, let us never forget, of our own free will to redeem our word which we had pledged to Poland. Of all the governments still freely engaged in this conflict, we are the only one that took such action. We are at war because we know that treaties must be observed and pledges kept if the world is to enjoy enduring peace. There could be no truer and therefore no nobler cause.

Let us for a moment review the war situation, for it is this which is uppermost in our minds. And let us contrast our position to-day with that which ruled little more than six months ago. Then the Axis forces were everywhere on the offensive, Rommel's armies were thrusting at the gateway of the Nile Delta, the pivot of our whole Middle East position, the loss of which would have broken our Empire communications and opened the back door to Russia. On the Russian front the Germans were threatening the Caucasus, and beating hammer blows on the heroic fortress of Stalingrad. In the Far East the Japanese were consolidating and extending their conquests in the Pacific islands.

To-day the enemy has been completely expelled from all Africa. In Russia and on the southern flank the Axis forces besieging Stalingrad have been destroyed with a completeness unparalleled in the history of the German Army. The whole of the Caucasus has now been swept clean of the enemy, save for a small area in the Kuban where the battle still rages. Farther north huge areas of territory have been re-occupied by the indomitable Red Army. In the Far East China has maintained her steadfast resistance to

CONSERVATIVE PARTY CONFERENCE

the Japanese invaders. In the meanwhile Allied forces in the south Pacific have brought Japanese expansion to an end and have begun the task of reconquest. In the far north Pacific, even as I speak, American forces have made progress in operations which will, we trust, drive the Japanese from the Aleutian Islands.

These are vast operations. But that they have been brought to a successful conclusion in so short a time has only been made possible by the close unity of purpose and action of the United Nations. The sea, land and air arms of our Allied forces have been welded into a single, effective instrument of war. More than this, the energy and vision of our leaders and the courage and good sense of our peoples have bound together the United Nations in a brotherhood of arms whose single purpose is final victory over the Axis in every part of the world.

During these six months the enemy has suffered major strategic defeats on all fronts, and he has also sustained losses of men and material which he can never replace.

Let me give you one example. In the Mediterranean and North African theatres of war alone, Axis losses since the beginning of the battle of El Alamein and the landing of Allied forces in North Africa have, as a conservative estimate, certainly exceeded 305,000 killed, wounded and prisoners, 41 warships, including 2 cruisers and 24 submarines, and a large number of light craft, 500,000 tons of merchant shipping sunk, 200,000 tons seriously damaged, 3,000 aircraft and 1,000 tanks destroyed, a vast quantity of guns, ammunition, vehicles and other military equipment captured.

To these stupendous figures must be added the numerous Axis losses in men, material and ships on the Russian and Pacific fronts.

We are a people with the sea in our blood. We could not meet to-day without paying a tribute to the Royal Navy and the Merchant Marine. During the whole period of the war the Royal Navy has fulfilled its time-honoured task of keeping open the ocean routes upon which all else depends. Methods of attack and defence develop and alter. In the last war it was U-boats and the convoy system. In this war it is air attack in relation to U-boats. But the fundamental importance of the control of sea communications in the conduct of war is unchanged and unchangeable. The enemy overestimated the success of their U-boats. They did not believe therefore that the North African campaign was possible. Yet, punctually, in accordance with a prearranged plan, the vast armada sailed to North Africa and delivered its precious freight with hardly a casualty at the appointed destinations. Meanwhile the battle of the Atlantic continues. At the moment construction is mounting, merchant shipping losses are decreasing, the sinking of U-boats are increasing. These are the trends we wish to see. More than that I cannot say. The battle of the Atlantic is not yet over.

A tribute must be paid in any survey of recent months to the contribution of the R.A.F. They have played their part, maybe a decisive part, in Tunisia. At the same time, relentlessly, night after night, Bomber Command has belaboured Germany with bomb and fire and more recently with water. Several of our recent raids upon the Ruhr have dropped a tonnage greater than the tonnage dropped at Cologne in a 1,000-bomber raid last year, a tonnage three times as heavy as the heaviest air attack ever delivered on any British city. Twelve months ago a raid which could drop 1,500 tons would have seemed phenomenal, to-day it is almost a routine operation of Bomber Command. And Bomber Command is still steadily gathering strength. As the months pass our enemies will feel its blows more heavily. Nor is this all. Almost every week now, to a rapidly growing extent, our American allies are joining us in the day offensive by launching day assaults on military objectives in Germany. It would be futile to waste time in arguing which is better, night or day bombing. We know what is best for Germany. Neither night bombing nor day bombing, but day and night bombing, ceaselessly, relentlessly, hour by hour bombing. That is the programme we have prepared for Germany. In this connection it is most encouraging that our great ally the Soviet Union is joining in the offensive on Germany from the other side. Formations of heavy Russian bombers now carry out night attacks on the towns of East Prussia and targets in enemy-occupied territory. So Germany is being bombed, not only round the clock, but also round the map. Nor I can assure you will Mussolini be forgotten, or Italy overlooked.

Let me now say a word about ourselves, the Conservative Party, in conference. From the outbreak of war we pledged ourselves to give the utmost support in our power to national unity, so that victory may be won. Not one of us regrets this decision, and each one of us can say from a full heart that we have done our utmost to observe loyally the conditions that such a pledge involves. Let me speak for one moment not as a member of the Conservative Party, but as Foreign Secretary. Looking ahead, as it is my duty to do, into the future, I pray that this country may hold to its present unity not only for the immediate tasks of war, but until the foundations of peace have been truly and firmly laid. There are some who appear to think that once victory has been gained in the field, the greater measure of our anxieties will be at an end. With all the emphasis at my command I must warn you that this is not so.

The task of reconstruction, national and international, will be infinitely more baffling and more complex this time than it was twenty-five years ago. The nations of Europe have been stripped and battered out of shape by the Nazi and Fascist oppressors. The loot that Goering has stolen from the private and public collections of the world and has heaped up at Karinhall like treasure in a pirate's cave, is but a minor symptom of the wreckage that has been wrought. It is easier to return a Reubens than to feed a people, to reclaim a stolen statue than to free a nation's soul.

There are times when I contemplate the nature and extent of the problems which will confront us, when I am, I must confess, almost daunted by the immensity of our task. This at least is certain: if we are to emerge from this war truly victorious, if we are to succeed where we failed before, then our own country must play its full part. No other country can play just that role to which our traditions, our position as a member of the British Commonwealth and our island geography have called us. Therefore my message to you to-day is, when this business is over, we must neither weaken nor relax. We must show in the post-war years the same courage and devotion the British people showed in the darkest moments of 1940. It will not be easy to do this. The strain has been great and the temptation to slacken will be strong. But it must be resisted. To win the peace requires as strong and concerted a national effort as to win the war. And we must win the peace this time.

Though a conference of this kind is inevitably concerned with home affairs and with the direction in which our national institutions will develop, when we emerge from our present troubles, there are wider issues which must face every party. Apart from international affairs, there is the question of the future of the British Commonwealth of Nations and Empire. The Conservative Party has never been the spiritual home of what used to be called little Englanders. We have always believed that Great Britain itself was only one of those dominions of His Majesty the King, some of them self-governing, some of them non-self-governing, which straddle the world and which represent what is known as the British point of view. The value to civilization of the great agglomeration of territories has never been more strikingly shown than in the last four years.

At a time when other nations were cracking and crumbling, the British Empire remained firm and immovable in defence of the principles of Freedom in which it believed. It would have been easy for the great Dominions to have stood out of this war. Under the Statute of Westminster, they had no obligation to come in. They were most of them far off from the area of conflict at any rate until the entry of Japan. They were not immediately threatened. Yet one and all, with the melancholy exception of the Government of Southern Ireland, they flocked to the colours, they came thousands of miles to fight, and die, for certain fundamental rights without which, in their view, life would not be worth living. And it was the same with the Colonies. When our fortunes were at their lowest ebb, the Colonial peoples, whatever their race, colour or religion, hastened to put their lives and their resources at the disposal of the British Crown. And why was this? It was, I believe, because they realized that we stood for something in which they trusted. The magnificent record of the British Empire in this war imposes a special obligation upon us. We, the peoples of these islands, and in particular the Conservative Party, to whom I speak to-day, must be worthy of that trust. We must seek to multiply the links that bind us to the Dominions. Imperial Conferences are all very well. They are most valuable institutions. But they occur all too seldom. We must bring the Dominions ever more into our councils. We must seek their assistance in the formulation of policy. We must always move forward together. It is not for me to suggest to-day ways and means. That is a matter for discussion between the Governments concerned. But with the invention of the aeroplane, the world has become infinitely smaller. We must take full advantage of this.

Equally we must lead the Colonies forward to self-government, in order that in due course they may take their full place in the structure of the Commonwealth. The British Empire is not static: it is dynamic. It is constantly changing and constantly developing. That is its life and its strength. It is for us here to learn about it, to know about it, so that we can stimulate its development. In this essential task the Conservative Party must play a full part.

One final word about ourselves. We call ourselves Conservatives. What do we mean by this? In seeking to define the word we must distinguish between natural Conservatism and political Conservatism. Natural Conservatism consists in preferring what one is accustomed to, old habits, old customs, old surroundings, old opinions. That is the characteristic of our country as a whole. There are perhaps more natural Conservatives in other political parties than in our Conservative Party. It is not our role to give expression to that attitude of mind. On the contrary, we have always to be ready to consider objectively new problems as they arise, to adapt ourselves to changing conditions. It is because we have done this that our Party has survived. Indeed, when we examine the basic principles of our Party, there is only one which is entirely synonymous with what I have called natural Conservatism. It is respect for tradition. Nor is this a characteristic of which we need be ashamed. For this great British tradition, which has influenced not only our own history but the history of the world, is a tradition, not of reaction but of quiet ordered progress. What is it that we are most proud of in our history? Not that we preserved the Feudal system longer than any other country, but that we were the first to discard it in favour of modern parliamentary government. Not that we were the last nation to uphold the Divine Right of Kings, but that we were the first to transform it into constitutional monarchy. Not that we are the latest and the greatest example of a centralized Empire of the old type but that we have been the first nation in the world to admit to equal status His Majesty's Dominions overseas.

This process of gradual beneficent evolution has continued throughout our history. In widening our parliamentary franchise, in extending our social services, we have always been ahead of other nations. We have throughout the centuries fought for freedom of speech and thought, and they are still our most cherished privileges. It is for that steady, wise evolution, which is continuing now and will, I hope, continue in the future, that Conservatism stands. We Conservatives must not be afraid of it. It is the British tradition. It must guide and inspire our policies. We have many and great problems to solve. These must be attacked energetically and realistically. They can best be solved by the British method.

During your deliberations you will no doubt examine and discuss many proposals for the betterment of the nation. Some of your projects will be good, some very good, some perhaps not quite so good. But that is our British method. Often you will criticize the Government, occasionally in a temporary lapse of memory you may even praise it! But whatever your expression of opinion, it is to the good that it should be ventilated here. That is the way our democracy works.

CONSERVATIVE PARTY CONFERENCE

At the same time, you will allow me to say, on behalf of you all, that in his broadcast speech a few weeks ago when he dealt with domestic affairs, the Prime Minister expressed the true feeling of each one of us who are members of the Conservative Party. We may argue methods, we may debate ways and means. But fundamentally that speech expresses your mind and mine. It is for no man to peer far into the future, but this is certain. In the last century our Party has played a dominating part in the councils of the nation. This was no chance happening. It was because, despite our failings and shortcomings, and we have them like other Parties, we did in some way express the national consciousness. It is be-cause of my conviction that we have no less a part to play in the future that I sincerely welcome this Conference and cordially wish you well.

28

CHINA DAY—7 JULY 1943

Mr. Churchill returned from Washington via North Africa, where he was joined by Mr. Eden at the end of May. Together they had conferences with General Eisenhower and with General Marshall who had flown with Mr. Churchill from Washington.

June 11. Pantellaria surrendered, followed the next day by Lampedusa.

June 18. Field-Marshal Wavell was appointed to succeed Lord Linlithgow as Viceroy of India.

June 29. In the Pacific, the American attack on the Solomons began.

July 5. German offensive opened in Russia. The Red Army counter-attacked three days later.

General Sikorski killed on his air journey to U.K. from Gibraltar.

On July 10, Mr. Eden addressed the Salute to China meeting at the Albert Hall. Dr. Wellington Koo, the Chinese Ambassador, was the other principal speaker and Mr. Attlee presided.

We are met here to-day to pay tribute to our ally China, who now enters upon the seventh year of war against our common enemy, Japan. It is six years to-day since the Japanese, by their treacherous attack on the Chinese troops near Peking, provoked the whole Chinese nation to resistance. This was to have been a punitive expedition, short and sharp, quickly over, but bringing gain and loot to the Japanese. It was, the world was assured, a mere incident. Now, after six years, the Japanese army which so light-heartedly embarked on this adventure, can take note that Chinese resistance is unbroken, and that the "incident" has become merged in a world war in which China finds herself allied with the British Commonwealth of Nations, the United States of America, the Netherlands, and the other United Nations. Six years of war is a harsh and exacting ordeal for any people however brave. We here in Britain have been at war for nearly four years, for some of the time, like China, alone; and we have suffered much. But we have been spared the horrors of actual invasion by a barbaric and ruthless enemy. For six years the armies of Japan have been murdering, pillaging and looting on Chinese soil. Against these armies the Chinese have put up a resistance which has stirred the imagination of the world.

It is not always easy for us here to grasp the intensity and significance of the war in the East. Living in Europe as Hitler's next neighbour, we have ever since his rise to power inevitably been preoccupied, though not always preoccupied enough, with the menace of Nazi Germany. As the German gangsters developed their technique of smash and grab, we saw that, unless the process could be stopped, there must be an end of freedom, toleration and good faith between man and man. We were perhaps slower to see that the same was true in the Far East. The danger was more remote; but it was not less real. The first major blow at the structure of peace, which the nations had tried to build after the last war, was struck by Japan. The stark reality of Japanese aggression became plain as thrust after thrust was made against China and as Japan set out to establish her merciless sway over the eastern hemisphere.

Then suddenly, while we were hard pressed in the West, the danger came nearer still with the attack on Pearl Harbour, Malaya and the Philippines. There followed grievous disasters, terrible in their extent and unexpected in their swiftness: Malaya, Singapore, the Philippines, the Dutch East Indies, Burma and much else beside. We were now sharing China's experience. Fully engaged at the side of our Chinese allies, we were learning what they had learnt of Japanese perfidy and brutality. Australia and India found themselves face to face with a threat whose deadly nature none could deny. And so with increasing force it was borne in upon all that present-day Japan, like Nazi Germany, does, in stark reality, represent the forces of evil. Japan has run up a long account, a very long account, of evil-doing; and that account must and will be settled. These thoughts lie deep in the consciousness of every one of us in this country, however close and menacing the German scourge may be.

It is natural that the momentous happenings of recent months and the sense of greater things to come should be foremost in our minds. But there is, I can assure Your Excellency, a full understanding that the completion of our task in Europe is only the beginning of the end. There is in our hearts a fixed and grim resolve to teach Japan once and for all the lesson that co-prosperity, as she calls it, is not achieved by cruelty and oppression and that he who draws the sword shall perish by the sword.

We of the British Commonwealth and Empire have a duty to our own people in the Far East who are imprisoned and enslaved by the Japanese. We have a duty to those territories of the British Empire which have been overrun; a duty to restore to their peoples the freedom and prosperity which they previously enjoyed and to assist in their development towards still better things. Finally, we have a duty towards our allies, and in particular our Chinese allies, to destroy the present Japanese menace in the Far East and to join in making a contribution to create a better order in which all just men may live in peace.

We can never forget that to preserve order and to maintain definite standards of civilized international intercourse is as vital to this country in the East as in the West. All other considerations apart, the peaceful development of commerce, which has always been the chief interest of British policy in the Far East, is impossible. Without such conditions there can be none of that two-way traffic between East and West which can bring to both sides enduring benefits.

I have no doubt that our united efforts will bring about the defeat of Japan. But we in this country have no illusions about the magnitude of the task involved. For the defeat of Japan, if it is to lead to lasting peace, means not only the physical defeat of her armed forces, which in itself will involve no mean effort, but also the defeat of those ideas which for more than a decade have been cultivated in the minds of the Japanese by their militarist leaders to the exclusion of everything that is reasonable and humane. Those leaders stand for the suppression of so-called "dangerous thoughts"; by which significant expression they mean all liberal tendencies and any trend which might lead the Japanese people away from the militarist programme of shameless aggression and exploitation. Those leaders stand for the creation of a police force and gendarmerie which rival the Gestapo in barbarity. These evils

CHINA DAY

flourish to-day, and so thorough has been the eradication of sane thought, that the Japanese armed forces fight in the blasphemous conviction that they are inspired by some divine spirit in their orgies of devastation. We are committed to the destruction of those forces and we shall destroy them.

It would be wrong to divorce in our minds the battles which we and our allies are fighting in the West from the battles which you and your allies are fighting in the East. War, like peace, is indivisible. The recent successes of the Chinese army play their part in the common struggle, just as the successes which have crowned our arms in North Africa brought aid and must have brought hope to our sorely tried allies in the East. In Europe the tide of aggression is ebbing. Our great bomber offensive is only the prelude to heavier blows. Every thrust against the Axis in Europe brings us nearer to the day when the full force of the United Nations can be brought to bear against Japan. Already the long-accumulated weight of Allied power has forced open the gates of the Mediterranean, and I can assure our Chinese friends that the day will come when, its work in Europe done, that Allied power will flow eastwards and overwhelm the Empire of Japan.

The war in the Far East has thus far fallen into three phases: first, a swift and deadly Japanese advance; secondly, desperate defence by the Allied nations, which preserved the bases from which a counter-attack could be launched; and thirdly, the beginnings of that counter-attack, which have already won victories holding promise of better things to come. So it is that a new hope begins to rise in the hearts of those peoples now experiencing the benefit of the Japanese "Co-prosperity sphere". Those of them, if any there were, who put faith in Japanese promises have already learnt their lesson. It is a curious fact that, as Japan's power and prospects begin to dwindle, she begins to abound in glittering promises of independence for the miserable peoples whom she has overrun, whose economies she has ruined and whose function is now only to supply and support the Japanese war machine. I should hardly be surprised if these peoples were to scrutinize these Japanese promises somewhat closely, in view of Japan's record. To those peoples who have hitherto lived under the flags of Great Britain and other freedom-loving nations, I send the assurance that the British people will not slacken for one moment in its efforts until their liberation has been secured.

As to the future of operations in the East, this is neither the time nor the place to make any detailed forecasts. But this assurance

CHINA DAY

I wish to give: the re-opening of communications with China remains a prime allied objective. I take this occasion to repeat the words used by the Prime Minister in his address to the Congress of the United States this year: "I regard", he said, "the bringing of effective and immediate aid to China as one of the most urgent of our common tasks." It merely remains for me to say that our determination to send aid to China is not limited by any political or financial considerations, but by physical problems alone. The task of finding and organizing alternative routes to supplement the air route has fallen largely upon us. We are doing our utmost to meet it. Apart from earlier credits which we have made to China we have extended Lend-Lease facilities to her. Such facilities cover arms, ammunition, military equipment, military freight, payment of Chinese troops in India and so forth. In short, I can say that wherever it is possible for China to obtain in the sterling area the supplies which she needs for waging our common war against Japan, there has been and will be no financial obstacle, still less any political obstacle.

And here I should like to pay a tribute to the magnificent work of private organizations in this country directed to the relief of distress and suffering in China. I refer in particular to the organizations comprised in the United Aid to China Fund and to the Joint War Organization of the British Red Cross and the Order of St. John.

The United Aid to China Fund started its appeal to the public one year ago to-day under the presidency of Lady Cripps. It had been intended that the appeal should run for three months, but such was the response from the public that it was decided to continue this combined effort indefinitely while the need lasted. Up to date the Fund has collected close on £7,000,000 and the proceeds are already being handed over to Madame Chiang Kai-Shek in instalments to be distributed where the need is greatest.

In addition to being a part to the United Aid to China Fund, the Joint War Organization of the British Red Cross and St. John has recently decided to establish a Red Cross Commission in China and to extend considerably their humanitarian activities there. Their work for the first year will cost not less than a quarter of a million pounds and as the need grows, I am told that more will be forthcoming. Through the means of these excellent and impressive activities of private bodies, the individual citizen of this country has an opportunity of expressing to China his personal sympathy and admiration. I look on this as of the utmost value for the future of Anglo-Chinese relations, for it means that the people of the one country are directly helping and succouring the people of the other. Direct personal contacts between large numbers of the inhabitants of this island and large numbers of the inhabitants of China are difficult to achieve. Perhaps they will become easier in a much shorter space of time than we now imagine. In the meantime such visits as we can exchange in the present difficult circumstances have a special value. A notable contribution to Sino-British relations was made by the recent visit to China of our Parliamentary Mission, one of whose members has spoken to us tonight. They were able to learn much, at first hand, of conditions in China, and were able, in return, to give a picture of Great Britain at war to their Chinese hosts. It is superfluous to add that they were everywhere received with that hospitality which is one of the most deep-rooted and most engaging characteristics of the Chinese. I am glad to say that we hope shortly to be able to repay some of this hospitality, on the occasion of the visit of a Chinese goodwill mission to England. Meanwhile, in two weeks' time it will be our privilege to have among us as our guest Dr. T. V. Soong, the Chinese Minister for Foreign Affairs, who has lately been in the United States of America. Dr. Soong may be assured of a warm welcome by the Government and people of this country.

I must take this opportunity to tell the Chinese Ambassador with what deep gratitude we noted the part he took in recently welcoming our Parliamentary Delegation to China. He is an ambassador in the best sense of the term in that he has a deep knowledge and a convinced friendship for both our countries.

This brings me to the general subject of the future of Anglo-Chinese relations, viewed in an altogether larger sphere of space and time. Although we have had our troubles in the past, like most countries, there are very real reasons why we and the Chinese should be friends, now and always. This year has indeed seen one very important historic step forward in the improvement of our mutual relations. I refer of course to the abolition of extraterritoriality, and the simultaneous signature of Anglo-Chinese and American-Chinese treaties. With the passing of the old treaties, China and Great Britain now stand on that footing of perfect equality and reciprocity which must be the basis of any real and lasting friendship. We can henceforward work together, in war or in peace, unhampered by reservations that are a legacy of times past.

CHINA DAY

From time to time our enemies suggest, either to China or to ourselves, that Great Britain does not wish to see China strong. Such suggestions are no doubt intended to be mischievous. They are in fact ludicrous, and I am sure that our Chinese friends are the first to resent them. The truth is that the interest of the British Empire has always lain in the existence of a strong and united China. So it has been in the past, so it will be in the future. Without a strong and united China there is no prospect of lasting stability in the Far East. When the present struggle with Japan is at an end we shall all be faced with vast problems of reconstruction. We shall be concerned to secure a lasting peace in Far-Eastern lands. It is obvious that whatever plans are devised to bring this about, China must play a leading part. It is equally clear that friendship between the British Commonwealth and Empire, the United States of America, China and the Soviet Union must be the foundation of any such peace. Just as we contemplate collective arrangements in the West to maintain an orderly development of civilized life, so in the East we shall need to build up a collective system of security. To that system the United Nations, and especially China and all those nations directly concerned in the Far East, will each have contributions to make.

But before we can build the peace we have to win the war. We are now witnessing the Second Act of this stupendous tragedy. In the First Act the powers of evil were everywhere triumphant, and it seemed hard to believe that they could do other than win in the end. In the Second Act they are being hurled back, and ever stronger reinforcements are being brought to bear against them. In the Third Act the wheel will have swung full circle, and they will be driven finally from the stage which they have held so long. We can all see that this will be the end of the story. But that is not enough. We must also pledge ourselves to see to it that this story shall never be enacted again. Twice in our lifetime the powers of darkness have threatened to overwhelm us. This time their defeat must be final. Just as we all here are determined, no matter from whence we come, from the West or from the East, to batter our common enemies, wherever they be, into unconditional surrender; so let us all dedicate ourselves to the task, which will one day be ours, of making real that great message which has been turned into a mockery by our enemies:

"Peace on earth and goodwill towards men."

29

MOSCOW CONFERENCE—1943

QUEBEC CONFERENCE

August 10–14. The Quebec Conference: attended by Mr. Churchill, President Roosevelt and Mr. Mackenzie King, and their advisers. Mr. Eden was at the last part of the Conference and returned to England on August 27.

RUSSIA

Orel fell to the Red Army on August 4, and advances continued all along the front; Smolensk fell on September 25. By the end of October, Dnieperpetrovsk had been récaptured. Two-thirds of occupied Russia had been cleared of Germans by the beginning of November.

PACIFIC

In the Pacific the last of the Aleutian Islands had been finally captured by August 20.

On August 25, Lord Louis Mountbatten became Supreme Commander in South-East Asia.

ITALY

July 10. The invasion of Sicily began. The island was cleared of the enemy by August 17.

July 25. Mussolini resigned and Marshal Badoglio was appointed Prime Minister.

MOSCOW CONFERENCE

September 3. The Eighth Army landed in the toe of Italy.

September 8. The Salerno landings begun by the Fifth Army under General Mark Clark.

September 17. The Fifth and Eighth Armies linked up near Salerno. Foggia, with its large airfields, was captured on September 27, and Naples on October 1.

October 12. Announced that Portugal agreed to grant Great Britain facilities in the Azores. Mr. Eden had negotiated this agreement.

October 13. Italy having declared war on Germany, was accepted as a co-belligerent.

October 30. Germans flooded the Pontine Marshes.

Mr. Eden left England on October 11 and spent the next four days in Cairo, inspecting troops and in discussions with statesmen and diplomats. He reached Moscow on October 18 at the same time as Mr. Cordell Hull for a Three Power Conference. He travelled back through Cairo, where he had conversations with the Turkish Minister of Foreign Affairs. He gave the House of Commons the following account on 11 November 1943:

I welcome this opportunity of giving to the House some account of the proceedings of the Foreign Secretaries' Conference concluded in Moscow a few days ago. It will not have escaped the observation of my hon. Friends that the communiqué and the published documents which accompanied it were unusually full. We, in fact, included in them all those portions of the work of the Conference about which we felt it possible to make public statements at this present time. This was done, of course, by agreement between the three of us, and so the House will understand that I cannot now add much fresh matter to the published declarations on the work of the Conference. There are, however, some comments that I would wish to make upon that work and one or two personal impressions that I would like to give to the House.

Let me say at the outset that the results of the Conference exceeded my hopes. As we worked, the sense of confidence grew, and this, in turn, seemed to give an added momentum to our progress so that it was better in the middle than at the beginning, and better at the end than in the middle. So it is, that looking back across

those fifteen days of the work we did in the Soviet capital, I can
say with absolute assurance that they have brought new warmth
and new confidence into all our dealings with our Soviet and American friends. We met twelve times in full session, but, of course, that
did not represent by any means the whole of the work done. Apart
from those meetings, we each of us had a large number of informal
conversations with our colleagues. I had such talks with Marshal
Stalin and Mr. Molotov, as well as with Mr. Cordell Hull and
Mr. Harriman, the American Ambassador. The actual achievements of the Conference, about which I want to say a word or two
in a moment, seem to me solid enough, but it was the friendly
atmosphere of mutual interest and mutual confidence in which all
these conversations took place, which, to me, will always make the
Moscow Conference memorable.

The first difficulty—and it was quite a stubborn one—which Mr.
Hull and I encountered was to persuade Mr. Molotov to preside at
our meetings. He was anxious that we should undertake that task
in turn, but we succeeded in convincing him that an army has
probably a better chance in battle if it does not change its general
every day, and we certainly could not have made a happier decision. As the House knows, I have in my life attended a good many
international gatherings and not always, I am sorry to say, have
they been conspicuously successful, but I have yet to sit under a
chairman who showed greater patience, skill and judgment than
did Mr. Molotov, and I must say that it was to his handling of a
long and complicated agenda that must go a large measure of
the credit for whatever success we achieved.

I think, too, that my friend and colleague Mr. Cordell Hull must
feel that the results of the Conference have justified his efforts and
his very gallant venture in making this long flight. Certainly we
were fortunate to have him with us, and his sincerity and singleness of purpose were a great encouragement to us at every step.
The House will understand from what I have said that the relations between colleagues were good and that they were equally
good among the staffs, but, apart from military matters, on which
I want to say a word in a moment, I must pay a special tribute to
the work of His Majesty's Ambassador in Moscow, Sir Archibald
Clark-Kerr. Much of the preparatory laying of the ground that is
necessary for such a Conference fell to him, and he has rendered
remarkable services to Anglo-Soviet understanding. I must also be
allowed to pay my tribute to the brilliant Foreign Office leader of
our team, Mr. Strang, who indefatigably helped us at every stage.

MOSCOW CONFERENCE

I believe that all of us who were at that Conference were conscious from the beginning of its work how much the future of millions of people depended upon the outcome of our labours, and we were, in consequence, all the more determined to do everything in our power to make it a success. Thus we met round the table on a basis of complete equality. We were able to discuss our problems and to state our views, conscious that we were each of us striving for one purpose and one purpose only—to try to bring the war to an end in victory at the earliest possible moment and thereafter in full co-operation with each other to ensure that the peoples of the world might live at peace.

Now a word of what the Conference did. We all agreed to start the talks with a discussion of measures for shortening the duration of the war. Though this topic is one of direct interest to all hon. Members in this House, they will not, for obvious reasons, expect me to give an account of the conclusions reached on this chapter of our work beyond the very carefully chosen words of the communiqué itself. The results of our discussions on this head can only be made public as they develop at the expense of the common enemy. I can only say that I have confidence that that development will be found generally satisfactory by hon. Members in all parts of the House. But this I can say about our military discussions, that I believe that perhaps they did more good to our mutual relations by the frank and exhaustive examination which was made of them than any other phase of the Conference. There was no tendency on the part of any of the delegates to dodge any of the difficult and important issues that these military matters raised, and I am deeply indebted to General Ismay, whom the Prime Minister generously lent to me, for the invaluable part which he played in this sphere of our work.

Now I would say something about the first of the published decisions of the Conference—the four nations' declaration. Nothing could give a better proof of Mr. Hull's vision and statesmanship than that declaration on general security, of which he is the parent. The principle which we agreed to in this declaration constitutes, on the whole, probably the most far-reaching of the decisions to which we came. These decisions cover the whole future organization of world security, and for that reason we were happy that the Government of China could associate itself with us and approve with us this document and be a common original signatory to it. A word on the significance of this document. As within nations, so between nations, when the immediate common effort needed for victory is over it is hard to hold the same unity in the years that follow. That is a lesson of which we are only too well aware, and the importance of this declaration is in the emphasis it lays on the decision of our Governments to continue our co-operation and our collaboration after the war. This, I emphasize, does not apply only to certain measures required for the defeat of the enemy and to see that the business does not start again, but it also applies to the whole long-term organization of security. Good as that is, the four nations' declaration would not have been, in my judgment, quite enough by itself. It is absolutely essential that there should be between us special machinery, over and above the ordinary machinery of diplomatic interchange, through which this country and its great allies can work continuously together, and concert rapidly and efficiently their views on the many political problems which arise out of the war. Our whole experience during this war has shown the urgent need for some such machinery, but there have always been geographical or other difficulties which have made it difficult to set it up.

It was a great—perhaps the greatest—achievement of the Conference to take the first steps in establishing this machinery. What we need most urgently and most immediately is some body, some organization to act as a clearing house for the exchange of information and ideas between us upon certain questions that will certainly arise as the war progresses. It is for this purpose that the Conference decided to set up in London a European Advisory Commission composed of responsible representatives of this country, of the United States and of the Soviet Union. This Commission, I must emphasize, is advisory in character. It will be set up at once. It will be its duty to study and to make joint recommendations to the three Governments on any question which the three Governments agree to refer to it. The object we have in mind is to be able by this machinery to look ahead and to make agreed plans for dealing with problems that will face us in the future. If we can do that, we shall be able to keep in step at every stage, and thus we can avoid some of the delays and some of the misunderstandings which inevitably occur when each of us makes his plans separately, however good those plans may happen to be. I think the House will understand what were the practical reasons which made us think it desirable to limit the initial members of this Advisory Commission to the three Powers, but I must emphasize again that this is an advisory and not an executive body. It is a piece of machinery set up for the convenience of the three Governments themselves; it is not an instrument for imposing their views on others. It is designed to concert political planning among the three great Powers, for the truth must be faced that it is upon these three Powers principally that will rest the responsibility for ensuring that this war is followed by a lasting peace. If we can agree together, we three, there is no problem that is not capable finally of solution. If we do not agree together there is no international event which cannot become an international problem. I felt that very strongly when we examined the question of this machinery, but of course setting up this machinery does not mean that we exclude other methods of consultation between the three Governments. We did at the Conference set on foot what is, I think, in diplomatic procedure something of a novelty, that is to say, we agreed that on occasions there might be problems which we should wish to submit to one of the capitals where the Foreign Secretary concerned and the two Ambassadors could meet together and discuss and advise upon it. Sometimes that might happen in London, sometimes in Washington, sometimes in Moscow. It would be something in the nature of an *ad hoc* tripartite conference of the Foreign Secretary and two Ambassadors which might be given a special task in any one of the capitals. I think that may prove to be a useful piece of machinery.

Now I come to another piece of machinery we set up, and that is concerned with Italy. We have set up an Inter-Allied Advisory Council to deal with Italy. This body is quite independent of the European Advisory Commission which is to sit in London and it has a specific, definite task to perform. Its duty will be to deal with day-to-day questions other than, of course, military operations, and to make agreed recommendations for the purpose of coordinating our Allied policy in regard to Italy. It will be set up at once, with representatives from this country, the United States, the Soviet Union and the French Committee of National Liberation, and we have also made provision to add to it representatives of Greece and Yugoslavia as soon as we possibly can. The whole House will feel that these two countries have a special interest in Italian affairs as a consequence of the acts of aggression which they have suffered. It is my belief that this Council will be useful in ensuring and maintaining a common policy among us in regard to Italy.

We took occasion, Mr. Hull and I, at the Conference to give our Soviet colleagues an account of the history of Allied military government in Italy, about which there has been some little misconception in this country and elsewhere. We gave an account of that and of the principles on which we had based it, and as a result of that and the discussions on it we had no difficulty at all in reaching agreement on the declaration regarding policy in Italy which has now been published. This declaration I think is also in itself an important element in creating understanding between our three countries. That is all I have to say about the various items of machinery which the Conference set up. They have a big job to do, but if this machinery works well, as I have every hope it will, it can make a substantial contribution to winning the war and still more to winning the peace.

I turn for a moment to one other important branch of our future responsibilities—economic. During the Conference Mr. Molotov and I had the chance to hear at first hand from Mr. Hull about measures of economic co-operation which, as we know, he has always had very much at heart. Indeed, after security, these economic questions constitute the most important field in which the lot of man can be improved. We had a useful exchange of views on these questions, and I am glad to say that we all three of us found ourselves in agreement on the programme for handling these vast problems, on many of which work has, as the House knows, already begun.

While we were in session we noticed with some interest that German propaganda was extremely active. It kept suggesting that every kind of difference had arisen between us and tried to sow dissension by every means in its power. I should like to report that all these attempts failed utterly, and in that brief fortnight the last chance of creating disunity between the three Allied Powers was completely and finally destroyed. The Nazi leaders must now look somewhere else. They must now understand that they have no hope by this means of escaping the fate which is overtaking them. I hope as the end draws nearer they will read the warning issued at the end of the Conference in the names of the Prime Minister, the President and Marshal Stalin that those German officers and men and members of the Nazi Party who have had any connection with atrocities and executions in countries overrun by German forces will be taken back to the countries in which their crimes were committed to be charged and punished according to the laws of those countries.

As regards the remainder of the agenda, it is sufficient to say there was no major political question in Europe which was not the subject of discussion between us in some form or other. I am not going to pretend for a moment that we were agreed on every point. That would indeed be the international millennium and we are nowhere near that yet. But what I can say is that we do now know each other's points of view on all these subjects. We discussed them with the utmost frankness, and I believe that in the spirit of goodwill which is now being established we can reasonably hope to make progress with even the most stubborn among them. As many Members will know, it is a common diplomatic experience to find that problems which seem to present insuperable difficulties when there is no confidence and no mutual trust can fall into a different perspective when once a real basis of goodwill has been established. Then perhaps you can get that reasonable compromise which in other conditions appears hopeless of realization. I count it, and this is the impression I would like to leave, as the major success of the Moscow Conference, not that we agreed these documents, not even that we set up this machinery, great though the importance which I attach to it, but that they did provide a basis of goodwill and confidence between us. I believe that has been won and I believe that it ought to endure, and that it should enable us to deal together with the problems that will lie ahead. Of course there will be set-backs and disappointments, we must expect them, but what is important is that the differences should be honestly and frankly faced and that we should together try to bring about their solution.

The Anglo-American-Soviet association which has found encouraging expression in this Conference is based on the firmest of all foundations, a common interest. The three countries have the same strong interest in peace, they have the same interest in securing that no aggressor shall again break the peace. I have seen fears expressed that as a result of this there will be some dictatorship imposed by the three Powers on others. I can assure the House that nothing of the kind is in our minds at all. Of course, we want association with others. Of course, we want the opportunity of full discussion, but, as I have said, special responsibilities do rest on our three Powers, and we did at Moscow try to devise machinery and agree on a policy which would enable us to give expression to that sense of our responsibility. Of course, we shall need the advice of others, and, of course, we shall welcome the advice of others, but the first essential is that we should get our machinery working between us three. We must proceed by stages. That does not exclude further developments in the future if all goes well.

At all times it is extremely difficult to assess the value of work in which one has been engaged oneself. It is not very easy to get the perspective right. But I have given the House my reasons for thinking that this Conference has produced concrete results. We three Powers discussed any and every subject with exactly the same ease and freedom as any three Members of this House could do, and sometimes with a good deal less controversy. We had no formalities, we had no set speeches at any time, we had no wrangle as to which subject was to come before the other on the agenda, or any of those familiar difficulties which those who attend Conferences know so well. I find all this heartening for the future, and I feel that we can enter the closing months of 1943 with a greater measure of confidence than seemed possible a brief while ago.

What is our country's role to be? Surely to use all our strength and all our authority to promote the growth of this confidence. We are not going to do that by some new subtle tricks of diplomacy but merely by treating our Russian and American friends as we treated each other in Moscow, that is to say, as loyal colleagues in an equal partnership. We can let our imagination play a little on what may be the consequences for good in this close association of three great Powers, the United States with over 135 millions, the Soviet Union with an even larger population, and these islands, the heart and centre of a great Commonwealth, and Empire.

There is one matter to which I must now refer. On my return journey I was glad of an opportunity of meeting the Turkish Minister for Foreign Affairs. We exchanged views on the general situation in the light of the Moscow Conference. My Turkish colleague has now returned to Ankara to report on the outcome of these conversations to his Government. In the meantime, there is nothing further I can say.

There is one final reflection I would like to leave with the House before I close. When I was in Moscow—and I think those who were with me would bear me out—I could not but be conscious of the quiet confidence of the Red Army in itself and of the Soviet people in the Red Army. Twice in our brief stay notable victories had been won, and they were celebrated in the traditional manner with salvoes of artillery and fireworks. But it seemed to me that as the guns of Moscow thundered out their congratulations to the Army their note was not only one of exultation but, even more, a stern warning to the enemy of what was yet to come.

On my return flight, or rather just before it, I made a request to my Soviet hosts. I asked them whether they would be good enough to agree to our aircraft circling low over Stalingrad. This was readily agreed to, and we were able thus to get a close view of this city of imperishable fame. We most of us have seen devastated areas in our time, either in this war or in the last or in some other experience of our lives, but none of us in that aeroplane had ever seen destruction on a scale to parallel the destruction of Stalingrad —none of us. Every house must have been a fortress, every street must have been a battle ground. There could have been no encounter more fierce in all history and, I should imagine, few, if any, more costly in human life. When you see that, when you see for miles and miles mounds of machinery twisted and flung about as though some great giant had dealt with it, factories completely destroyed, then you begin to understand that passionate earnestness which the Russians feel for an early conclusion of this war. Our own people who have endured the suffering and punishment of war now for more than four years share that resolve. I am confident that the Russians know they share that resolve, and I could not help reflecting, as we flew over Stalingrad: is it not possible that out of it all we shall be able together so to order the world that these cities that have been utterly shattered shall live again and that this time they can live their lives in lasting peace?

30

THE TEHERAN AND CAIRO CONFERENCES
1943

November 25. In Italy the Eighth Army crossed the River Sangro. The Fifth Army continued the offensive, crossed the Volturno and by the end of the year was able to launch a large-scale raid across the Garigliano.

November 27. One third of Berlin was reported to be wrecked as the result of large-scale air raids.

At the end of November, President Roosevelt, Marshal Chiang Kai-Shek and Mr. Churchill conferred in Cairo. This was followed by the Teheran conference between the "Big Three". Mr. Eden was present at both these conferences and also at the discussions with Turkey held in Cairo after Teheran.

Mr. Churchill became seriously ill with pneumonia shortly afterwards and remained in the Mediterranean but fully in touch with affairs; he returned to the United Kingdom on 18 January 1944.

Mr. Eden returned to London at the end of the discussions and gave the House of Commons an account of the conferences on December 14.

M y first sentence must be to express my warmest thanks to this House for their generous treatment of me in so kindly re-arranging Business as to enable this Debate to take place in the last week before the Christmas Recess. I understand, of course, that that re-arrangement must have been incon-

venient to many of my hon. Friends in all parts of the House, and
I am the more grateful to them. The fact is that it would not have
been possible for me to take part in these recent Turkish conversations in Cairo and get back, despite the best efforts of the Royal
Air Force, in time for a Debate last Thursday. Again I express my
thanks. Let me say also that I only too well understand the disappointment that hon. Members must be feeling that the Prime
Minister is not able to be here himself to give a first-hand account
of these three Conferences in which he has played so leading a
part. My right hon. Friend asked me to express his regret to the
House, but there is still important work for him to do in the sphere
where he now is, and he is sure the House would wish him to see
that work through to the end. So this poor substitute "struts and
frets his hour upon the stage".

We have spent three very strenuous weeks. Into that short time
have been compressed three Conferences of world significance any
one of which in the ordinary leisured times of diplomacy would
have taken a full month. But, with the rapid development of air
communication, methods of consultation have been transformed,
so it was possible within only a month of the meeting of the Foreign
Secretaries in Moscow to open the yet more authoritative Conferences of the heads of Governments in Teheran. These meetings
between the three men who bear the chief responsibility in their
respective countries must be a rare event. Their value can hardly
be exaggerated. They impose a considerable additional burden on
those who travel or take part in them. It is not so much the intensity of the work that has to be done as the wide range of subjects
through which the mind has to move from one to the other which
adds so heavily to the burden. I do not believe even my right hon.
Friend the Prime Minister, ardent as we know him to be for work,
has ever devoted more hours of the day and, alas, of the night to
unremitting labour than during these Conferences. I am glad to
be able to report to the House that, in spite of that, I left my right
hon. Friend, though perhaps a little tired, in good health, stout of
heart and most confident in spirit.

Now let me describe our work. It fell into three main, easily
defined chapters. First, the first Cairo Conference for the prosecution of the war against Japan, next the Teheran Conference for the
prosecution of the war against Germany, and then the second Cairo
Conference for discussions with the President and the Foreign
Secretary of Turkey. I propose to say something about each, and
also about a number of subsidiary and important matters which

were discussed and dealt with in both Cairo and Teheran. The greater part of the time of the first two Conferences in Cairo about the Far East, and in Teheran about the war against Germany, were taken up with military matters. It was possible for us to bring these matters to a state of complete and collective preparation far exceeding anything that had hitherto been realized in this war. The thought is, I think, quite well expressed in two sentences of the Teheran communiqué, to which I draw the attention of the House because they are, I think, the most important of all. It states:

"Our military staffs have joined in our round table discussions and we have concerted our plans for the destruction of the German forces. We have reached complete agreement as to the scope and timing of the operations which will be undertaken from the East, West and South."

That is a message which it has never, as yet, been possible to give to the Allied peoples in this war. The words must ring ominously in German ears and in those of Germany's unhappy satellites. They could be applied textually to the earlier Conference at Cairo in respect of the Far East. That Conference had certain special features. It gave the Prime Minister, for instance, his first opportunity of meeting the Generalissimo and Madame Chiang Kai-Shek. I think it was also the first time the President had met the Generalissimo. By the luck of good weather I arrived in Cairo on the evening when the Prime Minister was entertaining the Generalissimo and Madame Chiang Kai-Shek, this leader of indestructible China and his most gifted wife. It was a most memorable experience when the Prime Minister took his guests and Admiral Mountbatten, who is Supreme Allied Commander South-East Asia Command, and who, of course, also came to Cairo for the Conference, into his map room, where for some hours we dived deep into war plans and projects.

If I may just strike one personal note, I would say that it is difficult not to be deeply impressed by the Generalissimo, even at a first meeting. Some of my hon. Friends have already met him. I had never met him before, and that impression deepens as time goes on. Under the outward gentleness and gracefulness of this remarkable personality there is a core of supple steel. His is a strength, you feel, that cannot be broken; it can only be bent and then strike back with even greater force. From what I have said, the House will understand how readily the Generalissimo and our Prime Minister understood each other. They speak just the same language of determination, and all through that evening and many

228

subsequent discussions and meetings Madame Chiang Kai-Shek was always there to help us with her sagacious counsel, her unrivalled experience of East and West, and her brilliant gifts as an interpreter. I am sure the House will not wish me to apologize for giving just this personal impression of meeting these very remarkable personalities. As I have said, our Military Mission agreed in Cairo upon future military operations against Japan, but we also thought it well to take this opportunity to set out the political principles for which we are fighting, and we did so in these words:

"The three great Powers are fighting this war to resist and punish the aggression of Japan. They covet no gain for themselves and have no thought of territorial expansion."

Such being our purpose, it is our determined intention that Japan shall be deprived of opportunities for further mischief; that she shall be expelled from all the territories, to whomsoever they belong, which she has taken and that reparation shall be made to China for the wrongs which have been done to her. We thought it well, too, to take this opportunity to tell the people of Korea that we had not forgotten them and that their country would, in due course, become free and independent again. The House may say and it is true, that there is, in all this, no new declaration of British policy. The House will remember that even before Pearl Harbour, the Prime Minister warned Japan that if she attacked the United States we would declare war within the hour. From that moment we have been committed to the objectives which are set out now, for the first time, internationally, in the Cairo Agreement. We are committed to them because we understand that to destroy Germany and then make a compromise peace with Japan, would only sow the seeds of a third world war.

Let me emphasize. The war with Japan is not one in which we in this country are playing the part of benevolent assistants. Even if we are compelled, for the time being, to devote the greater part of our human and material resources to the task of defeating Germany, we are still principals in the Far Eastern war. Japan is just as great a menace to the security of the British Commonwealth as she is to the security of either the United States or China. Ask any one of the splendid fighting men from Canada, Australia or New Zealand who are in this country, whether they have any doubts on this score or whether they could contemplate any future for their countries unless the power of Japan were broken. They and thousands of their fellows came here in 1939 to help us in our defence here. Many of them are still here, in spite of the dangers to their own countries and we should be utterly unworthy of our heritage and traditions, if we did not, at the earliest possible moment, deploy all our resources for the purpose of establishing their security on a firm basis. For that we have to fight Japan to the bitter end whatever the cost and however long it takes.

I have no doubt that this meeting between the leaders of the three great Powers, upon whom rests the heaviest share in the conduct of the war against Japan, has been of the greatest service to our cause in the political as well as in the military sphere. I was able during these conversations to have some discussion with our Chinese friends on another matter in which I know the House takes an interest—post-war collaboration between our two countries both in policy and in commerce. I told our Chinese friends that it was the desire of this country that that collaboration should be as close and as cordial as possible. I found that to be their attitude also, and I hope, in fact I feel sure that we are going to be able to make steady progress in both those spheres.

Now, I invite the House to leave Cairo and the Far Eastern Conference and, if they will, to take their places with me again upon the magic carpet—in this instance the good aircraft "York" —and fly across the Dead Sea over Iraq and the Persian Hills to Teheran. This long journey which many, like my noble Friend opposite, have performed in the past, we performed in the incredible space of five and a half hours. The Teheran Conference lasted four full working days and they were crowded days. We had, every afternoon, a plenary session of the heads of the Governments and their principal diplomatic and military advisers. All the mornings were devoted to preparation and to those numerous consultations which have to take place between delegations in the course of any successful conference. There was a welcome absence of formality about all our meetings. Both lunches and dinners served for the further prosecution of business, except, perhaps for the Prime Minister's birthday celebrations. The party at these meals never totalled more than eight, with the necessary addition of interpreters. In this way, it is fair to say that all the waking hours and many hours normally devoted to sleep, were during these four days and nights, devoted to discussions on any and every topic between the leaders of these three countries.

When I came back to this House from Moscow I ventured to give the House a message that I was confident that the foundation had been laid for enduring collaboration between this country, the

United States and the Soviet Union. I am many times more confident of this to-day. The work of Teheran began just where the work of Moscow left off, but the Teheran Conference, being a conference of leaders, carries a still more stirring message to the world. I would like to quote just one extract about the Conference from the Soviet newspaper *Pravda*, and I quote it because it expresses exactly my own feelings at the end of this Conference. They say this:

"Only a short time separates us from the Moscow Conference of the three Foreign Ministers of the Allied Powers, the decisions of which not only demonstrated the strengthening of friendly co-operation between Great Britain, the U.S.S.R. and the U.S.A. in the war period, but laid the basis for fruitful work together after the war. But what a tremendous step forward has now been taken along this path."

I am convinced that that is true. Let me try to sum up the results of the Teheran meeting. The first result is that the war will be shortened. The close co-ordination of all our military plans which was reached at the Conference will ensure it. Clearly, we can do better when there is a close interplay at every move, which we have not had until now. The Teheran Conference laid the plans to this end. All is now agreed. Every plan is now agreed, and the timing is now agreed, and, in due course, the decisions of the Teheran Conference will be unrolled on the fields of battle.

Even this is not all, because victory is a means to an end, and the end is a peace that will last. More than once before allies have stood together in war and fallen apart in peace. In the last year or so many hon. Members in all parts of the House must have said to themselves: "Is this going to be our experience once again?" Well, that will certainly be Germany's game. Let the House not doubt that. She will play it with all she knows from the moment the last shot is fired—to sow confusion, to sow doubt and division. That will be Germany's game, and thus to prepare for the next war. This recurrent threat of war can only be met if there is an international order firmer in strength and unity than any enemy that can seek to challenge it. Is there or is there not the possibility of creating such an order? Do the foundations exist?

Six months ago I could not have given any certain answer. It might have been so; it might not have been so. But to-day I can give the answer. It is an emphatic "Yes". The foundations do exist, and I am truly confident that there is a possibility, and more than a possibility, a desire, among the three Powers for continued co-operation not only during the war, not only in reshaping Europe when the Armistice comes, but also, thereafter, in maintaining in the world an orderly progress and continuing peace. The foundations of that understanding were laid by us in Moscow. They have been strengthened and confirmed in Teheran. We three worked together. We have set our hands to the task, and heavy is our responsibility to ensure that we do not fail.

I would like to give two illustrations of the beginning that has been made. When I came back from Moscow a month ago I told the House that we had set up there an Advisory Council for Italy, on which there would be representatives of our country, the United States, Soviet Russia and France. That Committee—that Council —has begun its work. Its members have had a number of meetings. They have been to Italy and surveyed the position there. I had the opportunity when I was away to see the representatives of all four of the countries, and each and all told me that the work was proceeding smoothly and well. That is the first step. And then there is the Advisory Commission for Europe, the Commission agreed on in Moscow, which is to sit here in London. That has now been completed by the nomination by the United States of the American Ambassador in London, Mr. John Winant, a most admirable choice. I understand I am not telling secrets about another body which is to have its first preliminary informal meeting to-morrow. That is the beginning. These two bodies were planned in Moscow, but the scope of their work was greatly increased by the decisions taken at Teheran.

I will now pass to another matter—Turkey. It was decided in Teheran to invite the President of the Turkish Republic to attend a Conference with the representatives of the three Powers—the United States, Soviet Russia and ourselves—in Cairo, on what was our homeward journey. The Turkish President accepted, and he was accompanied by his Foreign Secretary and the Secretary-General of the Turkish Foreign Office. The British, the American and the Soviet Ambassadors in Ankara accompanied him. Unfortunately, Mr. Vyshinsky, who was to have been the Russian representative to join us in that capacity, was away at the front in Italy, and he could not reach us until after the close of the talks, but I was able to see him before I left Cairo, and I gave him a full account of all that had passed, and discussed with him the outcome of our work. These conversations were in the nature of a fuller and more complete development of the earlier meeting which I had had with the Turkish Foreign Secretary in Cairo five weeks ago. I clearly cannot at this stage give details of these confidential discussions—too many people might be listening—but I can say that I have good hopes that they will be found to have established a sound basis for future co-operation between the four countries—ourselves, Soviet Russia, America and Turkey.

Since his return to Ankara, the Turkish Foreign Minister himself has made a statement which the House, perhaps, may not have noticed in which he said that the conversations in Cairo were so intimate and far-reaching that he could now say that Turkey's relations with the United States and the Soviet Union were almost as cordial and as strong as with Great Britain. Those who know the past history of this business will realize what an important statement that is. It augurs well, I think, for the progressive development of future relations between us four, and were it on account of this development alone I should feel justified in telling the House that we regard the Cairo Conference No. 2 as encouraging. Further than that I cannot go to-day.

While we were in Cairo my right hon. Friend the Prime Minister and I were able to discuss the recent crisis in the Lebanon with my right hon. Friend the Member for Stockton (Mr. Harold Macmillan) and with my hon. and gallant Friend the Member for Carlisle (Major-General Sir Edward Spears), who is our Minister at Beirut, as well as with the Minister of State in the Middle East. The House has already been informed of the development and of the conclusion of that crisis, but, if the House will allow me, I want to take this, my first opportunity, to say something about it. Our interest in this matter is twofold. We have sympathy, deep sympathy, with the national aspirations of the Arab world.

We are the only country that has ever concluded a Treaty with and withdrawn from an independent Arab State. Yet at the same time the preservation of order and tranquillity in the Lebanon is an Allied interest, for it closely affects the whole of our war effort in the Middle East. I understand that General Catroux is going back to Beirut on behalf of the French Committee of National Liberation, and he is to conduct negotiations to try and bring about a *modus vivendi* in the Levant States. No happier choice of representative, I think, could have been made by our French friends, and I am sure the House will share the earnest hope, which we have expressed already through diplomatic channels to the authorities concerned, that these negotiations will be conducted in a conciliatory spirit on both sides and that they will lead to early agreement. I am confident that all our allies, all the members of the United Nations, share that view.

It so happened that on my return journey one of the engines of our four-engined aircraft became tired of operating, luckily when we were getting near the aerodrome of Algiers, and so we were landed there and delayed. As a consequence I had opportunities of meeting both M. Massigli and General Catroux himself and of conversations with them about this situation. Here let me say just one word—which I hope the House will endorse—to the people of France. We are at the heart of the fifth winter of this war. The suffering of the French people has been harsh and cruel. She has spent a long ordeal, which perhaps, but for the hazard of geography, the British people might have had to share. We believe that this great people, 40,000,000 strong, enriched by the moral and intellectual qualities that have been theirs throughout history, will find the spirit to lift them up again from the heavy blows which have been dealt them during the last four years. We believe that in the Colonial and French Forces in Tunisia and in Libya, of which I have heard from our own officers who served with them, and in the heroic and ever-increasing resistance movement in France, some of whose representatives I have met within the last few days—we believe that in those people we have the real soul of France. So I say at this time that despite all the difficulties we extend to France our sympathy and our confidence.

What I have said, and said deliberately, applies not only to France but to all those nations now under German occupation. What we are seeking, what we are working for, when we approach these matters in harmony with the United States and Russia is not to impose a three-Power will upon Europe. We are seeking to liberate those countries so that each and all can take their place in the European family again. There could not be anything exclusive in the arrangements between the three Powers. We want to restore the liberty of these nations of Europe, great and small, so that they can play their part in Europe. I am one who believes that Europe has still perhaps the greatest contribution of all to make to the future of mankind.

Having said that, I must come to one or two of our troubles, for it would not be fair to ignore our troubles. There are two countries in the Balkans about which I must say a word or two—Yugoslavia and Greece. It is, perhaps, inevitable that after three years of enemy occupation and guerrilla fighting there is not a little internal confusion and chaos. It must be remembered that German propaganda, day and night, is trying to increase that confusion, trying to spread false reports of our intentions, trying to divide us from our allies and play one off against the other. So I hope I may say to the House that in approaching these matters in public discussion we should use all possible restraint and above all, if I may add it, resist the temptation of fighting our own elections in all these Balkan lands. I laid down some time ago, with the assent of the Cabinet, of course, three rules to try to guide us in this state of affairs, and I will give them to the House. First, to give all the practical help in our power to those elements in these countries which are actively resisting the enemy. Second, to make clear that so far as we can exert any authority it shall be used to ensure that these countries shall be free to choose their own Governments when they are liberated. Third, to work in the closest possible concert with our allies.

Having said so much, may we, on the basis of these rules, look at Yugoslavia? For many months past the head and front of resistance to the enemy in Yugoslavia have been the partisans under their Commander-in-Chief, General Tito. From all the reports which we have received it is clear that these partisans are containing and engaging a large number of German divisions. We are doing all we can to supply them with munitions and to support them in every possible way. Our action in this respect has, of course, been endorsed by our allies.

MR. BELLENGER (Bassetlaw): By whom has it been endorsed?

MR. EDEN: By the Soviet Government and the United States Government several times over, at various conferences. Now if I may I would like to go back a little into past history. I want to show the House the development in this matter. As a result of information which we had we decided as long ago as the spring of this year that we should ask General Tito to receive a British Military Mission. He replied "Yes", and British officers have been with him ever since. Our Mission has been and, as it happens, is under the leadership of a Member of this House, my hon. and gallant Friend, the Member for Lancaster (Brigadier Fitzroy Maclean), who has established most excellent relations with General Tito. As the House will have seen from the newspapers to-day, the Soviet Government have decided also to send a Military Mission to the partisan Commander-in-Chief. I want to make it quite plain where we stand in this. Mr. Molotov was good enough to discuss this project with me, both when I was in Moscow and more recently in Teheran. He said: "You have a Mission with them, and we think of sending a Mission, too." We, of course, endorsed this proposal—the Prime Minister and I—and Mr. Molotov and I agreed that our two Missions shall work together in the closest collaboration when the Soviet Mission reaches the country. That is the position.

Now for another development since I left Teheran. As the House is aware, a Supreme Legislative Committee and an Executive National Committee of Liberation have recently been set up under the auspices of the Commander-in-Chief of the partisan forces. So far as I am aware, this National Committee does not claim authority outside the borders of the area in which it operates. It has certainly not claimed any form of recognition from His Majesty's Government. As I understand the position and as it has been reported to me by our officers, the partisans emphasize the provisional nature of this administration, and they hold that it is for the Yugoslav people, as soon as their country is liberated, freely to choose the form of Government they prefer. If that is the position, this, too, is the view of His Majesty's Government. It is also, as I know, because he has told us so, the desire of King Peter himself and the policy of his Government. [Hon. Members: "Oh."] They have publicly declared it as their policy. We must be fair in all this. A public statement was made by the Government that the moment the war was over they would lay down their portfolios and the country would choose what Government they preferred.

Mr. A. Bevan (Ebbw Vale): Do the radio pronouncements of the Yugoslav Government from Cairo confirm that statement?

Mr. Eden: Certainly, Sir. I am not trying to say that the Government in Cairo agree on all points with the partisans. Clearly that is not so. I am trying to make a fair approach to this very difficult question, and what I am saying is that all, including the Government in Cairo, have declared that the moment their country is liberated they will lay down their offices and it will be for the country to choose its Government. That is a point on which all are agreed—the King, General Tito and the Yugoslav Government. [Interruption.] I feel myself the greatest sympathy for this young king. He came to his responsibilities at a most critical hour in his country's history. He did his best to rally his country to the Allied cause, and he is now faced with the most difficult problems that any young monarch could be faced with. I repeat that we must try to be fair, and, if I may use the word, not too partisan in our actions in the literal and not the military sense of the word. Finally on that subject, let me tell the House this. We are in consultation with other Allied Governments on this policy, and the Prime Minister and I devoted no little time to it while we were in Cairo. We are now at work in conjunction with our allies to bring all those in Yugoslavia or out of it together who want to fight the common German enemy. I hope that the contributions of this House will be made to that end.

One word about Greece. The position there is not on all fours with the position in Yugoslavia. There there are warring bands, all of them in different degrees hostile to the Germans. There are also political controversies which cut right across the matter. It is our aim there to try and unite all these bands, or almost all of them, in common action against the enemy. We have some hope that we may have a measure of success in that. The recently published letter of the King of the Hellenes which he had written last November to his Cabinet, shows clearly that the King is anxious to make his contribution so that his position shall not be a matter of controversy or get in the way of unity. I am not without hope that we may see some progress in the near future, though I do not pretend that the task is particularly easy.

I want to say something about the progress of the fighting in Italy, because it is wrong that we should adjourn for Christmas without the House being informed of the latest information that the Government have. We must admit, first of all, that the advance of the Allied Armies in Italy during the third and fourth months of the campaign has not covered quite the spectacular distances we achieved in the first two months. That, of course, is not due to lack of initiative on the part of our armies. The truth is that we have now reached what is the narrowest part of the Italian Peninsula. The Apennines stretch almost from coast to coast, and where the Apennines stop the swollen rivers take over. That is the position which confronts us. These natural facilities afford exceptional opportunities for skilful defence, and the Germans, as they are forced relentlessly back, are making good use of these advantages. Add to this heavy persistent rains which swell every river and turn every approach into a sea of mud, and we have a fair picture of the background against which the Italian events should be reviewed. On November 8, after a surprise sea-borne attack on Termoli, the Eight Army pressed on and secured a bridgehead over the river Trigno while inland their left flank was moving up through the Apennines. Meanwhile, on the west, General Clark's Anglo-American Fifth Army crossed the Volturno and fought their way to the next river obstacle. By the 8th, by a lightning thrust most characteristic of him, General Montgomery swept the Germans back across the Sangro River. The whole of the rest of his line moved forward at the same time while the Fifth Army kept pace in the Western Apennines. It was then when, as I know, our commanders felt the campaign to be developing as they wished, that we had another deluge and steadily worsening weather conditions which called a halt along the whole group of armies. That time was spent building up stocks, preparing rivers and roads and getting ready for the next offensive, General Montgomery waiting for a spell of fine weather.

At last it came and on the night of November 27 the Eighth Army, further strengthened by the arrival of the Second New Zealand Division, that most gallant veteran division, was able to launch its main assault. It was preceded, as has become almost the custom now, by a familiar and shattering bombardment and the full support of the Royal Air Force. The 78th and the 8th Indian Divisions advanced and secured Fossa Cesia Ridge. Down came the rain again and still our troops fought grimly on, as they are doing now to the line of the Moro and beyond. Far on the left Canadians have now relieved the 78th Division and they are pressing on towards Ortona. Inland the New Zealand Division is trying to gain the high ground which will help the Canadians further in their advance. Meanwhile, on the west the Anglo-American Fifth Army began the battle for the Mignano Gap. There was a struggle to secure this mountain feature and the enemy had plenty of time to prepare formidable defences. But thanks to the gallantry of the Allied infantry all the more important of the hill features are now in our hands and it seems that the Germans may be forced to withdraw further. It would be unjust to make these references to the fighting in Italy without paying tribute to the Royal Engineers and the administrative services. Theirs has been an immense task to keep communications open and to reconstruct them where they are destroyed, and yet throughout this fighting the Army has never lacked for a moment a shell or food or supplies of any kind. It is my duty to give the House the casualties from the moment of the landing on the mainland to November 23. The British casualties were 3,212 killed, 9,709 wounded and 3,153 missing. Total 16,074. The American casualties were to November 25: 1,603 killed, 6,361 wounded, 2,685 missing. Total 10,649. Up to the most recent counting the German prisoners taken by the Allies total just over 6,000.

Let me sum up my impressions of these three weeks. My right hon. Friend and I were greatly encouraged by the outcome of our three conferences. So I believe were all our Allied colleagues. To that extent I bring the House a message of good cheer. These events, of course, give no cause for easy optimism—far from it. If I were to do that I would give my message falsely. The truth, on the contrary, is that the very magnitude of the plans to which we have set our hands, to which the heads of other Governments have given their approval, will call for an immense effort in the coming months from each and all of the United Nations. Plans, however good, can only yield results if the force of the citizens in all the lands is behind them. We have set ourselves a hard task in our determination to achieve victory at the earliest possible date. Great battles are impending. For this effort we shall need all our strength, all our courage, all our unity in greater measure perhaps than ever before. I ask this House to give the pledge that for our part that effort will be forthcoming.

1944

31

MORAL PRINCIPLES AND FOREIGN
AFFAIRS

JANUARY–MARCH 1944

During the winter the Red Army continued to advance victoriously. In the first week of the New Year the Polish frontier was crossed and farther south the end of March saw Bessarabia in Russian hands and the Army on the Roumanian border.

In Italy the Fifth and Eighth Armies were held on the Gustav Line, and the Anzio bridgehead, though it resisted fierce German counter-attacks, was unable to make headway.

In the Far East successful land, sea and air operations brought Australian progress in New Guinea, cut off 80,000 Japanese in New Britain and led to the American capture of the Marshall Islands. On the Burma front the Japanese were being held.

At home it was a time of "preparation, effort and resolve". Ever-increasing raids on Berlin and other parts of Germany and occupied Europe prepared the way for the Second Front. On March 26, Mr. Churchill in a broadcast said: "The hour of our greatest effort is approaching."

On March 28, Mr. Eden addressed the Free Church Federal Council.

For four years the greater part of Europe has lain under German rule. Nations have suffered, have writhed, have rebelled and been repressed with Nazi tyranny and ferocity. Small powers whose territories gave valuable strategic or industrial prizes were the earliest victims, Austria and Czechoslovakia were

242

among these. Pretexts were found or invented and the German armies marched in. Poland by her refusal to yield first challenged this paralysing process. But we and France could not bring her effective help and the German armies marched on. France herself fell and still the dirty brown patch of Nazi tyranny spread wider until from Norway to Greece, from Brittany to the shores of the Black Sea no land save only Switzerland was free.

But in these last weeks there has been a new development. The process is being carried still further. Germany's satellites have now to suffer with her other victims. Hitherto these wretched countries have been called upon to make a heavy contribution in life on every German front, but they have been left at least the semblance of control of their own affairs. And now all this too has been swept away. No shred of self-respect is left to these miserable henchmen of Nazi power. And so all occupied Europe is to-day in torment and in ferment under the thinning crust of German domination.

Many of these invaded countries have suffered to an extent and with an intensity of pain it is difficult for us to picture. These tragedies will leave their mark, scars cannot be healed all at once even when the day of liberation dawns. The problems that beset south-eastern Europe to-day are a forewarning of those that will confront us in many forms in many lands. After the last war the problems of European reconstruction were immensely formidable. But this time the suffering has struck much deeper, the confusion is more widespread, and so the work of healing will require more time and patience. There will be many mistakes; all cannot run smooth. Courage, perseverance, infinite patience will be needed. Above all, an understanding that we cannot at all times and in all places, wholly impose our judgment upon others.

None the less it must be our task to do everything in our power to help these countries of Europe who have endured so much, to liberty and independence, to help them by encouragement and example and by every means in our power to build for themselves a new life from the wreckage of the old. We must be clear about one factor. We must not expect the clock to start to strike again at the hour at which it left off when German invasion fell upon Europe. Many of these countries have been in the grip of the enemy for three years or more. They will not revert to the old life, we must help them to find the new.

In such conditions it is right that we should consider from time to time our own underlying purpose as a nation and how we propose to give it effect. It is certainly true that unless we set certain moral principles for our guide we shall be lost. One can only navigate a ship by some fixed guide, a compass or, more roughly, the Pole Star. But the very act of navigation, down to the hands of the man at the wheel, is a constant correction of drift. A ship, at any given moment, is hardly ever dead on her course; it is only by a multitude of approximations that she makes her landfall and is saved from disaster. But these approximations would only make confusion worse confounded unless they were designed to hold and keep one right line. To apply this conception to the present situation I would say that the British people are convinced that they are fighting not only for their own liberties and the freedom of their own land but for the good of the world as a whole. This is their landfall, and they are as determined to make it to-day as they were in the darkest hours of 1940. It is very easy, I know, to be cynical about the moral principles which the greater part of our countrymen regard as being involved in the present struggle. It may be argued by some that they do not enter into it at all and that we are simply engaged in a struggle for existence and nothing else. It is indeed a struggle for existence in which we are engaged. If Hitler had overwhelmed this island our national life and all those liberties which our ancestors have won over the centuries would have been utterly destroyed. But we should not have been the only ones to suffer. The victory which preserves our own independence will do the same for that of many other nations. It is not a reproach to us that we are fighting this tyranny on our own behalf when we are playing our part in saving others from it.

The philosophy of the naked struggle for existence—*der Kampf ums Dasein*—is the declared philosophy of Hitler. In *Mein Kampf* he has made it clear that as between nation and nation there are no obligations and that the law of the jungle is the only one that can prevail. This is also the view of Spengler, who went so far as to declare that "man is a beast of prey". Here is a conception which I feel that everyone in this island would instantly repudiate, but it is nevertheless a conception which has had a profound influence on German philosophy and on the German way of life. It is a conception which must be utterly rooted out if the world is to enjoy peace.

But if we say that we reject such a philosophy what is our positive creed which in international affairs shall guide us in the maze of day-to-day affairs? I suggest that it can only be the total antithesis to the Hitler philosophy; a conviction that nations are interdependent and that there will only be enduring peace if they strive to keep faith with one another. This means, then, that our policies must be sustained by a moral purpose. I agree with the words of J. Quincy Adams, one of the most sagacious of American statesmen: "The more of pure moral principle that is carried into the policy of a Government, the wiser and more profound will that policy be." That, I feel sure, is also your conviction. There, also, you, the Churches, have your indispensable part to play, to marshal those moral and spiritual resources of which Christian humanity has accumulated through the centuries a store now maybe hidden, but certainly not buried, beneath the weight of war and the suffering it brings.

Just as this moral principle lies at the root of the social structure within any nation, so must it lie at the root of any workable and endurable international system. It is quite true that in the past efforts to apply it have only been partially successful, though they have occasionally succeeded for quite long periods. But this does not mean that such attempts will always fail, and even if they did fail it would still be necessary to pursue the ideal of interdependence, for only thus can we escape from perpetual war and from one nation preying as a wolf upon another. We tried to set out this conception in the documents which we agreed at the Moscow Conference and in the communiqué issued after the meetings at Teheran. These statements recognize that after this war nations great and small will continue to exist and lead their individual lives. In other words they accept that the world community will be composed of a number of independent States. They do not contemplate that there will be any kind of super State. But we must realize that in the world in which we live, the independence of States can only be secured through international co-operation; that the independence of States means, in effect, the interdependence of States.

We shall see in the future, as the Moscow declaration forecasts, a large number of States enjoying "Sovereign equality" varying from huge entities such as the Soviet Union, the United States and the British Commonwealth of Nations to very small communities such as Luxembourg. This being so we have to find a way by which all these separate units, each with its own history and aspirations, can work together for a purpose so indispensable to them all. These purposes may be described as peace, freedom and welfare. I put peace first because we know only too well that we cannot have the other two without it. But peace itself would be a sterile thing if it were not accompanied by the right of free expression and development, and for that purpose we need an increase in human welfare so that men may have the time and opportunity for something else than the mere struggle for existence. How should we do it? Not, as I have said, by imposing the will of one nation or group of nations on all the rest but by those processes of ordered discussion inside the framework of freely accepted institutions by which alone permanent advance can be won. This is the work upon which we are now engaged. All peace-loving States have both the right and the duty to share in it and we must find a place for them all, great and small, in whatever institutions we set up. Every State must have the right to make its voice heard in the discussion of the means by which we arrive at our common ends, if only because each has also a duty to contribute, so far as its power extends, towards the ends which we all seek.

When we speak of "peace-loving" States in Article 4 of the Moscow Declaration we do not mean by this definition merely to refrain from using physical force against others. We mean something more positive than that. We mean a readiness to contribute something towards the security and welfare of other States even at the cost of some sacrifice of immediate national interest.

But let us admit that though all States are equal in status they are not equal in power and consequently their duties must vary. The responsibility for the preservation of peace must fall in the first instance on the Four Powers who signed the Moscow Declaration, and I hope also on France when, as we all trust without long delay, she resumes her place amongst the great Powers. They must be able to confer together regularly on the major problems of the world and to give a decisive lead when action is necessary. They must of course associate other Powers with them in their task.

But we must recognize that those who bear the greatest responsibility, those on whose shoulders the burden will fall, must have the greater voice in deciding on any action to be taken in the general interest. All independent States must be free to declare their opinions and their grievances. And all may profit by that. But when it comes to deciding on action which only certain States, by their military power, are in a position effectively to take, we cannot simply count heads. The Great Powers have, and must have, special responsibilities in the field of security. This does not mean that there will be a dictatorship of the Great Powers. Every free nation will have its own responsibility for peace, and its own contribution to make to it. But agreement among the Great Powers must be the foundation; for we have seen what happens when the

Great Powers fall out among themselves. The immediate result is that the smaller States are overwhelmed. The next result is war. The first problem, therefore, is to secure and maintain the co-operation of the Great Powers. This can only be done if we have some common purpose, some common set of principles.

It was these that we sought to set out in our conference at Moscow. But even when principles are agreed the task is far from complete. Their application presents continuing problems. Consultation between the three Great Powers is daily and continuous to-day over the whole field of our relations. But for dealing with certain problems it is useful to have special machinery to help us in our task. This is taking shape; progress is being made. For the first time here in London in the European Advisory Commission, Representatives of the three Great Powers, the United States of America, the Union of Soviet Socialist Republics and ourselves, have started work upon the solution of some of the more immediate problems we shall have to confront together. Useful and indeed essential work is being done on these, the fruits of which will become apparent in due course.

I have been speaking to you of peace as a matter of political and military security. But peace is something more than that. Peace is a matter, too, of economic and social well-being. And here, too, the United Nations are working out a practical policy. The success of the Food Conference at Hot Springs, the signing of the U.N.R.R.A. Agreement and the many resolutions passed by the Atlantic City Relief Conference show not only that the Great Powers are prepared to give a lead, but also that all Powers, great and small, are willing and anxious to play their part in a world system. It is difficult enough for a few powers to reach agreement. How much greater is the difficulty in achieving positive results when forty or more United Nations meet round the table. That they have achieved such results is the remarkable feature of these economic conferences. Moreover, the organizations which they have brought into being show that there is room for every State to find its proper place as a part of the international machine and so contribute to its effective running. These achievements form only the beginning of what we hope to do by the same methods, but they give good ground for hope in the future. Certain it is that if the world is to undertake successfully the great task of ensuring an expanding economy there must be much more co-operation in economic questions than there has been in the past.

But institutions alone, however cleverly constructed, cannot ensure success and so I return to the thought with which I began, that this great effort to obtain a more ordered and prosperous world community cannot succeed unless it is sustained by a moral purpose. Here I am sure that the deep ambition of the mass of humanity is on our side and that you here in this Conference will help us. We need your prayers, your aid, your understanding. The task is arduous, the end is not in sight, but with faith we can win through.

32

FOREIGN AFFAIRS AND THE EMPIRE

By mid-May the Red Army had recaptured Odessa, had cleared the Crimea and advanced into Roumania.

Allied Bombers based in Italy bombed military objectives in Roumania.

In Italy the Fifth and Eighth Armies began a combined offensive on May 12, and by May 24 had broken the Gustav and Hitler Lines.

In Burma the Japanese were held at Kohima and Imphal and on April 24 the Kohima garrison was relieved.

Spain agreed to the restriction of wolfram supplies to Germany.

British aid to Mihailovitch ceased, and the Royal Yugoslav Government severed relations with him.

On April 17 the privileges of Ambassadors and Envoys in the U.K. were restricted.

On May 1 the first war-time conference of Empire Prime Ministers opened in London. Full agreement on strategy and foreign policy was announced on May 17.

On May 24 a two-day Debate in the House of Commons on Foreign Affairs was begun by the Prime Minister who said of the Empire Prime Ministers' Conference:

"Nothing was more remarkable than the complete agreement which was expressed by every one of the Dominion Prime Ministers on the general conduct of our Foreign Affairs and on the principles which govern that conduct, and, I should add, on the skill and consistency with which they had been treated by my right Hon. Friend, the Foreign Secretary."

Mr. Eden wound up the Debate on May 25. (The House was in Committee of Supply.)

249

FOREIGN AFFAIRS AND THE EMPIRE

The hon. Member for Maldon (Mr. Driberg) has asked me a question, to which I should like to reply at once, in respect to what the Prime Minister said about Rome yesterday. I thought it that was clear to the Committee at the time that what my right hon. Friend meant was peculiarly closely allied to what he said. It was that we hoped the city of Rome would be spared the destruction of its monuments or any other destruction, but he did not indicate any new approach in the sense of any new instruction to our military authorities.

I hope that the Committee feels that it has had two days of pretty good Debate. I have certainly had the impression that the discussion has ranged far and wide and that hon. Members have taken the opportunity, not merely of following my right hon. Friend the Prime Minister in his very conclusive review of our relations with various countries, but of going outside that and, as I think they should, of putting their own suggestions and ideas forward so that the Government may study them in their policy. At the conclusion of this Debate I would like to try to reply to the points that have been raised, and try, too, to carry matters perhaps a little further, as some of my hon. Friends have asked me to do, in one or two directions.

As I listened to this two-day Debate, I had the impression that there was a growing note of confidence about ourselves in the speeches. No doubt there are reasons for that outside these walls. Military events at the moment and the good news from our armies would account for it. But I thought there was more to it than that. I think that there was also the increased sense of unity which the meeting of the Prime Ministers of the Empire has given us. I felt an echo when the hon. Gentleman the Member for Seaham (Mr. Shinwell) said that international unity was difficult to achieve. I could not agree with him more whole-heartedly. I happened to be reading in a history the other day about one of my illustrious predecessors who had one period of office of about eighteen months. The history just noted the term of office of Lord —— by saying: "No event of any international significance occurred." I thought that that was a time when I would have liked to be Secretary of State for Foreign Affairs. We live in very different times.

I would like at the beginning of my remarks to say something about the meeting of Empire Prime Ministers. Many comments have been made in this Debate about that meeting, and I think it is right to say that it was probably at once the most successful

and the most significant meeting of that kind which has ever been
held. Both the men and the moment served to bring that about.
Here were gathered together five statesmen of widely different
character and experience, but all united with the one purpose of
trying to maintain and strengthen this Empire and Commonwealth and to ensure that the world should have the benefit of the
service we could render it together. Of course, that is the note, as I
conceive it, of the British Commonwealth and Empire. We are not
an exclusive organization, but we do think—and I make no apology
for saying this—that we are the one really successful experiment in
international co-operation that there has ever been. Out of that,
we may suggest with becoming modesty to others, there may be
something to be learnt.

As I attended these proceedings, I detected more than once what
a strange, indefinable and, if you like, what an illogical thing, this
British Empire is. Sometimes the links that hold it together seem
so frail as to be almost non-existent, or so frail that they would
snap at the first pressure. That is a mistake which foreigners often
make. It is a mistake that Ribbentrop made, though God knows
I and others tried hard enough to make him believe it was wrong.
This demonstration of the reality of the strength of that relationship comes at a moment when it may be of real service to the
world. Anyhow, it has so happened that, in two world struggles in
one generation, the British Commonwealth has shown itself to
have a unity which nothing can break. In the second of these
struggles it stood alone for a year or more.

How difficult it is to try to explain what brings these men together from these many corners of the world, and leads them to
feel such deep loyalty towards the British Empire. I cannot pretend to describe it, but perhaps, like all really deep forces that move
mankind, there is an element of mystery in it that cannot be put
into words. I believe that to be true. Of this meeting I must say
that it owed its special character more than anything else to the
leadership given to it by our own Prime Minister. Sometimes, here
within this island, with our vast controversies and frequent
Debates, it is difficult to stand back and view matters as they are
seen in perspective by other lands and other peoples. Certain it is,
that the immense advantage of my right hon. Friend's position in
the world was of quite invaluable aid in leadership in those discussions.

There is another advantage. In the stress of war—and there is
still a stress of war—nothing is more difficult than to avoid becoming

immersed in the daily details of one's particular task, be it on foreign affairs, economic affairs, the Treasury or whatever it is, and the burden is such that when you have a moment in which you are not occupied with your own affairs, the Cabinet is discussing somebody else's affairs that are just a degree more tiresome than your own. When one is living like that, it is invaluable to be able to look at the problems which we have to face in company with a man like the Prime Minister. It is then that his experience is more valuable still. I can only say for myself that the experience was one that gave the greatest encouragement.

There was, it seemed to me, a feature of our meetings this time which I had not perceived before. I was privileged to attend the Imperial Conference of 1937. Since then we have developed to a very large extent the practice of sending the greatest possible amount of information to the Governments of all the Dominions; so that to-day, it is not merely a question of consulting them from time to time and asking their advice on some particular problem that arises, but it is the practice to give them fully all the information that we have on the day-to-day developments of foreign policy. The growth of that practice was immeasurably helpful at these meetings, because the whole background of knowledge was present to an equal extent in the minds of all the men round the table. It may be that there is more we can do in that regard. If there is, we will gladly do it, for I am confident that this exchange of information is an indispensable element in true co-operation between the Dominions and ourselves. If, as a result of that, we get from time to time, when we give information about foreign affairs or whatever it may be, replies, questions, even criticism, we welcome them, because they are all elements of strength to the British Commonwealth.

Having made those remarks on that aspect of our work, I want to plunge into the details of some of the matters which were discussed. More than one hon. Member in the Debate, talking about foreign affairs, has said that in war-time, of course, foreign policy must take second place to the immediate military needs, and that is true. In war-time the Foreign Office has two duties: to help the military arm and, as part of that help, to maintain, as far as lies in our power, unity among those who are fighting the common enemy. Also, so far as we can during war-time, it is to lay the foundations for co-operation afterwards. Those are the tasks on which we are engaged now. In war-time it sometimes happens that military needs may even conflict with political needs. I will put it another way—you may have to take decisions for a short-term advantage which, in the light of long-term policy, you would prefer not to take—that does sometimes happen; but there is one aspect of the work we have done to which I would draw the attention of the Committee.

Despite all those difficulties, and I may say temptations, in this respect in war-time, we have not on any occasion in these four years of conflict, entered into any secret engagement of any kind with anybody. I want the Committee to understand the importance of that. Hon. Members, like the hon. Member for West Leicester (Mr. H. Nicolson) who were present when the Treaty of Versailles was negotiated, will remember what embarrassment was caused when secret treaties were pulled out of pockets and engagements, often conflicting engagements, were all put on the table together. There is nothing of that kind on our part this time. To that extent, we shall have an advantage.

I have said that one of our tasks is to try to help the Armed Forces. I will give briefly some examples of what I mean by that; for example, the negotiations with Portugal about the Azores, the negotiations with Spain over wolfram, the handling of our affairs with Turkey which led to the stoppage of chrome. I had, as one or two hon. Members have remarked in this Debate, the task of lending help to our allies, among others, in trying to smooth out differences which arise, even between allies. Those are our tasks.

Here let me say one word about the neutral Powers. My hon. Friend the Member for West Leicester was, I think, rather hard on us about the neutrals. He was inclined to criticize us for our treatment of them. I know they may sometimes regard our methods as harsh and arbitrary, and think that we take too little account of the rights of small nations. If they do, I can say truly we regret it.

I can also say that we have asked no nation to take any step which violates its neutrality and we have asked no neutral who is also an ally—of whom there are some—to take any step beyond that which is specifically within our rights according to the terms of our alliance, and we must insist to the limit on what are our rights. It is our duty to do everything in our power to shorten this struggle. And therefore, to the neutrals themselves I say, if sometimes we have seemed outspoken and urgent in our demands, I regret it, but it is a fact that such action as we ask them to take is in their own interests, as anyone in this hour can see, if only it shortens the conflict, which they, as much as we, wish to see brought to an end.

FOREIGN AFFAIRS AND THE EMPIRE

I must say that my sympathies and thoughts are more at the present time with the occupied countries. I felt that the Members of the Committee were many times right when they recalled the staunch allies whom we have in Europe to-day. I think that at a time like this the Committee would like to send a message to those occupied countries—the smaller occupied countries of Europe—a message of encouragement and hope that their liberation may not be long delayed. [HON. MEMBERS: "Hear, hear."] I would like to speak of one or two of these countries. We had a remarkable speech just now—there were not quite so many Members present— from my hon. and gallant Friend the Member for Blackpool (Wing-Commander Robinson), just back from first hand experience in the Balkans and the Mediterranean. He told us of his experiences in a Greek ship, and how its sailors had twenty-four or twenty-five times taken that ship back into the Anzio beachhead. We are greatly encouraged at the political unity which the Greek nation has, at last, achieved. We can neither forget the past of that country, nor its own amazing achievements in this conflict at an earlier stage. After all, the Greeks were the first to debunk Mussolini. It was not we who did that. They defeated him and repelled him from their land, and we of this Committee would like to tell the Greek people that we hope that they are now united, and that they will be able to work together and re-establish their reputation in the world.

The hon. Gentleman the hon. Member for Romford (Mr. Parker) was a little critical of our Ambassador to the Greek Government. I think he said he had an anti-Bolshevik bogy. Quite honestly, I do not quite know what that means, or its particular relevance to the present situation, because people have different definitions of Bolshevism and bogies almost every week. However that may be, I can tell him that our Ambassador has, in fact, rendered the most loyal service in all this struggle. I happen to have known him for many years. Whether he has been right or wrong—[An HON. MEMBER "Who is he?"] He is Mr. Leeper.

MR. WOODBURN (Stirling and Clackmannan, Eastern): That is not the Ambassador to whom my hon. Friend referred.

MR. EDEN: Whether he has done right or wrong, everything he has done has been on instructions from His Majesty's Government here in London. [*Interruption.*]

I wish to mention one or two other of these countries—Yugoslavia, Poland and Czechoslovakia. The suffering of all these countries has been great, and the prayer for liberation is there. In particular, I want to say a word about the north-western countries, if I may so call them, which have been referred to in one or two speeches—Belgium, Norway and the Netherlands. Within the last few days we have signed agreements with the Governments of all three of them. The hon. Member for Kidderminster (Sir J. Wardlaw-Milne) asked whether we could perhaps make them public. We considered that in conjunction with our allies who have signed similar agreements, and we have found a difficulty in it because the agreements are not only political; they also contain military clauses affecting action which must be taken if and when these countries are liberated.

MR. SHINWELL: No secret agreement?

MR. EDEN: No, it is quite proper. A secret agreement disposing of somebody else's belongings would be most improper, but if it is a secret agreement arranging how by military means you are going to free a country I think that is not very shocking. That is what they are. I can tell the hon. Member, to relieve him from any strain of anxiety, that so far as the political clauses are concerned, what they are designed to do is to give the Governments of those countries the full control of their own affairs at the earliest possible moment.

Now I come to a country which has been mentioned several times in this discussion—France. There is no part of our policy to which we attach more importance than the restoration of the independence and greatness of France. France is our nearest neighbour, for more than 1,000 years our histories have been interlocked, sometimes in conflict. Sometimes the French got help from our northern neighbours, if I may speak as an Englishman for just one moment. But I think that as inhabitants of this island we would acknowledge that no country has contributed more to the civilization of Europe in the best sense of that term. For the future we know that the French people will have their part to play in Europe, and we shall need them, as they will need us, if confidence and security are to live again in Europe. In the meanwhile, I would like, on behalf of the Government, and I hope of the Committee, to pay tribute to the spirit of resistance which the French people are showing—[HON. MEMBERS: "Hear, hear."]—showing all the more despite the necessary bombardments which we are unhappily compelled to inflict upon them. I agree with what was said by the hon. Member for Bridgwater (Mr. Bartlett) yesterday. He said we must hand over the full responsibility for the government of France to the French people as soon as is possible. I agree; there is no difference about that. There is not the least intention in our minds to inflict an A.M.G.O.T., as it is called, upon France, or indeed upon any Allied country whatever, though incidentally it is not in the least the kind of machine which the hon. Baronet the Member for Barnstaple (Sir R. Acland) so eloquently imagined yesterday. But be A.M.G.O.T. good or ill, it has no connection with France or any Allied country when they are liberated.

In the light of these observations, I come to the special problem of recognition, and I would like to try to put it in its true perspective. I regret that there is some misunderstanding as to the extent of recognition already accorded to the French Committee of National Liberation. For instance, the hon. Gentleman the Member for Maldon asked why we did not recognize the Committee, as though there was no recognition at all. Of course, that is not the position at present. We welcomed the unity of the Committee last year at Algiers. We were happy to recognize them last August as the body qualified to conduct the French effort in the war. We have gone much further than that since. We have dealt with the Committee as if they were the legitimate Government of all French overseas territories. We have made agreements with them— financial agreements, economic agreements—on that basis. Our representative in Algiers has been given the rank of Ambassador, and the French representative here, Monsieur Viénot, who is doing such good work, has been given a similar rank. More than that, we have dealt with the French Committee not only as if they were the Government in the territory where their writ runs already, but we are also dealing with them in matters which concern the Metropolitan territory of France, and as the French authority which will exercise leadership in France as her liberation proceeds.

Now I come to where I think the difficulty lies. In connection with these discussions certain conversations have been necessary, and these conversations, and the progress of them, have unhappily been interfered with by the restrictions which we felt compelled to institute over a wide area as a security measure on account of forthcoming operations. I say, frankly, that those restrictions are extremely troublesome to the conduct of foreign affairs, not in respect of one country alone. I would like to say at this Box how grateful the Government are for the spirit in which the Diplomatic Corps as a whole have taken these quite unprecedented measures. But the House will understand, as I am sure our French friends will understand, that, vexatious as these restrictions are, the needs of absolute military security must come first.

FOREIGN AFFAIRS AND THE EMPIRE

That being so, we think that the best way to deal with the question of civil administration in France is to have direct conversations. It is for this purpose that the Prime Minister has invited General de Gaulle to come here and General de Gaulle has accepted. He will receive, I know, a warm welcome from all of us here. I feel confident that nothing but good will come out of that meeting, and that, when the whole situation can be surveyed, we shall be able to clear away all misunderstandings, however formidable they may seem now. At least, that is what we wish to do.

I will turn for a moment to another matter, to which I want to refer because of one or two speeches which were made, about our attitude to Europe. I do not know whether hon. Members happened to see a two-column article, which appeared in *The Times* on May 13, containing an analysis of German propaganda. If not, I commend it as quite good reading. That analysis showed that German propaganda had just two themes. One was that the Empire was breaking up. That is not working awfully well just now. The other was that we were disinteresting ourselves in certain parts of Europe: in other words, that, at some place or other, never specified—it may be Moscow, it may be Teheran—we had done a deal, it may be with the Soviet Government or it may be with somebody else, by which we would cease to interest ourselves in certain parts of Europe. That is absolutely and categorically untrue. I would like to go further. In the first place, no arrangement of such a kind has been come to. In the second place, no arrangement of such a kind was suggested to us. In the third place, if anybody had suggested such an arrangement to us, we would not have agreed to it. Otherwise, the report is approximately accurate.

It is, of course, true that there are certain parts of Europe— Western Europe and the Mediterranean—where our interests are more directly concerned than others. But, as the right hon. Gentleman the Member for Devonport (Mr. Hore-Belisha) emphasized in his speech, we are, above all, Europeans, and our interest in Europe is not limited to any single part of Europe. What we seek is the security of a continent which has suffered so much, but which has given so much light and leading to the world in the past, and could do it again, if only it could recover its unity and prosperity. I am confident that the Governments of the Dominions perfectly well understand our position in this respect, and that they endorse it. No great country should attempt to do more in its foreign policy than its strength will allow. But, having said that, I think I can

R   257

add that, as a result of this meeting, and as a result of the events in the war, the British Commonwealth's authority and influence in the world is at least as high as it has ever been; and that influence we should use, can use, and will use, to promote the prosperity and unity of Europe.

What do we want to achieve in our foreign policy? I would put it like this. We want, in our relations with other countries, to try to maintain a standard of honesty, of fair dealing, and of international good faith. Foreign affairs are really not so very different in those respects from domestic affairs. Human intercourse is based on good faith, on the keeping of promises, on honouring the pledged word between man and man. I agree so much with what my noble Friend the Member for Lanark (Lord Dunglass) said yesterday—we are very glad, all of us, to welcome him back—about the consequences of a lowering of international standards. I remember myself venturing to make, some years ago, a speech in this House, in which I said that I thought that we were in the presence of the progressive deterioration of international standards. I say, frankly, that I think that that process was one of the main contributory causes of the outbreak of this war. Why did the war become inevitable? It was because Hitler and Mussolini refused to observe the ordinary standards of international conduct in the day-to-day conduct of international affairs. It was more than that, because they used the desire of other nations to maintain those standards to obtain concessions, to profit by those concessions, and then to proceed to their next demand. They were encouraged by the desire of the peace-loving countries to avoid war if ever they could.

I remember an occasion, in a conversation with Hitler—I think it was 1933, or thereabouts—when he spoke to me of the Versailles Treaty, and he explained how that Treaty had been imposed upon Germany, and how, therefore, he could never accept it. I said: "What about the Treaty of Locarno?" He said: "That is another thing. That was a freely negotiated Treaty. Germany signed that of her own free will. By that I stand"—or words to that effect. He said it with a fervour and an eloquence which, I confess, entirely convinced me. I came back thinking: "That is not such an unreasonable attitude," and so forth. Eighteen months after that, Locarno had gone the same way as the Treaty of Versailles. That was the method, that was the technique, of those men. If those methods and those techniques are practised, whoever practises them there cannot be an enduring peace. So I say to the Committee: We cannot say to the world "You have got to do this; you

have got to do that." That is beyond the power of 45,000,000. But
what we can do is, in our own conduct, and by our own leadership,
to try to establish and maintain those standards of international
conduct without which there cannot be peace. That I conceive to
be the duty of British foreign policy.

May I, for a moment or two, look a little into the future? When
the victory is won, the first task will be close collaboration between
the British Commonwealth, the United States, the Soviet Union
and China—but in the main, so far as Europe is concerned, between the first three—to ensure that Germany cannot start this
business again. I want to speak for a moment about co-operation
between the three in particular—ourselves, the United States and
the Soviet Union. If I emphasize it, it is because I am convinced
that, if we can establish real understanding, all else, though difficult, will be possible. But, if we cannot establish that understanding, then the future is very dark indeed. Having said that, I am
not suggesting that these three Powers should seek to impose some
three-Power dictatorship on the world. That would be bad, very
bad. But what they should do is to serve the world in assuring, at
least, from the outset, that these two particular aggressors, with
whom we are now dealing, are not in a military position to repeat
in a few years' time what they did before. I hope I shall carry the
Committee with me in that. There is nothing exclusive in our
desire to work together. It is indispensable that we should so work
together. May I mention a suggestion about co-operation in Western
Europe? I think it may be desirable that we should have close,
intimate and friendly relations with other countries in Western
Europe, but neither my hon. Friend nor anyone else would suggest
that on such a foundation alone lasting security could be found.
We have to stretch wider than that.

I would like to say a word about our relations with these two
Powers. My right hon. and gallant Friend the Member for Kel-
vingrove (Lieut.-Colonel Elliot) spoke about our relative size—
our 45 millions and these two countries, one with 140 millions and
the other with 200 millions. That is true, but, on the other hand, I
must tell the Committee that, though I have been in many negotiations with these two Powers alone, I have never felt any sense
of inferiority, and I honestly do not believe that they felt any particular sense of superiority. I do not mean individually towards me,
but towards this country. The reason is, of course, that, though we
are only 45 millions, we have in this island a unique geographical
position and a rather remarkable experience, and because we are

17 *   259

the centre of a great Empire. I would suggest that we need not overstress the size of our partners or underestimate our own signifi-cance. At any rate, of all our international troubles, that is the one that worries me least.

About the United States, I think I can say, that, at this time, our relations are as close and cordial as they have ever been. We had the other day the experience of a visit from Mr. Stettinius, the Under Secretary of State, who, I think, spoke to hon. Members upstairs. That visit was remarkable, not only because of his own personality, but because he brought with him a large number of representatives of the State Department, and they worked together with our own representatives in the Foreign Office, with the result that, apart from the understanding at the higher level, there is now interlocked, at every stage, an understanding by each of the other's policy. That is something quite new in our experience with the United States, or, indeed, with any country, and I think it will be of great service, because, although decisions must be taken by Ministers, it is good that all those down the hierarchy should under-stand each other's point of view. Recently, we have had, both from the President and Mr. Hull, statements that show that American leaders are thinking on broad, courageous and good neighbourly lines.

Now I turn to our relations with the other great Power—our ally Russia. There is, in our minds, no reservation when we say that we wish to work with the Soviet Union in the fullest and closest col-laboration, but it is also in the interests of our two countries that we should accept that there are certain difficulties in this task, and I agree with the right hon. Gentleman the Member for Wakefield (Mr. A. Greenwood) that we do not gain much by ignoring them. There is, first, the legacy of suspicion, difficult to describe and quite impossible to exaggerate. It is a suspicion which is not, as many think, of modern growth, but which dates back to, and existed in, the days of Tsarist Russia, and will be found many times in the records of the Congress of Vienna. Unhappily, it has always played its part in Anglo-Russian relations, and it has a habit of accumulating suspicions on their side which produce counter-suspicions on ours, and, before we know where we are, a mountain of suspicion is the result. For that, there is only one cure—that, bit by bit, our peoples get to know each other better. We are ready, I say to our Soviet friends, to do anything in our power at any time to further that result.

There are other things—differences in form of Government,

differences in the attitude to the individual, to the Press, and so on. These are all pretty wide divergencies and I repeat, that we do better to face them frankly, but, on the other side, there is something else to put in the scale. There is the fact that, in the three great world convulsions, in the Napoleonic war, in the last great war, and in this war, we have found ourselves allied and fighting together for the same purpose—to stop one man or one Power dominating the whole of Europe. On each of the last occasions when we fought together, we fell aside quickly soon after, but this time we have got to do better. We have an absolute conviction here in this country that the Soviet Union means to see this struggle through to the end. We have the same intention.

I have been asked about the extent of our collaboration now. For instance, are we consulted on such matters as the Soviet peace terms to Roumania and the negotiations with Finland? The answer is that we were consulted on both questions. In respect of Roumania, we thought M. Molotov's speech, and the offer made, fair and just to Roumania. In respect of Finland, we deplored the fact that the Finnish Government had turned down the peace terms. On both these matters, we were consulted. I do not want to belittle the extent of the effort which has got to be made in both these countries to make of this twenty-year treaty a lasting reality of value to our two countries and to the world, but, surely, the Committee will feel that the stakes for the future in this matter are so huge that both of us must make every effort that we may succeed. Personally, I believe we shall succeed.

I have been asked several questions about the situation in the Far East, particularly by the hon. Member for Kidderminster, the hon. and gallant Member for Renfrew (Major Lloyd) and many others. I think we are all conscious of the heavy burdens that China carries just now. We in this country are in the fifth year of the war, and, looking back on it, it seems a pretty long period. China is, however you reckon it, at least in the eighth year of the war. Her people have suffered greatly, and many of her cities have been destroyed. We have been unable to carry to her all the help we would like to carry, and it is only by the remarkable efforts of the Air Force—quite unique efforts—in crossing the Himalayas, that any assistance has reached her at all. Her ordeals have been long and stern. We pledge ourselves anew that we will not rest until Japan is defeated and China has restored to her all those territories wrongly seized from her. An hon. Member asked me about supplies. In the main, of course, the supplies have to be for the United

States Air Force which has been built up in China, and for the needs of the Chinese armies under General Stilwell's leadership; but, whatever space is left over, it is for the Chinese Government to say what priority they want for the goods that are sent to them.

We all wish we could send more, but we are sending already the limit of our capacity.

While speaking of the Far East, I would like to make a statement upon the position of our prisoners in the hands of the Japanese. What I am now going to tell the Committee arose from the suggestion made, I think, by the hon. Member for Seaham on January 28, when I spoke about Japanese treatment of our prisoners and it was suggested that the Soviet Government might be asked to make representations to the Japanese Government on behalf of these prisoners. I communicated later with His Majesty's Ambassador in Moscow, and he recently approached the Soviet Government and explained to them our anxiety. There were three points on which we particularly wanted satisfaction from the Japanese Government.

They were, first of all, that the right should be recognized of the protecting Power, in this case Switzerland, and of the International Red Cross, to visit all the camps in which British subjects were held and to report freely and frankly on the conditions prevailing. [An Hon. Member: "And civilians."] Yes. Secondly, we should be given complete lists of our prisoners of war and internees in their hands, together with a list of those who had died; and thirdly, that the Japanese Government should agree to receive Red Cross supplies which would be sent at regular intervals in neutral ships to Japanese ports, and facilities should be given to distribute those supplies. The Soviet Government replied that, while these matters fell directly within the competence of the Protecting Power, they were, nevertheless, prepared to approach the Japanese Government in regard to them, and they have now done so, and I want to thank them and to express the thanks of the Government for their action. I ought to add that this action does not in any way express any lack of confidence in Switzerland as the Protecting Power. We know that our Swiss friends have done everything in their power and we hope that this additional action may assist them in their work in this connection and in what they will do for us hereafter.

My time is nearly up. I want to say a word on economic affairs. I want to tell my hon. Friends that it is true that the Foreign Office has taken over certain fresh activities in the economic field. We have not snatched them—as an hon. Gentleman suggested—the Foreign Office never snatches—but we have negotiated. We have these additional opportunities now. We shall need them, I am confident, and perhaps in a later Debate I may be able to describe the set-up for dealing with these activities to anybody else, either to the United States or anybody. We maintain our organization in that respect. As a result of this arrangement, we shall receive at the Foreign Office now, the economic intelligence which used to go to the Ministry of Economic Warfare.

That will be of great value to us in our political work, and also a new Department which I am setting up will be able to make use of the economic intelligence that we receive. There will be, as a result, a closer relation between our political and economic policies as a whole, and, I hasten to add, it does not mean that I am attempting to take any duties away from my right hon. Friend the President of the Board of Trade or my right hon. Friend the Chancellor of the Exchequer. But it is the truth that foreign policy and economic policy are now more closely related, or perhaps, what is more probable, there is a better understanding now than there used to be of how closely they are related. But however we express it, there is no doubt of the need for an organization such as I have described, and which I would like to describe more fully at a later time.

I want for a few minutes to look into the future, as some other hon. Members have done. There has been much said about the League of Nations, where it succeeded and where it failed. I am not going to argue that now. There is not time, and even if there were, it would take many hours of discussion and there would be many divergent opinions. The Prime Minister explained yesterday that we do not want to impose upon others in detail whatever our ideas may be; at the same time we are entitled to say what our general ideas are about the world organization.

I would like to leave with the Committee just a few principles on which we suggest this future organization should be based. They are these: first, that the world organization must be designed, in the first instance, to prevent a recurrence of aggression by Germany and Japan and must be fully equipped with forces to meet the purpose; secondly, that to ensure this there must be close political and military co-operation between the United States, the Soviet Union, the British Commonwealth, and China—[An Hon. Member: "And France."]—and other Powers; thirdly, that the responsibility in any future world organization must be related to power, and consequently the world organization should be constructed, on and around the four great Powers I have mentioned, and all other peace-loving States should come in and play their part in the structure; fourthly, that the world organization should be flexible and not rigid, that is to say, that it should grow by practice and not try straight away to work to a fixed and rigid code or rule; and, fifthly, that all the Powers, great and small, included in the world organization, should strive for economic as well as for political collaboration.

I understand only too well the difficulties in any attempt to translate into practical experience the principles I have outlined. What I can say is that we have already begun informal conversations with other Powers about these propositions and I hope that in the coming months we shall be able to make more progress with them. At least we are convinced that it is only by translating into the period of peace the confidence which we have built up and the machinery we have built up for collaboration as Allies in the war, that we can hope to save the world from a repetition of those conflicts, which, twice in our generation, have caused so much misery to mankind. I have tried to give the Committee some account of our policy, and I can only repeat, as I began, that, despite the difficulties to which hon. Members have referred, we shall persist in our course and do so with a greater measure of hope as a result of the meetings of Prime Ministers held in London in these last weeks.

33

THE CONSERVATIVE PARTY POLICY

JUNE–OCTOBER 1944

June 6. D-DAY AND THE SECOND FRONT.

WESTERN EUROPE

Cherbourg fell on June 25. The British, Canadian and American forces broke out of the enlargened bridgehead on July 18. Paris was liberated on August 24, Belgium entered on September 2, and the outposts of the Siegfried Line reached on September 14.

Meanwhile, an attempt had been made on Hitler's life on July 20.

Allied forces under Field-Marshal Wilson landed in the south of France on August 15 and advanced quickly north.

Airborne landings started in Holland on September 17 and by September 20 the Second Army had reached the south bank of the Waal. Efforts to reach the 1st Airborne Division at Arnhem failed and the survivors were withdrawn on September 26.

The flying bomb attacks on London started on June 12.

MEDITERRANEAN

In Italy, Florence fell on August 11, the Gothic Line was pierced on September 1, and Rimini was captured on September 22. The withdrawal of the French Corps and the American Corps for the Southern France landings had weakened Field-Marshal Alexander's power.

On October 5 British forces landed on the mainland of Greece.

RUSSIA

The Russians signed an armistice with Finland on September 19

265

and captured Tallinin in Estonia on September 22, and Riga on October 30. They had reached Praga, on the outskirts of Warsaw, on September 17. They entered Czechoslovakia in mid-October. In the south, Bulgaria secured an armistice from Russia on September 7, and Roumania had accepted an armistice on August 23. By October the Red Army was fighting in Hungary and Yugoslavia; Belgrade fell to them on October 20.

Mr. Churchill was in Canada with Mr. Roosevelt from September 10 to 25. Mr. Eden joined the Conference from September 14 to 17. On October 8, Mr. Churchill and Mr. Eden reached Moscow for a further meeting with Marshal Stalin.

In the afternoon, before leaving for Moscow, Mr. Eden addressed the Bristol Conservatives on October 2.

In contrast to the dire peril in which we stood four years ago, it is fair to say that our feet are now set firmly on the road to final victory.

In these conditions it is natural that we should begin to consider some of the problems which will confront us when the victory is won, and in particular it is right that we, as Conservatives, should consider now the contribution which we can make as Conservatives to the future well-being of our country. We have a long tradition of service behind us. We have a long future of service before us.

There is one general comment that I should like to make to you about ourselves in relation to the problems which lie ahead. We have as members of the Conservative Party our own approach to world and domestic affairs, our own line of thought, which we believe is as vigorous and progressive as that of other parties. But our faith is a distinct faith. It is not a watered-down edition of any other faith; it is not a diluted socialism; it is not a red wine into which we have put a little water. It is as British and distinctive as good British beer, with a great deal more body to it than the war-time beverage.

During the life of the present Government, despite preoccupation with the conduct of the war, which in itself, you know, takes up quite a little time, we have set on foot proposals for social reform which would certainly have been regarded as a programme of unrivalled scope and thoroughness for any Government in piping times of peace. As a Conservative, I rejoice that we have been able to do this. We can claim that from the days of Lord Shaftesbury our party has always stood in the forefront to champion proposals for social reform.

But there is one word of warning that I think it only honest to utter in relation to all these proposals. The benefits which are received under these schemes are frequently described as State benefits. I personally have never much liked this phrase, because it assumes the existence of a beneficent State outside the community itself from whose bottomless purse these flowing benefits can be drawn. This is not in truth and in honesty the position. These are in truth community benefits earned by the community and paid out for the assistance of those members who most need them.

We must realize that if we are to benefit from these great schemes we have also got to pay for them, and every section of the community will have to pay for them. If this is clearly understood, well and good, for the schemes in themselves are most admirable schemes. But I do not think it would be right for any great party to go to the country proudly referring to its record and promising yet more instalments in the same sense without honestly telling the electors at the same time what charges these benefits will levy upon them.

How then are these charges to be met? How are we to ensure that the community will be able to earn those benefits which we all desire the community to have? There is only one way in which this can be done. It is by ensuring that our industrial efficiency and productivity are as great as we can possibly make them. Unless British agriculture is prosperous, unless our exports are flowing from the Avon and the Severn, from the Thames and the Humber, the Tyne and the Tees, from the Mersey and the Clyde, in the fullest possible volume, unless our Mercantile Marine is re-established and unless we are able to build a new Mercantile Marine in the air, we shall be unable to accord those social services which we all, irrespective of party, desire and which we all indeed may regard as a social necessity. The issue which will confront this country when our German and Japanese enemies are laid low is whether or not British industry will be able, not only to re-establish itself at its pre-war levels, but markedly to raise those levels.

It is in relation to this main issue that questions of State control or private enterprise must be examined and debated. The truth is that both State control and private enterprise can serve the national interest. There is scope and opportunity for both; but this very fact makes it all the more necessary in our view that private enterprise should not be stifled. There are certain enterprises which are monopolies in their own sphere, such as the Post Office. Nobody disputes that this is properly a State enterprise. There are certain enterprises which are of their nature public services, though they may have been originally created by the enterprise of individuals. It should be for Parliament to decide whether enterprises or services of this type should be managed centrally or locally under private or State control. For our part, we would draw no rigid line: we would judge each on its merits.

But there is a third and indeed largest category. These are the industries which, by their variety and diversity of character, call in a special degree for the qualities of initiative, individuality and imagination. It is just these qualities displayed often in the past by small manufacturers that have created some of the greatest industries in our land and have enabled us to compete successfully in the markets of the world. It is just these qualities which we shall most need in the post-war years. Here it is clearly to the public interest that full play should be given to individual enterprise and leadership. As the Prime Minister has so well said in a speech you will all remember: "There is a broadening field for State ownership and enterprise, especially in relation to monopolies of all kinds. The modern State will increasingly concern itself with the economic well-being of the nation; but it is all the more vital to revive at the earliest moment a widespread healthy and vigorous private enterprise, without which we shall never be able to provide, in the years when it is needed, the employment for our soldiers, sailors and airmen to which they are entitled after their duty has been done."

I have spoken of State control and individual enterprise in the relatively narrow context of industry. But what, after all, is the Conservative conception of the importance of the individual, and the relationship of the individual to the State?

That is a more fundamental question.

It is possible to conjure up a conception of the State as an all good, all powerful institution, and to believe that we are making progress if only we will entrust more authority to the State. I believe that there is danger in such doctrine, though it is sometimes put forward in tempting guise. For instance, we are sometimes told that the procedure of Parliament is too slow; that more power should be given to the executive in order to free it from some parts of the prodecure which have hitherto in this country in times of peace largely controlled the rate at which legislation can be passed.

I repeat that there seems to me to be danger in such doctrine, and I for one should require much convincing before I should be ready to cast my vote in such a way as might in normal times diminish the effective scrutiny and watchfulness of Parliament over legislation. War-time is abnormal, and in war conditions the Government may be given abnormal powers. I should not care to see these powers or anything like them become our practice in times of peace. In this country, the elected representatives of the people must be the true repositories of power. Such control is indispensable in times of peace if legislation, often controversial in character, is to be fairly debated; and if account is to be taken, as it should be taken, of minority views and if balanced conclusions are to be reached.

Another issue much debated is the future of the war-time controls which have been imposed upon industry and upon every citizen in our land.

We are now at war with totalitarian states. To fight them we have had to use some of their weapons. To defeat them our people have accepted regimentation and controls to an extent never before known in our history.

But though we use these weapons we don't love them. Though we employ them for a specific purpose to defeat our enemy in war, we have no intention to perpetuate them for their own sake in peace. Such a course would be too much like canonizing the black-out or standing in a queue for the good of our souls.

It would be foolish to advocate the complete abolition of all controls the moment the war is won. Clearly any such attempt would land us in chaos; but their ordered reduction must be our object. Least of all do we wish to fall into the state of mind where controls are thought good for their own sake.

We have to make sure that the way we practise democracy is the most likely way in the changing circumstances of the world to guarantee the best and freest life to the members of the community to which we belong.

If we believe in democracy, it is surely because we stand for the rights of the individual, because our purpose is to assure freedom for the expression of thought, to encourage conditions in which the individual human personality can live and grow. Man was not, in our view, made for the State. The State was made for man. The duty of government consists in striking a just balance between the claims of the individual and those of the State to which he owes allegiance.

If when this war is won nations will understand how complete is their dependence each on the other, then we shall have made progress towards keeping the peace. In terms of communications, of means of transport and of modern weapons, Europe is to-day no larger than was the France of the Middle Ages.

None will dispute the need for some international authority to guide and direct the work which the governments of the world must do together if full use is to be made of the opportunities that victory will bring. It is equally true that if that authority is to have a fair chance of success it must command sufficient armed strength to enable it to enforce its decrees in a world not yet ready to accept control by international law. The more firmly established is the respect for law in any state, the less need has the policeman for weapons. Oftentimes his uniform is authority enough. But the converse is no less true, and in relations between States the events of recent years have proved clearly enough how overwhelming is the gangster's advantage when the nations who would resist aggression fail to act together and neglect their defences.

We have learnt another lesson during these war years. It is that if the new international order is to have a fair chance of success, it must be based upon the closest understanding between the three great Powers, the United States of America, the Soviet Union and the British Commonwealth of Nations.

There should be nothing exclusive about this association, nor does any one of the Powers concerned desire that there should be. But unless this foundation of understanding exists we shall soon find ourselves faced with many of the problems which previously baffled and finally destroyed the League of Nations.

I have spoken of these international problems because it is upon their solution that all reconstruction after the war really depends. Unless and until international relations are placed on a stable and satisfactory basis all efforts at national reconstruction are in danger of being brought to naught by a new outbreak of war.

I would like to say a word to you now about one of the members and, to me, the most important member of that trinity. I mean the British Commonwealth and Empire. This is surely the most remarkable community of free nations that the world has ever seen. We have no call to apologize for it; we have every reason to take pride in it. It must be our determination to do everything in our power to add to the measure of understanding, of confidence and indeed of affection, between its members. Thus can the British Commonwealth and Empire make an ever-growing contribution in its record of service to mankind.

We have led the world at its darkest hour; we can lead it too into the sun-splashed periods that break beyond.

1 8

34

ATHENS AND ITALY

OCTOBER–NOVEMBER 1944

The Moscow Conference. Mr. Churchill and· Mr. Eden for Britain, and Mr. Harriman representing President Roosevelt, conferred with Marshal Stalin and Mr. Molotov. During this conference, the British representatives strove to secure agreement in conjunction with the Russians, between M. Mikolajczyck and his colleagues representing the Polish Government in London, and the Lublin National Committee.

The Russian advances continued and gains included the nickel mines of Petsamo on the Finnish–Norwegian border, parts of East Prussia and the outskirts of Budapest.

Further gains were made all along the Allied Front in western Europe. Antwerp was opened to Allied shipping on November 30. French troops reached the Rhine at the end of November.

In Italy, Forli was captured on November 10.

Lord Moyne was assassinated in Cairo on November 6.

On November 8, President Roosevelt was re-elected President for a fourth term.

Mr. Churchill arrived home from the Moscow Conference on October 22. Mr. Eden did not accompany him but paid visits to Cairo, Athens and Italy. He received the Freedom of Athens at the Acropolis on October 27. In view of what was to come, his visit to Greece was of great importance. On his return to London, Mr. Eden gave the following account to the House of Commons on November 8.

ATHENS AND ITALY

My right hon. Friend the Prime Minister gave the House, a fortnight ago, an account of our conversation with Marshal Stalin and M. Molotov in Moscow. I have nothing to add to that account but if the House would give me leave I would like to make a very brief statement of the work that it fell to me to do after the departure of my right hon. Friend. In Egypt I met the newly appointed Egyptian Prime Minister, who assured me of his Government's loyalty to the alliance with this country, which alliance, as the House will remember, is enshrined in the Anglo-Egyptian Treaty of 1936, an instrument which has well stood the test of time, emergency and war. In the three or four days that I spent in Cairo I also had the opportunity to discuss with Lord Moyne—whose brutal and tragic assassination is such a blow to us all—all the manifold political and administrative problems which were in the area of his responsibility.

On October 25 I left, with Lord Moyne, by air, for Athens. I should have explained that, at an earlier stage, our Ambassador to Greece had telegraphed to the Prime Minister and myself urging that one or both of us should visit Athens on our way home, to meet the Ministers of the Greek Government and to see for ourselves the situation and the problems which to-day confront liberated Greece. The Prime Minister agreed that this should be my task. I do not believe that informed opinion in this country yet fully understands how complete, how merciless, how dastardly has been the devastation inflicted by the German armies in Allied lands as they are compelled to withdraw. The purpose underlying this systematic barbarity is clear enough. It is to bring to a standstill the whole life of the nation. That is what the Germans told the Greeks they would do as they left. All communications, all bridges, all telegraphs are destroyed; all means of transport, lorries and even, in many instances, pack animals are removed; all harbours are mined, blocked, blown up, every crane in the Piraeus destroyed. The essential parts of factories are removed and stocks of raw materials are either taken away or destroyed. For instance, there is, in Greece, a small but important textile industry. There is no means of getting that to work because there is no machinery left nor cotton.

In Greece, thanks to the heroism of the local defenders, the great power station near Athens was saved, but for the rest, one has to admit that the German plan was so thoroughly carried out that

problems of immense complexity confronted the Greek Government, and of these vexed problems, the currency situation was by
no means the least. Though much remains to be done, I am able
to report to the House substantial progress in dealing with these
problems. First and foremost, in respect to supply, as a result of
most strenuous efforts on the part of the Royal Navy and the Royal
Engineers, who sometimes do not get all the public credit they
deserve, and of the civilian population in the Piraeus, too, that
port has been got to work again, in part, at least. By the end of
October we had reached a figure of supplies unloaded at the
Piraeus alone of almost 3,000 tons a day—a truly remarkable figure
in the circumstances. A substantial proportion of what is unloaded
is foodstuffs for the civilian population and we are confident that
that figure can be improved substantially as the port capacity is
increased.

When the remaining obstacles are overcome, we expect to un-
load in Greece a monthly tonnage of over 130,000 tons and of that,
about 60,000 tons will be foodstuffs and 70,000 tons will be clothing, medicine and relief goods. I must make it plain that the
delivery of these very large supplies and the organization entailed
were only made possible by the careful work done in advance,
largely by all staffs of our military authorities and by those of the
United States in the Middle East, so that when the emergency
came we should be ready. It is also clear that an effective means of
combating this inflation—though I do not pretend to be an authority on this matter—is to ensure the import of supplies, and in
connection with that the Supreme Commander in the Mediterranean, General Wilson, Admiral Cunningham, the C.-in-C.,
Mediterranean, Lord Moyne and my right hon. Friend the Member for Stockton-on-Tees (Mr. H. Macmillan) and I have had
many consultations, as a result of which, certain arrangements
were made to bring urgently from the Middle East certain goods in
addition to the previously arranged military relief.

I would like to give the House just two examples which may
interest all. By air we arranged to bring some 200 tons of special
supplies urgently needed, and the Royal Navy and warships
brought over in addition some 600 or 700 tons in emergency pas-
sages. The arrival of these goods helped to restore confidence; and
we tried to deal with the problem of transport in the same way.
Admirable arrangements had been made by the military authorities, but owing to the complete removal of every means of transport inside the country, something further was needed, and we did

arrange for several hundred further lorries to be brought from the Middle East to help to restore some economic life inside the country, for that was wholly at a standstill. For example, olive oil, which is the diet of the Greek people, is produced in large quantities, but owing to this complete removal of transport and destruction of bridges it could not be removed from the country places, and in the towns it was not available.

In the last few days the first convoy has arrived in Athens bringing olive oil from the Peloponnese, and so progress is being made, and there is good hope for the future provided stable internal conditions can be maintained; but on this all successful organization of relief must inevitably depend. I could not close this brief account of what we saw in Greece without saying how much moved were all ranks of the British Forces by the truly warmhearted welcome given them by all sections of the Greek people. As we all know, our Greek friends are very politically minded, they have many parties, and I could find only one subject upon which they all agreed, a general and wholehearted welcome to the British Forces.

I should like also to say a very few words about my visit to Italy. The main purpose of this was to accept an invitation which General Alexander had kindly extended to me, to visit our front in northern Italy. I was unfortunate in that the days of my stay there coincided with those phenomenal storms, which the people of a country invariably tell you have never been known to happen since 1880 or some other date. As a result, all I could know was that the rivers were soon torrents, all low-lying land was a quagmire much more like Flanders than the Italy of the Florentine pictures, and all movement was a matter of the utmost difficulty. Even a day's hard work, in which we transferred ourselves from a jeep to a three-ton lorry in accordance with the depths of the flood at particular points —all the time slithering about and cursing and struggling a good deal—enabled us to cover only a very small percentage of the mileage we had planned to cover. Although this was naturally disappointing to anyone who wished to see much, it did enable me to understand, as I suppose nothing else could have done, the conditions under which our Allied Armies are living and fighting in Italy. No praise that we can utter can be too high for those men. They have had a prolonged struggle with a stubborn foe. They have had to contend not only with the fighting capacity of their enemies but with conditions of climate and terrain peculiar to Italy. Under the brilliant leadership of General Alexander and of his army commanders, the United States General Mark Clark and General McCreery, who has succeeded General Oliver Leese, they have persevered undaunted.

I hope that in a comparatively short space of time it will be possible to arrange for some Members of this House to visit that front. I know that such a visit would be welcomed there—I was so informed—and when hon. Members do go I am sure they will feel, as I do, that to meet those men, to see the conditions in which they live and fight, is to feel a deep sense of pride in our own people, a conviction of final victory and a confidence in the work we can all do together in the years that lie ahead.

35

PARIS—11 NOVEMBER 1944

Paris had been liberated on August 24. On October 23 General de Gaulle's Provisional Government of France had been recognized by the United Kingdom, the United States of America and the U.S.S.R.

In November Mr. Eden accompanied Mr. Churchill to Paris for the Armistice Day Ceremony. He returned before Mr. Churchill and on November 14 gave the House of Commons the following account of their visit:

Since my right hon. Friend the Prime Minister has not himself returned to this country, he has asked me to give, with the leave of the House, a brief account of our visit to the French capital this last week-end. The overwhelming impression left upon our minds by those crowded hours was of the sincerity and spontaneity of the welcome accorded to us by every section of the French people. The House will recall, perhaps, that for reasons of security no announcement was made of the Prime Minister's presence, even on the morning of the Armistice ceremony, in the French papers themselves; yet the news of his coming had spread overnight, widely enough at least for immense multitudes to assemble on the main thoroughfares through which he was to pass. It would be a great mistake to interpret this welcome as a momentary effervescence of spirit in a great capital city at last delivered from four years of foreign rule. It was something much deeper than that, it was rather the expression of a deep thankfulness for suffering at last ended. One felt behind the tumultuous greetings of these vast but orderly crowds the heart beat of a nation once again united with its allies and confident of its own future.

277

PARIS

It is difficult for us here to picture the life that is endured by a great nation under enemy occupation, completely severed from all contact with the outside world, dominated by enemy propaganda and able only to get encouragement from time to time from some clandestine listening to broadcasts from overseas. Here it is right that I should say that from countless Frenchmen we heard expressions of the inspiration and the will to live which they have drawn from the broadcasts of my right hon. Friend the Prime Minister and, let it be added, from the daily regular work of the B.B.C. and its contributors.

Most of the German propaganda was directed against this country but the fact remains—a fact of which we should take note—that the effect of this propaganda, taken together with the sufferings of the French people in this period of tyrannous enemy rule, has been to place our friendship with France on a surer foundation than has ever existed before in the history of our two countries. It seems indeed that the knowledge that our friendship has survived this, the most severe strain that could be put upon it, gives it a deeper and a more vibrant significance. That, I am convinced, is the message which Paris was giving to this country during that week-end.

In the course of his speech of welcome to us, General de Gaulle recalled Hitler's claim that his system would last for a thousand years. "I do not know", said General de Gaulle, "what will remain of his system in a thousand years, but I do know that in a thousand years' time France, which has some experience of blood, sweat and tears, will not have forgotten what has been accomplished in this war through blood, sweat and tears by the noble British people under the leadership of their Prime Minister." These are generous words. They were uttered by a man who himself to-day unquestionably inspires and personifies the unity of the French people. He has around him a band of young and vigorous colleagues who have proved their worth in the ordeal through which France has passed. Among them in particular I would like to mention M. Bidault, now Foreign Minister of France. It was a great pleasure for the Prime Minister and myself to meet this gallant man, who was himself the outstanding leader of the French resistance movement. We could see the same vigour, the same confidence in France's future expressed in the thousands of troops who marched past us in the Champs-Élysées, the great majority of whom are very recently enlisted members of the F.F.I., and every man of whom is a volunteer. No one can doubt that when time and opportunity offer, these men will give as splendid an account of themselves against the hated Nazi foe in the field as they have already shown in the bitter and bloody warfare in the interior of France itself.

I would like to make one reference to conditions in France, because I think we should bear in mind that, despite some outward appearances, life in Paris is a constant struggle with material difficulties. The almost total lack of fuel and of transport are, in themselves, a severe hardship in these winter months, but worse than this is the mental suffering which these people have undergone and continue to undergo. There are still over 2,500,000 French prisoners of war, political deportees and forced labourers in Germany. There is scarcely a family of France which has not a husband or a son still in Germany. All parcels and letters have ceased. In fact, deportees have never been allowed any communication of any kind with their families since they were taken away to Germany. When we consider these facts, we can perhaps estimate, too, what the absence of these men means to France, not only in the loss of a great part of what was best in the nation's manhood, with all the social, economic and military consequences entailed, but also in mental distress for those who are left behind.

It is not surprising that in these conditions, France, which after all these years has suddenly regained her freedom, should be like a man emerging from a darkened room into a blaze of light, dazed for a moment and grateful still to his friends for a measure of understanding and encouragement. Let us interpret this in the terms of France's position as a great Power. It was indeed appropriate that the three Allied Powers, the United States of America, the Soviet Union and ourselves were able to invite France, on this very Saturday, to take her place with us as a permanent member of the European Advisory Commission. The new situation which was thus created and the work that must flow therefrom was naturally the subject of discussion between us in Paris. Of these discussions, I will only say now that both the French Ministers and ourselves regarded them as eminently satisfactory.

I would conclude with this confident message to the House. France's determination to work together with her Allies expresses, I am sure, the heartfelt wish of the French people, and it is the will of the people which is the only sure foundation of a foreign policy in a free land. France will recover. Before now in her history she has shown powers of recuperation which have astounded the world. It is my belief that she will do this again, and she can be assured that in her endeavour she will have the constant friendship, understanding and help of the British peoples everywhere.

36

GREECE—CIVIL WAR 1944

The King opened the sixth war session of Parliament on November 29. During the Debate on the Address, an Amendment was moved regretting the British Intervention in Greece and other parts of Europe. The Amendment was defeated by 279 to 30. Mr. Churchill replied to the mover and Mr. Eden wound up on December 8.

The following are some relevant facts about British aid to Greece in the war.

April 1941. British **Empire** troops suffered 30,000 casualties in Greece.

May 1944. M. Papandreou met leaders of all parties from Greece, including E.A.M., in the Lebanon. A Greek Government of all parties was subsequently formed under his leadership.

September 14. Following discussions in Quebec between Mr. Churchill and President Roosevelt, Field-Marshal Wilson, the Supreme Commander in the Mediterranean, was directed to prepare a force to occupy the Athens area.

October 5. Allied troops landed on the Greek mainland.

October and November. Supplies of clothing and food were sent to different parts of Greece by the British Government and unloaded under their arrangements. (U.N.R.R.A. was to come in later.) See page 274.

November 9. The Greek mountain brigade, having taken part, with the Eighth Army, in the capture of Ravenna, reached Athens.

December 3. Civil war began in Athens.

Night of December 4–5. During the night, telegrams reached H.M. Government in the U.K. from Athens that E.L.A.S. troops were within 1,000 yards of G.H.Q. in the Grande Bretagne and no farther from the British Embassy.

December 5. British troops involved in the fighting in Athens.

I think each of us who has listened to this Debate must have felt a sense of melancholy, almost of tragedy, brooding over our proceedings. Whatever view we take as to the inevitability or otherwise of the events which have recently happened in Greece, every Member of this House must feel deeply the thought that there should be conflict now raging in Athens, in a land which means so much to every one of us. And if every Member feels that, I perhaps, not unnaturally, feel it more than most, for it is only a few weeks ago I was in Athens, and heard the cheers of the vast Greek populace, addressed in friendship to Britain, a welcome addressed to our own soldiers. I was one afternoon in Greece, where it so happened that a battalion of the regiment to which I still belong was stationed, and I heard from them that never had they experienced so much friendliness as greeted them in that country. It is a tragedy, however we look at it, that out of all this, these happenings should arise. I propose to try to give some account of how and why these happenings have come about, and what is the position of His Majesty's Government in regard to them. But I would like to say, at the outset, that it is a message from this House that we deplore these events, and that our feelings go out to our own forces who are called upon to deal with them.

MR. GALLACHER: Tell them to cease firing.

MR. EDEN: I am not going to be led away by the hon. Gentleman. What are the charges? The first charge which the hon. Member for Broxtowe (Mr. Cocks) put forward is that, as victory is approaching, British policy is inclined to support worn-out regimes against more popular forces. My right hon. Friend dealt this morning at length, and, I think the House will agree, faithfully, with those charges so far as concerns Belgium and Italy. I do not propose to say anything more about either of those two countries, but simply to concentrate what I have to say on the situation in Greece. The hon. Gentleman concluded his appeal by asking the Government immediately to put an end to all this fratricidal strife. I agree with the hon. Gentleman, and I really hope to show how that was precisely our purpose at every stage in the policy we have pursued, not only in these last days in Athens, but for many, may I add, weary months of attempting to secure Greek unity before the Greek Government went back. I will tell the House how we tried to follow that through.

I agree with my hon. Friend the Member for Oxford (Mr. Hogg), who, in a very remarkable speech, if I may say so, spoke of the honour it was for Britain to take part in the liberation of Greece. I think that is true; but I repeat that our purpose is to enable the Greek people to express their own will and their own decision. We must, though, insist that that expression must be through the ballot box, and not by the bomb. How have we tried to follow that course out? The first question I am asked—and it is a perfectly reasonable question—is, do the present Greek Government—or shall we say the Greek Government up to a week ago—represent the people of Greece? Have they a basis of popular support? How in the world can that be finally ascertained except by a method which is familiar to all of us—the ballot box—and how could that have been practicable in Greece in the last few years since the German occupation? The Government were perfectly conscious at one time that the Greek Government in Cairo was not wholly representative of the Greek people, and that is why we sought to bring out representatives of the various parties in order to make that Government representative. We brought out a number of persons from Greece, including, among others, the present Prime Minister of Greece— about whom a word hereafter—and, as a result of these representatives, including those of E.A.M. and the Communist Party, having been brought out, eventually a conference was held at the Lebanon among the Greeks themselves. They arrived at an agreement and a Government was set up.

Now, unfortunately—as in my experience sometimes happens and not only in Greek politics—though the leaders agreed on a policy in the Lebanon, when the E.A.M. representative got back to Greece they had not a little difficulty with their own followers. That is not unique in political life, and I certainly do not want to embarrass anybody by stressing it unduly. Such may be the proper expression of the popular will. After that slight hiatus, the ranks were closed again and, eventually, a Greek Government was formed at the end of August, the Lebanon Conference having been in May. Last August, a Greek Government was formed composed of all parties, including E.A.M. That is the Government which we recognize and which all our Allies recognize, and which eventually went into Greece. I want to draw the attention of the House to this, because the hon. Member for Broxtowe said that this is not a representative Government, but that it is an uneasy alliance and so on. I want to give the words used on September 15 before this Government went back to Greece, by Professor Svolos, leader of the E.A.M. Party, who called on M. Papandreou and assured him in the name of all the E.A.M. Ministers that, whatever readjustments might have to be made when they got back to Athens, it was their desire that a Coalition Government, on the lines of the existing Government, should continue in office under M. Papandreou's presidency until elections could be held.

I stress that because it was M. Papandreou's original intention, as I know, to resign as soon as he returned to Greece. As the result, however, of representations from the E.A.M. Ministers in the Government, he decided, and I think rightly decided, to continue in office when they returned to Greece. So much for the "uneasy alliance" of the hon. Member for Broxtowe. Nor do I think that his aspersions were in any way representative of the union which had been arrived at. What is the present Greek Government? It is well worth looking at. It is a Government consisting of 22 Members—quite a large Cabinet for a relatively small country. I will give the parties to which its members belong. There are the Social Democrats. The Prime Minister himself is a Social Democrat, and I am advised that that party is slightly to the Left of the official Labour Party in this country. I am very careful to say that I am so advised. I cannot guarantee it. There are four Liberals—and they are to the Right of the Social Democrats. There is a Democratic Union Party and a Party called E.K.K.A. I hope I shall not be asked to describe them, because I do not know a great deal about them. They have each one representative. Then there is the National Union Party and the Agrarian Party, and, finally, the Popular Party, which, I am told, is one which may be said to be somewhere between the Labour Party and the Conservative Party in this country. That is the composition of this Government. There are 22 members of this Government, and this is the point I wish to emphasize. Of these 22, so far as I have been able to discover, every single one is a Republican.

Here, I want to kill the story that the present difficulties or troubles in Greece are something to do with the quarrel between Royalists and Republicans. That is really not so; it is a quite ludicrous over-simplification of the matter. When the seven E.A.M. Ministers walked out of this Cabinet, in circumstances which I shall shortly describe, they left behind the remainder, who are the Government to-day. They are Republicans and none of them is more dangerously reactionary than the right hon. Gentleman the Member for Leith (Mr. Ernest Brown). I think that is a correct description of the Government, and I think the hon. Member for West Leicester (Mr. Harold Nicolson) was justified in the admirable balance which he brought into these affairs. When the hon. Member for Maldon (Mr. Driberg) talks about a reactionary group, he is making a fantastic travesty of the facts. When he says this is a war between the people of Greece and a few Quislings, backed up by British bayonets, I cannot believe that he really thinks this is so. And, if he does, how does he explain that every known Greek party was in this Government, brought there from Greece at great trouble by us and at some risk to our people, to create a national front? What is the good of describing that Government, even after the E.A.M. Ministers walked out of it, as a reactionary group?

Let me now say a word about M. Papandreou himself, because we have been told by one or two speakers that this is a conflict between the democratic forces of E.A.M. and a reactionary Government—I think I am being fair—headed by M. Papandreou who wants a dictatorship. If anyone will read the past history of M. Papandreou, he can disprove that story for himself. Reference was also made by the hon. Member for Broxtowe to the events of 1936 and especially to the Metaxas dictatorship. Where was M. Papandreou after that? The hon. Member did not appear to have looked that up. M. Papandreou was, from that date, in exile because he was in opposition to the Metaxas dictatorship. This is the man who, we are told, has now become a Fascist himself. This is going a little bit too far, until it seems that everybody who disagrees with the views of our sole Communist representative in this House, has become a Fascist.

MR. GALLACHER: May I ask the Minister not to follow the example of the Prime Minister and make all kinds of loose charges? The right hon. Gentleman has never heard me say that M. Papandreou was a Fascist, but there are very evil influences around him. Do not put the responsibility on me.

MR. EDEN: I am deeply relieved to find that everybody is agreed that M. Papandreou is not a Fascist. That, at any rate, is one step forward. But that he is surrounded by a number of other influences in the Cabinet; well, I have tried to describe these other influences. An hon. Gentleman spoke earlier about the Athens police and their Fascist tendencies. When I was in Athens nobody described them like that to me. I heard no such thing. Here was this Government composed of all the parties, including six or seven E.A.M. Ministers in the Government. They had been two months or so in Athens, and if there had been the least sign of such "Fascist tendencies", somebody in the Cabinet would have said: "This is a bad business. Let us have the police combed out." As far as I know, no one said that. It is rather late that these charges should be made when we were never told that either by a single member of the Cabinet, neither by a Communist nor by anybody else.

MR. GALLACHER: That is not correct. Is it not the case that one of the serious troubles between E.A.M. and Papandreou and others was that they absolutely refused to comb the Fascists out of the police, and out of other administrative bodies?

MR. EDEN: I do not think so, and I am coming to the case of the differences in a moment. I want to be really fair in regard to the facts which happened when M. Papandreou returned to Athens. He laid down the policy of the Government in a speech on October 18, a few days before I reached Athens, which was the subject of much public discussion. I will read one passage from this speech because it is important. He said this:

"First, anxious to re-establish a Free Greek State, the Government will pursue the task of reorganizing the country's armed forces on solely national and military criteria, as the National Conference at Lebanon laid down. Flags will be handed to the courageous fighters of our guerrilla forces, and their cadres will find a worthy place in the reorganized Greek Army. The basis of our national army, as it has always been in the past and as it is for all free peoples, will be the regular call to the colours. The whole Greek people claim the right to defend the country. The known *coup d'état* spirit of our armed forces shall be dissolved. It will be the rule and the practice that the army cannot be the master, but only the sovereign people whose will is expressed by the Government. The army shall be at the Government's order. It will be the rule and the practice that the army can belong to neither party nor a private individual. It belongs to the country alone and obeys the Government's orders only."

I must now tell this House of my own experiences during those few days in Athens. Among those who asked to see me—I did not ask to see them—were many leading representatives of the Communist Party in Greece. I asked M. Papandreou, as I thought it was only courteous to do so, whether it was in order that I should see them and he said: "Yes." I was glad, therefore, to see them at

285

reason55555555555555555555

the British Embassy. What did they tell me? In the first place they expressed their thanks for the help which the British Government had given to Greece during her time of trial under German rule, and for the supplies that were arriving, as a result of a great feat of organization, in the Piraeus. I asked them—it was only shortly after this declaration from which I have quoted was made—whether they were content with the Government, whether unity was established in the Government, and whether they had any complaints to make, and they told me just exactly what Professor Svolos himself had told M. Papandreou before agreement was reached, that they were perfectly content about the unity of the Government and the policy it was pursuing and completely loyal to M. Papandreou as Prime Minister. That was what I was told. I did not want to take any part in their politics, but after I had heard that declaration, I said that I trusted that unity in the Government would be maintained while we did all we could to support Greece with food and all the essentials of life. They replied that they were in agreement with that document that I have read out and which M. Papandreou said had been previously approved by all Ministers, and I hoped that the same agreement might be maintained.

MR. BOWLES: What date was that?

MR. EDEN: I think it was October 28. There is no catch about this. It is an account of what happened, and I think the House should know about it.

I pass from that to another matter which has been referred to, which is the arrival of the mountain brigade. That Greek brigade from Rimini arrived in Athens on November 9. It has been represented by some speakers in the House as if that was some form of sinister Fascist organization. That brigade received a welcome from the Greek people. One telegram that I saw described this welcome as only parallel to the greeting given to our troops on their arrival. What about the issues which have brought about this rift in the Greek Government? As to the discussion about the measures for disbanding the E.A.M. police and E.L.A.S. army, we knew quite well when I was in Athens that this was an issue which might cause a rift. In the discussions the E.A.M. Ministers had not, at first, said anything at all about the demobilization of the Greek brigade. The plan for demobilization, I must tell the House, was agreed to by the whole Government at this stage, including the E.A.M. Ministers. It was in two stages. On December 1, the E.A.M. police which had been established in Athens and a number of other towns, was to be replaced by the National Guard, which is composed of men of the 1936 class, who had been called up. On December 10, the guerrillas were to be demobilized and replaced by a national army formed by calling up three more classes and we had made arrangements when I was in Greece for the provision of 40,000 uniforms and equipment for this new national army. That was the plan agreed to by everybody. Since then difficulties have begun to arise. On November 30, a draft decree—I ask the House to note this—for the demobilization of the guerrillas had been drawn up at M. Papandreou's request by the E.A.M. Ministers themselves. They provided, in this draft decree—and this meets the point of an hon. Member who spoke earlier—that the mountain brigade and the Sacred Squadron were not to be demobilized and that E.L.A.S. was to retain one brigade of guerrillas, and I think E.D.E.S. were to be given some small force.

These were the proposals of the E.A.M. Ministers themselves. That was November 30. At the last moment these were changed again. The E.A.M. Ministers insisted on the demobilization of the Greek regular units instead of maintaining the agreement that the Greek Brigade should remain and the E.A.M. Brigade remain also. This changed the position. For they decided that the Greek Regular Brigade should be demobilized altogether. On this issue the other Greek Government Ministers all refused to agree. They were quite willing that an E.A.M. Brigade should remain if so desired. They made that concession to balance the Greek Regular Brigade but were not prepared to see demobilized this one regular Greek force —which many wished would go again into action against the Germans. It was on that that the split came, and it came within the Greek Government and it did not come on any move or instruction or advice from His Majesty's Government. Therefore, it is not, unhappily, true to say that agreement was ever reached about demobilization. I have taken a great deal of trouble to check these facts and to watch them, and I feel quite confident that the account I am giving the House is as correct as can be given in these very difficult conditions.

So it happened that the next day, as the result of this failure to reach agreement on demobilization, the E.A.M. police refused to hand over their arms in accordance with the Government's decision. Then it was that M. Papandreou circulated a decree enforcing the Government's decision. He circulated that decree and asked the Ministers to sign it. All the Ministers signed it except the E.A.M. Ministers, who resigned rather than sign it. Thus it was that the split came, and it was after that event that General

Scobie issued his broadcast, to which reference has already been made.

I must refer to one other matter, which is the relation of these irregular armies to our own Command. Before ever Greece was liberated, before our troops went in, we knew that there would be this problem of these irregular armies. In point of fact it has not played, so far as General Zervas is concerned, any great part in events in Athens because General Zervas's forces are in Epirus, far away from the capital. All the same, care was taken to bring together the leaders of the two armies—General Zervas and General Sarafis, who is the commander-in-chief of E.L.A.S.—and they came to see General Wilson at his headquarters before the start of the liberation of Greece. Agreement was reached with these two generals and with the Greek Government, that all Greek Forces, including all guerrillas—E.L.A.S. or E.D.E.S.—were to serve under the direct command of General Scobie as General Wilson's deputy. That was the agreement reached, and so I say again that this action of E.A.M. Ministers and the consequent action of E.L.A.S. was a breach of their own agreement with our military commanders, quite apart from the political issue altogether.

I will mention one other matter on which there has been a certain amount of talk in this Debate—the security battalions and the role they played. Whatever may have been the past of the security battalions, they do not enter into this business at all, because they are all disbanded and have been disbanded for some little time past. They have played no part in events, and they are not playing any part now, either in support of the British Forces or the Greek Forces in Athens.

I must now refer to the remarks made about our Ambassador in Athens, that he was inadequate and partisan. If any hon. Member of this House thinks that the present position of His Majesty's Ambassador in Greece is an easy one to discharge, he is welcome to that thought, but in actual fact, it is a matter of the utmost difficulty in a position like this for our Ambassador to maintain a fair and impartial position, and truly to represent the instructions which he receives from His Majesty's Government. It is the belief of the War Cabinet that Mr. Leeper has striven, most loyally and truly, to carry out those instructions. I could not accept any kind of strictures on him.

There is somebody else on the scene to which reference must be made, and that is the veteran leader of the Greek Liberal Party, M. Sophoulis, who has been pictured from time to time in the Press and in speeches as a sort of *deus ex machina*. It has been made out that if only the British Government had not butted in, this man would long since have settled the problem so that all Greeks would be able to live happily together for ever after. I have nothing at all against this most respected Greek elder statesman, but I am bound to say this: that he, and I am sorry to say the other members of the Greek Liberal Party too, have frequently criticized M. Papandreou for making too many concessions to E.A.M. and E.L.A.S. The latter have retorted in the last day or two by issuing leaflets; in which they most violently attack this most venerable elder statesman, and say that in no circumstances whatever, would anything have induced them to serve under his leadership. I am bound to say that that leaflet does not surprise me in the very least, and I do not think that there was ever the slightest chance that M. Sophoulis could have formed a government including all the parties. All that would have happened would have been the additional confusion of all trying to do a little cabinet-making, amidst all the troubles then surging round Athens. I do hope I have said enough to show the House——

Mr. Gallacher: What about——

Mr. Eden: The hon. Gentleman must let me finish—I hope I have been able to show that the Government which we have been seeking to support in Greece is not a Right-Wing Government but that it is, so far as we could contrive to help it to make itself so, a Government of all the parties which, until a few days ago, was accepted as such by everybody. The mere withdrawal of one section—seven members out of twenty-four—does not turn a representative Government into a dictatorship, any more than, let me say, the most melancholy departure of any part of the National Government from this bench would turn what was left into a dictatorship, supposing what was left had a majority of support in this House.

May I say a word more about the Greek brigade and the Sacred Squadron which seems to have dominated this Debate? We are told that the reason why E.A.M. had to leave the Government was because of the fear that this Greek brigade would dominate the proceedings if once E.A.M. were disarmed. I ask the House in all seriousness, could anybody accept that as being a real accusation? Supposing E.A.M. Ministers had remained in the Papandreou Government with all the authority of government, are we to be told that the mere existence of one Greek regular brigade, probably shortly to leave again for the battle front, was such a formidable thing that they could not dare to allow its existence to continue? That cannot be true if there were real popular support for the position which they said they held; it would be true though if the popular support had been greatly exaggerated. Are the Sacred Squadrons—there are two squadrons actually; one is at present in the Greek islands and the other is at Salonika—so terrifying to the E.A.M. Cabinet Ministers of Athens? We must be careful not to build up this imaginary military dictatorship where none exists at all. The truth is much nearer to what my hon. Friend the Member for West Leicester said earlier, that maybe we are to blame for not intervening at an earlier stage than we did.

What about the present position? The House has perhaps read the account in *The Times* this morning, and there are three items in it, to which I would draw the attention of the House because they help me to answer the right hon. Gentleman the Member for Wakefield (Mr. A. Greenwood). They are these. First, the writer said:

"The reception of our men when they rushed sometimes rather forcibly into Greek houses, trampled through bedrooms, dining-rooms and kitchens, most of which are occupied ... demonstrates popular feeling. Our men are welcomed as liberators, and people who have been terrorized for many months gladly point out where E.L.A.S. men may be concealed."

Now that would not happen if we were supporting a tyrannical dictatorship against the will of the populace. I believe that to be a true account. Let me read two other items which give me, as I want to give the House, some hope—if I may have the hon. Gentlemen's attention—that we may yet get out of these troubles. The next item is this:

"A general commanding 4,000 guerrillas in the Eleusis area"—twenty miles from Athens—actually some guerrillas which I happened to see myself—E.A.M. Forces—"refused to bring in his men to fight in Athens" to attempt to decide the issue there. There is, I think, a measure of encouragement in that—[*Interruption*]—I am sorry if I interrupt a little, but it would make it easier for me to be understood if my hon Friends would listen——

VISCOUNTESS ASTOR: They are not interested.

MR. EDEN: This report is of importance and I want hon. Members who do not agree with the Government to listen to this extract:

"Even General Sarafis himself... would have been ready to sign the order for disbanding the E.L.A.S. if it had not been for the fact that he was frankly afraid to do so."

GREECE—CIVIL WAR

I think that possibly that is true. I hope and believe, and it is the desire of His Majesty's Government, that this horrible strife will soon be ended, and that those who are engaged in it and are now attacking what is the only constitutional Government there is, will cease their activities. We do not say that this Government has to endure for ever. We have never based ourselves on that case. We say that there are people in arms against the only constituted authority. It is the only Government there is. As soon as arms are laid down, and peace is restored, then it is our hope that at the earliest possible moment free elections may be held. I go further. I say to the House that His Majesty's Government are ready to play their part, if it is desired, and invite their allies to join in playing their part, in doing all they can to ensure that these elections should be freely held. That is all we desire. We do not want to impose a Government headed by Mr. X or Mr. Y on the Greek people. Why should we? We have plenty of anxieties and troubles of our own. But we do say that we have a responsibility to the Greek people to let them declare their own will for themselves.

Why did we ever go there at all? An hon. Gentleman said: "It is not on our lines of communication," but the country was without any produce, and Germany had done all in her power to destroy it. The people in Greece would have starved. That is why we intervened, knowing full well the risks and the political disputes and passions of this war, and also the passions left over from the Metaxas regime. We knew all this would burst in our faces, but we thought it right to take the risk and responsibility. We repeat, order must be restored, and when order is restored let free elections be held. We desire to help in holding such elections, and we invite our allies to help us in doing that. Let us not bring in questions about the Greek King playing this part or that. The King never sought, in these months, to play any part in these affairs, and whatever our views about Royalism or Republicanism I think we owe him some token of respect for the manner in which he has held back, and not sought to complicate what he knew was a difficult position in his own country.

We do not seek to dictate to Greece what her Government shall be. We do not seek to order the Greeks to have this, that or the other Government. All we wish to do is to ensure conditions in which food and supplies can reach the Greek people, because we know that if we do not they will starve. I believe that the great mass of them are not interested in E.A.M., E.L.A.S. or E.D.E.S. They are much more interested in getting something to eat and their life restored again, and employment for their people. That is what we are trying to do. In the process we have become involved against our will, in this internecine conflict. We beg and urge that those carrying it on shall lay down their arms. When arms are laid down it will be for the Greek people to decide on their Government, and they will do it with our help and goodwill, and once again, I hope, democracy will play its part in the land of its birth.

1945

37

GREECE—A REVIEW OF THE CIVIL WAR

Fierce fighting continued in Athens and the Piraeus during the latter half of December and until January 5. Reinforcements arrived from Italy during December.

The British Government was subjected to strong criticism by Parliament and certain sections of the Press in this country and in the U.S.A., but held firmly to its declared policy.

A lively debate took place in the House of Commons on December 20, when Mr. Eden gave a full explanation of the Government's policy. In the course of his speech he said:

"We seek nothing for ourselves in Greece at all. We seek neither strategic nor economic advantages. . . . Of course it is true that we have an interest in the Mediterranean. That has never been denied by anyone, but I say that we took this action above all, and only, to try to bring food and supplies to Greece, because we knew of the condition in which we should find Greece. . . . We did weigh the alternatives. We knew that there were risks . . . but if we had not gone in, what would have happened? Supposing there had been civil strife, Greek against Greek, as a result of which no food could have been got in?"

On December 25, Mr. Churchill and Mr. Eden made a dramatic visit to Athens. Archbishop Damaskinos became Regent on December 31 and General Plastiras formed a new Government on January 3.

The Varkiza agreement was signed by the Greeks on January 11 and E.L.A.S. signed General Scobie's truce terms the next day.

On January 18, Mr. Churchill opened a debate on the war situation, dealing very fully with the Greek situation. Mr. Eden wound up on January 19 and confined his remarks to the Greek

294

situation. The debate was stormy throughout and interruptions were frequent. He spoke immediately after Mr. James Griffiths, but Mr. Aneurin Bevan had been speaking a little earlier.

Much of this Debate has concerned itself with the affairs of south-eastern Europe, and the hon. Gentleman who has just spoken has concentrated almost exclusively on that sphere. Therefore, I propose to devote the greater part of what I have to say also to these same topics. Before I come to south-eastern Europe, however, there are one or two other matters raised in the Debate to which I want to refer.

In particular, I want to say something about two allies of ours that are suffering at the present time perhaps more than they have done at any time in this war—Holland and Norway. These are two countries that set, perhaps, some of our allies something of an example in political unity, two countries which have contributed always to the fullest extent in their power to the Allied effort, and I think that the Committee would wish that, in this time of their greatest trial, a message from us should go to these people to tell them that everything that it is within our power to do to alleviate their suffering will be done, and that we shall not forget, either now or in future years, the glorious part that they have played.

My hon. and gallant Friend the Member for North Newcastle (Lieut.-Colonel Sir C. Headlam), in opening his speech made the observation that, sometimes, he was doubtful whether or not these Debates served a useful purpose. He will not be surprised if I tell him that, from time to time, that thought also flits across the mind of the Foreign Secretary when he listens to the Debates. It is not so much always what is said; it is the difficulty in which the Government spokesmen sometimes are in saying all that they would like to say in reply. But, about this Debate, in the two days on which it has lasted, and, in particular, the speech of the Prime Minister, I think the House will feel that it has done a real and much-needed national service. We must all have felt, in these last weeks—I know I have—how much easier it is to imperil a grand Coalition than to fortify it. Yet the problems which are now confronting us in liberated Europe have not come altogether as a surprise. The advance of victorious Allied armies is going to present us with many more such problems. I only pray that each one of them is not

GREECE—A REVIEW OF THE CIVIL WAR

going to arouse quite the intensity of passion which this Greek issue has developed. If so, I frankly say that I shudder to think how we are going to be able to play our part in the councils of Europe. There will be differences in respect of policy in all these countries, differences in this House and differences in the countries which have been under a foreign yolk for a period of years. Man is a political animal and, therefore, he likes controversy, and does not always agree with his neighbour. And so it is in this House, and so it is going to be in those countries. If we are to handle the situation, we shall need a measure of patience and understanding, tolerance and goodwill between the great Allies.

We need something more. Several speeches in this Debate have referred to the machinery of Allied co-operation for dealing with political issues. My right hon. Friend the Member for Devonport (Mr. Hore-Belisha), in a very forceful speech, asked whether we thought everything had been done about this situation, and whether we had any plan; the right hon. Baronet the Member for south-west Bethnal Green (Sir P. Harris) spoke in much the same strain and so did other Members also. I must say—speaking I think for the Government in this—that we are not fully satisfied with the existing machinery for international co-operation on the political plane. We have been troubled about this for some time. It was we who, more than a year ago, at the Moscow conference, first suggested the need for some further machinery. We first proposed the setting up of what has now become the European Advisory Commission to which the right hon. Baronet referred. That Commission has done invaluable work.

The fruits of that work will be seen after the defeat of the enemy and of the satellite countries, when these problems will have to be dealt with, but they have neither the authority nor the representation sufficient to deal with many of the other problems that confront us. It may be that we can improve on that machinery and that there ought to be more frequent contacts, not necessarily between the heads of Governments, who have heavy charges to bear and who cannot be constantly meeting, but perhaps between the Foreign Secretaries. The contacts might be very frequent, I do not know, but I can tell the House, in answer to the questions which have been put, that this issue of the machinery of our collaboration will certainly be among those which will have to be examined at the meeting, which rumour has it—I do not know—is to be held at some time or other somewhere or other. I would only add that, as far as our contribution is concerned, we are prepared bodily to place ourselves at disposal to any extent which may be required in order that that machinery may function.

Before I turn to the Greek issue let me reply to some of the questions which were put by the right hon. Gentleman the Member for Wakefield (Mr. A. Greenwood) yesterday. He showed some anxiety as to the part that my right hon. Friend might play at this meeting of the heads of Governments and he said he thought my right hon. Friend was in danger of appeasing some of his great allies too much. I do not know. It is always questionable how far it is wise in war time to express, on the public platform, or the Floor of this House, exactly what you feel about the various political problems on which you are in controversy with your allies. It is a question of appreciation. Sometimes it is good and sometimes it is not so good. I am bound to say that, though I have seen my right hon. Friend in many roles, I have not so far seen him in the role of the timid fawn. I do not think that the right hon. Gentleman the Member for Wakefield need be too anxious lest my right hon. Friend the Prime Minister's known diffidence of expression should in any way hamper the case of His Majesty's Government at the next meeting. We have many international anxieties but I admit frankly that that is about the least of those which beset me.

I come to the vexatious problem which has been the theme of almost all this Debate—the problem of the situation in Greece. As I listened to the speeches which have been made to-day, and to some of the speeches that were made earlier, I was forced to the conclusion that some hon. Members of this Committee painted themselves a picture of E.A.M. that really bears no resemblance to reality. I want to put the position of that organization in as fair a perspective as I can. Nobody has suggested that this movement at its outset did not enlist under its banner numbers of men who joined for purely patriotic motives. Of course that is so, but it is no less clear that from the very early days of the movement the leaders who control the E.A.M. were not prepared to tolerate rivals in the political field of resistance in Greece. It was that which first brought about our difficulties in the guerrilla movement. General Sarafis himself at one time tried to lead another rival guerrilla band and he was brought in by force to E.A.M. and was a prisoner for some time until he was good enough to be their general.

This rivalry between E.D.E.S. and E.L.A.S. cannot be explained on the ground that E.L.A.S. bands were purely democratic and E.D.E.S. bands were purely reactionary. That is not so. I have read the charter of E.D.E.S. I should say that it was as near as can be an attempt to describe a Socialist heaven, if such a conception can be expressed by anybody who is a member of the Tory Party. As near as might be that seemed to be their programme, and yet there was from the outset this rivalry—a rivalry which, I believe, is largely based on the determination of some of E.A.M. leaders that no one was going to share with them the resistance movement in Greece.

PETTY-OFFICER ALAN HERBERT (Oxford University): Will the right hon. Gentleman lay the document on the Table?

MR. EDEN: We are preparing a White Paper and I hope that we can make it quite interesting. There was another organization —a military band called E.K.K.A.—which was another guerrilla organization. This is worth noting as an indication of developments which take place. In February of last year our officers in Greece, who played a really magnificent part in trying to hold these warring guerrilla elements together, secured a truce and all these various bands agreed to join together and to think only about the Germans for the time being. What happened? A very few weeks after that E.L.A.S. broke this agreement and they attacked and destroyed this guerrilla band of E.K.K.A. They murdered its leader, one Colonel Psaros, against whom, as far as I have been able to discover, no plausible charge has ever been brought, even by E.L.A.S. itself. So, I say, even before the German withdrawal there were, it appeared to us, unmistakable signs that it was the ambition of E.L.A.S. to seize control of the country by force. Here, let me add, His Majesty's Government have never been opposed to E.A.M. becoming the Government of Greece, but what we have said, and what we do say is, that they have no right to that position except through the medium of the ballot box, whereas their attempt has been, as we see it, to seize power with the weapons provided for them to do battle against the Germans.

MR. COCKS rose——

MR. EDEN: I have all the notes of the hon. Gentleman's speech, and I will answer him as I go along. If I do not, by all means let him interrupt. As I said, this evidence of the tendency of E.L.A.S. to seize power, rather than to be elected to power, had its effect upon the organization itself. There were many in the ranks who did not like it and who began to see the effect of that. Even before the fighting broke out in Athens, and after the fighting broke out, all the more moderate elements of what is called the E.A.M. organization flaked away. That was very noticeable to me, who had been to Athens before, when I returned with the Prime Minister at Christmas time, because when this conference, which he summoned, took place, to which the E.L.A.S. representatives came, I thought that they would do their best to show as broad a representation as possible, obviously in order to impress us and the world of their representative character. It was not so. Their representatives to the Conference were three Communists, led and dominated by the secretary-general of the Communist Party—those were the men who came to negotiate at this meeting. What I submit—and I have little doubt of it myself, but I cannot prove it—is that in the progress of the fighting, all the elements except the hard Communist core flaked away in disapproval of the policy which the Communist leaders were adopting. [An HON. MEMBER: "What proof is there?"] No proof, but I will try to prove to the satisfaction of the House that the policy we have pursued was the only policy open to us, and was a just and correct policy.

SIR R. ACLAND rose——

MR. EDEN: I am going to answer the hon. Baronet's question too. I cannot answer all at once, they come in turn. Why do I say that there has been this flaking away? I submit to the House that the Socialists, the Agrarians and the Popular Democrats, all of whom formed part of E.A.M. in the earlier stages, have announced their decision to break away and have, in one form or another, denounced the activities of their former associates.

MR. S. O. DAVIES (Merthyr): By whom?

MR. EDEN: I am just going to say by whom. The hon. Gentleman is in a hurry and wants to make my speech for me. I am going to tell him by whom and, in particular, I am going to take the Greek Socialist Party, which is the most important of these parties, and one which I hope will appeal to the hon. Gentleman who interrupted. It is the S.K.E. That party issued a manifesto and I shall trouble the Committee by reading it because I think it important that we should try to assess what is the true feeling of the organization, and the whole basis of my contention is that E.A.M., as such, does not exist any more and what is left is just a hard Communist or, if you like, Trotskyite core.

MR. STOKES rose——

MR. EDEN: The hon. Gentleman wants to hear what is the manifesto of the Greek Socialist Party and I will tell him. It says:

"The political bureau of the central committee of the Socialist Party in Greece, after succeeding in restoring its organization, which it had not succeeded in doing owing to the recent tragic events, assembled with almost a full meeting and, with the co-operation of representatives of the party organization in Macedonia and Thrace, examined the situation as transformed by the rupture of the Government of National Unity, and after detailed discussion by members of all the burning political questions of the day, resolved as follows:

It utterly condemns the civil war and hostilities between Greeks and Allies. These unhappy events took place in our country contrary to the desires of the S.K.E. which did all that it could to prevent them. It considers that the civil war was organized solely by deadly enemies of our country and is contrary to our national claims and the interests of the Greek working people and to the common anti-Fascist goal of the united nations. The party adopts and approves the resolution of the regional party organization of Macedonia and Thrace, which had the courage to take the initiative in disapproving the civil war immediately after the outbreak of hostilities, in view of the fact that the central leadership of the party was unable to meet. It declares that it refused all responsibility for, and withdrew itself from the E.A.M. bloc as soon as it was informed of the armed breach which took place without consultation with the S.K.E.

It appealed to all kindred parties and organizations in the manual and clerical working class to contribute to the cessation of civil war with a view to the return of political peace in the country. . . ."

And so on in the same strain.

MR. S. O. DAVIES: By whom was that document signed?

MR. EDEN: Of course, I am going to tell the hon. Gentleman by whom it was signed; did he think I was going to read out a document like that without checking where it came from?

MR. DAVIES: I only wanted to make a comment that documents are being read out here, and most persons in this Committee know that they have never been authentic documents and this is one of them.

MR. EDEN: The hon. Gentleman says it is not an authentic document. I will tell him who are the persons behind this document, and I will leave it to the Committee to judge. I have been into this matter with some trouble, because we do not want to give the Committee incorrect information. What earthly advantage is it to the Government to do that? Let the hon. Gentleman look back to the Debates of last December, and he will be able to judge whether his information was correct or not. The Greek Socialist Party is directed by a political bureau of eight members.

MR. GALLACHER: It is a fake. There is no Socialist Party in Europe——

MR. EDEN: I know the hon. Member does not like Socialist parties anyway.

MR. GALLACHER: I put it to the Secretary of State that this demonstrates it to be a fake—there never has been a Socialist Party in Europe which had a political bureau.

MR. EDEN: Perhaps the hon. Gentleman will let me describe who these people are——

MR. GALLACHER: It is a fake.

MR. EDEN: ——and then the people who know the Socialist Party better than me can speak about it. This party is directed by a political bureau of eight members, all but one of whom are now in Athens—I know where the one who is not in Athens is, but I do not propose to say—and by a central committee of twenty, all but two of whom are also in Athens. Now it so happens that representation of this party at the moment is especially full because there are also in Athens four delegates from northern Greece who were all members of the central committee. I will give their names so that they can be checked if anybody knows them. A gentleman called Mr. Stavirides, Mr. Papanikolaou, Mr. Mylonas, and Mr. Dimitrakopoulos—my Greek is not very good—those four are all the representatives who came down from Macedonia, and the manifesto to which I have just referred was voted by all the members—that is 20 of the central committee in Athens—and three of them went up to our Ambassador and handed it over to him.

MR. GALLACHER: I still think it is a fake.

MR. EDEN: I admit that the conditions in Athens are disturbed. I admit the difficulty of substantiating exactly what this or that section of political opinion feels in a city which has been through what Athens has been through, but I submit to the Committee that the document I have read out, and the circumstances which I have described of its presentation to us, is at least a strong *prima facie* case that it represents something of substance in Greek Socialist opinion.

MR. S. O. DAVIES: Can the Foreign Secretary explain why the names of Professor Svolos and Professor Angelopoulos are not among the names he read out, because they are, and have been, accredited leaders of the Greek Socialist Party?

MR. EDEN: I will say why those two names were not there.

Professor Svolos was a member of E.A.M., but I do not know his present whereabouts, and I cannot tell why he was not a signatory to this document. All I can tell the Committee is that this is the report which came to us through our Ambassador. There is no secret about this. We ourselves asked Sir Walter Citrine and others to go to Athens and see for themselves what was the position of the trade unions there. During the last twenty-four hours we have suggested that the party of Members of Parliament now in Italy should, themselves, go on to Greece.

MR. GALLACHER: Oh!

MR. EDEN: Are not Members of this House to be trusted except the hon. Member himself? Have we reached a point of dictatorship when only the hon. Gentleman can represent Members of this House. We suggested that that party should go to Greece simply because they are half-way there already, in Italy.

MR. GALLACHER *rose*——

THE CHAIRMAN (MAJOR MILNER): The hon. Gentleman must not interrupt. He makes interjections which, on occasions, he is entitled to do, but he is not entitled to make continuous comments.

MR. EDEN: We are anxious that hon. Members should get information about the situation. Apart from the delegation which, as I have already said, may go on from Italy to Greece we are ready as opportunity offers for perhaps a further delegation to go from this House to Greece. We have nothing to hide. If hon. Members here had seen what the Prime Minister and I have seen I am sure that many of the speeches and criticisms we have heard would never have been made. What I have said about the Greek Socialist Party applies also to the Agrarian Party and to the Popular Democrats. I believe that they, too, have flaked away from E.A.M. I cannot prove it; I have not the documents to show it but I can tell the Committee that that is our belief, which the House will find justified in the next few weeks. But what I do know is that representatives of the Agrarian Party from Salonika have definitely broken away from E.A.M., and have taken refuge in Athens.

MR. J. GRIFFITHS: I gather that these defections, if they be so, must have taken place since the right hon. Gentleman last spoke. The last time he spoke, he wanted E.A.M. in the Government.

MR. EDEN: They have taken place since we were in Athens. Now I come to the events on which I have been challenged and the position of the Government in the present situation. I must remind the Committee that, for months before we went into Greece, we laboured to bring about unity in the Greek political parties. We got all the parties together, and we got a document signed at Caserta, agreed by the rival commanders-in-chief. We have been challenged as to the course of events which brought about the break-up of the Government. The hon. Baronet the Member for Barnstaple (Sir R. Acland), the hon. Member for Broxtowe (Mr. Cocks) and the hon. Member for Ebbw Vale (Mr. Bevan) referred to that in the course of their speeches. I will again tell the Committee, briefly, the events so far as we know them. It has been suggested that the arrival of the Greek Brigade, the Rimini Brigade, was the cause of the trouble. So far as I can test the evidence there is not a shadow for justification for that statement, and I will show why. The Greek Brigade arrived in Athens on November 9, not November 19 as the hon. Member for Broxtowe stated in the Debate yesterday.

Its arrival was universally applauded by all sections of the Greek population. I know that because we were told in Athens that they were the only people who had a bigger reception than the British troops, when they arrived in Athens. After the arrival of this Brigade, the Greek E.A.M. Ministers in the Greek Government could have objected if they had wished. Nothing would have been easier, but no objection was made. On the contrary, eight days afterwards—on the 17th—agreement was reached with the Greek Government, to which the E.A.M. Ministers subscribed, that all guerrilla formations should be disarmed and no mention was made at all of the Rimini Brigade. Later the E.A.M. Ministers began to argue that if the guerrillas were to be disarmed the Rimini Brigade ought to lay down their arms, too. But the other members of the Greek Government would not accept that, and I do not think that is very surprising, either in the light of the record of the Brigade or in the light of the fact of how few Greek troops there were under arms. Still, they wanted to reach agreement and M. Papandreou asked the E.A.M. Ministers, who were complaining of the existence of this Brigade, to draft a decree for the demobilization of the guerrillas, in which it was provided that a brigade of E.L.A.S. should be retained under arms in order to balance the Rimini Brigade. That compromise was offered; that draft was produced by the E.A.M. Ministers themselves. They drew it up, brought it to their colleagues and it was accepted by all the other members of the Government on November 27. How is it possible to say that the Rimini Brigade was the cause of the break?

Next day the E.A.M. Ministers went back on the draft which they themselves had drawn up and demanded that all forces should

GREECE—A REVIEW OF THE CIVIL WAR

be disarmed, including the Rimini Brigade. The Government refused and matters reached a deadlock. But it was not even this that brought about the final split in the Government. The final split was this: that on December 1, the E.A.M. civil police refused to hand over their arms to the National Guard. It is worth looking at this, because the decision that they should hand over their arms had been reached unanimously by the Government, including E.A.M. Ministers, as long ago as November 5. At this point the E.A.M. police had not been an issue during the negotiations about the disarmament of the guerrilla armies at all. It was also known that the same morning E.A.M. were going to call a general strike. It was faced with this, that M. Papandreou circulated to all his colleagues a draft decree re-affirming the Government's decision that the E.A.M. police should hand over their arms, a decision nearly a month old. The E.A.M. Ministers refused to ratify the decision and that night resigned.

I want to say one more thing about the E.A.M. police, because I want the Committee to note that it is my contention that it was over this issue of the E.A.M. police that the break occurred, and that it was the police themselves who were largely responsible for taking hostages and the methods of their custody. I must say that during the long negotiations about a truce, when every effort was being made to try to get agreement, the E.L.A.S. representatives said that they could not release their hostages because they could not answer for the actions of the E.A.M. police who had taken those hostages.

SIR R. ACLAND: Will the right hon. Gentleman confirm the Scobie leaflet? There is no reference in it to the agreement or to the steps that were taken.

MR. EDEN: General Scobie's broadcast was made on the afternoon of December 1. [HON. MEMBERS: "The leaflet."] The leaflet and the broadcast were the same. They stated his desire to maintain law and order, and to assist in the distribution of relief. Nothing in that leaflet could possibly have been so construed as to inflame passion, but it was a warning that, if it came to force, we should do our best to maintain law and order. I do not know what else a general in that position would be supposed to say.

Now I want to come to the present position, and to the matter of hostages, and to General Plastiras's position. Some hon. Members do not seem quite to understand why we spoke with such strength in condemnation of hostages. It was even suggested that the Greek Government have themselves arrested a number of

304

people in Athens. I want to clear that up. As far as the arrests that we have made are concerned, a decision has been taken as the result of agreement between General Scobie and the Greek Government, that all civilians arrested by British Forces for bearing arms against us should be released with the exception of those who will be exchanged to fulfil the terms of the agreement reached with E.A.M. As far as arrests by the Greek Government are concerned, it has already been made clear that prosecutions will only be instituted against those who have violated the penal code, or the rules of war, on charges such as murder, rape or looting. In other words, the act of bearing arms against the State will not be regarded as a crime in itself and will not be punished. I say this to make it plain that there is no question of hostages being held either by the Greek Government or by ourselves. We have not got one. I now demand, in the name of all parties and all Members of the House, that E.A.M. should release those hostages forthwith.

I now come to deal with reports in the Press that warrants have been issued in Athens for the arrest of prominent E.A.M. and E.L.A.S. leaders. This story first appeared on January 8 and was contradicted by the Greek Ministry of Foreign Affairs and by us at the Foreign Office. Subsequent investigation has shown that a police interpreter was responsible for the report. The story was revived two or three days ago. I have to-day received a telegram from His Majesty's Ambassador in Athens which states that no such warrants have been issued. He has obtained personal confirmation of this from the Greek Minister of Foreign Affairs. There have also been references to a statement made by General Plastiras to Press correspondents that he could not agree to an amnesty. I have stated that the declared intention of the Greek Government is to take action only against those guilty of crimes against the penal code or the rules of war. General Plastiras yesterday confirmed this to our Ambassador. He said it was still the policy of the Greek Government, and he specifically authorized me to tell that to the House of Commons to-day. Therefore, the only rebels liable to prosecution are those guilty of ordinary crimes against the criminal code. He repeated this instruction, which is an instruction of the Greek Government, to the military governor of Attica, to the head of the gendarmerie and the head of the police. He told them that no political arrests are to be made. People charged on such charges as murder, rape and looting are having their cases investigated immediately and, if no *prima facie* case exists, they are to be discharged. A panel of 75 judges or magistrates is already at work to effect that. I have only one thing to add about the various Plastiras reports. The report in the Press that General Gonatas is appointed Governor of Macedonia is not accurate. I think I have covered all the realm of charges.

MR. BEVAN: The right hon. Gentleman's statement is exceedingly important and, so far, has been satisfactory in detail, but I read out a statement made by the Greek Minister to British Press representatives in Athens in which he said they were going to release all prisoners except those who bore arms. Does the right hon. Gentleman assume that the Greek Government is going to make a statement which will satisfy opinion here on that point?

MR. EDEN: I could not have dealt more fully with the matter. I have explained that our Ambassador saw General Plastiras himself and it is on his authority and that of General Plastiras that I have made this statement, which covers precisely the issues which have been raised to-day. The position could not be clearer and the hon. Member has really no right to complain that I am not clear. He asks us to be objective on this matter. I have never heard anyone import so much prejudice into the subject of debate.

He threw taunt after taunt at General Plastiras. Who is this very wicked man who is held up like that? He was the man who, after the collapse of Greece in 1922, took over the Government, pulled his country together, arranged for a general election, and retired after the election, which resulted in the return of Venizelos. He was the man who was Prime Minister when Greece alone among the European countries accepted refugees and hundreds of thousands of Armenians, thus helping to relieve a problem which was haunting Europe. He is the man, we are told now, who played about with the Germans in France. He was in France in exile, and he was there approached by the S.S. who said: "Come and be our quisling in Greece." He refused to have anything to do with it.

All these stories are brought to this Committee to create prejudice. We are told that we wanted to deny freedom in Greece. Why should this country wish to deny freedom in Greece, this country which is fighting because it believes in just those very things. When I hear the hon. Gentleman speak like that I say to him, what do we in this country desire in Greece and in all these countries? We desire a decision by the ballot box, and I give the Committee this pledge. Wherever Britain's authority can carry, the decision will be by the ballot box. We cannot pledge ourselves that our power or authority will reach over every land. Our authority is limited, but where it can be exerted the decision will be by the ballot box, and not by the bullet or by attempts to seize power because by fortuitous circumstances you have the arms at that moment.

Let me sum up. We have discussed this matter, we have debated it now three times at great length. I have had some experience in my life of international affairs, and I have never known an issue where I have been more absolutely certain we are right. I am convinced that if hon. Members could have seen what I saw in Athens last time, their reaction would be exactly the same as mine. I am sure that it was our action, and only our action, unpopular and difficult as it was, hard as it was to explain to our American friends, I admit, which prevented a massacre in Athens. That is my absolute conviction, and I believe it is shared by virtually everybody who saw the situation as it then was.

I have something more to say to the Committee. The Government have been criticized, they have been maligned, they have been taunted for the policy they have pursued in Greece. In that matter, it has, admittedly, done us some injury in other lands, where it is not easy, in all respects, to understand the issue. I think that this afternoon I have for the Government the right to say to the Committee: "Have we your support or have we not?" I have set out our case as fully and fairly as I can. I have made plain that the whole of our authority will be used to see that there is nothing in the nature of proscription and no punishment because these people in their folly, if you like, have taken arms against the State. We will do our best to ensure that at the earliest moment there are free elections in Greece, but, meanwhile, we must have an expression of the views of this House. We are entitled to know whether, as a result of this discussion, the world is to believe we are supported by the overwhelming majority of this House or not. It is difficult sometimes when you read, as I have to, despatches from abroad. I read reports that the Government's position is shaken on account of its policy in Greece. We all know that that is not true. We know that the more it is explained, the more it will be understood and the stronger our position will be. But foreign countries do not know. It is all too easy for Goebbels and company to make use of the reported state of public opinion here and of the gossip of some journalist, in some column or other, which says that we are tottering to our fall.

I ask the Committee this afternoon to pronounce whether or not the Government are tottering to their fall, and to give us on the programme I have outlined, on the pledges I have given, and on my right hon. Friend's speech, a Vote of Confidence, so that the nation as a whole may know where we stand, and so that this policy which we have pursued throughout—let me say, with patience and with only the one purpose, to bring freedom to Greece—may be finally fulfilled.

[The Committee divided on a motion against the Government's policy: Ayes, 7; Noes, 340.]

38

CRIMEA CONFERENCE

The Russians encircled Budapest on Christmas Day and completed its capture on February 13. Hungary was granted an armistice by the United Nations on January 20. In the north, the Red Army reached the German frontier on January 30 having crossed the Silesian frontier from the south two weeks before. By the end of February they had captured Neu Stettin and part of Breslau.

In western Europe the German counter-attack in the Ardennes was initially successful and all Belgium seemed to be threatened, but the position was stabilized and the bulge was straightened out by January 26 after fierce fighting by the American armies. A German thrust in the Strasbourg area was halted. By mid-February, British and Canadian troops were on the Rhine and by the end of February, American troops were within six miles of Cologne.

In Italy, after the capture of Faenza there was a lull, weather was bad and troops were being regrouped.

The enemy was forced out of northern Burma and the attack on Mandalay began on February 8. Akyab fell on January 5. In the Philippines, U.S. troops entered Manila on February 3. Strong U.S. bomber forces attacked Japan.

On January 5, the Lublin Government was recognized by the Russians as the provisional Government of Poland.

On February 2, Mr. Churchill arrived in the Crimea with Mr. Eden. On their journey out they stopped at Malta where they had discussions with President Roosevelt and Mr. Stettinius, the United States Secretary of State, who also went on to the Crimea.

309

THE CRIMEA CONFERENCE

On February 12, the terms of the "Yalta" agreement were announced. The next day the Polish Government in London announced that they refused to agree to the terms.

On February 14, Mr. Churchill and Mr. Eden left the Crimea and arrived in Athens where they were given a wonderful welcome. Turkey declared war on the Axis on February 23.

On February 27 and 28, and March 1, the House of Commons debated the Prime Minister's motion:

"That this House approves the declaration of joint policy agreed to by the three great powers at the Crimea Conference and, in particular, welcomes their determination to maintain unity of action not only in achieving the final defeat of the common enemy but, thereafter, in peace as in war."

Mr. Churchill was the first speaker.

On the second day, Mr. Petherick moved an amendment regretting "the decision to transfer to another Power the territory of an ally country contrary to the Treaty and to Article 2 of the Atlantic Charter. . . ."

Mr. Victor Raikes spoke in support of this amendment just before Mr. Eden replied. After Mr. Eden's speech the House divided on the Amendment. Ayes, 25; Noes, 396.

The following is Mr. Eden's speech:

I think those of us who have listened to this discussion have been conscious that we are discussing an issue on which the House feels deeply. Hon. Members, whatever their point of view on the issue, have fully expressed themselves and that is as it should be, for after all there are very few institutions anywhere in the world which could conduct such a discussion as has been conducted here during the last two days.

I am sure that not one of our critics will deny that we have a right, as a Government, to come to the House and ask for their judgment on the work that we did in the Crimea. Let me correct one thing that my hon. Friend said, at the beginning of his speech. He referred to my right hon. Friend's speech, and to the position of the Prime Minister in this matter. I must make it absolutely clear to the House that at every stage of this anxious Polish business, lasting as it has now done over almost the whole of the war period—and indeed starting from long before that—at any rate, so

310

long as this Government have handled it—all the decisions have been taken by the War Cabinet; and the responsibility is the responsibility of the War Cabinet. We have worked together in all we have done, and my right hon. Friends in the War Cabinet want me to say that we have worked, in the Crimea and other occasions, as a united War Cabinet, and, be our treatment of this subject right or wrong, it is the treatment of a united Government, who took all their decisions with a knowledge of the facts put before them.

My hon. Friend also spoke of our relations with the Polish Government, and asked, was it true that I have not had direct contacts with the Polish Prime Minister or members of his Government? It is true that we have not had personal contacts with them, but it is also true that I have frequently seen the Ambassador who represents that Government. I have seen him, naturally, since I returned from the Crimea. Perhaps I ought to add, as a matter of historical accuracy, that I had arranged an interview with the Polish Prime Minister and his Foreign Secretary just before we went to the Crimea, but an incident occurred, which will be fresh in the mind of the House—that we had a sudden and unexpected Greek Debate; and I, therefore, asked my Permanent Under-Secretary, Sir Alexander Cadogan, to see them instead. I think the House will accept it that there has not been any discourtesy on the part of His Majesty's Government. I cannot, however, pretend that we have the same cordial relations with the present Polish Government as we had with the Government which preceded them, and which included, as, unhappily, this Government do not, all the main Polish parties represented in London.

I want to deal with this question, taking two main issues—first, and the more briefly of the two, the question of the frontiers, and, second, the question of whether under the arrangement which we have devised in the Crimea there can be and will be a free and independent Poland. A word about the frontier itself. My hon. and gallant Friend the Member for Epsom (Sir A. Southby) and others, including the mover of the Amendment, who raised this issue, always begin at the Treaty of Riga; but it is really completely unrealistic to begin this discussion at the Treaty of Riga. I admit that it is true—there is no question of it—that the Soviet Government ultimately accepted the Treaty of Riga, but nobody with a knowledge of the history of those parts is going to contend that Russia was content with that solution, or, indeed, that we were content with that solution. As the House knows, and as I have stated before, we more than once urged the Polish Government at the time not to extend their frontiers East beyond the Curzon Line, and for two years after the Treaty of Riga withheld our recognition of that arrangement. In 1923, when the Conference of Ambassadors did eventually recognize the Treaty, that Conference made it plain, on our initiative, that the responsibility for the Line rested with the two Governments concerned, and not with us.

More than that, the Conference made it clear that in their recognition of the Riga frontier, two years after the Treaty had been signed, there was called for—put it this way—the setting-up of an autonomous regime in Eastern Galicia for ethnographical reasons. In point of fact, that autonomous regime was never set up. What happened was that, after fighting between the Poles and Ukrainians, the Polish armies were victorious and obtained control of the country. I hope the House is not going to assume that, on account of that, what happened at that time was accepted by the population as a whole. It was not. Although the area was placed under the Minority Treaty, because of the disputes and the anxieties about it, the provisions of that Minority Treaty were never fully carried out, and disturbances, as the House will see if they look up the records, were unhappily frequent. What happened was this. It is not in any way surprising or a criticism of anybody. As the Eastern Galicia area—which is the one, I think, in most dispute—was an area of mixed population, with Poles in the minority, the Poles sought to increase their own population in that area by bringing other Poles in, with the result that that, in its turn, led to friction. Further, there was the issue which, the House must bear in mind, underlies the whole of this frontier problem: the religious issue between the Roman Catholic elements and the Orthodox Church. The religious difference in that area is far older than the national issue, and it is religion which lies at the root of much of the feeling on this issue.

I have explained before, and I am not going over it again, the basis on which the Curzon Line was delimited, but this at least can be accepted by everybody, whatever else we dispute—that east of the Curzon Line there are no areas where the Poles are in the majority except the two cities of Vilna and Lvov, which, in their turn, are surrounded by large non-Polish areas. On that particular aspect of the question there is no dispute between us at all. I, therefore, say that when the Soviet Government say that they will accept the Curzon Line, with certain adjustments, minor adjustments, but all in favour of Poland—the importance of which

I must emphasize, for the Curzon Line, it is true, is not a frontier but a line drawn on the map, and it is of importance to the Polish Government that all adjustments, and there must be many, shall favour them—I cannot stand at this Box and say that I regard that as a gross injustice to Poland. It is the position which successive Governments in this country have consistently taken. I would put this to my hon. Friends. Are they absolutely convinced that the structure of the Polish State is strengthened by the inclusion of large, or considerable, non-Polish elements in it? I wonder.

MR. A. BEVAN (Ebbw Vale): On the West, too?

MR. EDEN: The assumption in regard to the West is that the populations shall be removed. That is the whole basis. In most cases, I can tell the hon. Gentleman, they have gone already. But let me deal with this matter—I am sorry the hon. Gentleman has put me off my stroke—about the minorities in the Polish State. I should have said that there were two weaknesses in the Polish State, as it existed before the war. One was these very considerable minority elements, who came frequently and made their complaints before the International Tribunal at Geneva, and the other was the Corridor. I am amazed that in the speeches which the Mover and Seconder of the Amendment made neither of them—I listened carefully—made even the slightest reference to the significance to Poland of the fact that this Corridor problem would cease to exist. If my hon. Friend's concern is solely for Poland, surely they must take some account of that?

May I ask them this? Which Poland would be stronger—the Poland with Vilna and with the Corridor as it was, or a Poland without Vilna and without the Corridor? I have not the slightest doubt, nor, I believe, has any student of international affairs the slightest doubt, which Poland would be the stronger. I am going to say a word or two about this Corridor business. I made one reference to it before, but, if the House will allow me, I am going into it a little deeper, because I had to handle this myself year after year at Geneva, when the unfortunate British representative on the Council was *Rapporteur* for Danzig. I promise the House that I never chose the job; I inherited it, and it was the most thankless task that ever fell to the lot of man, because, at every single meeting, we were faced with these issues, demands, charges and counter-charges between Poles and Germans. I think the only other person who had this experience to the same extent is the present Lord Chancellor. We were never able to obtain a solution of real value, because no solution was possible as long as the Corridor existed.

I remember one occasion—it will probably be fresh in the minds of many hon. Members—when the German representative had behaved in a particularly insulting manner to the Council. After he had withdrawn, I thought it my duty to say to the Council, in private, of course, the Press having withdrawn, that, in view of his behaviour, we ought to know whether the Polish Government would take action in the event of a German infraction by violence of the Free City, for which we were responsible. I put that question, and the Polish answer was "Yes". I mention that only to show that it would be a cardinal sin on our part to perpetuate that state of affairs. I have been engaged in these last years in this Polish-Russian dispute, and, for what my own judgment is worth, I have come to the decision that there are two alternatives. Either you must deprive Poland of all outlet to the sea, or East Prussia must cease to be German and the Corridor must go. Of these two alternatives, I unhesitatingly commend the second to the House; but do not let anybody say that that is not something of importance for the Poland of the future, and do not let people merely say: "You are taking half Poland away," without putting into the balance what this means.

I turn to another aspect. It is not only the question of what the elimination of the Corridor means. The House must also put into the balance the position of Upper Silesia, which we are all agreed should go to Poland, and which is a territory of great value industrially. Poland tried hard to get it after the last peace settlement, but her claim was rejected. That must be put into the balance, too. I believe that, when a settlement is finally reached —and here let me say again that what we have expressed is our view of what a settlement should be with our ally, a settlement which we would wish to discuss with the new Polish Government when it is created—I believe it may still be found—and I say this with respect to some of my hon. Friends—that the new Poland when so constituted, will be as strong as, or stronger than, the Poland that existed in 1939. That depends, of course, on how the agreement is carried out.

Therefore, I turn to that, and to the setting-up of the new Government. I was asked by my noble Friend the Member for Lanark (Lord Dunglass) yesterday, and I have been asked to-day by both the Mover and the Seconder of the Amendment, why it was that, when we approached this problem in the Crimea, we did not make an end of the Lublin Government, as it were, "de-recognize" the Lublin Government and "de-recognize" the Government here, and start entirely afresh. Of course, that is an attractive suggestion, and it was, in fact, the point from which we started our examination of the matter, but this is the difficulty with which we were faced. The Russians said to us, and it is inescapable, that they must have some authority on their lines of communication through Poland. Whether we like or dislike the Lublin Committee—and personally I say I dislike it—for the moment it is the authority which is functioning there in fulfilling the requirements of the Russian military authorities. What they said to us was: "We do not know how long it will take to form a new Polish Government; it may take weeks, it may take months." I do not know, either; it takes quite a long time to form a British Government. Nobody can say. During that time there could not be a vacuum in Poland, and so it is that we agreed, eventually, that pending the creation of the new Government—and I beg the House to note that the phrase "new Government" occurs twice in the Declaration—the Soviet Government will continue to recognize the Lublin Government and we and the United States will continue to recognize the Government here. I hope I have been able to remove the doubts expressed by my hon. Friends to-day.

The right hon. Member for Wakefield (Mr. Greenwood) yesterday complained that we had taken our decision, or come to our agreement behind the back, I think his phrase was, of the Polish Government. As I understand his argument, it was that we ought to have summoned the Polish Government to our councils in Yalta when we reached a certain point in our discussions and talked matters over with them. Of course, we thought of it. Let me therefore ask the right hon. Gentleman which Polish Government were we to summon? Were we to summon the Lublin Government, for both we and the United States Government hold that that Government is not fully representative of the Polish people? Or were we to summon the Government here in London, which the Soviet Government hold is not representative of the Polish people? Or were we to summon both Governments? Apart from certain physical difficulties, this last arrangement would not have been satisfactory. Moreover in my belief, probably, those Polish statesmen who have most following in Poland—and all this is a matter of one's own conjecture—are Poles in Poland and Poles in London, who are members neither of the Lublin Government nor of the London Government. What did we do? We could not bring them all to Yalta; if we had done, no doubt we should still be there. It was impossible to do that, and so we decided to appoint this Commission to carry through the task for us.

My right hon. Friend said something about this Commission of the Soviet Foreign Secretary and two Ambassadors, and one of the speakers seemed to indicate that he thought that there was a weakness in our position; but let me assure the House that our Ambassador will act under instructions of His Majesty's Government and will not deviate from those instructions. The hon. and gallant Member for Berwick and Haddington (Captain McEwen), said that our Ambassador had said that the Lublin Government should be recognized. I do not know when he said that. He never said anything of that kind to me, to my right hon. Friend the Prime Minister, or to any one of our colleagues, and, certainly, he knows well enough what is the attitude of His Majesty's Government in that respect.

Let me now try to answer some of the questions that have been put. My hon. and gallant Friend the Member for Berwick and Haddington, and indeed, the hon. Gentleman who has just spoken, really put what was the only alternative course. They said that better than what we have done, would have been to have left it alone. I cannot accept that view. That really is an absolute policy of despair. What would that have meant? It would have meant that the Lublin Government would have continued to operate with the support of the Soviet Government. We do not know what the conditions are there at the present time, and I am not by any means sure all the information that hon. Friends get about the state of opinion in Poland is accurate. I am not even sure that the politicians who have been five years out of the country know exactly what their country feels. There have been revolutions in thought as well as in spirit in Poland in these last years. There was an account the other day—one has to be very careful from which newspapers one quotes—in the *Manchester Guardian*—whose foreign correspondents I have always found very reliable, so far—which gave an account of some American officers who came out from Poland. They said they saw the first Russian forces drive on, the Poles, delirious with delight, cheering both the Russians and their Western Allies. I do not know whether it is true or whether it is not. I should think that very likely it was so. Maybe it was only so at the beginning and it may be so now, but one cannot tell, as one cannot be sure. But I beg of hon. Members not to accept every report that comes and is suddenly thrust upon us in the House of Commons by our friends.

MR. PETHERICK: Would not a perfectly simple solution be for the Russian Government to accept British war correspondents and British correspondents to look after the interests of civil affairs in Poland?

MR. EDEN: That is going a little ahead of what I was going to say. I would like first to answer two questions asked by my Noble Friend yesterday about our desires in connection with this Polish situation. He asked for two specific answers to his questions. First. Is it our desire that Poland should be really and truly free? Yes, certainly, most certainly it is. In examining that Government, if and when it is brought together, it will be for us and our allies to decide whether that Government is really and truly, as far as we can judge, representative of the Polish people. Our recognition must depend upon that. We would not recognize a Government which we did not think representative. The addition of one or two Ministers would not meet our views. It must be, or as far as it can be made, representative of the Polish parties as they are known, and include representative national Polish figures. That is what we mean. There is only one consideration—I do not think we could call it more than that—that we would ask of the new Polish Government; that is that they would enter into a treaty of friendship and alliance with Russia. I do not think that anybody would think that unreasonable because at the same time that Government would have treaties of friendship and alliance with us and the French Government.

The second question was: Do we favour the establishment of machinery for Allied supervision of elections? That was a question which was also discussed. The Greek Government have asked for such supervision and we have invited, or shall invite when the time comes, our Russian and American allies to join in it. It may be, if and when this new Polish Government is formed they will also ask for international supervision. I hope so. If they do then we shall certainly be prepared to join in it. We could not agree to any inter-Allied supervision to which we were not parties in view of our treaty relations with Poland. I think the House will agree that the final decision on that cannot be taken until the moment comes, if and when this new Polish Government is formed, because that new Government must have a say as to their supervision and, if they desire it, as to its nature and the conditions. But I will make plain our own position, as it is made plain to our allies, that, if there should be such supervision, we shall be glad to take part in it ourselves. There is one more question which my Noble Friend

THE CRIMEA CONFERENCE

asked. He said that, in the arrangement for Yugoslavia, we included a provision that the acts of the Yugoslav Committee should be ratified by the new Parliament, and he asked why we did not include a similar provision in the Polish Agreement. But to be honest with my hon. Friend, we did not think of it. We did not think we had got to a stage far enough for that to be operative but I see no reason whatever why that proposal should not be made. In view of the fact that it was at once accepted by our allies in relation to Yugoslavia, I have no reason to think that it will not be accepted in relation to Poland, and I think it is a good thing that that proposal should be put forward. It would be an additional safeguard.

Let me turn to the question of information from inside Poland. We should certainly like people from this country to have an opportunity of seeing for themselves conditions inside Poland. There have been newspaper correspondents, but apart from them, we would like other opportunities, and I have every reason to believe that our Russian Allies would certainly not object to it. Indeed I am inclined to think from something I have had to-day that they would probably welcome it, but I would rather not go further at the moment than to say that we are in correspondence with our Russian allies about making arrangements so that people from this country can go to Poland to see what is going on. We shall do all we can to bring these arrangements to early fruition. I feel that nothing would give more reassurance to this House than a sense that there would be an opportunity to see what was going on in Poland.

I come on to the other questions. My hon. and gallant Friend the Member for Berwick and Haddington said: "Why, when you are signing the Anglo-Soviet Treaty, do not you consider this Polish matter and did not you put special provisions into your agreement about it?" There was a similar question asked in another form by my hon. and gallant Friend the Member for Epsom (Sir A. Southby). The answer is that, at the time the Anglo-Soviet Treaty was made, fortunately Soviet Russia and the Polish Government here were in relations. It was one of the few comparatively calm and encouraging periods of Soviet-Polish relations, and they were in relation very largely as the outcome of the efforts of His Majesty's Government to bring about the agreement of 1941. Of course, the Soviet Government are aware of our engagement towards Poland on which I propose to say a word. I must repeat and make plain —I am not sure that it is plain to some hon. Members—exactly the

318

position about recognition. I hold the House out no pledge. No one can be certain how it is going to work out but we hope that the discussions in Moscow will be attended by representative Poles from inside Poland and from outside Poland and that as a result of those conversations a thoroughly representative Polish Government will come into being. If it does and if it is in the words of the communiqué, "properly constituted" then we and our allies will recognize that government as the provisional government of Poland—provisional until the elections take place. If it does not come into being then we remain as we are to-day, we and the United States recognizing the Government in London and the Soviet Government recognizing, I presume, the Government in Lublin. That, may I add, would not be a very happy state of affairs either for Poland or for unity between our allies.

Now may I say a word or two about the Amendment which we are now discussing? The Amendment suggests that the recommendations which the three Great Powers have made for the solution of the Polish problem are contrary to treaty. That is not so. We have at no time guaranteed Poland's pre-war frontier. Nor, let me add, can I accept that to agree to recommend the line which was worked out at the time as giving as near as might be an ethnographical boundary is to run directly counter to the terms of the Atlantic Charter. As to the last part of my hon. Friend's Amendment, I must say that I am frankly puzzled as to how that can be regarded as a criticism of the policy which we are now advocating. If my hon. Friends will read the wording, it seems to me to be a precise description of what we are seeking to do in Poland. We are seeking to ensure to Poland the full right to choose her own Government free from the influence of any other power, or any other powers, let me add. So that in that respect I do not understand where we are open to criticism. As I have said, whether we shall succeed or not I cannot pronounce upon now, but I have not the least doubt, and I hope the House has not the least doubt, that it is not only our right but our duty to make this attempt.

I come to a criticism made by my hon. Friend the Member for Penryn and Falmouth (Mr. Petherick) who maintained that in the course which we have jointly agreed, we have in some way violated the Anglo-Polish Agreement of 1939, and he referred to a secret Protocol in this connection. I can assure my hon. Friend that his fears are entirely unfounded. There is nothing in the Anglo-Polish Treaty, or in any other document, which guarantees the frontiers of Poland. The Government of 1939 gave the House, of course, full information about the Treaty but, quite rightly they went further than this and made clear the effect of the secret Protocol from which my hon. Friend quoted. I must read to the House the reply given by my right hon. Friend the present Minister of Education who was then Under-Secretary for Foreign Affairs.

MR. BELLENGER (Bassetlaw): Has the Protocol been published?

MR. EDEN: No, sir.

MR. BELLENGER: Will the right hon. Gentleman do that?

MR. EDEN: I will now have to consider that. Naturally I had it in mind as my hon. Friend has raised the question—I do not make any complaint about that. I am now going to read the answer which was given to Parliament at the time. I was not a Member of the Government myself. This is what he said in reply to a Parliamentary Question on 19 October 1939, asking whether the references to aggression by a European Power in the Anglo-Polish Agreement were intended to cover the case of aggression by Powers other than Germany' including Russia, and my right hon. Friend replied:

"No, sir. During the negotiations which led up to the signature of the agreement, it was understood between the Polish Government and His Majesty's Government that the agreement should only cover the case of aggression by Germany, and the Polish Government confirm that this is so."—[*Official Report*, 19 October 1939. Vol. 352, c. 1082.]

That is the exact position of the Agreement. There was no question whatever of any engagement having been made about the eastern frontiers at that time or at any other time.

MR. PETHERICK: May I interrupt the right hon. Gentleman? He is referring only to the main Treaty of mutual assistance. I asked about a Protocol of which I read out an extract and it was perfectly plain. I will do it again if he likes. Clause 3 of the secret Protocol says:

"The undertakings mentioned in Article 6 of the agreement, should they be entered into by one of the contracting parties with a third State"—shall we say Russia or some other State?—"would of necessity be so framed that their execution should at no time prejudice either the sovereignty or territorial inviolability of the other contracting parties."

MR. EDEN: I do not know that my hon. Friend has got the complete document. In fact I do not know what he has got. I must frankly say, if he has got the complete document, he will see that that refers to an earlier Article, and the earlier Article makes it

THE CRIMEA CONFERENCE

quite plain——[An Hon. Member: "What are these?"] My hon. Friend did not tell me he was going to read out from a secret document, but, naturally, as he did so, I have looked it up, and I have seen exactly what the position is. I can assure my hon. Friend, and my right hon. Friend the Minister of Education will confirm it, that the answer I have just given was precisely intended to cover that secret Protocol. I can assure him there is no catch about the matter at all and that what that Clause refers to, if he will look back, is to Article 3 of the agreement which refers to certain undertakings that might in the future be made——

Mr. Petherick: I am extremely sorry but Clause 3 says "undertakings mentioned in Article 6". Nothing could be more specific.

Mr. Eden: I beg the hon. Gentleman's pardon but I have taken the trouble to look up this matter since he raised it. I was not even a member of the Government then, but I consulted those who were and I think my right hon. Friend will bear me out that they spared no pains to tell the House exactly what the position was, and it would have been wrong if the Government had not done so. What they made absolutely plain was that these measures only applied to aggression by Germany, and it does not in the least surprise me, if I may say so. I am now going to look into these documents and lay them on the Table. I do not ask my hon. Friend how he obtained this secret Protocol.

Mr. A. Bevan (Ebbw Vale): Is it not rather disquieting, during this period when there was so very much interest in foreign affairs, that His Majesty's Government should be making secret commitments with other Powers?

Mr. Eden: I really do not think so. We must not let a wrong impression go out. I have consulted my legal advisers and in their judgment, and in the judgment of those concerned at the time, the effect of this secret Protocol was to limit—precisely to limit—the obligations put before the House, not to increase them.

Let me now come back to some of the points which have been raised, because I want to carry the House with me in the remaining arguments I have to make. My hon. and gallant Friend the Member for Epsom asked what were the reasons why we failed to conclude a treaty with Russia in 1939. Here, again, I am dealing with matters which I did not handle, but I think the correct answer is something like this: Russia said at that time that if she was to conclude a treaty, she must have the right to move her troops across Poland, or across the Baltic States, in the event of war with

Germany. The Polish Government at that time were consulted on this point, and would not agree to the Russian demand. Although I do not pretend to be an historian, I think that that was, approximately, the main cause of the breakdown of those negotiations.

SIR A. SOUTHBY: Do I understand my right hon. Friend to mean that our failure to come to agreement in 1939 was due to Russia's demand for those portions of territory which I mentioned in the question I asked him in my speech?

MR. EDEN: Perhaps my hon. and gallant Friend will put down a Question about it on the Order Paper; it is a little difficult for me to give a detailed answer at short notice. But I have consulted those who were concerned, and I think the answer I gave was the main cause of the breakdown.

Now I come to the main issue. Some of my hon. Friends have said, with warmth, that the decisions we arrived at at Yalta have become a matter of world anxiety. I really cannot accept that that is true. So far as I know, the deepest anxiety of all was caused to Goebbels. If the House will read some of the stuff put out by Goebbels, after the Yalta Agreement, they would see in that the measure of the success of that Agreement. But not only that. If the House would look at reviews of the American Press and, still more so, of the Swedish Press—Sweden has had a long traditional friendship with Poland—and of the Turkish Press, they would find in them a general and wide endorsement of what we set out to achieve at Yalta. It really is a wild exaggeration to say that the work we did there was a cause of anxiety. I cannot tell how these matters will work out in their later stages. I know how infinitely difficult the problems will be. It may be that we shall not succeed, but I think some of my hon. Friends would have been wiser had they reserved judgment until a later stage. There is no such thing as a perfect solution of this problem, but surely it is a step forward that the three Great Powers have agreed upon a method of handling it.

Since the Polish-Soviet Agreement of 1941 was unhappily broken by an incident which is fresh in the minds of the House, I have been faced with two main anxieties in dealing with the problem. First, what would be the effect of failing to restore relations to Poland with Russia and, second, what would be the effect on the three great countries joined together in the prosecution of the war? Those are the problems we have to confront. If we are to restore Poland as a true, independent State she will need the help of each one of the three Great Powers to restore her devastated frontier. She cannot do that unless there is agreement between them. Some of my hon. Friends have said that a policy of continuing to recognize the Government here while the Lublin Government is recognized by Russia is of no assistance to Poland, although it may give us a great moral position. I am surprised at my hon. Friends using that argument. My hon. Friend the Member for south-east Essex (Mr. Raikes), who has just spoken, chided me once, I remember, for being an idealist. I am not so sure that he would do that to-day, because he himself once said:

"As has been so often proved, those who are prepared for the sake of ideals to disregard the realistic facts of the present situation, may indeed, as has been the case in the past, cause more unnecessary suffering than perhaps any other people."

MR. RAIKES: Perhaps I have gained a little idealism while my right hon. Friend has lost a bit of it.

MR. EDEN: It seems then that we must be near agreement at last. Let me put the issue broadly. I share the feeling which my right hon. Friend expressed yesterday. It is difficult at times not to be oppressed by the weight of problems which lie upon Europe. They are infinitely greater than they were after the last war. There have been six years of war on an unparalleled scale; there has been the devastation of air bombardment, which there was not last time, and the dislocation caused by the movement of millions of workers to slavery in Germany. If any life is to be restored to Europe, if it is to be saved from anarchy and chaos, it can only be done by the three Powers working together. The right hon. Gentleman opposite spoke yesterday of the difficulties of maintaining unity in peace. Of course, he is right, but after what we have endured there is no duty more incumbent upon statesmanship than to try and strengthen that unity, and to try to find together in good faith a full solution of the problems which confront us all.

In conclusion, I would like to say a word or two to some of my hon. Friends. As I listened to their speeches I felt the sincerity of the feeling which underlay them. Some of them expressed the view that my right hon. Friend the Prime Minister and I did not stand up with sufficient authority for the point of view of His Majesty's Government. I repudiate that and I would ask my hon. Friends to question themselves a little, if they would. The foreign policy of this country has been based for centuries on the determination that no one country should dominate Europe. We believe in Europe, we are a part of Europe and I myself am convinced that no one country is ever going to dominate Europe. It is too big for any one nation to succeed in doing that. It is because of that instinct of our own that we have a special position in Europe, and that a special measure of confidence is extended to us. It is for that reason that there were the wars with Philip II of Spain, with Louis XIV, with Wilhelm II, and now with Hitler and the Third Reich.

As I listened to some of the speeches I could not help feeling that some of my hon. Friends, in talking about Poland, had not only Poland in mind, but the fear that Russia, flushed with the magnificent triumphs of her armies, was also dreaming a dream of European domination. This, of course, is the constant theme of German propaganda. It is poured out day by day and night after night and comes to us in all sorts of unexpected forms and guises. It was their theme before the war. It was then the Bolshevik bogy, and how well Hitler used it. How often visitors to Nuremberg were told by the Germans they met, of the fear of Russia. I have had plenty of it chucked at me at interviews with Hitler myself. Can anyone doubt that that theme, before the war, was an element in making it difficult for us to establish an understanding with Soviet Russia? Can anyone doubt that, if we had had in 1939, the unity between Russia, this country and the United States that we cemented at Yalta, there would not have been the present war? I go further. Can anyone doubt that, so long as we hold that unity, there will not be another war? We do not say that we can establish conditions in which there will never be war again, but I believe if we can hold this unity we can establish peace for twenty-five years or fifty years or—who can say? But unless we can hold it there will be no peace for anything like that period of time.

Finally may I say this word, again to my hon. Friends? Make no mistake. The moment this fighting ceases, Germany will be out on the old theme of propaganda again. She will again try to play us off against Russia, and Russia against America and ourselves. She will play on all their pity, which she knows so well how to do. The whole orchestra of German self-pity will work up again to fortissimo. Let us be very careful that we do not fall victims to that.

What is my conclusion? I say that, while we must be watchful, active and vigorous and do all in our power to secure the real freedom and independence of our Polish allies—while that is our right and our duty, do not let us at the same time fall victims too easily to suspicion of another ally. I think we have to be on our guard. I assure the House that the Government will do all that lies in their power to see that the objectives the Prime Minister and I described are carried out. We are in the midst of this business.

We are not through it. We have many difficult stages to fulfil. Neither my right hon. Friend nor I can give any undertaking what our measure of success may be, but unless hon. Members feel that we should not try—and I cannot believe that they do—I would ask them to give us the encouragement to go forward. I would ask them to give it with a really strong and definite voice, otherwise we are going to confuse the mind of the world and the minds of our Polish friends for, after all, this cannot be solved at all unless the elements which represent Poland can be brought together. I would ask the House to consider again and give us full support for the work we are doing and, in the light of the assurances that I have given to the House, to say that in what we have done we have their confidence, and in what we are going to do we shall have their confidence, provided we fulfil the engagements that we have given. I in turn will tell them that we will report ourselves faithfully to this House.

[Question put: "That those words be there added."
The House divided: Ayes, 25; Noes, 396.]

When, one day later, Mr. Eden replied to the Debate on the main question, in the course of a further reference to Poland he said:
My hon. Friend the Member for Cambridge University and others who have been a little critical again to-day—and I must reply to them—really have not told us what alternative course we ought to pursue. What they have said is: "We do not think you ought to have got into this position." Let me assure the House that we did not want to get into this position. It was because we did not wish to arrive at this position that, a long time ago, my right hon. Friend and I began our efforts—the moment when Polish-Russian relations were broken off—to try to restore them. I repeat what the Prime Minister said, that if little more than a year ago the Polish Government had felt able to come to a decision about the frontier position in the East I am quite certain it would have been possible for us to make arrangements with our allies whereby that Government would now be in Warsaw with Mr. Mikolajczyk as its Prime Minister. It is just because we feared this present situation was going to arise that we made those efforts. Faced with that situation, neither my hon. Friend, nor anyone else in this Debate, has told us of any course we could pursue, except to sit still and take no action at all.

39

THE SCOTTISH UNIONIST CONFERENCE
—1945

MARCH 1945

Marshal Zhukov's forces captured Kustrin on the east bank of the Oder. The Baltic was reached at several points and further gains were made in Hungary.

In the west, Cologne was captured on March 6. The U.S. First Army crossed the Rhine at Remagen and by March 20 had established a bridgehead of twenty miles.

In Burma, Mandalay fell to the Fourteenth Army on March 20. The Burma Road had been cleared by the second week in March.

At home the Prime Minister addressed a Conservative Party conference for the first time since he became leader of the Party. In the course of his speech he said, with reference to the holding of a General Election:

"I regret to say that the public declarations of our Labour and some of our Liberal colleagues and of the party organizations which they represent, leaves us no doubt that they will feel themselves bound to resume their full liberty of action and thus bring this famous Coalition to an end."

On March 21, Mr. Eden spoke to the Scottish Unionists in St. Andrew's Hall, Glasgow. In this speech he referred to the future of Europe; on 29 September 1944, he had said in a Debate in the House of Commons:

"The principal danger to Europe—this may not be agreed by all, but this is my conviction—after the defeat of Germany, will be the re-emergence of Germany. You may disagree about how you wish to avoid it but that is the problem which will be a continuing one for the foreign policy not only of ourselves but of all those who come after us."

In his speech at Glasgow, he covered home as well as foreign policy:

SCOTTISH UNIONIST CONFERENCE

W e, in Britain, have never liked to be rigid in our policy whether in our domestic or foreign affairs. We dislike being confined by a fixed code of rules which are often out of date as soon as they are drawn up. We have the most flexible of Constitutions. There is hardly any difficulty it may not surmount. It comes and goes, appears and disappears, with a suddenness which foreigners find as bewildering as Alice did the habits of the Cheshire Cat. Anyway, it suits us very well. It is long tried and well proven. Our Constitution has always been able to adapt itself to any emergency and to carry forward into the future the lessons of the past. There could be no better example of this than our relations with the great Dominions. These have been transformed in the last fifty years, but meanwhile our ties of affection and common interest have been strengthened. Of all the events of these last years none has been more remarkable than the free and spontaneous declarations of war by the Dominions and their determined stand with us in the darkest hour when but for them and our Colonial Empire we stood alone.

What I have said of the British Constitution holds good of our foreign policy. It has never been possible to fit so complex a matter, dependent on the wills of other governments and peoples as well as on our own, into a body of rules which we can issue as a directive to those engaged in the conduct of international affairs. But that does not mean that our foreign policy has not rested on firm principles. The overriding principle has been the responsibility of the executive to Parliament. Without that constant check on the power of ministers and cabinets I doubt if the continuity of our policy could have been preserved.

Of course, the system has certain disadvantages for those who have to conduct foreign policy with other Powers who have no such checks imposed upon them and do not have to explain everything all the time. Sometimes one feels a little like a man playing a difficult hand of cards whose earnest friend says in a loud voice behind him: "Why don't you play that Queen of Spades?" At the same time Parliament has recognized that unless an alternative government can replace that in power, the government of the day must be given sufficient backing to put its policies into practice. It is for governments to propose and carry out policy but there must be constant consultation between the government and Parliament. Recently, for instance, the Prime Minister and I have laid before Parliament the results of our work with our allies in the Crimea.

The debates which followed were, I think, worthy of the best traditions of Parliament. We are now able to go on with our heavy labours, fortified by immense majorities derived from all the great parties in the State. I trust that in the difficult days to come after the war, for they will be very difficult days, however much our political parties may differ in detail, we shall preserve a sense of common purpose. That is one of the most valuable of our traditions. We ourselves may be scarcely conscious of it, but it is the envy of many other less fortunate lands.

There is another principle of our foreign policy which has not such a long history but is, none the less, one of the most important. I mean the practice of constant consultation with the Dominion Governments. This is something unparalleled in history. Our methods were reviewed at the Conference of Dominion Prime Ministers last spring and we shall do all we can to continue to expand and improve them. But it is especially valuable to be able to supplement our machinery of consultation, however smoothly it works, from time to time by meetings round the table. I need not say, therefore, how glad I am that we are soon to have a meeting with the Dominions in London so that we may all be made fully aware of each other's point of view before we join the other United Nations at San Francisco.

I come to the third great distinction which marks us out from most other lands. We live on an island and our insular position has determined our policy. Almost every other State in Europe has in the last hundred and fifty years had its capital entered by foreign troops or, at any rate, been dominated by a foreign government. We have been spared this. We have guarded our island well through all its perils. Meantime, across all the oceans of the world our ships go forth to bring home to us the food and raw materials of industry without which we cannot live. I need hardly insist on the overwhelming importance of this fact here in this great port of Glasgow from which more than ever in time of war ships sail to all quarters of the globe. For here we stand in the home of the shipbuilding industry, which has made an indispensable contribution to the victory that now draws near.

It has always been a cardinal principle of our foreign policy to keep open the highways of the sea. The unrivalled skill and indomitable glowing courage of the Royal Navy and the Merchant Marine, have done this throughout the war, assisted, let me add, by the devotion and vigilance of the Royal Air Force. But let us remember a fact which we too often forget. There were periods in our history when we could claim the command of the seas, all the Seven Seas. Our naval superiority was then so great that we could concentrate overwhelming force in any quarter of the globe and yet retain the mastery of our home waters. But that time is long past. In the twentieth century we have only been able to ensure the control of the seas and the power to import our necessary supplies because we could rely on friendly States acting with us, or at any rate not against us, in some vital areas of the world. We have indeed, in this sense, always lived dangerously. But not, I think, so very dangerously, because we have always pursued a just and reasonable policy in this sphere so that it has been to the interest of other powerful States to be on our side. Now that the air has introduced a new factor into naval strategy, it is still more impossible for any one Power to maintain the control of the Seas as we once did. These are considerations which no Foreign Secretary of this country should ever allow himself to forget. There is another principle of which we must take account. Every State tries to prevent other States combining to menace its own safety. That is why we have always, though sometimes too tardily, as recent history well shows, striven to prevent Europe falling under the domination of one Power. We have never sought such a position of domination for ourselves and we have never allowed any other State to obtain it, for we knew that if this were to happen our own liberties would soon be gone with those of the rest of Europe. We have fought three great world wars for this end. We are determined that Europe shall only be united by the free will of its separate States. When that happy day comes we shall hope to be in partnership with it. But we have never sought to create coalitions against great European Powers unless they have pursued a policy of aggression. Bismarck's new Germany after 1870 was the most powerful State in Europe, but we made no attempt to seek allies against it until under his successors Germany tried to dominate and even subjugate all Europe and we had to defend the liberties of Europe with our own.

It is for the freedom of Europe, nay of all nations, that we are fighting at this moment, because we are determined to beat down the monstrous tyranny of the Nazis in Europe and in the Far East the hideous overlordship of the Japanese. Surely we may hope that the overthrow of these two tyrannies and the miseries which they have brought upon their own peoples as well as upon their victims will prevent the renewal of any such attempt. But if ever such a threat comes into existence again, I am certain that the same result will follow and free men all over the world will combine together again as they do now to protect their liberties.

But there is another side to the picture. Rather than secure their country's safety through the dissensions of others, British statesmen have generally preferred another method. They have been amongst the foremost to try to set up in the world practical institutions by which the great Powers, instead of jealously watching each other, should meet together to settle their differences by discussion and compromise. I do not want in any way to suggest that this method is the prerogative of any one party: it certainly is not. But I think that I may point out here that this policy is in the line of a great Conservative tradition. It was followed by Castlereagh, by Lord Salisbury and, in our own time, by Sir Austen Chamberlain. It was never more necessary than now. We have to preserve in peace that unity of purpose and action amongst the great Powers which they have achieved in war. I have no illusions as to the difficulty of that task. But I am encouraged to hope, because for the first time all the peace-loving Powers of the world share our conviction that they must continue to work together.

It is idle to think that you can have security by agreeing to join together to put down aggressors whilst each Power acts in all other respects independently of the others. If peace is to endure there must be a harmony of policy and the constant recognition of the fact that there is a common interest above and beyond, but not on a long view antagonistic to the policy of each individual Power. We must beware also of collective insecurity where each peaceful power looks to the other and makes little attempt to do its share. That way lies disaster. But here let me say that it is against all the tradition of our policy and of our party to allow unity among the great Powers to become a means to bully the smaller. There can be no freedom in the world unless the smaller States can be joined with the great Powers in the protection of their common interests. Their right to their own way of life must be respected. They must have their due share in making the great decisions. To find the right method by which this problem can be solved has puzzled the world for over a century and I would not say that we have found a final solution to-day. But one fact stands out. Responsibility and power must be related if institutions are to survive the test of experience. But if this be true, it is also true that it is the duty of all great Powers to use their exceptional strength with restraint. "It is excellent to have a giant's strength but it is tyrannous to use it like a giant." We are about to embark on a new experiment in international practice. We hope to lay the foundation of this at San Francisco. This endeavour may well prove to be the world's last chance. How far we shall succeed will depend in large measure upon those who have power recognizing that they must exercise it not roughly but in accordance with the principles to which they have subscribed. Well would it have been for Germany when she became one of the most powerful nations in the world if she had remembered the words of her own great thinker, Goethe:

"The Master first reveals himself in limitation and only law can give us liberty."

Let no one underrate the immensity of the problems, economic as well as political, that will confront us when the victory is won. Just as this war has been more violent and terrible than any war in history, so as the tide ebbs all over the world the wreckage that is left behind will be more appalling than ever before. That is true not only of the world outside these islands; it is true also of this country itself. We have been spared the clash of armies on our soil, but we have known destruction from the skies.

Unhappily, the effects of war are wider and even deeper than this. In the past six years warfare has taken on an entirely new meaning. This is total war. I have seen an example of this this afternoon. I have seen hundreds of Norwegians, men, women and children, who have been rescued from the extreme north of their country, from Finnmark, where they were homeless and at the mercy of the German invader. British, Canadian and American forces have brought them here to sanctuary in Scotland. We shall not rest until these hapless and innocent people can return home to a Norway freed from the defiling touch of a merciless and odious enemy.

Here in this country we have been mobilized for war as we were never mobilized between 1914 and 1918. There has been a far greater dislocation of man-power and woman-power. There has been a far greater shortage of civilian goods, a far greater shrinkage in our export trade by which we must live, a far greater proportion of our productive capacity has been devoted directly to war. So it is that the transition from war to peace will be a much more complex and difficult process than it was last time. Immense problems confront us. Here in this island are grave issues of demobilization and re-employment of men and of industry. These issues would be hard enough to resolve if the world were normal; they are made infinitely more difficult by the widespread disruption which is the consequence of total war. I state these problems not to daunt you, for I am a convinced optimist in respect of the future of our people. I believe in their future because I believe in them. But in what temper shall we face the future? War is a moral as well as a military conflict. It is the firmest will no less than the strongest armament that wins the war. But peace is a moral problem too. It would be very easy to abandon ourselves to those airy Utopias which the Prime Minister so rightly condemned last week, but you don't win wars by dreaming dreams and you cannot make a peace, you cannot build houses, you cannot build schools, you cannot ensure full employment or social security or a national health service simply by seeing visions. You win these things by hard work, by courage and by enterprise, by free enterprise. Why do we, as Conservatives, lay such emphasis on free enterprise? It is because we know that each individual among us has his own special gifts and because we believe that each one of us should be free to use those gifts for his own benefit and for the benefit of the community. If men were machines there would be no scope for freedom of enterprise, there would be absolute uniformity, there would be absolute regularity, there would be absolute identity of function. All that would be necessary would be for the Chief Engineer, seated at his desk in Whitehall, and I can imagine many applications for this post, to turn the appropriate switch and all our problems would be solved.

But men and women are not like that. We are individual human beings and, thank God, no two of us are alike. We respond to different impulses. We have different contributions to make to the common life which is the community. We have differing hopes and differing ambitions. How shall we best harness these different and highly individual capacities to the service of the community? Shall we be wise to try to make each man and woman conform as closely as may be to a common pattern, a cog in the wheel of the machinery of the State? I think not. I think that we should be wiser to permit, and indeed to encourage, the individual to develop his or her own personality in his or her own way. We should be wiser to encourage each citizen to indulge his own hopes and to try to fulfil his own ambitions, only seeing to it that these hopes and these ambitions do not clash with the interests of the community as a whole.

Now there is in certain quarters a tendency to think that the hopes and ambitions of the individual must necessarily be at odds with the interests of the community. I do not accept this. On the contrary, a social theory which postulates that the community can only be healthy when the individuals which compose it are directed and controlled, encouraged to conform to pattern and discouraged from enterprise and experiment, a social theory of that kind means stagnation. It is the direct denial of the British spirit.

We have built up this great Empire of ours not upon vast combines, not upon municipal undertakings; not even upon directions from Whitehall. We have built it up on a spirit of adventure.

In his admirable book *The English Spirit*—if you can forgive that title—Mr. Rowse writes these words about the British Empire:

"You might say the British Empire was a product—almost a by-product—of adventure. It certainly was not planned; it came into being naturally, gradually, as the result of the adventurous spirit, the stout heart and courage of our forefathers looking for a livelihood and an outlet for their energy and spirits across the ocean."

How true that is. Great Britain is a Power in the world to-day just because the ordinary man amongst us has always been free to take his own future in his own hands, has been free to venture forth to the farthest corners of the earth, has been free in the last analysis to make himself an extraordinary man. Britain has become great because of free enterprise, which is another name for courage. That does not mean, as some of our critics would have us believe, that the Conservative Party, the moment the war is over, will seek to abolish every control or seek to create a situation in which the rich and powerful will prosper and the weak and unlucky will go to the wall. When the war is over there will be shortages, there will be scarcity both of men and material. In such a situation it is clear that some controls will be necessary, just as rationing is necessary to-day. But we do not regard these controls as desirable in themselves. We seek to free ourselves of them as soon as we may because we believe that it is man's destiny to order his own life and that the community is healthiest when man is fulfilling his destiny.

But there is one control which, let me say as a parliamentarian and a Conservative, I hope that we shall be most watchful to maintain, that is control by Parliament over the executive. I have spoken of this in connection with foreign affairs. It is no less significant in relation to domestic affairs. One hears much in these days of the slowness of the machinery of Parliament, that this or that particular method requires overhaul. I would beg you to proceed in these matters with the utmost caution. It is on the vigilance of Parliament that the liberties of our people rest. In this sphere it is far better that Parliament should sometimes spend too much time on this bill or on that, rather than that there should not be full opportunity for the closest scrutiny, and if need be challenge of every measure that comes before it.

And now a few words about the continuance or otherwise of the National Coalition. First let me observe that it is not members of the Conservative Party who have given notice to end the present Government. Personally I make no secret to you that I shall profoundly regret that event, which is certainly none of our seeking. But our Socialist and some of our Liberal allies having served us with notice that they will quit, does not alter the problems of making and preparing the peace and of making a new and better form of national administration. I have no doubt that many men and women of all parties and of no party share that view. I have no doubt that many agree with Major Lloyd George and will support such a national administration and Mr. Churchill as leader. Certainly no man is better qualified than the Prime Minister to call the nation to the great tasks of peace—to inspire it to master them. Nor is there any mystery as to what the programme will be. Its main outlines have already been firmly drawn by the Prime Minister in his famous broadcast of the Four Years Plan given exactly two years ago to-night.

In those two years, the hard preparatory work has been accomplished and it remains for the Government returned at the election to implement and carry forward the work which has been put in hand. The Prime Minister's programme included schemes for social reform, wider in scope and more ambitious in character than we have ever attempted in our history. That programme has been worked out and approved by all three Parties in the present Government. The Prime Minister said in his speech two years ago:

"When this plan has been shaped it will have to be presented to the country either by a National Government formally representative, as this one is, of the three parties in the State, or by a National Government comprising the best men in all parties who are willing to serve." There is therefore nothing new in the declaration of the Prime Minister last week. It was all foreseen and forecast two years ago. The plan will certainly be carried through by Mr. Churchill and the Government he will lead if we are returned at the General Election. Whether we are to carry out this great task or not will be for the people to decide. This Parliament is ten years old. While many will deplore the return to party warfare at this time, no believer in democracy can deny that it is healthy that Parliament should soon be refreshed by contact with the electorate. When that time comes, we, as Conservatives, will state our faith and propound our programme and fight for it with all the strength that is in us, and I am confident also without personal rancour or abuse. It is our fundamental national unity which has carried us through these last five years, the most dangerous years in all the history of these islands. We will engage in our domestic controversies with all the strength we can command, but we shall do so, I believe, without any weakening of that underlying unity which binds men of British race the world over. Thus can we best serve the State by proving once again to the nations of the world that Britain can practise democracy in peace as she has fought for freedom in war.

It is not given to us to penetrate the veil that shrouds the future. But this at least is sure, whatever the coming years may hold, there will be a future in them for Scotland, your great country, a future in them for our great party, a future for the British Commonwealth and Empire as a leader of the world.

40

THE SAN FRANCISCO CONFERENCE

GERMANY

March 24. 300,000 British, Canadian and American troops cross the Rhine and 40,000 land by air to the east.

April 1–11. Three quarters of a million Germans captured in the west, bringing the total from D-Day up to two million.

April 18. Russians launched a nine-armies attack on Berlin; the Russian flag was hoisted on the Reichstag on April 30.

April 25. American and Russian troops linked up on the Elbe.

May 1. Hitler's death announced.

May 3. Hamburg captured by Second Army.

May 4. German troops in the north-west of Germany surrendered to Field-Marshal Montgomery.

May 5. Cease Fire on the British Front.

May 7. Unconditional surrender of all German armed forces signed by General Jodl at Rheims.

AUSTRIA

April 13. Vienna fell to the Red Army.

May 6. British troops entered Austria.

ITALY

Field-Marshal Alexander's final offensive started on April 9. The Po was crossed on April 24. German troops in Italy surrendered to him on May 2. Mussolini was captured by Italian partisans on April 28 and executed.

WAR AGAINST JAPAN

Rangoon was captured on May 3 and on the next day Admiral Mountbatten announced that the Battle of Burma had ended.

April 5. U.S.S.R. denounced the Russo-Japanese Neutrality Pact.

U.S.A.

April 12. President Roosevelt died.

Mr. Eden attended President Roosevelt's funeral in Washington. He subsequently headed the U.K. delegation to the San Francisco conference. The other principal U.K. delegates were Mr. Attlee, Lord Cranborne and Lord Halifax. The Conference began on April 25 and on the next day Mr. Eden made this speech:

(I) THE SECOND DAY OF THE CONFERENCE

No more suitable setting could have been found for this assembly than the splendid city of San Francisco, one of the main centres of the United Nations war effort, San Francisco, whose confidence in the future is only equalled by its sense of comradeship to-day.

Our deep gratitude is due to the city itself and to the whole State of California, which with traditional hospitality has opened its gates to us, and also to the Government and the people of the United States who in a wider sense are our hosts at this momentous conference.

We are met here in the shadow of a grievous loss. No one can speak in this assembly without recalling the memory of Franklin Roosevelt, the friend of free peoples, the good neighbour. He looked forward to continuing in peace that close association of the free nations which has brought us to the very edge of victory and from which the meeting of to-day has sprung. It was he who named us the United Nations, and we shall best honour his memory by proving ourselves worthy of that proud title.

Let us be clear about the purpose of this conference. We are not met here to draft the terms of the treaty of peace. We are met to agree to set up a world organization which will help to keep the peace when victory is finally won over Germany and Japan.

At intervals in history mankind has sought by the creation of international machinery to solve disputes between nations by agreement and not by force. Hitherto all these endeavours have failed. Yet no one here doubts that despite these earlier failures a further attempt must be made, and this time we must succeed. All the causes that made some form of international machinery desirable after the last war make it indispensable to-day.

In the last hundred years, and in particular the last twenty-five years, the discoveries of science have served to enrich and sometimes endanger the world, but above all to contract it. We have entered an age when no natural barrier, whether mountain or ocean, can guarantee security against the new weapons which science has placed at the disposal of mankind. This hard fact is now biting deeply into the consciousness of all peoples, and they are, I believe, ready to accept its implications and to shoulder the responsibilities which it imposes.

Herein lies the main difference between to-day and the lost opportunity at the end of the last World War. To-day this fact is patent to us all. Whether we will or not we are all now one another's neighbours. San Francisco is as close to Berlin or Tokyo as New York to Washington a century ago.

The world of to-day is one large city and our countries are its several parishes. We are the citizens. Either we must find some means of ordering our relations with justice and fair dealing while allowing nations great and small full opportunity to develop their free and independent life, or we shall soon head for another world conflict which this time must bring the utter destruction of civilization in its train. It is, therefore, no exaggeration to say that the work on which we are making a start here may be the world's last chance.

That is why the governments of the four powers who sponsored the invitations to this conference asked their representatives to meet and work out proposals which might later form the basis of an international agreement. They did so, at Dumbarton Oaks. Their work was examined and completed in the Crimea. The final outcome is now before you.

Here there are a few general observations which I would make. In the first place these proposals admittedly constitute a compromise. In the second place they do not constitute an attempt by the four powers to dictate to the rest of the world what form the future world organization should take. They are the suggestions which we unitedly present to you, for your consideration. Nor are they intended to stand unchanged until the end of time.

For our own part His Majesty's Government and the United Kingdom are prepared to accept and to endorse them and to do their best to give them life because we believe that they can form a basis for a future world organization which will help to provide that security which is to-day mankind's greatest need.

Security is not itself a final end. But it is indispensable if we are to make true freedom possible. Not otherwise can we hope to realize a world in which justice for nations as well as for individuals can prevail.

But this security cannot be created in a day nor by any document however admirable. It must be the product of time and of constant effort, of learning to work together, of practising and upholding accepted standards of international conduct. The important thing is to begin now.

Here let me sound a warning note and make a suggestion. Let us not attempt too much. We cannot hope here to produce a complete scheme perfect in all its elaborate details for future ordering of the world. I am persuaded that we should be wise to set ourselves a goal more within the compass of our immediate possibilities.

We shall have taken the indispensable first step if we can now draw up a charter within the framework of our principles. The details can then be left to be filled in in the light of experience. I know that this is an Anglo-Saxon conception, which may possibly be challenged by others, but I am convinced that in this particular case it is right, and I would claim that its merit is capable of proof by reference to historical facts.

Now let me turn briefly to the proposals themselves which we are met to discuss. They impose obligations equally on all powers great and small. But I am conscious that a special responsibility lies on great powers in these days when industrial potential is so decisive a factor in military strength.

Great powers can make a two-fold contribution. They can make it by their support of this organization. They can make it also by setting themselves certain standards in international conduct and by observing those standards scrupulously in all their dealing with other countries. The greater the power any State commands the heavier its responsibility to wield that power with consideration for others and with restraint upon its own selfish impulses.

What was the most sinister feature of the years which preceded the present struggle? It was the deliberate debasement of international conduct in which Germany, Italy and Japan engaged to further their own selfish plans. It was the practice of these powers not only persistently to violate their engagements, but to use the new engagements they so readily undertook after each aggression as a cloak to cover their next crime. This was their technique.

But what was the result? There came a time when the outraged forces of civilization had to call a halt to these practices and so inevitably the world was plunged into another war. Great powers have a special responsibility to guard against the recurrence of such practices.

I have laid emphasis on that portion of our task which is concerned with the provision of international machinery for the settlement of political disputes. But of equal importance with this is the solution of economic problems, which, if untended, can themselves sow the seeds of future wars. This will be the task of the social and economic council which finds its place in the proposals now before you. It is our duty to ensure that this council shall be well adapted to play its full part in our new structure of peace.

Here then are our two immediate tasks, political and economic. Let us press them vigorously to a conclusion. World events of unprecedented magnitude both in the east and in the west crowd upon us every hour.

If we order our labours efficiently and work to the utmost of our strength, it should surely be possible for us to agree upon our charter within four weeks from now. We cannot afford to delay. Sir, I hope that we shall set ourselves such a target date and determine to reach it. This conference bears heavy responsibilities. It has also splendid opportunities. Let it seize them now.

In the early days of this war I went to Egypt to greet soldiers from Australia and New Zealand who had come to that country to protect the Suez Canal against the imminent threat of Mussolini's aggression. On the evening of their arrival I was speaking to a number of the men of the motives which had made them volunteer for this adventure. Of the group one man remained silent. At last I turned to him and said: "And what made you come here?" He replied: "I guess there is a job of work to be done."

In the last six terrible years unnumbered men have died to give humanity another chance. We too have a job of work to do if we are not to fail these men. Let us do it with courage, modesty and dispatch. Let us do it now.

(II) BROADCAST TO U.S.A. AND U.K., MAY 7

From time to time in human history events occur of such magnitude that it is difficult for the human mind to grasp their full significance all at once. The defeat and surrender of German armies which has brought fighting in the west very near its end, the death of Hitler and of Mussolini together with that of a number of their notorious accomplices in crime; all these events crowding upon our minds make this a bewildering but majestic and triumphant hour.

The collapse has been as swift and complete as the struggle of the years that preceded was long, harsh and cruel. Inevitably one's mind goes back to-day to that month of May five years ago when the Nazi avalanche first burst over the lands of the West, sweeping so much before it, clamping down tyrannical Nazi rule upon the free lands of Norway, Holland, Belgium and France. The free nations were then indeed near to the abyss. Now five years later Allied arms have driven the Nazi foe into the abyss. To-day as the hour of victory over the Nazi foe draws near our first thought is one of deep thankfulness to Almighty God for His mercies to us, and our strength for the final overthrow of that other enemy, Japan.

For us at home in Britain the defeat of Germany will end a period of five years and eight months during which large parts of the United Kingdom have been at all times open to air attack. During long periods attack from the air has in fact been heavy and continuous. Moreover, throughout these years Great Britain, a country which can only exist by imports, lived under the constant threat of the interruption of vital supplies by sea and air attack on shipping. It was only by a supreme effort and by unbending fortitude on the part of the whole nation, that the British people, in defiance of those two threats, continued to prosecute the war to the full limit of their strength in Europe, in the Mediterranean, in Africa and in Burma.

During these long war years the whole nation at home in Britain has been mobilized for war to an extent unsurpassed by any of our allies.

Six and a quarter million men and women of the United Kingdom have served in the armed forces. This figure does not include one and a quarter million who served in the Home Guard while carrying out their daily civilian tasks. Over two and a quarter mil-

lion of its men and women in the armed forces are overseas, and
one million have become casualties. Sixty thousand civilians have
been killed, and eighty-five thousand have been seriously wounded
in air attacks on the United Kingdom. You will, therefore, I am
sure, understand me when I recall to-day with pride the grim endurance of the people at home, their unflagging resolution, and the
deeds of British men and women the world over.

It seems fitting that at this moment when the final defeat of
Germany is about to release us to turn the full energies of our
nations against Japan, news should just have reached us of the
fall of Rangoon and the liberation of Burma. The Burmese campaign has been arduous in the extreme. It has called for exceptional
courage and endurance. The turning point of the campaign was
a year ago when the Japanese forces broke into the Imphal plain
and sought to inflict defeat upon British and Indian troops. Had
this plan been carried through the road to India would have been
forced open and the supply route to China must have been cut.

Fortunately that Japanese plan was defeated at Imphal by the
Divisions of General Slim's Fourteenth Army of British, Indian
and African troops, and at Myitkyina by General Stillwell's victory. After that the tide began to turn, until to-day British forces
are in Rangoon, 600 miles south of the Imphal Plain.

This stupendous advance has been achieved in a few months in
conditions of the utmost physical difficulty against a ruthless and
resourceful foe. In the course of it 12 Japanese Divisions have been
destroyed. 100,000 Japanese dead have been counted by our troops.
The total Japanese casualties in Burma amount to over 300,000.
But these feats of our land forces would have been impossible but
for the unexampled organization of Anglo-American air supply by
which means alone our troops have been kept fed and supplied.

Now all these considerable resources in men and material which
have been devoted to the destruction of the Japanese armies in
Burma will be free to carry on the good work in other lands until
the bell tolls for the Japanese as it has already tolled for Hitler.

As the great world conflict draws more nearly to an end we begin
to look forward into the future. Here at San Francisco we have
been charged with an essential task. Our work, if it is to be successfully concluded, as I believe it will be, cannot by itself alone
ensure the peace of the world. But all the same some such organization as we are striving to set up here is indispensable if we are
to keep the peace which our fighting men are winning. That is not
only my view, it is the view of all the nations assembled here. So

far, though progress has perhaps inevitably been slow, it has on the whole been encouraging. I am confident that we are going to agree on a Charter, and I have hopes that it will be a better document than anything of its kind that has existed in the world until now. Of course, it will not be perfect, but the great thing is to get going.

If the Fathers of your constitution had gone on debating whether it would work instead of seeing that it did work; well, you would not have been the great nation that you are to-day. Alexander Hamilton, for instance, did not think that your constitution was strong enough, but he threw himself wholeheartedly with others into the task of getting it adopted.

It is certainly important to get the best possible machinery but what really counts is whether we continue to be determined to make it work or not. In democratic countries it is the people who finally settle the question of how much strength and vigour Governments are going to put into any particular piece of work. That is why you in the United States and you at home in Britain and in other parts of the British Commonwealth and Empire have all a job to do as well as we who are sitting round the table in San Francisco.

After all, what we want to do is something fairly simple. We want to set up some decent standards of international conduct. If any nation defies these and tries to do what the Nazis and Japanese have tried to do, and failed, we want to be able to stop the trouble before its starts. That is much better than waiting till it has caused such misery and ruin as we see in the world to-day. We are proposing to set up a Security Council whose chief charge it will be to do this very thing. All the Great Powers will sit on this Council and the other powers are to have six representatives. Of course the larger powers must agree among themselves if the scheme is to succeed. There is an old Latin tag which may be translated: "Who is going to police the policemen?" Unless the police behave themselves with restraint and with a proper regard to their responsibilities, the scheme won't work. Everybody knows that. But everybody also knows that no single power, not even the strongest, can assure itself against such suffering by its own efforts alone. That is the vital lesson of the last twenty years which we must surely have learnt and please God will not forget.

But this problem of security is not our whole task, though no progress is possible so long as it remains unsolved. The Economic and Social Council has an immense part to play. With all our new resources and inventions there is no reason why we should not soon make life much better for us all.

But these good things will come not through material things alone but from the spirit and mind of men. There lies the real solution of our great problem of living and working together instead of destroying one another. In its fundamentals it is a moral problem.

Men may differ in many things. But there are deep moral forces which bind us all together. Man is a social animal; he wants to live with others, not by himself. Slowly and painfully he is learning that he must do to others what he would have them do to him. Selfishness can never really satisfy any nation any more than it can satisfy the deepest instincts of individuals. That is the principle on which our new organization must rest. If we are true to it, we cannot fail.

(III) V.E. DAY BROADCAST

On May 8 Mr. Eden broadcast to the world in company with Mr. Stettinius, the Secretary of State of the U.S.A., Mr. Molotov and M. Bidault.

The hour for which we have waited so long has struck. The unconditional surrender of Germany is announced.

At such a time, I have no doubt that the feeling that will be uppermost in all our minds will not be one of triumph but of thankfulness, of thankfulness first of all to God, who has brought us through so many and great perils, and next to our fighting men, to whom, under God's guidance, we owe our deliverance.

In this moment of victory, our minds go back to the dark days of the past. Through those grim years what was it that sustained us? It was surely faith in the justice of our cause, a passionate conviction that liberty should not, must not, perish from the earth.

It was that unquenchable faith, which inspired the people of London to face the worst that the air forces of the enemy could do to them, which brought young men from the ends of the earth, from the nations of the British Commonwealth and Empire not themselves directly threatened, to fight and to die. It is that same faith that must inspire us now.

I speak in particular to my own countrymen. The British Empire

344

has battled for nearly six years to see this day. For twelve hard months we stood alone.

Since then we have seen the United Nations grow year by year. To-day, a great company, we celebrate the victory of our cause. With you in Britain we greet the dawn of our deliverance.

May it give us strength to go forward to victory over our remaining enemy, Japan, and to the shaping of that new world which we are here to build.

41

THE GENERAL ELECTION

Mr. Eden and Mr. Attlee returned to the U.K. from San Francisco on May 17.

The Labour Party Conference was held in Blackpool in the week beginning May 20. On May 21, Mr. Attlee rejected the Prime Minister's offer to continue the Coalition until V.J. Day.

On May 23, it was announced that Parliament would be dissolved on June 15 and that polling for the General Election would take place on July 5.

Ten days later it was announced that Mr. Eden was ill and was under doctor's orders to keep to his bed for six weeks.

Mr. Eden was, therefore, confined to bed throughout the Election campaign which was conducted for him in his own constituency by his wife; but he was able, from his home, to make an Election Broadcast on June 27.

I have not spoken to you since I returned from Russia in the dark days of the winter of 1941. Then I gave you some account of the endurance of that land and of the courage of our sailors who manned the convoys that carried supplies to Russia through the Arctic night.

Those dark days of 1941, and others like them, now lie behind us, a nightmare of the past. The victory in Europe is won, at a price most grievous in the quality of the men we have lost. We have now to apply ourselves to win victory over Japan in the Far East and to the tasks of peace in Europe.

THE GENERAL ELECTION

I should much have preferred the Coalition to continue together until the end of the Japanese war. I realized the difficulties of such a plan. But I am sure that it was the best plan and I am sorry for personal as well as political reasons, that our friends of the Socialist Party could not agree with it. But since they could not, an early election was inevitable. I say inevitable, because you can hold a coalition together for a purpose; the defeat of Germany or the defeat of Japan is such a purpose, but you cannot hold a coalition together merely for a date. An autumn election would simply have meant a continuous manœuvring for position from now until the autumn, with devastating effects on the authority of the Government at home and abroad. So that the choice was the end of the Japanese war or now. Our Socialist friends preferred now. I regret their decision, but nobody who professes to believe in democracy should cry out too loud because a ten-year-old Parliament is dissolved in June and not in October.

And so it is that within a few days you will be called upon to choose a new parliament. Lying here in the country and forbidden to take any active part in the Election campaign, for which failure I ask the forgiveness of my generous Warwickshire friends, I have listened to the rival speakers. As I have listened I have felt great sympathy with the voter whose one wish it is to cast his or her vote in the best way to serve the country. That, after all, is what we all want to do. There has been so much advice, so many appeals, so many charges and counter-charges and it has all gone on for so long. I shall do my best to-night to put before you as fairly as I can the world scene and the domestic scene, as I picture them, and their relation to each other.

Clearly the first duties of the new parliament will be to win the war against Japan and to make and keep the peace in Europe. Both are immensely formidable tasks. We should make the gravest mistake if we were to underrate the extent of the effort that is still called for from us in the Far East. When I was in Washington a few weeks ago I found no inclination there to regard the Japanese war as any less formidable than the German war has been. In many ways it is a heavier task. The giant distances, the natural obstacles and the fanatical character of the foe, make it a struggle without precedent in all the history of war. And surely there can be no doubt who is the man who should lead us in that war as Prime Minister and Minister of Defence. Through all these years I have sat in the Defence Committee with the Prime Minister, as one of his civilian colleagues. Every one of us who has watched him there,

347

whatever his party politics, will agree that he is above all others the man for that job, and a stern job it is likely to prove. He is the master-builder, unmatched for such a task.

But I want to speak to you also of the other principal task of this new Parliament, to make and keep the peace in Europe. On our success or failure in this sphere everything depends. Housing, new schemes of social insurance, the future of education, whether this industry or that is to be run by the State or by free enterprise, which controls must be kept on and which can be allowed to lapse; all this and much more besides depends upon our ability to maintain peace.

How are we to do it? Firstly, we must establish a strong world organization which shall provide a forum for the discussion and settlement of disputes and which shall promote international effort for social and economic welfare. We have made a good start with this work at San Francisco. Secondly, if such an organization is to be successful, it must command the military strength to enforce its decisions. We must be prepared to contribute to that strength, as also to make provision for our own defence against any emergency that may arise. Thirdly, we must take steps to ensure that Germany and Japan are not in a position to engage again upon a war of aggression. Fourthly, if this world organization is to succeed, its strength will in a large measure depend upon close friendship and understanding between ourselves, the United States and the Soviet Union. We must continue to do everything in our power to promote this friendship. Our unity has enabled us to win the war; if maintained and developed it can keep the peace.

These objectives which I have set out will, I think, be generally endorsed by most of you. They were well expressed about three weeks ago by Lord Samuel in his broadcast. I agree with all he had to say on this subject. Indeed, I had hoped that foreign affairs would not be an issue at this election, not because I am at all frightened of controversy, but because I had thought that the nation was broadly agreed upon what that policy should be.

But some observations have been made by critics of the Government which raise important issues with which I must deal. Over and over again Mr. Laski repeats that he doesn't believe in the continuity of our foreign policy, though he never tells us which part of the present foreign policy won't continue. It has been suggested by Sir Stafford Cripps and others that in order to have good relations with the Soviet Union we should have a Socialist government in this country, because, so the argument runs, British

Socialists are more sympathetic to the Russian objectives than are Conservatives and Liberals. My friends, such an argument is not merely false, it is dangerous. It would be just as reasonable to argue in reply that in order that this country should have good relations with the United States, the home of free enterprise, it is essential to return to power in this country a government which believes in free enterprise, that is to say, a government drawn from the Conservative and Liberal Parties. But, personally, I would never use such an argument. International relations are not governed by such considerations as these. They are governed by the policy of any given foreign country on the main international issues. To attempt to align your international friendship primarily with governments who share the same domestic political creeds, whatever their foreign policy may be, is just crazy.

M. Herriot, the distinguished French statesman who has been released from German captivity, summed the whole matter up very well the other day when he said: "In foreign policy . . . you can do nothing constructive if you subordinate that policy to considerations of home policy." That was the lesson M. Herriot told the French people that he hoped they had learnt from their calamities. To judge by the unhappy intervention of Mr. Laski, it seems that we have need to learn it also. In the seven years that I at different times have been Foreign Secretary it has never once occurred to me to say to any foreign representative of the countless foreign Powers I have met: "Are you a Conservative? Are you a Liberal? Are you a Socialist?" What interests me is the foreign policy that the country concerned is pursuing, its attitude towards the problems of peace and its attitude to my country.

But I said just now that this doctrine was not only false but dangerous, and I will now tell you why it is dangerous. If you accept that in order to be on good terms with any given foreign Power you must choose your own Government to match the political complexion of that foreign Power, you are, in fact, allowing a foreign Power to dictate the political colour of the government of your own country. That would indeed be a lamentable departure from all our island habits and traditions. We do a lot for foreign countries; we might at least be allowed to choose our own government for ourselves. But now a new argument has been brought up. We are told that though the Prime Minister and I, together with our Cabinet colleagues, may have pursued a foreign policy of which the nation has approved all through these war years, once we are left on our own without our Socialist and Liberal colleagues to guide us, we shall swerve from the straight and narrow path and be misled by the Tory Party. This prospect Sir Stafford Cripps tells us he finds "terrifying". Well, we live in dangerous times but of all the many perils that confront us I can assure you that the one that at this time troubles me least is the prospect of the Prime Minister and the Foreign Secretary of this Government being cudgelled and cowed into policies of which they do not approve by the party to which they belong. But, lest anyone should share Sir Stafford Cripps's fear, let me assure him or her that the foreign policy we have been pursuing during these past five years has not only had the approval of the Liberal Party and the greater part of the Socialist Party, but also the approval of the overwhelming majority of the Conservative Party, as numerous debates and divisions in Parliament will attest. If we are returning we will continue to pursue that policy.

It is true that our foreign policy has come in for some criticism from Socialist press and speakers. For instance we are still being blamed for Greek dissensions. Personally, I am very ready to defend our policy and also our intervention in Greece, as to the necessity for which I never had the slightest doubt. On this Greek issue I would only ask my listeners who have friends or relations among our armed forces there to consult their letters. I am ready to abide by the judgment of the fighting men who went through it all. But on this as on all other issues in these war years the Government was pursuing an agreed foreign policy. It is perhaps not known that every telegram of any importance on foreign affairs, either outward or inward, is circulated to all the members of the War Cabinet. Therefore there is a much wider knowledge of every move in foreign policy among members of the Cabinet than in the work of any other department. It is right and proper that this should be so. But to attack the Prime Minister and myself for the policy pursued in respect of any particular country is not just, unless our critics are prepared at the same time to attack Mr. Attlee, Mr. Bevin and Mr. Morrison, who were full partners with us and have never shirked responsibility for the decisions we took together.

My friends, whichever party or parties forms the government of this country as the outcome of the present general election, will have a very heavy task in the field of foreign affairs. Let no one minimize its extent or its gravity. The devastation of Europe wrought by this war is something much wider and deeper than was wrought by the last world war. There are acute international difficulties to be solved and vexatious territorial issues to be adjusted. In a large part of Central Europe to-day there is a vacuum, by which I mean that there is no organized national life, there is a desperate want of the bare necessities of existence, a ruined transport system and, most serious of all, a general lowering of standards. All this has got to be rebuilt, for, in the last resort, it is on these things, on our ability to maintain certain standards within States and between States that preservation of peace and life depends. No one in this country can really be eager to undertake these heavy tasks if they understand what they entail. I can only tell you that if you charge us with them, we shall use such authority and influence as we possess to make and keep the peace in Europe. And surely it is our duty to reduce our own differences to a minimum so that by the widest possible measure of agreement at home we may exert the maximum influence abroad.

I want to turn now to domestic issues, and I would like to talk particularly to the younger members of the community, on whom the burdens of the future will fall and whose voice will rightly be heard in this election. Especially am I thinking of the young men and women in the services who have had to bear the heaviest burden of sacrifice during these years of war. Many of you have never before had an opportunity to vote in a national election, but I believe that you are now firmly determined to have a voice in shaping the future and in making the best use of the victory, which you have done so much to win. You are not interested in the old party war cries, in electioneering slogans, or in extravagant promises, which you know that neither side can fulfil; nor do you want to listen to lengthy recriminations about the past, for it is easy enough to find in the record of every party much that can be criticized. It is with the future and not with the past that we are concerned at this election, and I would ask you, therefore, to consider with me for a moment the common tasks and the common opportunities, to which we must turn together, if we are to see the happy and prosperous Britain which we all desire.

We in the National Government understand very well that the problems of to-day cannot be tackled by the methods of yesterday. War experience has taught everybody lessons. We have every intention of profiting by them. But just because we recognize the need for the improvement and reform of the old system, we do not believe that the country should embark upon a revolutionary change, which will sweep away the good along with the bad. Our problems after this war are going to be most formidable.

THE GENERAL ELECTION

I am only too conscious of the extent of our difficulties. But I cannot believe that we shall improve our chances of finding employment, at good wages, for our people by adding to the problems of transition from war economy to peace economy the transference of many of our great industries from free enterprise to State control. We have surely troubles enough at this time without that.

The system of free enterprise (which is sometimes called capitalism) was responsible for the enormous increase in material wealth which flooded this country during the last century, to the great benefit of every section of the community, thereby providing the foundation of the relatively higher standard of living which Britain enjoys to-day. But, in spite of the many real advantages which it brought, unrestricted private enterprise in commerce and industry did not always work to the public advantage and it could not solve all the economic problems of the modern State. Monopolies came into being, which sometimes tended to promote high prices and artificial scarcity; there was widespread unemployment and social insecurity; the lack of proper control over building development contributed to create the slums, which are a blot on many of our great industrial cities to-day.

All these things represented a terrible cost in human suffering, but do not forget that there was also another side to the picture: the national wealth was increasing steadily, wages were rising, hours of work were being reduced and improved opportunities of leisure and recreation were being offered to all. Surely this is not the time to scrap all that we have and replace it by something entirely new and untried, but let us rather seek to improve and develop the inheritance that is ours. Because there are still many imperfections and injustices in our economic system, it does not follow that the principle upon which it is based is wrong, but only that there is need for constant progressive adjustment and reform.

Frankly, I cannot follow Sir Stafford Cripps when he speaks as he did the other night as though State control was all that was virtuous and private enterprise all that was evil. There is no moral issue in this. The issue is which system will give our people more prosperity at home, whether in agriculture or in urban industry, which will give us the better chance of selling our goods in the markets of the world, as we must sell them if we are to maintain and improve our standard of life in this country, as we all want to do. It is no good just to hiss out the word "profit" as if it were the equivalent of "sin" and to think that you have proved anything thereby. It is not necessarily sinful to make a profit, especially in these days when the Chancellor of the Exchequer takes it nearly all away, any more than it is sinful to try to improve your position in the world so that your children may have better advantages than you have had yourself.

My friends, a few weeks ago I flew to San Francisco to attend the conference of the United Nations. The flight across the American continent was a revelation. I had never spanned the whole breadth of the United States before. Only on such a journey can you get an impression of the size, of the resources, of the wealth, of the United States, now the greatest industrial country in the world. You cannot make that journey, you cannot spend any length of time anywhere in the United States and escape the sense of vitality and confidence, freedom and frank friendship, which has become the birthright of the American people.

But, more remarkable still, the United States has transformed itself in a brief space of five years from a comparatively unarmed State, save for its Navy, to the greatest military arsenal and most formidable military power on earth. And as you contemplate this and reflect that the greater part of all development in the United States has taken place in less than a hundred years, you ask yourself how has it all been done? The answer is by enterprise, by courage, by taking risks, by competition; certainly not by Socialism. No country believes more firmly in free enterprise than the United States. They have less State control to-day than we.

The National Government stands for free enterprise and for the encouragement of individual initiative here at home, but these tendencies must not be allowed to develop in a way that conflicts with the public interest. Do not imagine that the choice before you at this election lies between complete State socialism, as expounded by the Socialist Party, and an anarchy of unrestricted private enterprise. Private enterprise and government control can and should exist side by side. Already in this country we have entrusted to public bodies the conduct of certain essential services. It was a Conservative Government which in 1926 set up a public board to undertake the wholesale distribution of electricity through the grid and in the same year granted a charter to the British Broadcasting Corporation. Our postal services have long been run by a government department.

There are certain enterprises which are by their nature public services though they may have been originally created by the enterprise of individuals. It should be for Parliament to decide whether enterprises or services of this type should be managed

z   353

singly or *locally* under private or State control. For my part, I would draw no rigid line. I would judge each on its merits. But there is a third and by far the largest category. These are the industries which, by their variety and diversity of character, call in a special degree for the qualities of initiative, individuality and imagination. It is just these qualities, displayed often in the past by small manufacturers, that have created some of the greatest industries in our land and have enabled us to compete successfully in the markets of the world. It is just these qualities which we shall most need in the post-war years. Here, it is clearly to the public interest that full play should be given to individual enterprise and leadership.

Unlike the Socialist Party, we are not wedded to a rigid economic doctrine, which takes no account of the diversity of our industrial system. We are as anxious as the Socialists that our national resources shall be fully harnessed to the task of supplying in abundance first the necessities and then the luxuries of life, but we do not believe that the methods which they suggest will achieve the ends we all desire. In a Socialist State the Government is in the position of universal producer, universal employer, universal monopolist. How then can it any longer act as referee or protect the rights of the individual citizen, who has become merely an employee of the State? Is it even likely that such an all-powerful Government will listen to criticism from its own civil servants—for that is what we shall all be, if the Socialists have their way?

It is the policy of the National Government to find a middle way between the extremes of completely uncontrolled free enterprise and bureaucratic tyranny. For instance, it is sometimes suggested that one has got to be either for or against controls, but really the issue is not as simple as that. Some controls and priorities are still useful, and should be kept; others will soon have outlived their utility, and should be dropped. We intend, if we are returned to power, to retain war-time controls only just as long as the necessity for them exists. When food and clothing are scarce, rationing and price control are the only means of preventing soaring prices and unfair distribution, but as soon as more abundant supplies are available, these controls can be safely removed.

Now take the example which is in all our minds and which troubles us most. The country is desperately short of houses, and the supply of materials and labour is insufficient to meet all our building needs at once. The Government must therefore decide which of these needs are the most urgent and allocate the available resources accordingly. This is just what we propose to do. Otherwise we shall find cinemas and hotels and war memorials being built, while there are still people without houses to live in. As building materials and labour are in short supply, it is also necessary for the Government to control prices. We do this to protect homes. And here I will give you the only pledge I propose to give to-night. We will do everything in human power to get the maximum number of houses in the shortest possible time.

To sum up, then, I am sure myself that we can continue to secure the advantages of competitive and enterprising business while at the same time protecting ourselves against its abuses. If you doubt the Government's sincere concern for the general well-being of the nation, examine, I ask you, carefully the extensive measures of social reform put forward during the war by the late Government, in which we took our full share. Read the White Papers on Social Insurance and Full Employment, study the Government's proposals for a national health service, and remember the great advance in education, which is already on the Statute Book.

We in this country must look to our own soil. Food is scarce here and in the world to-day. British agriculture must be maintained in a condition to enable farmers to get a fair return for their produce and farm workers a fair wage.

Our task now is to harness the immense energy and singleness of purpose which the nation has displayed during the war, to conquer the evil of poverty, ill health and unemployment, and to guarantee to every man, woman and child in this country the necessities of a decent life. It is because I am convinced that the present National Government under Mr. Churchill's leadership is best fitted to lead the nation in this great quest for peace and work for health and happiness that I ask you to give it your support on polling day.

Good night—to you all.

42

FOREIGN AFFAIRS IN THE NEW PARLIAMENT

During June and July the fighting continued in the Far East. British Forces maintained their advance through Burma to Siam. The Australians invaded Sarawak and attacked in the East Indies. Okinawa was cleared by the Americans. Japan was bombed on a terrific scale.

On July 26, Britain, U.S.A. and China addressed an ultimatum to Japan calling for immediate unconditional surrender or complete destruction; this was rejected two days later. By the beginning of August the Australians had trapped 50,000 Japs on Rabaul and the Americans had completed the mopping up of the Philippines.

August 6. Atom bombing of Hiroshima.

August 8. Russia declared war on Japan.

August 9. Atom bombing of Nagasaki.

August 10. Japanese surrendered. This surrender was conditionally accepted by Britain, U.S.A. and China the next day.

August 14. Final and complete surrender was later accepted from the Japanese, and announced in London, Washington, Moscow and Chungking.

July 17. Mr. Churchill, President Truman and Generalissimo Stalin met in Potsdam. Mr. Churchill was accompanied by Mr. Eden and Mr. Attlee.

July 25. The Big Three meeting in Potsdam was suspended and Mr. Churchill, Mr. Eden and Mr. Attlee flew back to the U.K. for the declaration of the results of the General Election. After the results had been declared, Mr. Attlee returned to Potsdam with Mr. Bevin for the conclusion of the Conference.

FOREIGN AFFAIRS IN THE NEW PARLIAMENT

AT HOME

July 5. Polling Day.

July 26. The results of the General Election were declared. Mr. Churchill resigned, and Mr. Eden ceased to be Secretary of State for Foreign Affairs after a second term of office of four and a half years. Mr. Attlee became Prime Minister and later Mr. Ernest Bevin was appointed Secretary of State for Foreign Affairs.

August 1. The new House of Commons met.

August 15. H.M. the King opened Parliament.

August 16. The Debate on the Address began.

On August 20, continuing the Debate on the Address, Mr. Bevin opened the discussion of Foreign Affairs. Two more speeches followed and then Mr. Eden, as the Member for Warwick and Leamington, made his first speech from the Opposition front bench.

I think I may be allowed to congratulate the hon. and gallant Member who has just spoken upon the vigour and eloquence of his maiden speech. It is clear that he has been at great pains to examine the subject about which he was informing the House, and I trust that many times in the future we may have the pleasure of hearing contributions from him. May I also be allowed to congratulate my hon. and gallant Friend the Member for Lancaster (Brigadier Maclean) on his maiden speech? We know that for a long period in the late war he carried out a personal service of the greatest value to the Allied cause, and it is fitting that he should be here now to help us with his advice. We are now in the third day of the Debate on the Address, and I confess, having listened to the greater part of it, that I have been much impressed by its quality, and by the standard of the speeches delivered, and I share with my right hon. Friend the Leader of the Opposition the feeling of confidence in the contribution that this new Parliament can make to the very difficult tasks that lie ahead of us. It is fortunate for the nation and for this Parliament that the Japanese war should have ended as suddenly as it did, just at the moment when the new Parliament assembled. It has enabled us to pass at one stride to the tasks of peace, and we are spared that anxious period when the Government would have had to make the maximum contribution it could to the Japanese war while at the same time trying to carry through a heavy reconstruction programme at home. I had always

357

thought that that period would be one of the greatest difficulty for the nation and I hope that I shall not be considered too tender to right hon. Gentlemen opposite if I say that I am glad that they have not got to go through that period and that none of us have.

As one looks round this Parliament one is impressed by the number of new Members on both sides of the House who have seen active military service in the war. I think that is an advantage to us all, and I think perhaps that it would have been better after the last war if, in the early period after it, we had had more here who had experienced what so many young Members of this House have experienced in this war. The Debate on the Address has ranged over a large number of subjects, and to-morrow we go back to general issues, but you, Mr. Speaker, have guided us to-day in indicating that we should concentrate, in the main, upon issues of foreign policy. Therefore, this is perhaps our most important day of all, for upon the successful solution of these most difficult problems depends our ability to deal with all our domestic issues which, heaven knows, are wide and complicated enough.

So I would like to begin my remarks on foreign policy by congratulating my right hon. Friend the Foreign Secretary—if I may still call him "my right hon. Friend"—upon the speech which he has just made. In its wide sweep, and in its breadth of judgment and in its forthrightness, it was worthy of my right hon. Friend, and worthy of the occasion. I wish him, cordially, all good fortune in the heavy tasks that now fall to his hands. He will be served at home and abroad by a most loyal and experienced staff. As a former Foreign Secretary, I should like on this, the first, occasion of speaking in Opposition, to pay my tribute to them. I know something about the diplomatic services of other countries, and I believe ours to be second to none. If I may say so, I think that their only fault is that there are not enough of them, but as my right hon. Friend has been Minister of Labour, he will know how to make up for that deficiency. He and I served four years together in the War Cabinet——

MR. CHURCHILL: Five.

MR. EDEN: Well, I was not in the Cabinet all the time. During that period there were many discussions on foreign affairs, but I cannot recall one single occasion when there was a difference between us. I hope I do not embarrass the Foreign Secretary by saying that.

MR. BEVIN: No.

MR. EDEN: There were no differences on any important issue

of foreign policy. My right hon. Friend helped me during those critical war years, and, in the same spirit, I should like to try to help him now. As my right hon. and hon. Friends and I see it, now when we are in Opposition—we cannot tell for how long; no one can tell—it will be our duty on these difficult foreign issues to ask questions, to make comments and occasionally, perhaps, to voice criticisms. But I can assure my right hon. Friend that we shall do so, being scrupulous to avoid, as far as possible, adding to the difficulties of his task. It seems to me that it is not our duty to emphasize the divergencies that may exist between us on foreign policy, but rather to state those divergencies frankly, in order that we may try to reach agreement as a result of discussions, so that Parliament may, in these difficult years of foreign policy, function largely as a Council of State. I am convinced that the greater measure of agreement there is between us at home, the greater will be the authority of my right hon. Friend abroad.

It is in that spirit that I address myself to one or two remarks which my right hon. Friend made during his speech. I am glad that agreement was reached to set up a Council of Foreign Secretaries here in London to prepare the peace, and carry through other tasks which may be charged to it. I ought to say, perhaps, in passing, that as I understand the position, the previous arrangement for meetings of Foreign Secretaries, agreed in the Crimea, may very likely be merged with this new plan. I have seen it stated that these suggested meetings in the Crimea never came to anything. That is not quite accurate. We did not have our summer meeting in London, because all three Foreign Secretaries were in San Francisco at that time. But the intention to have those meetings has never been changed, and I, naturally, greatly welcome this development as it now is. I welcome it, among other reasons, because I am sure that the task of preparing a peace, such as the Government and our allies have now to prepare, cannot best be done at one great assembly. The matter is too complicated; the work at a great assembly is too heavy for it to be done well. The right way to do it is by a permanent staff, who will serve the Foreign Secretaries, and by deputies who will replace them, and who will prepare the work for subsequent submission to the Government.

I have had this project in mind for a long time, and it was be_ cause I thought that we should work in this way, and not through some great peace conference, that at Moscow, in the autumn 1943, we suggested that the European Advisory Commission should be set up and should meet here in London. That was the first

359

occasion when the great Allies met at a meeting, other than heads of Governments or Foreign Secretaries. That body has been criticized for failing to achieve more than it did. It was a body that had to prepare the ground for others, and those who carried through that task never expected to get much credit. But they did valuable work for us in preparation of the Armistice terms and other matters, and I would like to pay tribute to the American Ambassador in London, the Soviet Ambassador in London and Sir William Strang for the part they played in the many months of weary work that was quite indispensable, if there was to be Allied unity in this period.

Now I come to further remarks which my right hon. Friend made. He said, in reference to the Mediterranean and the Middle East—if I have got his words right—that this was one of the most vital areas affecting the British Empire and Commonwealth. We entirely associate ourselves with that remark. If I may speak about some of these countries I will do so in turn, beginning with what my right hon. Friend called that most popular subject—Spain. I do not propose to make any political observations about Spain, only to make a suggestion. My right hon. Friend the Member for Woodford (Mr. Churchill), some little time ago, addressed a communication to General Franco which was at the time approved by the War Cabinet and if there be no objection, I think it might be useful if that document were, at some convenient early date, made public. I do not know what the diplomatic procedure and so on may be, but, if it were possible, I think it would be a good thing.

Mr. Churchill: It has been largely made public.

Mr. Eden: It was largely made public in the United States, but if it could be officially made public here, I think it would be a good thing, because I think it would serve to remove some of the misconceptions which seem to lurk here and there about my right hon. Friend's views on that subject. Now I pass to other countries, to the Mediterranean, and first to Greece. I agree entirely with what the Foreign Secretary said on that subject. I am glad that the Government have invited the Archbishop to come to London. I am sure that that is a wise thing, for the Archbishop certainly impressed my right hon. Friend the Member for Woodford and myself, when we saw him, as being one who possessed a physical stature, a mental stature and other gifts as well which made him the most considerable figure in Greece. I feel that conversations and discussions with him will be of assistance, in attempting to settle the tangled affairs of that country.

FOREIGN AFFAIRS IN THE NEW PARLIAMENT

I do not want to enter into any controversy about the past in regard to Greece. I would only say, for ourselves, that in all the troubled time in Greece, about which there is so much dispute, Greece has, at any rate, been the one country in the Balkans from which, and about which, everyone was free to comment as much as ever he liked. Indeed, this was done. Messages poured out from Greece without any kind of political censorship even at the height of the fighting and the worst of the period. That is something. I agree with the Foreign Secretary's words on that. My right hon. Friend and I spoke of this also at Potsdam. We should like to see other countries give exactly the same facilities. We ask nothing more. It is not very much to ask. Anybody can comment on our elections. Why should we not comment occasionally on other peoples? We cannot do any harm, unless there is some reason why we should not or which is not apparent to us now. With a situation such as we have in these countries, which the Foreign Secretary so well described at the beginning of his speech, it will be a gain to them and to Europe if there is as little as possible political censorship and as much as possible freedom to speak and criticize.

I want to say a word or two now about an important matter— the radio campaign which has been going on against Greece from Sofia, Belgrade, and, I think, Moscow, and the charge, among others, that the Greeks have aggressive military intentions against their northern neighbours. I am glad that the Foreign Secretary has arranged for this mission to go to that frontier. I am sure that is a wise step. I have little doubt what their report will be. Frankly any suggestion that Greece has aggressive intentions against her northern neighbours does not bear a moment's examination when you look at Greece's own military capacity. Some of this radio propaganda seems to have overlooked the fact that the Greek Army was destroyed in 1941, in playing a most gallant part in the Allied cause. It has, for various reasons, never been reconstructed. Greece's liberation is not so long ago. There have been internal disturbances in the country. It has not been possible to create an army that could form an aggressive force against anybody, certainly not against her fully armed northern neighbours.

If there is one country about whose radio campaign and criticisms of Greece I feel badly, it is Bulgaria. I have no sentiments of tenderness towards Bulgaria at all. Her record in this war, and in the last, was bad. In 1941, at a critical period, she allowed German troops to come into Bulgaria, which greatly complicated our task in trying to help Greece with our slender resources. I do not think that that country has any ground to speak as she does or for the making of claims against her southern neighbours. Treatment of our prisoners has been very bad, and she is not one towards whom we have any cause to feel tenderly at all. I also agree with the statement of Mr. Byrnes which, I understand, was endorsed by the Foreign Secretary to-day, about the present government of Bulgaria. We had, in fact, stated that that was the view of His Majesty's Government at the time of the Potsdam Conference. All that Mr. Byrnes, the Foreign Secretary, or anyone asks, in any of these countries, is that elections should be, as far as possible, freely held, and that the countries should be allowed to express themselves as they wish. If they choose one form of government or another we shall not complain nor, I presume, will the other side of the House. But what we do ask is that they shall have a fair chance of doing it. The Bulgarian elections cannot possibly be described as free elections or as giving a chance to candidates from all parties to play their parts.

One word about Yugoslavia, because His Majesty's late advisers have certain responsibilities there. We joined with our Russian and American Allies who recommended the recognition of the present Yugoslav Government, on the basis of what was known as the Tito-Subasic Agreement. That Agreement had in it very wide guarantees for freedom of the Press, freedom of political parties, and so forth. Not much has appeared in our own Press, but from what I can learn there is not now the amount of freedom there should be, if that Agreement is being carried out. In particular, at the time, the three heads of the Governments addressed a message to Marshal Tito, from Yalta, suggesting that it would be good if the National Council of Liberation could be enlarged at an early date to include members of the previous Parliaments, and that was agreed to then by Marshal Tito, but, so far as I know, it has never been carried out. I would ask the right hon. Gentleman who is to reply, whether he has any information about that in recent weeks. As we did recommend the recognition of this Government on the basis of certain assurances, we have a proper right to ask that those assurances should be fully carried out.

I turn to another country about which we are much concerned. That is Poland. I agree with the right hon. Gentleman that the most important internal issue in Poland now is the question of the elections—as in so many other of these lands—and that the elections should be free, and the world free to comment upon them.

FOREIGN AFFAIRS IN THE NEW PARLIAMENT

The right hon. Gentleman mentioned a number of assurances which the Polish Government had given them, and I think I ought to say, because I endorse what he says, that my right hon. Friend the Leader of the Opposition and I received the same assurances from the Polish Government when we saw them, and also the same assurances from Marshal Stalin about the withdrawal of Russian troops. All that is satisfactory. When I saw the Poles the last night before I left Berlin—not being quite certain I was not coming back again—I did not finish up the conversation as tidily as I ought to have done. I was not sure myself what the position was about the parties. What we asked from the Polish Ministers was that all four main Polish pre-war political parties should have a right to run their candidates in the election.

The right hon. Gentleman mentioned the Socialist Party, but the four pre-war Polish parties were the Socialist Party, the Christian Socialist Party, the Peasant Party, and the National Democratic Party. We know that the Peasant Party is in the Government; M. Mikolajczyk is there. We know the same about the Socialist Party; M. Stanczyk is there and is now, I understand, in this country. They also have complete freedom. As to the Christian Socialist Party, I do not know what their position is, and I do not know whether they have freedom to run their candidates. No one suggests that they are collaborationists, and we think they should have their chance. More difficult is the National Democratic Party. I was told by some of the Polish representatives that some members of that party had been collaborationists. That may or may not be so. I am bound, however, to say that Poland is almost the only country where no Quisling was ever produced. Even supposing it were so, I do not think it would be right that the whole party should be excluded from taking part in the election because some of them had been collaborationists or behaved in some way they should not during the war.

MR. SYDNEY SILVERMAN (Nelson and Colne): Was it not a Fascist Party?

MR. EDEN: No, I do not think I have ever heard that suggestion. I have always understood that term could not be applied to that party, but if the Government have other information I shall be glad to hear it. There is one small section of it which might be so described, but certainly not the party as a whole. It has been represented in the Government from the earliest days that the Polish Government came here. I ask that the Government should do what they can to ensure that they are all allowed to run candidates, always excluding those who have been collaborationists, if any, and to have a fair and free chance at the election.

I would like to say a word about the question of the Western frontiers of Poland. It is an immensely tangled and difficult question. May I tell the House my own feelings about it? I do not desire to commit anyone else, but this is a matter on which everyone is allowed to have his own opinion. There was originally the age-old problem of the Corridor. It was my conviction, and I stated it to the House in the last Parliament, that it was impossible to continue with the policy of the Corridor if there was to be enduring peace in Eastern Europe. Therefore, either you had to say to Poland: "You cannot have access to the sea at all," or the Corridor had to go and East Prussia had to go to Poland, save the Königsberg area, which goes, by agreement, to Russia. In addition to that, the Polish claim to Upper Silesia is a strong one. I think Poland should have it, and also some parts of the land of Eastern Pomerania. We were never really happy about the Polish frontier going even up to the line of the Oder. When in Moscow we discussed this matter and there was the question of Mr. Mikolajczyk going back to Poland as Prime Minister, we agreed upon words which said: "Land that Poland may desire, up to the line of the Oder." We thought it would be unwise even to go up to the line of the Oder or even along its frontier.

Now we have this further demand to go right through to the Western Neisse. I think the population was about 11,000,000 in the whole area, but let us take it as 8,000,000 or 9,000,000. I find it hard to believe that the Polish population who would come out of Russia will be much more than 4,000,000. There you have these agricultural areas of Germany, of immense importance to the feeding of Europe and its industrial areas, and I cannot see how the Polish population is going to be able to settle this problem, man these industries, look after that agricultural land and produce, as they should, food for the other parts of Europe. This question, I understand, will not be settled until the Peace Conference. I would only say to our Polish friends that as, last time, they made a mistake in insisting on going too far East, so this time, I fear, they are making a mistake in insisting in going too far West. I think it only fair to make that statement to the House.

Now I come to a word on the economic conditions about which the right hon. Gentleman spoke. I agree with his analysis of that problem. It is going to be a desperately difficult one not, perhaps, even so much this winter as the early part of next year, before the harvest is brought in. We have to make every contribution we can within our very straitened limits, and not so much because we want to be generous, but because, in our own interest, the economy of Europe should not collapse. We know how straitened are our circumstances and how small our contribution can be, with the best will in the world. I should be grateful, if the right hon. Gentleman is going to reply, if he would give us any further information about U.N.R.R.A. and its development and what the prospects are there. They have indeed a heavy task. The right hon. Gentleman referred to France and there, too, I would wish him all success in his endeavours. We hope they will be fruitful.

Then, I come to another country farther away, about which I want to speak for a few moments if the House will bear with me, because I regard it as a country of great importance because of the special responsibility we have undertaken there. That is Persia. In 1941 Persia became suddenly, as a result of Germany's attack on Russia, a most important strategic area. She was on our lines of communication, and the only route open to us save the Arctic route, the full story of which has never yet been told—a superb piece of gallantry by the Royal Navy and the Merchant Marine. Save for that, we had no route except through Persia. The Germans were fully aware of that, and did everything they could to sabotage our attempts to get supplies through that country. The result was a diplomatic duel, long fought out until the Treaties made between us and Persia and between the Soviet Union and Persia by which we got permission to station troops over the period of the war, and a number of other facilities, in return for which we undertook to respect the integrity of Persia and withdraw as soon as fighting was over.

Persia has loyally carried out these Treaties by us and the Soviet Government and, therefore, for some time past, I have been anxious that we should begin to do our part of the bargain. Although, strictly speaking, we were not called upon to withdraw until hostilities were over, we did recognize as long ago as the Crimea Conference, my right hon. Friend and I, that such a beginning should be made and it was agreed that the first withdrawal should take place at Teheran, both by us and by the Russians. It was further agreed that further stages of the withdrawal would be discussed at the Foreign Secretaries' meeting next month. I certainly think that it would be good if they were so discussed, because the Japanese war is now over, and there is no object for any of us to stay in Persia any longer; and certainly this country would like us to get out as rapidly as possible. We have only one interest in Persia and that is to see that country prosperous, united and strong, and the last thing we want is a recurrence of the practice of zones of influence and matters of that kind which there were in Persia long ago, and which made us so intensely unpopular in that country for a generation. I hope that the policy of withdrawal will be carried out by the Allies and carried out rapidly.

As to China, I wonder whether the right hon. Gentleman who is to reply can tell us whether the former Foreign Secretary and now Prime Minister of China, Mr. T. V. Soong, is going to carry out his intention of paying a visit to this country. It would be very good, I think, if he did so. He would have a great welcome here from the people of this country who understand what China has endured during the war years and are anxious to see China and the friendship which we have had for her in the years gone by as steadfast and enduring in the years that lie ahead. I endorse what the right hon. Gentleman said on the question of Hong Kong. I think the position taken up is a just and fair one, and one which everyone in this country would wish to uphold. What he has said has received, I think, the approbation of the House as a whole, and we feel that what he has said represents a foreign policy on behalf of which he can speak for all parties in this country.

I say only this in conclusion. I repeat my best wishes to the right hon. Gentleman. Every section of the House will endorse those wishes. Two successive generations have given of their best that the world may be free. This time, victory has come, together with this stark and unparalleled warning. I said at San Francisco that it was the world's last chance. I meant it in the light of the knowledge that we then had. We pray that the world will seize this last chance, and any efforts which the right hon. Gentleman makes wisely to guide and encourage it, we shall support to the utmost of our strength.

1946

Mr. Eden had not confined his Election Appeal to his constituency or his nation-wide broadcast to Foreign Affairs. It was significant that his vote in a three-cornered contest was 1,500 more than in 1935 when there was a straight Conservative *v*. Labour contest. Even during the war he had found time to attend to the problems of reconstruction at home. In many of his speeches in the country and in his speeches during Debates on the Address in the years 1940, 1941 and 1943, he had shown a deep insight into the needs of the future. Following the General Election, there was a number of By-Elections, and in each of these Mr. Eden took a part. First at Monmouth, which was won by Mr. Peter Thornycroft, and then at Bromley which was won by Mr. Harold Macmillan, he made his contributions to the attack upon the Government's declared policy.

Just before Christmas it was announced that Mr. Churchill would spend the first three months of 1946 in America for health reasons and that in his absence Mr. Eden would be Deputy Leader of the Opposition. In this capacity he led the Opposition in the House of Commons in the important debates on Coal Industry Nationalization, Trade Unions and National Insurance, and in the country at the By-Elections and at week-end mass meetings.

During the autumn and winter he became a Freeman of Durham City and was installed as Chancellor of Birmingham University.

43

THE COAL INDUSTRY

The King's speech on 15 August 1945 foretold the presentation of bills to nationalize the Bank of England and the coal-mining industry. The Bank of England Bill was discussed in the House of Commons before Christmas. On January 29, Mr. Shinwell, Minister of Fuel and Power, moved the second reading of the Coal Industry Nationalization Bill. Mr. Eden, as acting Leader of the Opposition, replied:

I have always regarded the right hon. Gentleman the Minister as an ardent controversialist, and one who enjoys the cut and thrust of debate more than most. In the light of that recollection of his previous performances, would he allow me to offer him my congratulations on the comparative restraint with which he has contrived to handle this subject which, unhappily, in the past has been the cause of no little controversy in this House? May I also be allowed to congratulate him on something else—on a precedent, which I hope the Lord President and Leader of the House will see is followed. The right hon. Gentleman told us, and rightly, in the concluding words of his speech that we had had ample time to consider this Measure. I take this opportunity to ask the Leader of the House to give the House equally ample time to consider other equally important Measures.

I shall not begrudge either the right hon. Gentleman or the serried ranks behind him any satisfaction that they can generate on this occasion; all the more so because I think it will not last awfully long. Nor can anyone who has watched the politics of this country for many years past deny that the miners of this country have been pressing for the nationalization of the industry. I certainly cannot deny it, because it is now nearly a quarter of a century ago, as the right hon. Gentleman the Parliamentary Secretary to the Treasury knows very well, since I stood before the electors in a mining constituency and was soundly beaten for my pains. What I am wondering now, and what I would ask the right hon. Gentleman and others who remember that contest to consider, is whether the nationalization that the miners want, or think they want, is in fact the nationalization they are going to get in this Bill.

We have had from the right hon. Gentleman some reference to the past, and he was pretty severe, as he was bound to be, on private ownership. He said that we on this side of the House were always saying that things had gone wrong with the mining industry between the wars and that this was under a form of nationalization. I do not think we have ever said that. Certainly I have never said that, but what I would say is that this industry more than any other in the land has been subject to political controversy and the victim of Government interference. Hon. Members may put it this way if they prefer, that Government interference has resulted, from their point of view, in better conditions than would otherwise have existed, but the point I am seeking to make is that no other industry in this country has been subject to so much debate, legislation, controversy and political upheaval generally——[Hon. Members: "Why?"]——I am going to deal with "why" in a moment. Hon. Members opposite think that the period of trouble is past, because the ownership is to be changed. I hope they are right. We shall see.

The Lord President of the Council made a little journey the other day on the other side of the Atlantic, and in the course of it made several speeches; some quite good, which got him into trouble with his own friends, and some not so good. Among the speeches with which I did agree was one in which he said that, in the past, the Conservative Party and the Liberal Party had had a responsibility for Measures of nationalization which had been put through in this country. The right hon. Gentleman is quite correct, and I presume he will not complain if, after our past experience of adapting industry to changed and revolutionary conditions, we examine this Bill for its effect on the industry and make that examination both stern and critical. The right hon. Gentleman said:

THE COAL INDUSTRY

"Let the argument be directed to the merits, and let the test be public interest."

Let it be so. We would choose no other battleground, and we are perfectly ready to credit hon. Members opposite with a sincere belief in the virtues of nationalization. Indeed I do not know how many times we have had those virtues put forward to us in political controversy. But the scheme put forward in this Bill is not, of course, nationalization in the sense, for instance, in which a State-administered Post Office is nationalization, and it is not syndicalism. The old cry which one used to hear of "The mines for the miners" has no place in this Bill.

MR. TOM SMITH (Normanton): The miners, as an organized body, never preached syndicalism.

MR. EDEN: It is a cry which the hon. Gentleman will have heard. I never suggested that he uttered it. I suggested that both of us have heard it, and that it has no place in this Bill. What this Bill proposes to do is to set up a State monopoly for the production of coal, and that is all. Are hon. Members opposite really certain that the bulk of their supporters are enthusiastic for such a monopoly; and are they sure that the evils of monopoly disappear, once it comes under the *aegis* of the State? Here we have this Bill of 58 Clauses and three Schedules and yet, from the national point of view, the most surprising thing about it is the issues which are not dealt with in it, and were not dealt with by the right hon. Gentleman. The right hon. Gentleman has told us very little about the future organization and working of the industry under this Bill. It is quite true that in this Bill with its many Clauses there is evidence of much work having been done and much effort devoted to arrangements for the transfer of ownership of the mines to the State. But there is nothing here to show how the industry is to be run when it is thus transferred. Surely that is the essential problem not only for the industry but for the nation?

The right hon. Gentleman made a very brief passing reference to the Reid Report and to the work of the Committee set up by my right hon. and gallant Friend the Member for Pembroke (Major Lloyd George) when he was holding the office which the right hon. Gentleman now holds. Speaking, without any of his expert knowledge, I must say I regarded that Report, and still regard it, as a most remarkable document. I have in mind particularly Chapter 6 and the conclusions of that chapter in which the contrast is drawn between the coal industry of this country and the coal industries of certain other countries. These conclusions are set out under 12

THE COAL INDUSTRY

headings with proposals as to what should be done for the betterment of the industry. The Bill does not tell us, and the right hon.
Gentleman has not told us, how the proposals of the Reid Committee, which I presume he endorses—the Coalition Government
did endorse it—are to be brought any nearer fruition by the transfer of ownership, which is all that this Bill does.

If the right hon. Gentleman will look at Appendix 1 of that
Report, he will see there the comparison between the coal industry
of this country and the coal industries of certain other countries.
That comparison—and here I think I must challenge the right hon.
Gentleman on his remarks about the conduct of the industry in this
country—shows quite clearly that up to the war of 1914–18, the
industry in this country compared very favourably with the coal
industries in all other countries, except the United States of
America, where exceptional circumstances existed. The actual
passage is this:

"Before the 1914–1918 war, the output per manshift in Britain
compared favourably with that of practically all the major coal-
producing countries other than the United States. In particular
it was higher than in the Ruhr which was Britain's only important
rival. This fact, combined with relatively cheap rail hauls from
mine to port, enabled Britain to dominate the seaborne coal trade
of the world."

I think it would have been fair when the right hon. Gentleman
was making his strictures on the industry, if he had referred both
to that fact, and to the fact that after the 1914–18 period there were
new circumstances, the payment of reparations for instance, to
what had formerly been British markets in France and Belgium,
from Germany, and the fact that a number of countries, which had
been our markets before, began to get their own coal. There was
the change-over from coal-burning ships to oil-burning ships, and
all kinds of conditions which I think might, in fairness, have been
mentioned by the right hon. Gentleman. If we are to face this
problem we should remember to put the picture as fairly as we
can. If private enterprise is always at fault, how can the right hon.
Gentleman explain the recent developments in the United States?
I am not referring now to the richer and happier coal conditions
as regards the actual mineral which exist there. But not only is the
coal production in the United States per man something like five
and a half times what it is here, but the extraordinary thing is that
during the war the improvement per output per manshift was just
about equal to our actual production. That is a very remarkable

and for us a very disturbing figure, and it cannot be got rid of by saying that every fault here has been the fault of private enterprise, because that figure shows exactly what is happening under private enterprise there at the present time.

I think the House ought also to consider some other figures which I have taken from the Reid Report and which I give to the House for the purpose of putting to measure the right hon. Gentleman's problem. In Poland, in the nine years between 1927 and 1936, the output per manshift increased by 54 per cent, as compared with an increase here of 14 per cent. In the Ruhr, as compared with 1925, the increase was 81 per cent., and in Holland 118 per cent. [*Interruption.*] The mines in Holland are not wholly State owned. Some are privately owned, and some are State owned. Some of the export mines are State owned, and some of the other mines are privately owned. The hon. Member can take whichever suit his purpose. I am not trying to argue on the basis of which mines are State owned and which are privately owned; I am trying to show that during that period those competitors of ours went ahead of us, whereas before 1914–18 we had held our own.

MR. T. SMITH: This is an important point. In making a comparison with a country like Holland, it must be borne in mind that the comparison is between a country with relatively modern new mines and a country which has been honeycombed with pits for 300 years. If the output of the Dutch mines were compared with that of similar pits in this country, the production figures would be different.

MR. EDEN: That is a very fair point, but it does not meet the situation in the Ruhr or in Poland, where the contrast is the same. I do not want to labour the matter; it is from the Reid Committee's Report, and is not my argument. I want only to point out to the House that this is a situation with which the Government must deal if we are to recover our position and that of the industry. The question we have to put to the right hon. Gentleman, and to the Minister who will reply to this Debate for the Government, is: How does the Bill, as it has been introduced, ensure that the British coal-mining industry will regain its position not only as an essential producer of raw material for our industries, but as a successful competitor in the world market? I want now to examine the organization of the industry so far as it has been revealed to us to-day. I apologize for referring so often to the Lord President of the Council, but I intend to quote him in aid for the purposes of my examination. Some years ago he wrote a book—a very good book from his point of view—entitled *Socialization and Transport,* in which he indicated that a board managing a public undertaking must be appointed by and clearly accountable to public authority; but he also insisted that it must be left, in every possible respect, free to conduct its operations on business lines. He wrote:

"The board must have autonomy and freedom of business management. It must not only be allowed to enjoy responsibility; it must even have responsibility thrust down its throat."

No one can pretend that is the position under this Bill. I shall quote from the Bill, and ask the Minister how he reconciles the Bill with what I have just read. Under this Bill, the Board has no autonomy. Its powers are not anywhere clearly defined. On the contrary, the right hon. Gentleman has given himself extremely wide and extremely vaguely defined power of control over the proposed National Coal Board, which is set out in Clause 3 of the Bill. I will read the provision to him, and hon. Members can decide how it squares with the Lord President's definition:

"The Minister may give to the Board directions of a general character as to the exercise and performance by the Board of their functions in relation to matters appearing to the Minister to affect the national interest."

What in the world could be wider than that? What does not appear to the Minister to affect the national interest? Almost any conceivable subject concerning the industry could be covered by that. The right hon. Gentleman must find a narrower definition than that if he wishes to say that the Lord President's book expresses his philosophy. May I make a suggestion? Right hon. Gentlemen on the Government Front Bench should read one another's books. It is clear that there is no clear line of demarcation in this Bill between the Board and the Minister. I ask the right hon. Gentleman to answer one or two questions about the Board. I had thought he would tell us all about it to-day, but he told us absolutely nothing about it. I had thought he would say: "Here is my board, with none of those discredited politicians on it." But he did not tell us who the archangels are. He did not give us a name or a hint. Is it possible that they do not want to come on to the Board? I can hardly believe that the Minister would have wanted to move the Second Reading of the Bill without telling us who were the Board.

I am driven reluctantly to the conclusion that he may not have been able to scrape them together before the appointed day. We shall be interested in these illustrious gentlemen when their names are put before us; but before they do come before us, may I ask the right hon. Gentleman one or two things about them? What is to be the security of tenure of the archangels when they come on to the Board? Are they to be removable at the behest of the Minister, or are they to serve for a term of years, and if so, for how many years? There is nothing about that in the Bill. I think we ought to be told, and I have a suspicion that these gentlemen might want to know before they join the Board. I know that discredited politicians would want to know. Will the right hon. Gentleman accept responsibility in this House for the Board's actions, or will he disclaim responsibility, as once or twice we have heard Ministers do in the past, for instance, in respect of the B.B.C.——

THE LORD PRESIDENT OF THE COUNCIL (MR. H. MORRISON): The right hon. Member for Bournemouth (Mr. Brendan Bracken).

MR. EDEN: ——a perfectly proper constitutional position in relation to the B.B.C. I want to know what will be the Minister's relation to the Board. Will it be like the B.B.C., or will it be like Mussolini? We must know where the responsibility lies. Will hon. Members be able to table questions to the right hon. Gentleman about the decisions of the Board? There is nothing about that in the Bill. Last Thursday the Minister made a speech in which he suggested that he did not intend—and he rather emphasized it again this afternoon—to put the mining industry in the hands of civil servants. He said this was a fair field for men with business capacity, and that in the hands of such men, the coal-mining industry would be placed. All I can see is that the Board, in practice under the terms of the Bill as it is now framed—and I ask for the contradiction from the right hon. Gentleman in due course if I am wrong —will be unable to initiate any policy at all, without reference to the Minister, which is important, having regard to the extremely sweeping powers laid down under Clause 3.

Let me take an example, and perhaps whoever is replying will tell me what the position will be. Suppose the Board, as the right hon. Gentleman indicated might well happen in many parts of the country, decide, for sound technical reasons that a pit must be closed, and that the labour in the pit must be transferred to a more productive pit, say twenty miles away. Suppose, and it is also not an unnatural thing, that the men concerned object to such a dislocation of their lives. What will the Minister decree? Will he reply that it is the responsibility of the Board and has nothing at all to do with him; will he overrule the Board; or will he leave it, in the

THE COAL INDUSTRY

perfect Ministerial parlance, that the case should be judged on its merits? Which is it to be? We have not the slightest indication in the Bill or in the right hon. Gentleman's speech. I have a slight suspicion that the right hon. Gentleman is trying to make the best of both worlds, that he is trying to tell those behind him that he could use wide powers to introduce the Socialist control of industry, while he can reply to critics over here that the Board is an entirely independent enterprise, only subject to general direction.

The truth is that this Bill is a new kind of animal in all nationalization experience. It is a hybrid animal. The main objection urged to the Foot Report was that it failed to provide any guarantee of technical reorganization or any safeguard for consumer interests. Can the Government really say that this type of monopoly can be justified on the grounds of the improved technical efficiency that it is going to bring? The Ministry was not really convincing about that to-day. He knows better than I that there can be no comparison here with, say, the water, or the gas services. He knows better than I, that you cannot even compare the coal-mining industry with Government factories producing on a war basis. The obvious parallel perhaps is in agriculture, in farms which vary from field to field. How is this Bill going to help the industry to deal with this state of affairs? I must warn the House. What we fear will happen, is what often happens to monopolies. The consumer will be fleeced in the interests of the producer, or the Coal Board will have to go to the Chancellor of the Exchequer for financial assistance to keep prices down and then the taxpayer will pay.

Will the right hon. Gentleman tell us something more about the £150,000,000. He said he was putting this in for capital equipment in the industry. I thought he was going to tell us something more about it but there was not another word. How did he arrive at that sum? It is a considerable sum even for these days. How has it been calculated? The Government just throw in £150,000,000 and say it is going to be spent in the first five years. How did they arrive at the figure? Has it been related to the vast sums which the Chancellor—as he knows only too well—has to find. Has it been related to what the right hon. Gentleman has to find for national insurance, for re-equipping other industries? Has the right hon. Gentleman taken into account the fact that he has committed himself to stabilizing the cost of living? Has he realized that we have to build 5,000,000 houses?

Is this really going to be done without a wages policy at all? I suggest, on the information we have now, that this £150,000,000 has just been thrown into the Bill as a frivolous piece of publicity. [*Interruption.*] All right, perhaps the right hon. Gentleman will be good enough to answer me on some of those points. I suppose the £150,000,000 is to be spent on partly re-equipping the mining industry. But where is the machinery to be obtained? According to my information, the output of the mining machinery industry in this country before the war was about £2,000,000 to £3,000,000 worth a year. What arrangements have been made for so greatly increasing the output of this industry as to enable even a small part of this vast sum to be expended? I suppose the Government have a plan? There must be a plan. How can they just put £150,000,000 in the Bill, and hope for the best? I want to help the right hon. Gentleman. Perhaps this machinery is to be got from the United States as part of the loan expenditure. That might be a good plan. But what I am saying is, that we ought to be told.

I turn to another essential aspect of this industry, to which the right hon. Gentleman only gave a passing reference, the question of export. There is no reference to the word "export" anywhere in the Bill. Yet it is true, as everybody knows, that coal remains potentially our greatest export asset. We are making great efforts, and the President of the Board of Trade is doing everything he can, to increase the export of manufactured goods. But supposing we could have a coal export of 50,000,000 tons per annum. What an immense contribution that would be to the restoration of our trade balance! On that, there is no difference between us, but how is this Bill going to facilitate such an export? Here I want to put to the Chancellor of the Exchequer, one point, on which we are not quite clear. There is a reference in the First Schedule to taking over wharves, etc. Is this confined to this country? I should like that to be confirmed because for obvious reasons it would not be wise to extend that principle abroad.

Now I come to the main contention the Government bring forward. The Minister said, in view of the past history of this industry and what has been happening, in view of the troubles of the past, and all the disputes, the Bill would be an advantage, because by it we are going to obtain a new psychological approach to these problems, and a new feeling in the industry. Nationalization has long been proclaimed as the objective of the Socialist Party. I hope the right hon. Gentleman is right in what he says about the new psychological approach by the industry, because if this Bill is to be judged on its results—and they will be regarded as serious to some of us—then, I am bound to tell him that, so far, there has been very little evidence to justify his hopes. The policy of nationalization was proclaimed six months ago. The Government then got their mandate, but there has been no favourable reaction so far, and no response to the Minister's appeals which have succeeded each other with increasing urgency and with increasing ineffectualness. The output figures continue to go down—more than proportionately to the decline in the labour forces. I hope what the right hon. Gentleman said will prove true, but that, time alone can show.

Now I must say a word about price policy, on which the Bill is disturbingly obscure. I must ask the attention of the House to this point. I thought, on my first reading of the Bill, that it was for the Board to settle its own price policy, because the Board is required to make coal available "in such quantities and at such prices as may seem to them best calculated to further the public interest".

Surely, it is possible that the Board, the Government, the miners, and the consuming public, might all have different conceptions of the public interest, in relation to the price of coal. As *The Times* points out, suppose, for instance, that the Board were to reject a particular demand of the miners for higher wages or other rates of pay, on the ground that it was against the public interest to raise the price of coal. There is nothing in the Bill, so far as I can see, to prevent the Minister of Fuel and Power from overriding the Board, by using the power under Clause 3 to which I have already referred, and giving "directions of a general character . . . in relation to matters appearing to the Minister to affect the national interest".

We want to know where, in this respect, responsibility would lie.

Now a word about the Consumers' Councils. The right hon. Gentleman was very proud of his Consumers' Councils. I think he must have had his tongue in his cheek. He is going to appoint those Consumers' Councils, and they are to be entirely responsible to him.—[An HON. MEMBER: "What is wrong with it?"]—It is horribly reminiscent of the burglar lending the householder his dog and saying: "There you are. Go and make the best of that one." Surely, at the very least, the Consumers' Councils should have the right to publish recommendations which they have made to the Minister, if the recommendations are not accepted. The House of Commons and the country should know what those recommendations have been. It is not provided for in the Bill. I understand that the right hon. Gentleman does not agree. I ask him to show me whether it is in the Bill.

MR. SHINWELL: If the right hon. Gentleman is challenging me——

MR. EDEN: I only want to know.

MR. SHINWELL: It is a persistent challenge. The right hon. Gentleman will be answered adequately and faithfully before the end of the Debate. We cannot answer every question straight away. The right hon. Gentleman is asking me why this point is not in the Bill. The answer is that it is impossible in this or in any other Bill to put in every precise detail of organization.

MR. EDEN: I did not want to challenge the right hon. Gentleman in an unfair way. I thought he said it was in the Bill.

MR. SHINWELL: No.

MR. EDEN: Then that is all right, and we are all clear. The position remains unsatisfactory, and will be a subject for discussion on the Committee stage on the proposals that we shall have to put forward.

There is another point in connection with prices. It is quite possible for the Government to differentiate prices between various classes of consumer. By favouritism in the speed and quality of delivery the Board could exert an immense influence on all the industries of the country which depend upon coal. The Board could influence profit and could influence location of industry. The Coal Board will itself, as the right hon. Gentleman knows, be the owner of a large number of plants in those coal-using trades. Is the Board to be free to discriminate against privately owned competitors? I ask this question because there is no Clause in the Bill requiring strict impartiality in price-fixing. Parliament in the past has been careful to include just such a Clause in Statutes dealing with monopolies. The Government must be familiar with that fact. In the Railway Clauses Act, the Docks and Harbours Act, and in any number of other Acts, there has always been such a Clause. There was such a Clause in the Coal Mines Act, 1930, which was introduced by the Labour Government. I want to know where there is any such Clause in the Bill, and whether the Government would consider inserting such a Clause?

I apologize for being so long, but there are many things I must mention on this subject. I come to the question of compensation. It will be more fully dealt with by my right hon. and learned Friend the Member for Hillhead (Mr. J. S. C. Reid). I will content myself with making the observation that, when introducing an experiment of this kind, the Government should be careful that the compensation should be fair and should be seen to be fair and in the public interest. [An HON. MEMBER: "Why?"] It is just as well to appear to be fair, but I do not want to put the standards of the hon. Member too high. I must say that I do not regard the arbitrary method of calculating the global sum as fair, or the freezing of the compensation money as in the public interest. This country is still the largest holder in the world of property overseas. I know that the Chancellor of the Exchequer will agree with me when I say that we should be careful before we lay down precedents for Government purchases of property. The most extraordinary feature of this proposal is that it deals with inalienable—I cannot get that word out. The right hon. Gentleman the Chancellor of the Exchequer, who is a scholar of King's, must dislike it as much as I do.

THE CHANCELLOR OF THE EXCHEQUER (MR. DALTON): I say "non-transferable".

MR. EDEN: I thank the right hon. Gentleman. It is not the first time that Cambridge has helped Oxford. "Non-transferable" is much better. What is the position? I ask the right hon. Gentleman to give us some explanation for this quite unprecedented procedure in our financial practice. If a company—and no doubt he will tell me later if I am wrong, but this is how I understand the position —goes into liquidation, the stock with which it is compensated becomes negotiable in the hands of the individual shareholder. He can do what he likes with it. On the other hand, if the company does not go into liquidation, its compensation becomes un-negotiable. How can that be called equitable or just as between two sets of companies? According to the terms of the Bill the stock is inalienable if the company remains and does not go into liquidation. The direction or the management of such a business cannot use its capital and business experience to launch out into any new enterprise at all. All it can do is to sit still and receive the annual interest. The *Economist* seems to express it correctly. I do not always agree with the *Economist*. I think it was at one time the pet paper of the right hon. Gentleman the Chancellor of the Exchequer.

MR. DALTON: No.

MR. EDEN: I hope that he will agree with me that this quotation seems a fair summing up of the position:

"If Mr. Shinwell"—I apologize for the reference to the right hon. Gentleman by name—"cannot pay for the mines without upsetting Mr. Dalton's drive for cheaper money, they should decide between them which should wait for the other."

That is a pretty fair statement of the Government's position. In
any event I would ask the Minister whether, in respect of those
companies, he regards it as a fair idea of a business transaction to
give a man a cheque for his property and then to stop it at the
bank? So far as I can discover, that is exactly the position in which
these companies will be, so long as they exist as companies.

MR. BOWLES (Nuneaton): Is the right hon. Gentleman not
aware that no company can buy its own shares, that the present law
is that no company can buy in cash the shares of its shareholders?

MR. EDEN: That is not the point I was raising at all. May I try
to give an illustration? Suppose, for the sake of argument, that I
have a picture which is valuable and rare. A gallery comes to me
and says: "That picture is of national importance. We want to
acquire it for the State." I say: "I am prepared to do that. Will
you appoint an arbitrator? I will accept whatever the arbitrator
says is a fair valuation for the picture." The arbitrator says: "I
think £15,000 is a fair price." Then, after the whole business is
concluded, the gallery turns to me and says: "That is all right, but,
of course, you cannot cash your cheque, and we cannot tell you
what interest you will have on your money." That is exactly the
position here. If my illustration is faulty, I should be only too glad
to have the error pointed out to me.

Let me try to sum up. For six months the coal industry has been
drifting, as the right hon. Gentlemen admit, rudderless, with the
tide of declining output. How long is it to be before the vesting
date? I believe there are to-day about 850 separate undertakings.
Everybody agrees that number should be reduced. Is it to be hoped
that the nine wise men of the Coal Board, in the few weeks between their appointment and the vesting date, can assimilate sufficient knowledge of the industry to take over active direction?
Why could not the Government put first things first? Why, before
the drive for production is under way, have they introduced this
intricate Measure with all its legal and financial complications over-
burdening the Civil Service, the National Board, and industry
itself, for two years with these secondary problems? The duty of the
Government was to free them to concentrate on the very material
problem of coal production. The case was very well put, not by any
wicked Tory but in a production by a Liberal Committee. It is
true they have been denounced since, but people are quite good
sometimes even when they have been denounced. They said this.
It is a quotation I would leave in the minds of the House and of
my hon. Friends below the gangway:

THE COAL INDUSTRY

"The real danger is that questions of valuation may give rise to a delay in the initiating of an adequate development programme at a time when the growing need is for an immediate increase in the production of coal. The real need of the industry, as has been pointed out in the Foot and Reid Reports, is to increase not merely gross output but output per manshift. In other words, to increase the efficiency of the industry the urgent need of to-day is to proceed at once to overtake the arrears in modernization of the mines which have increased during the war by difficulties of supply."

I maintain that that is precisely what we ought to do and that this Bill makes no contribution to that end. If the Government disregard that work, they cannot avoid responsibility for the utmost hazards into which our economy is likely to fall. The right hon. Gentleman himself gave, very fairly, a warning at the outset of his speech about that, and he has already received a warning against facile optimism in the utter failure of his appeal for an additional 8,000,000 tons this winter. There is nothing in this Bill which would lead any impartial critic to believe that the Government scheme is going to put the coal industry on to its feet. The right hon. Gentleman said the other day, perhaps in a jovial mood—I do not know, it was before Christmas—that after a forty-years' study of nationalization he had never realized the complexity of compensation. Let me tell him that this is going to be the least of his complexities. If he failed to foresee the minor difficulties of acquiring the ownership of the mines, what assurance is there that he has foreseen the major difficulties of running them?

I forecast that a year or two from now, hon. Members opposite, who so lustily cheered the introduction of this Bill, will be thinking of it as "the Act that nobody loves", and because this Bill will fail in its purpose, the Government must accept full responsibility for that failure, with all the repercussion I fear it will inevitably have upon our national life and our country's future prosperity.

44

OUR RELATIONS WITH RUSSIA

Following the Potsdam Conference of July and August the Foreign Ministers met in London in the autumn. A further meeting was held in Moscow at the end of December. The United Nations Organization met in London in January; during the meeting of the Security Council, Mr. Bevin and Mr. Vishinsky, Mr. Molotov's deputy, had some sharp clashes.

Mr. Harold Macmillan opened a two-days' Debate on Foreign Affairs on February 20. Late that evening, Mr. Noel Baker, the Minister of State, gave the House a survey of U.N.O. Mr. Bevin was to wind up on the second day. Immediately before him, and just after Mr. Seymour Cocks, who had opposed the Coalition's policy towards Greece and now criticized Mr. Bevin's policy on Greece, Mr. Eden made the following speech:

W e are drawing near the end of what has been a very important Debate. I shall not follow the line taken by the hon. Gentleman who has just spoken, or accept his invitation to answer a speech on Greece which he said I did not answer during the last Parliament. I will make only two comments on his Greek observations. It is not true to say that we went into Greece to prevent a Left government being returned. It is true to say, as the records will show, that we went there at the invitation of all Greek parties, including those of the Left. To over-simplify the Greek issue is to risk not presenting the facts fairly to this House.

OUR RELATIONS WITH RUSSIA

The Debate has been marked throughout, on the part of all Members who have spoken, by a sense of responsibility, and indeed, by a sense of anxiety as to the international situation which is now confronting us. Two reflections came to my mind, as I listened to my hon. Friends and to hon. Members opposite, as to the feelings which dominated our discussion. The first was the anxiety felt by hon. Members in all parts of the House, and expressed by the hon. Member for Broxtowe (Mr. Cocks), about the international situation in general and about Anglo-Soviet relations in particular. The second reflection was that there is in all parts of the House a deep fund of goodwill from which I can fairly tell the Foreign Secretary he can draw. All parts of the House have shown it.

I must mention one or two speeches, particularly the maiden speech yesterday of my hon. and gallant Friend the Member for Carshalton (Brigadier Head). All of them—and I hope the right hon. Gentleman will agree—showed a constructive desire to help the right hon. Gentleman with his formidable task, which he is shouldering with characteristic courage and determination. At any rate, it is certainly in that spirit that I shall try to address my observations to the House this evening. I have not been altogether happy about the form the Debate has taken. It is a pity, as my hon. Friend the Senior Burgess for Cambridge University (Mr. Pickthorn) said a little while ago, and unfortunate, that we have had to wait until the very end of the Debate to hear a statement of policy from the Government.

I did not understand, when the business was announced last Thursday, that neither the right hon. Gentleman nor the Minister of State would give us on the first day any broad survey of the international situation as, I think, we naturally expected. I do not complain of the right hon. Gentleman not doing it, because I know what a hard time he has, but I did hope that the Minister of State would do it yesterday. Instead, he gave us a very clearly stated account of the work of the different United Nations organizations. I do not want to be disrespectful, but, so far as that statement was factual, most of us could have obtained every word of it from a newspaper. I shall comment upon his statement in detail, but I think that the Minister was definitely over-optimistic in the view which he took.

As to the work of the various United Nations organizations, it is very difficult for those of us who have not been at the meetings to form a just assessment of what happened. The best which could be said about it is that I believe few organizations could have supported so severe a strain as the United Nations organization has sustained from the outset, and the fact that it has survived is an encouraging start.

It is equally true that those discussions have also left in the public mind what *The Times* this morning describes—I think, rightly—as a sense of great uneasiness. As I listened to this Debate and realized that it would be my task to sum up before the right hon. Gentleman the Foreign Secretary spoke, I was conscious of that position too. Though I am afraid I have inflicted far too many speeches on foreign policy in my time, I do not think I have ever known one where it was more difficult to offer some constructive suggestion in a situation which is, none the less, I am certain, troubling every hon. Member in this House.

If I may, I want to try to look at the causes of this unease and make one or two suggestions which might help to remove them. Let me start first with what, I think, troubles us all most—the present state of Anglo-Soviet relations. It has been said many times in this Debate—and I think with truth—that it is difficult for us to understand the profound impression that has been made upon the minds of the Soviet Government and the Soviet people by the wide and deep invasion of their land by the German armies and by the distress and suffering that accompanied that event. That is perfectly true, and it is perhaps difficult for an island people entirely to understand it because, despite the fact that modern inventions have resulted in our being militarily no longer an island, it is, none the less, true that our mental approach to this question is still the mental approach of an island people. Physically, perhaps, if I may, I could give one illustration. I happened to be in Moscow in the winter of 1941, about Christmas time, when conditions were about at their worst for Russia, and pretty bad for us at that particular phase of the war. During an interval in our discussions, Marshal Stalin arranged that General Nye and myself should go up to what our Russian Allies called the front—which was as near as they thought it reasonable for any foreigner to go, because they were always anxious we should not get into trouble—so that we could see the prevailing conditions in that area. I wish I could give to the House the sense I got—and several hon. Members in this House have seen many battles—of what the Russians were feeling about this German tidal wave which had not, perhaps, up to then, so far as they knew, reached the high-water mark, though it was only fifty miles from Moscow.

I am convinced that it is the scourge of that invasion—and not the only one in that country—which is the dominant motive in Soviet foreign policy. It does not excuse some things which I shall talk about in a moment, but it is there. Coupled with it is the memory that it was only 80,000,000 Germans who nearly dealt a mortal thrust to 180,000,000 Russians, and a determination that, so far as lies in the power of the Union, Germany shall not be in a position to do that again. That, I think, is the second dominant note of Soviet foreign policy. I say those things, not to excuse, but so that we may try, in fairness, to set out the position as it seems to be. The determination not to allow Germany to be in a position ever to do this again and this alarm—I think that that is the right word—which the near approach of the Germans to Moscow created, have resulted in Soviet determination to have as friendly neighbours as they can. And there, almost at once, their policy results in difficulties and complications for the Soviet Government's allies.

It often happens that those whom the Soviet Government think they can trust among their neighbours are not those whom the majority in those countries wish to govern them. That is undoubtedly true. Inevitable friction results, and it is really too oversimplifying the issue to speak like the hon. Gentleman the Member for the Forest of Dean (Mr. Price) spoke in the Debate yesterday. He complained of American reluctance to recognize the Governments set up in Roumania and Bulgaria. Russia, no doubt, regarded it as legitimate to set up those governments in those particular countries, but it is pardonable that other countries should have their doubts as to whether those Governments are truly representative of those countries. If they have those doubts, it is inevitable they should hesitate to recognize them.

Now a word about the relation of the Soviet Union with the other two Powers—ourselves and the United States. I believe that the Soviet Union is sincere when they say to us that they want to collaborate with ourselves and the United States, their two great partners in the mortal conflict from which they and we have only just emerged. I think, also, that the Soviet Union are sincere in wishing that the United Nations Organization should function. It can only function if there is a measure of understanding between the three great Powers. That far, I think, we are agreed. But here comes the rub. While Russia wants this collaboration—as I say, I am convinced sincerely with the other two great Powers—she appears only to want it on her own terms. That will not work.

Sooner or later, that must land us all into difficulties. It cannot be acceptable to the allies of the Soviet Union that the Soviet Government should just repeat that formula of the need for unity as a sort of abracadabra and then, having said it, pursue any policy she likes, quite regardless of the feelings or interests of those who have been her allies. That is the heart of the problem, and it is only right that we should fairly state it to our allies. There can be no true understanding between Governments which permanently stand a strain of that kind.

I hope I may be allowed, without conceit, to introduce for a moment a personal note. It is nearly eleven years since I first went to Russia and had my first conversations with Marshal Stalin, M. Molotov and M. Litvinov. We had very long, exhaustive conversations about the relations between our two countries, but I will not weary the House with an account of them. We afterwards issued a document which I would rather like hon. Members to look at again, because it is of interest in our present state of relations. I am not going to quote it except for one short passage which shows where we ought to be in our relations with the Soviet Union and where we are not at the moment. It says:

"The representatives of the Government were happy to note that there is at present no conflict of interest between the two Governments on any of the main issues of international policy and that this fact provided a firm foundation for the development of fruitful collaboration between them in the cause of peace. They are confident that both countries, recognizing that the integrity and prosperity of each is of advantage to the other, will govern their mutual relations in that spirit of collaboration and loyalty to obligations assumed by them which is inherent in their common membership of the League of Nations."

I say substitute the word "charter" for "League of Nations", and that is the basis upon which our policy with our Russian Ally ought to rest, but I cannot truly say that it is the basis on which it rests now. I am bound also to say—and I say it as one who has long been anxious for collaboration with the Soviet Union—that the fault, in the main, is that of our Soviet Ally. I am now going to give one or two reasons. I wish to take up the remarks made by the hon. Gentleman the Member for the Forest of Dean about the situation in the Middle East. He complained that our policy in Persia, for example, was to keep in power what he called the nobility—I will quote his words—those

"who have been to Eton and Balliol, to Harrow and Trinity, Cambridge, who know the Persian classics."—[*Official Report*, 20 February 1946; Vol. 419, c. 1174.]

That is all right, but let me tell him, incidentally, that knowledge of the Persian classics is not confined to what he is pleased to call the Persian nobles, any more than, so far as I know, a knowledge of the classics is very widespread among the same kind of people in this country. However, he is quite wrong in his definition of our policy. We have never sought to back one particular government in Persia, or, indeed, any particular government in Persia.

Here, I think, is the fundamental problem which the House has to face about these countries. We did not elect the Medjliss. The system under which the Medjliss is elected may not be a good one, but I am not responsible for that, and neither is the right hon. Gentleman the Secretary of State for Foreign Affairs. The hon. Member for the Forest of Dean asked: "How can you expect to have our conception of democracy in the Balkans and in the countries of Eastern Europe?" If he does not expect to have our conception of democracy there, why does he expect to have it in the Middle East? It suited his argument with regard to the policy of Russia in the Balkans, but he used an argument exactly to the contrary with regard to Persia. I will tell the hon. Gentleman what we have to face. In none of those Middle Eastern countries is there a democratic government in the sense that we understand it—a parliamentary one—nor is there likely to be one. The hon. Gentleman spoke of our attitude to the League of Arab States. I think that was a perfectly correct attitude—one of encouragement, but not of interference in their arrangements. We have tried from time to time to encourage these Middle Eastern lands to broaden the basis of their prosperity, to increase the wealth of those who have far too little substance on which to live. I know—and so does the right hon. Gentleman—that many times ambassadors—or some of us, at least—have given that advice on instructions, when we have had actual contacts with these people, but that is as far as we have gone, and the House ought to consider whether we would be justified in going farther.

MR. PRICE (Forest of Dean): Would not the right hon. Gentleman admit that, if we and Russia took action together in Teheran, we would get a somewhat different government there than there is now?

MR. EDEN: I am not sure about that. Let us look at this carefully. I think this is important and fundamental to our Persian policy. Supposing we and the Russians did agree that one party was better than another, is it really our business to impose that party on Persia, and ought we to? The hon. Gentleman will remember, for instance, that in the time of Edward Grey, in 1906, we tried to do that sort of thing. It was a terrible failure and we got ourselves absolutely detested by every section of the Persian people. If we ourselves, or in conjunction with Russia, said to any of these other countries: "This and that is what you should do"—in fact, in other words, if we tried to govern them—we would be opening ourselves to the very charges which were hurled at us yesterday by the hon. Member for West Fife (Mr. Gallacher). I think the Russian attitude is wrong. I think their interference in the internal affairs of Persia is contrary to the treaty they signed, and if we did it we would be acting contrary to the treaty which we signed. Persia should work out these things for herself, with any encouragement and assistance we can give, but without ourselves or our Ally saying: "This, that, or the other party is the one which should be put into power."

I apologize for that digression. There are one or two other things to which I would like to refer. I have one other point of criticism to make to the hon. Member for the Forest of Dean. I am sorry for talking so much about his speech, but it was one of great interest. I did not like the regrettable sneer at Congress. After all, Congress is the elected Assembly of the United States, and, anyway, this is not a very good time for such sneers. It is difficult to minimize the part that America can play, if she will, to help to lead the world at a time like this; nor, if I may say so in passing, do we improve our relations with one ally by sneering at another. In this present serious and anxious position, it is obviously the desire of His Majesty's Government to pursue a constructive policy, and to try and bring about an improvement.

I would like, if I may, to make one or two suggestions to the right hon. Gentleman on this subject. We would be glad to hear, if he can tell us, any information, first of all, about the general Far Eastern situation? I myself am not going into that; it has been touched upon by so many other speakers. But, coming nearer home, I would like to ask him whether he can tell us anything about the prospects of some form of closer understanding between the countries of Western Europe? I know what the earlier difficulties were. Until those countries were liberated, and until, in some cases, they had had their elections, they did not want to enter into commitments—I think rightly so—but now that period is passed, and, while nobody cares more than I do for good relations with the

Soviet Union, I cannot now or at any time admit that they have the right to complain if we choose to make arrangements with our near neighbours in Western Europe.

It is only fair that I should add, so far as I can remember, that no statesman of the Soviet Union has ever raised to me any objection to such a course. I have seen plenty of it in the newspapers, but I do not think any such objection was raised by any statesman of the Soviet Union. On the contrary, I can remember one particular occasion when the Soviet Union took exactly the opposite line and made it clear that they did not take any objection to our making such an arrangement. However, whether they do or not, we are obviously entitled to make such an arrangement, and it is clear to us all that it is in the interests of the peace of Europe that we should do so. Therefore, any information the right hon. Gentleman can give us—not forgetting that all these arrangements are allowed for and arranged for in the Charter itself—would be very welcome. There is no question of replacing the authority of the Charter.

Can the right hon. Gentleman tell us anything about the other subject which he touched upon—with regard to Germany and our policy towards Germany? I feel that perhaps one ought not to raise that question without trying to make at least one constructive contribution on the subject. I will try to make one. I believe it would be to the long-term advantage of Europe if the Ruhr were internationalized. I can see no disadvantage—although I do not know what the position is in respect of our allies—in our making that arrangement. Of course, that by itself would not be a guarantee of security in the West, but it would be a step which would assist to create a sense of security, and I can conceive of it being so worked out as to be to the economic advantage, not only of Germany's neighbours, but also of Germany herself.

There is one other matter to which I wish to refer before I close. There were occasions during the war, as the right hon. Gentleman will remember, when we had the opportunity of full discussions on foreign policy with the Prime Ministers of the great Dominions. Those discussions were of immense benefit to us. The position is quite unique in the world now. The Prime Ministers of the Dominions, and, of course, the Ministers of external affairs, have access to all the information to which we have access.

They know exactly as much as we do on every subject. Yet they bring to our problems a fresh mind and a different angle of approach. For my part, I was never so heartened by any experience during the whole of the war as by the meetings—which the Prime Minister and the right hon. Gentleman will remember, because they sat through them all—of the Dominion Prime Ministers held in London in 1944. If it were possible—I do not know whether it be so or not—to create the opportunity for another such meeting in the course of the next few months when developments and foreign policy are certain to be so important, and when the right hon. Gentleman's task is so complex and difficult, I believe he would find it of inestimable benefit.

Let me conclude as I began. We are at an anxious moment in the state of relations between the great Powers. Any hon. Member could feel the sense of that weighing on us while listening to this Debate. We have all pledged ourselves to observe the Charter which we drew up at San Francisco. If we carry out that pledge, not only in the letter, which is always so capable of argument and interpretation this way and that, but in the spirit, then the nations can move forward to an era of prosperity greater than has ever been known. My hon. Friend the Senior Burgess for Cambridge University was, I submit to the House, right in what he said in relation to the rule of law. Unless there is an observance of the rule of law none of our plans however well conceived, and none of our Charters however well drawn up are going to be worth very much. If we can work in that spirit our problems can be solved. But if we do not, there is a real danger that suspicion will grow, until it hardens into lasting misunderstanding. That is the anxiety which I feel to-day, which might be an immeasurable calamity for the human race. What steps the Government think it right to take to meet the situation is for them to say. I am not suggesting who shall see whom or when anybody shall meet anybody. That is for their initiative. There is the problem. With all our hearts and minds we seek to help the Government in their task. Any endeavours which the right hon. Gentleman makes to this end will have the support of the House and the people. From the bottom of our hearts we wish him God speed in his harsh task.

45

THE CONSERVATIVE PARTY AND ITS OBJECTIVES

Following the failure of the Conservative Party at the General Election, many party supporters clamoured for a new declaration of policy. As the Socialists' plans began to unfold and the results of Socialist administration began to be felt, there was an increased demand for an up-to-date statement of the Conservative Party's attitude to modern problems.

Mr. Eden made the first of his 1946 speeches on the fundamentals of Conservative faith at Hull on March 7.

Britain now has to face a grave financial and economic situation. It is the primary duty now of Government and people alike to find some solution to these problems, to find some new incentives that will in some measure restore the will to work hard and the desire to take risks, without which we cannot solve our problems. I will suggest a few.

Firstly, it is clearly a matter of the utmost urgency to increase the supply of consumer goods in the shops of this country. Of course, it is true that we have to build up our export trade in similar goods as quickly as possible, and that one article cannot be sold in two places. But it is possible to carry to excess the policy of diverting a fixed proportion of the total home production to the needs of the export market. It is essential in most industries that manufacturers should have a flourishing home market on which to base their ventures in competitive world markets. But, at the present it is even more important to increase the total amount of goods produced for both purposes, home consumption and export, and in particular to increase the amount of production per man week throughout industry. It seems clear that to-day the scarcity of consumer goods available to the home purchaser is having its effect in restricting production. This, in turn, will be reflected in our export achievements. A great measure of austerity will be inevitable for some time to come, but if you carry your austerity too far it will defeat its own purpose. That is precisely what is happening to-day.

Secondly, there is the problem of taxation. It is undeniable that present high levels of taxation are a serious obstruction both to enterprise and to productive effort. Present taxation rates freeze the development of new enterprise. They discourage the taking of risks, for it is impossible under existing circumstances for the prospect of rewards to balance the hazards that must be faced. The Government should regard it as a first charge upon their attention to achieve a substantial reduction of present rates of taxation. More than that, they must be careful when they succeed in achieving such reductions that they are so framed as to give the maximum incentive to initiative and to sheer hard work. Tax reductions must be framed, not on party political considerations, but to meet the grave and urgent economic needs of the whole community. They must, moreover, be based on equivalent reductions in expenditure if the existing level of inflation is not to be gravely increased.

My third point is this: that it is of great importance to clear away the fog of propaganda that hangs about the question of profits and their relation to wages. Even Mr. Herbert Morrison proposes to allow some 80 per cent of British industry to remain in private hands for some years. How can you expect private industry working for profit, to give of its best so long as the profit motive is continually held up to derision and defamation by every Left Wing propagandist?

I say that a profit honestly earned is as right and morally desirable as a wage honestly earned. Both are payments for services rendered. It is not an ignoble motive for a man to desire to provide for his wife and children fairer opportunities than he may have enjoyed himself.

The proper task is not to spend our efforts in decrying the immoral exceptions, but to recognize that a profit is as proper a reward for enterprise and risk-taking as a wage is for manual or clerical labour. It has for years been preached by the propagandists of the

Left that profits and wages are essentially at odds and that wages can only be increased by abolishing profits. The results of this foolish and pernicious doctrine can now be clearly seen.

Working people in many industries have been led to believe that there is some vast fund on which they can draw and which would enable them to obtain more even though working less. They have been taught by Socialist propaganda to believe this myth. But can a Socialist Government blame them if they expect it to be realized now? The truth of the matter, of course, is that it is only out of industry's rising earnings that rising wages can be paid. Capital and labour alike have a fundamental interest in increasing the productivity of industry. It is by increasing productivity, and only by increasing productivity, that either profits or wages can be substantially and steadily increased.

Therefore, let the political propagandists of the Left turn from their imaginary Marxist bogies to the real problem of immediately increasing the production of goods and services. For upon this the whole well-being of our people depends. Let the trade union movement continue to discharge, as it does so well in this country, the function of ensuring that organized labour obtains its proper share of the rewards of increased production. Given the continuation of the system of collective bargaining whereby this is achieved, surely it is the high duty of the trade union movement to concentrate next on the removal of all possible obstacles to the expansion of production in this country and on the encouragement of their members to a renewal of the effort of 1940.

Finally, we have need of a vigorous administration on the part of the Government. There are many practical and urgent problems of administration that merit their attention. There are many things that only the Government can do, which must be done before we can see a restoration of full output in British industry. I will give two examples.

Firstly, there is the problem of labour supply. Here indeed is a problem of supreme urgency for the Government to tackle.

Secondly, there is the problem of releasing management from some of the controls and restrictions that at present gravely hamper normal commercial planning. Of course, so long as vital resources remain in short supply some system of controls must be maintained, but let it be as simple as possible, let it be flexible and, above all, let it work with speed.

The number of Government Departments is many, the uncertainties as to final approval are numerous and perplexing. This problem needs to be tackled swiftly and with imagination. This Government declares its belief in planning. No one realizes the importance of practical planning for production better than the individual manufacturer, whose constant business it is. Yet at this moment his planning is undoubtedly being restricted and hampered by the operation of the Government's cumbrous and slow moving administrative machine. The truth is that the Government is attempting more in this sphere of day-to-day industrial life than it is in the power of any central authority to carry through.

Now I would turn to our more long-term problems. It is often alleged by our opponents that the Conservative Party lacks a policy; or, that if we have a policy, it is purely a negative opposition to Socialism. Nothing could be farther from the truth. We have, as I will endeavour to make clear, a policy that is both positive and practical. It is neither a watered-down form of Socialism, nor is it a doctrinaire opposition to Socialism. We do not base our policy on opposition to Socialism.

Our policy is determined by the practical needs of our people, and its relation to Socialism is of secondary importance. The fundamental political problem that faces us is that of the relation of the individual to the State. This is a problem to which every age has to find its own answer. It is not a problem to which one can give a simple answer in one sentence. It is essentially a problem of balance and evolution. The individual can only develop a full and satisfactory life within the context of a community. That much is clear. Only by participation in organized society can the individual develop into the whole man, develop his talents, his economic ability and his social life, or enjoy his relaxation.

Membership of a community carries with it obligations to the State in return for the benefits that the State can give. Complete individualism is an impossibility. Yet, on the other hand, complete State domination is utterly repugnant to our democratic traditions and to the whole political instinct of our people. The function of the State is to give the fullest possible scope to the free development of the individual, and it is to me anathema to hear it argued that the individual liberty exists primarily for the purposes of the State. We must, therefore, choose our course avoiding both extremes. This does not mean compromise. It means that we must find a just balance which is a very different thing from compromise. Indeed, it has been our genius for finding this balance that has been the foundation of our long history of political achievement.

It is our aim, as a party, to develop the science of government so that the full benefits that can be achieved by modern administration may be freely available to every individual. But, at the same time, we are determined to ensure that the fullest opportunity shall be given to the individual to lead his or her own life, in his or her own way. Nor do I believe that the way of progress lies in a change of our political system. I believe that a better world can come only when that world is peopled by better men and women. I believe that character grows in the environment of freedom and personal responsibility.

To turn now to the practical application of this principle. Let us, for a moment, review the problems of industrial organization. They are, indeed, in the forefront of political controversy, and let me say at once that anyone who expects the Conservative Party to produce an industrial policy that can be summed up in one word or even in one phrase will be disappointed. Our problems are not so simple that they will admit of a solution by such a single talisman. Slogans settle nothing. I know that the Socialists consider that the single word "nationalization" will solve all our economic difficulties. But when you examine this word "nationalization" which serves Socialists both as a common principle of political thought and as a comprehensive solution for practical problems, we find that its varying forms agree only in being negative. All that we can draw from the word "nationalization" is the abolition of individual initiative, individual enterprise and competition, and the establishment of a State monopoly. How that monopoly will be organized, how it will work, how it will solve the practical problems of industry is not made clear.

In reply I would say that in our industrial policy we will uphold the same principle as we maintain in considering the relations of the individual to the State. We will seek to achieve the proper balance between the organizing power of the State and the drive and force of free enterprise.

We, as a party, believe in free competitive enterprise. We believe that British industry can best develop if those who are directing its activities are left to act upon their own initiative and their own responsibility so far as possible in the conduct of their business. And we believe that the only true guarantee of efficiency, the only sound protection for the consumer, is that afforded by competition. But we do not seek to apply one single remedy to all our problems.

It cannot be gainsaid that over a certain sector of industry free competition in the traditional manner no longer operates. We have never denied the problems that this creates. It is clear that the

State must exercise some degree of supervision where the interests of the consumer are not protected by the normal means of competition. But State supervision must not be confused with State management and ownership.

Our approach to these matters is essentially practical. We believe that the manner in which the State should intervene in the development of these industries is a matter that must be decided in each case, on a wholly practical basis free from any doctrinaire considerations. By far the largest category in industry is that in which competition still remains and must be encouraged. These are primarily the industries which, by their variety and by their diversity of character, call for a special degree of initiative and enterprise. It is to the new industries and particularly to the quality industries that as a nation we must look.

Many new ideas which to-day are but tentative, even speculative, will develop into the great British industries of the future. As other nations overseas enlarge the scope of their industries, we here must concentrate more and more upon producing goods of higher quality, for it is in this sphere that our opportunities and our markets lie. It is in the provision of skilled labour and highly developed capital equipment that we have excelled, and must excel in the future if we are to expand our economic capacity to the full. In this sphere of new ideas and new development, the most important sphere of all, the fullest possible freedom for individual enterprise and initiative is indispensable.

And so I repeat that we of the Conservative Party have a policy that is both definite and positive. We avoid both the extreme of individualism, and the folly of total State domination. But this does not mean that our policy is merely one of compromise. We recognize that wise government and competent administration can bring increasing benefits to the citizens of this country as the science and practice of politics develop. But, at the same time, we will never forget that the fundamental purpose of government is to ensure the full development of the individual. Our aim is to harmonize the full development of individual tastes and talents with the desires and needs of the whole community. This, we believe, can be done. The pursuit of this end constitutes a policy to which we can devote our full energies. If realized, it will bring the organizing power of the State and the free play of individual enterprise into the service of us all.

That is our policy. That is our objective. It is in pursuit of those endeavours that we ask your help and work.

46

EGYPT

On May 7, Mr. Attlee announced that:

"It is the considered policy of H.M. Government in the U.K. to consolidate their alliance with Egypt as between two equal nations having interests in common. In pursuance of this policy, negotiations have begun in an atmosphere of cordiality and goodwill. The Government of the U.K. have proposed the withdrawal of all British naval, military and air forces from Egyptian territory, and to settle in negotiations the stages and date of completion of this withdrawal and the arrangements to be made by the Egyptian Government to make possible mutual assistance in time of war or imminent threat of war in accordance with the alliance."

Mr. Churchill moved the adjournment of the House that day and a Debate took place. Subsequently Mr. Eden asked the Prime Minister a number of questions about consultations with the Dominions on this subject. A further Debate took place on Friday, May 24. Mr. Eden who, as Foreign Secretary, had concluded and signed the Treaty of Alliance between Great Britain and Egypt in 1936, opened the Debate:

I think that the Foreign Secretary will agree that, in the last ten months since the accession of the present Government to Office, we, on this side of the House, have certainly not sought to promote controversy on foreign affairs. On the contrary, we have done what we could, not only in public speech, but in private action, to help the right hon. Gentleman in his task, the difficulty of which none of us would seek to deny. In stating that, I would like to make it plain that we are not, of course, asking for thanks or, still less, for favours for the course which we have pursued. We have simply pursued it because we considered it to be in the broad national interest. It is my conviction that, if a Foreign Secretary of this country, speaking in the councils of the nations, can speak with the knowledge that he has the support of all the principal parties in the State, his hand will, correspondingly, be strengthened. Of course, there will be occasions when difficulties arise, but, broadly, that is true, and, therefore, broadly, we conceive it our duty, so far as we can, to keep foreign affairs out of political controversy.

In passing in that connection, I would like to refer to what is, as the Committee may have observed, an interesting development in relation to the conduct of foreign affairs in the United States. In doing so, I would like to assure the Government that I am not making suggestions that they should necessarily follow the same course. It is interesting to notice that, ever since the San Francisco Conference, the American administration have always taken with them leading figures of the Opposition to the big international conferences. I have noted in the last few days, since the return of the American delegation from Paris, that a very powerful speech has been made in support of the Administration's foreign policy, by no less a person than Senator Vandenbergh, who is a leading Republican figure in the United States. I am not suggesting that the Government should follow exactly that precedent, least of all am I angling to attend any more international conferences of any sort; I have had enough. It is, I think, broadly speaking, in a democratic State an advantage that, wherever we can, we should seek to find agreement on international policy. In that spirit I turn to this Egyptian situation.

I begin by referring to the matters in respect of which, as I understand the position, there is agreement between us. There is no dispute between us as to the importance of the Canal zone as an artery of our Imperial life. Therefore, I am not going to take up the time of the Committee by explaining why I believe that Canal zone to be of vital significance. I use the word "vital" in its correct sense. In reply to some observations which I have seen in the Press, I would say to the Committee that it is not merely, or even principally—if I might have the right hon. Gentleman's attention for a moment——

2 6

EGYPT

THE SECRETARY OF STATE FOR FOREIGN AFFAIRS (MR. BEVIN): I am listening.

MR. EDEN: A question of the use of the canal in war. It is that the Canal zone lies in a unique strategic position, being, for all practical purposes, the junction of three continents. It is that which creates its significance, from the strategic point of view. As I read the recent Egyptian demand, and some of the statements made in this country, I have regarded as entirely unjustified, suggestions that the 1936 Treaty in some way inflicted humiliation upon Egypt, or was in some way derogatory to Egyptian sovereign status. That was certainly not thought by any one at the time. It was not thought by anyone in this House, and it was not thought by any Egyptian citizen. In fact, they all said the contrary. Not only did they say it then, but I shall show in a moment that they have said it many times since. So far as this House is concerned, the Treaty received unanimous assent, and the right hon. Gentleman the present Chancellor, in following me at the time, used words about the Treaty which I must say expressed my view then as they expressed his, and express my view now. He said:

"We hope that this Treaty will close for ever an old chapter in Anglo-Egyptian relations which was marked by misunderstandings on both sides from time to time and by certain apparent conflicts of purpose. We hope that that chapter is closed and that this Treaty is going to open a new chapter based on mutual respect, sincere co-operation and abiding friendship, not merely between governments, but between the British and Egyptian peoples themselves."—*Official Report*, 24 November 1936; Vol. 318, c. 268.

That is what the present Chancellor of the Exchequer said then. It was certainly my view of the Treaty at the time and the view of the Egyptian signatories who represented all parties in the Egyptian State. Therefore, I cannot accept the language which is now quite suddenly being used that this Treaty, which was then regarded by everyone as being made between two equal States without derogation of sovereignty, suddenly becomes something which, in some fashion or another, places Egypt in an inferior position.

Let me add this on that subject. Throughout the time that I was Foreign Secretary, on many occasions during the war when I went to Egypt I naturally discussed Anglo-Egyptian relations with Egyptian statesmen of all kinds. It is quite true that, once or twice, references were made in those conversations to the fact that, in due course, a revision of this Treaty would have to come about, and I have never disputed that. Indeed, it is provided for in the terms of the Treaty itself. But never was language used to me to indicate that the existing Treaty was in any way derogatory to Egyptian sovereignty. On the contrary, all the expressions on the point were warmly in another sense. In fact, this sentiment that the 1936 Treaty is in some way derogatory to Egypt, is quite a recent one. I have no doubt that it arises, in large part, owing to the continued presence of British troops in the great Egyptian cities after the end of hostilities.

Since the speech by the Chancellor of the Exchequer from which I have quoted, and which was made at a time when I was in Egypt in 1940, a Wafdist paper—and I mention the Wafd because it is, of course, very important in connection with these negotiations and the future of Egypt—has used words which I would like to quote to the Committee. I apologize for referring to myself, but I cannot help it because it is a quotation from the paper. It says that I was

"one of the most important factors which helped to clear the situation and adjust the account in the interest of Egypt and the restoration of her complete sovereignty".

That, again, is a reference to the 1936 Treaty showing that, at that time, the Wafd did not consider it injured their sovereignty at all. Another paper, *El Masri*, the paper with, perhaps, the widest circulation in Egypt—although it is not for me to show how a wide circulation and influence do not necessarily go hand in hand, said:

"The war has rather provided many links which emphasize the benefits of this alliance which tend to strengthen it in the interest of both parties. This is what is said and believed by every one of the delegates of both States who signed the Treaty in 1936."

I will not weary the Committee with more quotations, but that shows that at that time, at any rate, no one in Egypt, as did no one here, thought that the 1936 Treaty was derogatory to Egyptian sovereignty at all. It is no doubt true that Egyptian public opinion, like public opinion here, perhaps, has changed in a measure since 1940, but both Egypt and ourselves should beware of transient emotions if they run counter to fundamental truths which are really in the interests of the two countries. I cannot resist the conviction that, if the Government, after the conclusion of hostilities with Japan, had taken early steps to remove our troops from the great cities to the Canal zone, and had made it plain, at the same time, that they were prepared to negotiate a revision of the Treaty with a united front in Egypt, as we negotiated in 1936—I can only express an opinion we should have been spared these extreme demands which have now been made, the realization of which, I am convinced, is neither in the interest of Egypt or of ourselves.

Let me now say—because one must be fair about these difficulties where one knows they exist—that I know something of the technical difficulties in realizing the programme which I have suggested. I know something of the extent to which staffs have been built up in Cairo, and the amount of accumulated headquarters of various kinds which have been built up there, and I have no doubt that it was extremely difficult, immediately after the Japanese war, to make those arrangements. Still, I repeat that had those difficulties been overcome, and had the troops been removed, we would not have been faced with the demands with which we are now confronted. Let me say this about the 1936 Treaty. I feel strongly about this, because I maintain that the Treaty embodied a fundamental truth both for Egypt and for the British Empire. The security of the Canal zone is, at one and the same time, an Egyptian interest and a British Imperial interest. Therefore, I cannot accept the argument that British troops or air forces in the area of the Canal zone, remote from the large centres of Egyptian population, can really be regarded as a derogation of Egyptian sovereignty. There are parallels in other parts of the world. The United States continue to use bases in British territory, in the West Indies, at this time. None of us regards that as derogatory to our national status.

MR. SYDNEY SILVERMAN (Nelson and Colne): What about occupying London?

MR. EDEN: The hon. Gentleman says that if they occupied London, we would regard it as derogatory to our national status. That mentality shows a wrong approach to this question. First, it is not a question of occupation. If the hon. Gentleman had read the first Article of the 1936 Treaty, he would see that by agreement between the Egyptians and ourselves that was not the purpose for which our troops were in Egypt. With regard to occupying London, I have just said that, in my view, the great capital cities should be evacuated, and that is exactly what the 1936 Treaty did.

Let me give another example. The Soviet Union has sought and obtained the use of bases in Finland. In both cases, the American bases in the West Indies and the Soviet bases in Finland have been secured on account of vital strategic interests of the Powers concerned and for the freedom of their communications. The Panama Canal is in an entirely different position because the Canal zone is United States territory, but nobody doubts that the continuation of this state of affairs is not only an American interest, but a world interest. Nor, so far as I know, has anybody suggested that, on account of modern strategic developments or the discovery of the atomic bomb or anything else, the area is any less important than it was before. I come back to what I maintain is a fundamental truth enshrined in the 1936 Treaty, namely, that the defence of the Canal is an Anglo-Egyptian interest, using the word "Anglo" in the broadest Imperial sense. Neither of our great allies has ever denied that to me or to the right hon. Gentleman, nor has anybody else denied it, so far as I know.

Can that broad Imperial interest—the Anglo-Egyptian interest in the Canal zone—be secured except by the presence of an Anglo-Egyptian force in the Canal zone? That is a strategic question to which a strategic answer is required. I am no expert to give an answer to that. All I can say is that I know of no such plan. If there be such a plan, I think we should know it. I do not mean that the Government should divulge details of the plan publicly if that would be against the Imperial interest, but, at any rate, everything possible should be told us of the plan, and, at least, we should be told that there is a plan, if there is one. So far we do not even know that there is one. Here, perhaps I may be allowed to utter a warning, which it is easier for me to give without the responsibilities of Ministerial Office than it might be for the right hon. Gentleman on the opposite Bench. It may be thought that if the necessary preparations can only be made in advance, the actual movement of Forces can wait the sounding of the hour of menace. That may be strategically sound—I am not qualified to pronounce, although I have doubts about it—but I am quite sure that it is politically unsound and even politically very dangerous. What happens? When tension grows and peril menaces, it is not fair to put too much strain on a small country by saying at that very hour: "You must agree that danger threatens and you must let us come, publicly before the world, into your country in order to share with you the averting of that danger."

It is difficult for any country to agree to that, and if anybody doubts it they have only to look at the experience before this war, not as far away as the Middle East, but here in Western Europe. The right hon. Gentleman knows very well how impossible it was to get even the necessary staff conversations ready which might have enabled us and our French Allies to afford protection to their smaller neighbours. There is always the hope when danger draws nigh—and the less the power of a State perhaps the greater the hope—that the scythe of war will pass them by. That makes the temptation to find some excuse to say: "No, when the hour of danger comes." It was thus, in fact, that Hitler was able to take so many nations one by one. I am conscious of the right hon. Gentleman's difficulties, and I will say what I believe to be one of his principal difficulties. I know that many times successive Governments in this country have expressed their intention of withdrawing their forces from the great cities of Egypt and even, indeed, from Egypt itself, under certain conditions, and that for one reason or another, there have been delays. Of course, that is so, but Egypt cannot say that it is our fault that there has been delay in the fulfilment of the 1936 Treaty so far as evacuation from the great cities is concerned; it was certainly not our fault up to the time of the defeat of Japan. I cannot tell how the negotiations will go, and we shall be glad of any information that the right hon. Gentleman can give us to-day about the situation at the present time.

It would be wrong if I were to conclude what I have to say without stating what I would be inclined to do if I were in the right hon. Gentleman's place. I would advise the Government to complete the withdrawal from the great cities to the Canal zone at the earliest possible moment. I believe by doing that they will reduce the temperature. I cannot believe the anxiety of the average Egyptian is about troops and establishments he does not see in the Canal zone. It is about the troops he does see, as the hon. Gentleman said just now, and the staff cars he sees driving about the capital city, with all that it means. Secondly, I would make it plain to the Egyptian Government that, if a revision of this Treaty is to be agreed upon, it is in the interests of both countries that it should be negotiated, accepted and signed, as was the Treaty of 1936, by all parties in Egypt. I think that is important. Otherwise, we shall be in danger of making some arrangement which has no finality. I say that, not in any criticism of the authority of the present Egyptian Government. I say it because, if I remember aright—no doubt the right hon. Gentleman will check it—in 1935, before we began our negotiations, it was Sidky Pasha himself, who was not then in the Government, who first made the statement that the Treaty should be negotiated by a united Egypt and that all the parties in Egypt should come in. Therefore, I do not think he should be one to complain of that suggestion now. I believe it would immeasurably enhance the conclusion, if it is reached, if all the parties, including, of course, the Wafd, are in agreement about it.

Thirdly, I would make it plain—as I think it has already been made plain, if I understood the Prime Minister aright the other day—that any new agreement must, in the terms of the 1936 Treaty itself, provide for the continuation of the Anglo-Egyptian alliance. Above all, if I may make this appeal, I think the Government should do everything in their power to get this discussion back into its true perspective. This is not an issue of the British Empire against Egypt, nor is it an issue of rival national interests. It is a question of how these two countries, whose friendship has been tried and tested in war, can give expression in the revision of a Treaty to the reality, namely, that each has need of the other. We live in a troubled world. No one can pretend that international conditions are settled. In that troubled world we have need of Egypt's friendship, and Egypt also has need of the friendship of the British Empire. The task of the right hon. Gentleman is to find a new expression for that, an expression which will enable him, at the same time, to carry out the purpose of the 1936 arrangement; that is to say, to enable us together to ensure the security of a zone upon which the life of both our peoples depends.

47

GOVERNMENT AND INDUSTRY

Throughout the summer, controversy between the Government and the Opposition on domestic issues grew more and more marked. Even the Coalition measures, the National Insurance Bill and the National Health Service Bill, though the principles were agreed, aroused long and keen debate on major detail. The Coal Industry Nationalization Bill passed through the Commons and later received a number of improvements in the Lords. Housing progress and the policy of Mr. Bevan were debated more than once, but the Housing shortage did not abate. The Government's handling of the food crisis, and in particular the lack of information given in time, and finally Bread Rationing which came into force on July 21, gave rise to further stormy controversy.

In April, Mr. Wilmot announced the Government's intention to transfer appropriate sections of the Steel Industry to the ownership of the nation. This was followed by a critical campaign in the Press, and a Debate in the Commons six weeks later.

Parliament rose for the summer recess on August 2. Recent by-elections had shown no marked swing back to the Conservative Party, but had given them some encouragement.

Meanwhile Mr. Eden had, in addressing mass meetings in the country, urged the importance of the correct balance between Government and the individual.

In June he visited Bermuda as a member of the U.K. delegation to the Empire Parliamentary Association's Conference, which included representatives of the U.S. Congress. After the Conference, he went on to U.S.A. and later to Canada. Whilst in Canada he was given an enthusiastic welcome and Mr. Mackenzie King referred to him as "No. 1 Goodwill Visitor".

GOVERNMENT AND INDUSTRY

On his return to London he took part in the By-Elections and in the Debates on food shortages. On August 1 he attended a crowded meeting at Walthamstow organized by the London Conservatives, and made the following speech:

There will be no dispute, even in quarters friendly to the Government, that discontent with the Government's record in administration is widespread and is growing.

Many examples of this can be cited. The confused and contradictory orders that preceded bread rationing are unhappily familiar to you all. Many instances of this have been cited in Parliament and in the Press. I will add one more.

On May 2 the previous Minister of Food cut the sugar ration to the bakers by 25 per cent. He allotted this sugar to confectionery and ice cream instead. The bakers protested that the result of this cut must mean a greater consumption of flour, and this at a time when bread rationing was already threatened. The Minister, however, persisted in his decision.

Ten days ago Mr. Strachey reversed the decision of his predecessor and restored the sugar level to that which had ruled before May 2. No one will deny that such chopping and changing in a few weeks betrays a lamentable absence of proper planning, and the Socialists are always setting themselves up as a party of planners.

And then in Housing there have been many disappointments. I will give you one example in that field. The programme of temporary houses has been lagging painfully.

Last March Lord Listowel, the Postmaster-General, told the House of Lords, that the Government were "now contemplating the erection of temporary houses at the rate of 4,000 to 5,000 houses a month, a speed of construction in the off-season that will undoubtedly be accelerated during the spring and summer months". (*Hansard*, 13 March 1946. Col. 115.)

This acceleration was naturally to be expected, but unfortunately it has not happened. The figures for May and June are little better than those for January and February and worse than those for March and April.

These are the figures: In January and February 6,615 temporary houses were completed in England and Wales, an average of

3,307 a month. In March and April 8,019, an average of 4,009 a month. In May and June 7,133, an average of 3,567 a month.

Lord Listowel's forecast has not been fulfilled.

There is a reason for these repeated failures to put first things first. It is that the Government is absorbed in its pursuit of Socialism. There is no more unhappy example of the folly to which the blind pursuit of an ideology can lead an administration than the Government's decision to nationalize the iron and steel industry.

Let us look for a moment at the record and present position of this industry. There is no dispute anywhere that its contribution to the war effort was a proud one. Nor can it be denied that its contribution to our export trade is a great and growing one. In the second quarter of 1946 iron and steel exports exceeded exports in the second quarter of 1938 by 35 per cent in volume, and 120 per cent in value. During those three months exports of iron and steel were running at an annual figure of no less than £92,000,000. There is no doubt that if more coal were available the industry could do better still.

Furthermore, this is an industry which happily has a long record of industrial peace. There has been no serious dispute within the industry for a generation. Moreover, the industry has prepared and is ready to engage upon an important programme of modernization designed to equip it to play a leading part in our national economy in the coming years. And this is the industry which the Government now choose to threaten with nationalization and all the confusion and uncertainty which that sentence must involve.

The action is so crazy as to be almost unbelievable.

Some time ago Mr. Morrison said that the question whether or not an industry should be nationalized must be decided on its merits. The nationalizers must make their case. I do not quarrel with that, but nothing of the kind has been attempted here. No serious argument of any kind has been put forward to show that the country will benefit if this great industry is nationalized.

Either Mr. Morrison has gone back on his principle or he has been repudiated by his own colleagues.

As an Opposition we shall do everything in our power to prevent the nationalization of the iron and steel industry.

Now let me state our attitude to this industry. What would we do? We do not deny that in any industry of this fundamental importance, an industry which has developed such a closely-knit structure, there must be a measure of public supervision. There must be control in the public interest to ensure that the consumer is not exploited, for example, by excessive prices. But such control already existed before the war in the shape of a Government appointed body, the Import Duties Advisory Committee, who maintained a general supervision of the price structure of the iron and steel industry. It may be that the machinery of control which has been exercised by the Ministry of Supply during and since the war could be improved upon, and this problem we should have examined as a matter of urgency. But certainly we should not have gone out of our way to harass and impede the leaders of industry.

On the contrary, we should have done our best to assist them in carrying out their development plans.

Between 1934 and 1939 the industry had spent no less than fifty million pounds on the provision of new capital equipment. At the request of the Coalition Government they have recently evolved schemes for further development on a vast scale. We believe this further development, which could have been financed by the industry itself with the assistance of the normal capital market, could best and most efficiently be carried out by the industrialists who devised the plan. They alone have the necessary knowledge to carry it out. They would act, as they themselves would agree to be desirable, with the full knowledge and agreement of the Import Duties Advisory Committee, or any similar Government body established for the purpose.

Our method of approach to the iron and steel industry is based on principles which govern our attitude to industry as a whole. We accept that there is a field for State action in relation to our national economy and to our industrial life. But that certainly does not mean State ownership, for ownership is only one, and usually the worst, form of State intervention in the affairs of industry. We believe that it is essential to leave the day-to-day operation and management of industry in the hands of normal industrial and commercial management and to confine State control solely to what is necessary to protect the interests of the consuming public.

There is a further point which I should like to emphasize. State action in the economic sphere is normally thought of as wholly negative and restrictive. We think of State action as a matter of controls, licensing, forms and so forth. And, indeed, under the present Socialist Government it is not surprising that we should look on State action in relation to industry in this light. But I believe that should be only part of the story. Governments will be called upon in the future to exercise a restraining influence in some circumstances upon industry, for example, to prevent the development of harmful monopolistic practices.

There is, however, far greater scope for Governments to give positive and constructive assistance to industry. I am thinking in particular of that 80 per cent of British industry which even Mr. Morrison condescends to leave to private enterprise. There is to my mind no doubt that close and genuine co-operation between Government and private industry in these post-war years can bring valuable financial and economic benefits to this country.

I would like to give one or two examples of what I have in mind. Let us first consider international trading arrangements. The flow of international trade has been increasingly affected by Government action, both in the regulation of foreign exchanges and in the development of commercial treaties. This tendency is likely to increase rather than to diminish in the future. More than any other country, we in this island depend upon a free and steady flow of international trade, and I believe that the schemes for regulating international trade and international exchange that are at present being discussed can bring great benefits to this country.

On the other hand, there is no doubt whatsoever that a false step in negotiation can bring upon us dire disaster. In particular, the whittling away of Imperial Preference without any corresponding gain to this country and the Empire could do untold harm. It is of the utmost importance that the Government, in the long and complicated negotiations that will develop in the months which are to follow, should take British industry and British commerce fully into their confidence and should be guided by those who know from personal experience what are the best markets for this country, and what are the advantages we need to gain and the concessions that we can afford to give.

Then again, there is to my mind scope for improvement in industrial taxation policy. Sir John Anderson, when he was Chancellor of the Exchequer, made a considerable step in this direction when he introduced special allowances designed to encourage the installation of new capital equipment. No one will deny that British industry can survive only if it maintains its capital equipment at a level of efficiency and modernity that will stand comparison with any other country. This cannot be done at present punitive levels of taxation without willingness and anxiety on the part of Governments to frame their taxation policy so as to encourage rather than to discourage enterprise and industrial development.

GOVERNMENT AND INDUSTRY

We have, I said, taken some steps forward along this road, but the Government should consider as a matter of urgency what further help can be given to industry by these means.

Thirdly, the Government should assist private enterprise by the provision of economic information about this country and foreign countries, which only the Government can possess. The Central Statistical Office, established under the Coalition Government, is rendering a most useful service. We have already a clearer picture of the total economic condition of the country than ever before. And the work of the Office is developing. Clearly it is impossible for a man engaged in a single industry to have full knowledge of all the factors affecting the economic life of the nation. But his calculations on future production and sales must be intimately affected by general economic developments such as, for example, the probable level of employment or national income. This information the Government alone is in a position to provide. I believe that close co-operation between the Government and industry in this matter will be of considerable mutual benefit, both by allowing the Government to make plans for a high and stable level of employment throughout the country and for a balanced distribution of industry, and by providing industry with invaluable information for the planning of future production.

I have given you some examples of the constructive help that a Government can give to industry. How much better it would be for our national life if the Government would pursue and develop these and similar constructive aids to industry instead of abusing those whose responsibility it is to lead it, and threatening the industries themselves with nationalization.

In my observations on the iron and steel industry and upon the industrial situation as a whole, I have set before you our point of view. If you agree with this, then I ask you to join with us in an effort to ensure that these constructive policies are pursued and that a halt is called to the ever-widening scope of Socialist experiment. Even at the last General Election the majority of the people did not vote for Socialism. But if we are to save this country from the doom of becoming a Socialist State we have to marshal all our forces and proclaim our faith. If we do this boldly we shall not lack friends. We are justified in finding a measure of encouragement in the recent By-Election results. It is also encouraging to learn of the large number of branches that are being formed and of the enthusiastic membership which is joining our Young Conservative and Unionist Organization. Since the General Election 843

411

branches have been formed in England and Wales and another 215 are in the process of formation.

All this is good news, but we must regard it not as an excuse to relax our efforts but as a stimulus to redouble them. Much work yet remains to be done in reorganization and in policy. That work can and will be done. I feel sure that I can count upon you for a full share in a united effort which will carry our cause to victory.

48

RESTRAINT IN FOREIGN AFFAIRS

During the summer the nations of the world had prepared for the Peace Conference which was to be held in Paris in August. The Foreign Ministers of the United Kingdom, United States of America, U.S.S.R. and France had prepared draft treaties with Italy and the minor partners of the defeated Axis. After the Paris Peace conference had been in session for a few weeks, the United Nations had divided themselves on most of the important issues into two blocs, the western bloc and the Slav bloc. Outspoken comment was followed by outspoken reply and the glare of publicity went to accentuate the diversion of opinion.

Mr. Eden's first speech following the summer holidays was made at Watford on September 23. He said:

As you know, I have never considered that foreign affairs should be or need be an issue of party politics, and it is certainly not in any party strain that I speak to you to-night. None the less, the international situation is so much in all our minds that I make no apology for devoting the greater part of my remarks to that subject this evening.

We have all felt a sense of disappointment and growing concern at the course of events in Paris. I had hoped that after the four Foreign Secretaries had agreed the main points of the draft treaties to be submitted to the Peace Conference, progress thereafter would be smoother. It seemed reasonable to suppose that having agreed the main principles of their drafts together, the four would also co-operate with the body of the Peace Conference to secure a final agreement on these principles. Nothing of the kind has happened. On the contrary, the world has been the uneasy witness of a series of debates held in public with an unparalleled lack of patience or restraint. There may be some who consider that no great harm is done by such methods, and that everyone is in the end rather the better for a little letting off steam. There is something to be said for this method in special cases; there is nothing to be said for public bickering as a practice.

What makes it so particularly tragic in the present situation is that a little more than a year ago the armed forces of these same nations were dying together on a common battlefield. Are all the revelations of Nuremberg and Belsen, and the other camps of horror, where whole populations were murdered, already forgotten? And all this bitter controversy is taking place before the victorious powers have even begun to discuss the major issue of Germany. In such conditions it is foolish to seek to minimize the seriousness of the situation. It is profoundly disquieting. It is not so much that I see in this state of affairs an imminent threat of war. That is not the immediate danger. But anyone who reads the reports of the Paris Conference can judge for himself how vehemence and antagonism have grown with every passing week. In an atmosphere such as that every incident is magnified and every suspicion becomes a sinister fact. And so the area of controversy widens, while the more extreme the statements, the more certain are they to catch the headlines.

If you want an example of how those who speak the same language can misunderstand, it is only necessary to read some recent references in the United States to "British Imperialism". I do not propose to comment upon them in detail, for no answer could be more complete or appropriate than that which Field-Marshal Smuts gave in Aberdeen last week. I will only say this—the British Commonwealth is a family of free nations; free to stay, free to go. Admittedly, this has been a gradual development. It is still continuing throughout the British Empire. I cannot help thinking that the world has something to learn from this experiment. It is a melancholy reflection that there should be anyone among our American friends who clearly does not understand it yet. But in this there is also a warning of the pitfalls that beset international understanding.

I want to speak to you in the main to-night of our relations with the Soviet Union. In three great conflicts the Russian and British people have been allies. After two of them we fell away with unhappy consequences for mankind. We do not want that to happen again; yet it is happening now before our eyes, with no benefit to anyone. Let us see if we can make any constructive contribution tonight to mend this state of affairs. I observe that in a speech the other day, M. Molotov said: "It is a dangerous path to ignore the Soviet Union, or China or France in international affairs." Of course that is true: no one disputes that. So far as France and China are concerned, I well remember that we repeatedly proposed their inclusion on a variety of occasions while I was Foreign Secretary. I cannot recall any ardent support for these proposals from our Russian Allies; on the contrary, they frequently opposed them. So far as the Soviet Union itself is concerned, I am sure that the overwhelming majority of the people of this country has desired and still desires the most friendly relations with the Soviet Union. Nobody who knows the British people should doubt that for a moment. We have not forgotten, we never can forget, Russia's glorious contribution to the common victory. We know how heavy were her losses in men and material. We have a Twenty Year Treaty of Alliance with the Soviet Union. We have expressed a willingness to prolong that Treaty. We want to work with the Soviet Union, as with our other allies, in peace as in war.

If our Soviet Allies are building their foreign policy on any other premises than our friendship, as I fear that they now are, then they are building on a false reading of the facts. The British people are not fickle friends. But there is only one foundation for enduring friendship in international as in domestic affairs, and that is sincere co-operation based on mutual understanding. Can Soviet statesmen truly feel in their hearts that they have been acting in that spirit recently towards ourselves and towards our allies? I take one example, Bulgaria's preposterous claims against Greece. Bulgaria's record in this war and in the last is indefensible. It was Bulgaria's defection in 1941 by admitting German troops into her territory that immeasurably increased the difficulty of Greece's task in defending herself, with such help as we could give her, against Hitler's armies when they came to the help of Mussolini's defeated legions. The Greek campaign was thereby shortened and Germany was able to attack Russia in the end of June 1941. That date would have been earlier still but for Greece's gallant resistance and the Yugoslav *coup d'état*. All this is fully borne out by captured German documents and by the evidence of German generals at the Nuremberg trials. Russia knows all this very well. She knows that Bulgaria should be punished; she has many times told us so. Yet the Soviet Union is now apparently lending the full authority of her support to Bulgaria's claims that she shall be rewarded for her misconduct by the cession of Greek territory to her. How can our Russian Allies be surprised that such an attitude causes concern and resentment here?

But even this is not the whole trouble. Nobody in this country contests for an instant the right of the Soviet Union to any form of government she likes. We prefer our own, but the fact that Russian soldiers are Communists does not cause us to value any the less their magnificent fighting qualities or to forget that they played their full part in tearing the guts out of the Germany Army. There is no reason why the two ideologies should not live together in peace if both will accept not to back their fancies in every other land. Restraint may be difficult to practise, but surely this is not too much to ask as the price for enduring peace. If we found it possible in war, in order that we might defeat a common enemy, to relegate ideological differences to a secondary position, why cannot we make a like contribution in order to secure an enduring peace? This is every whit as important. Indeed, it was to win this enduring peace that millions in every country gave their lives.

Surely it must be plain to all that we cannot continue as we are now without consequences which may be fatal to all. What is required is a new spirit and a new approach. Only too often suspicions, however groundless at the start, harden into facts, and these facts in their turn breed new suspicions and so the vicious circle widens. A positive effort to dissipate these suspicions is required from the Four Great Powers. They cannot be content with the day-to-day wrangles of the Paris Conference and the Security Council. Unless and until the underlying suspicions as to their respective intentions can be shed by the United States, Britain and Russia, such meagre progress as it is possible to make on matters of detail has little value.

Let the victorious powers get back to the spirit which once animated them, the realization that another world conflict would involve the final destruction of civilization. I have no doubt that this is the sincere desire of His Majesty's Government, as of everyone else in this country. Starting from this point, let them and the Governments of the other Great Powers see what they can each do in their respective spheres to understand the susceptibilities of the other, to remove suspicions and to build up confidence. The fact that it is possible for Americans and Britons, for Russians and Frenchmen to work together has been shown in a limited field in the trial of the war criminals at Nuremberg. To extend this co-operation and mutual trust to the wider field of our political and economic relations throughout the world is no policy of weakness. It is a policy of common sense which must appeal to all who realize to what destiny the present disputes and misunderstandings are leading us. It is for the Governments to judge how such a new approach could be undertaken. The decision on methods must be theirs, but the objective is clear. It is the right and the duty of the whole world to call upon the Governments to make this new approach. Mankind has need of it.

In the meantime, while we strive all we can to improve relations between the great victorious Powers, there is a task nearer home, on which we can surely concentrate. The nations of Western Europe who fought together in the late war have special interests in common, both political and economic. Twice in a generation they have had to withstand the onslaught of German armies. It would be helpful and timely that these common interests should find expression in some agreement between them. There are, no doubt, difficulties, but given a common effort I am confident that they could be overcome. Such an arrangement should not be construed as hostile to anyone else. There are similar arrangements in other parts of the world. The American continent embodies them in the Agreement of Chapultepec and the Soviet Union also has arrangements with her own neighbours. The San Francisco Charter specifically provides for such regional agreements. Whatever wider European arrangements may later become possible, as we would all ardently wish to see them become possible, here is a task in a given area to which we can bend our efforts. By doing this we shall help to bring cohesion and prosperity to wide areas of Europe and the globe, and we should thus make a constructive contribution to a distracted world. And, who can say that the example may not be catching?

49

A NATION-WIDE PROPERTY-OWNING DEMOCRACY

The Annual Conference of the Conservative Party opened at Blackpool on Thursday, October 3. This was the first Conference to be held by the party outside London since 1938, and a large number of delegates both men and women, representing people of all ages and all walks of life, applied itself enthusiastically to a discussion of the elements of Conservatism. Throughout August and September there had been speculations in the Press and in other places about the possibility of the Conservative Party adopting a new name—New Democratic Party and Unionist Party were suggested. There was also a discussion as to an alliance between all sections of the Liberal Party and the Conservative Party; and about the advisability of a detailed opposition programme. But at the root of all the doubts and questionings lay the demand for a clear statement of the differences in 1946 between the Socialist and Conservative outlook on Domestic affairs.

Mr. Eden spoke in reply to a resolution ably moved by Mr. Aubrey Jones, the defeated candidate at the Heywood and Radcliffe By-Election. Two days later in his speech at the Mass party meeting, Mr. Churchill endorsed Mr. Eden's demand for a nation-wide property-owning democracy. Meanwhile this speech had been most warmly welcomed at the Conference and in the Conservative and Liberal Press. Mr. Eden had later enlarged upon his ideas for industrial policy at a crowded meeting at Liverpool.

In his speech at Blackpool, Mr. Eden said:

A good service has been done to the Conference and to the party by Mr. Aubrey Jones and others in tabling these Resolutions. Their point of view is not identical but their purpose is the same. They seek to give expression to a way of life for the British people under which industry may prosper and men may be free. I have noticed that much abuse has been showered upon our party previous to this Conference. Mr. Clement Davies accuses us of being too amorous. He indignantly repels our alleged advances. I respect his political chastity which I note is only equalled by its political futility. And then there is the Attorney-General. I never know whether he is coming or going. One day it is abuse, the next day it is apology. It is immaterial to us under which threat we live to-day. Our concern at this Conference is with ourselves. We are not supplicants to anyone. We seek to state our faith and by that faith we would be judged.

Until a few months ago the Socialist had one advantage in any discussion of domestic policies with his Liberal or Conservative rivals. He had a soverign remedy which he was always ready to put forward, nationalization. And as that experiment had never been tried in a productive industry in this country, the Socialist was likely to receive that benefit of the doubt which a man with a heavy cold will often extend to a new remedy, even though he knows in his heart that there is no escape from working the wretched thing through. But now all this is changed or changing. We are moving from the realms of advocacy to those of practical experiment. The nationalization of the coal mines is already law, and other industries are under sentence. Experience up to date is not heartening for the nationalizers. Progress in the coal-mining industry is not encouraging. The approach of the appointed day has brought no upward surge in output. We may be sure that, as the evidence of failure accumulates, the search among the more intelligent and less bigoted voters for constructive alternatives will grow. It is in this sphere that we have an essential job of work to do.

Long experience has taught us that to offer to the people any single panacea as the Socialists offer nationalization would be merely to delude ourselves and them. Life is not as simple as that. For the manifold and diverse problems that face us, manifold and diverse solutions must of necessity be required. But this I believe we can say, that there is one single principle that will unite all the solutions that we shall seek and propound. There is one principle underlying our approach to all these problems, a principle on which we stand in fundamental opposition to Socialism. The objective of Socialism is state ownership of all the means of production, distribution and exchange. Our objective is a nation-wide property-owning democracy. These objectives are fundamentally opposed. Whereas the Socialist purpose is the concentration of ownership in the hands of the State, ours is the distribution of ownership over the widest practicable number of individuals.

Both parties believe in a form of capitalism; but, whereas our opponents believe in State capitalism, we believe in the widest measure of individual capitalism. I believe this to be a fundamental principle of political philosophy. Man should be master of his environment and not its slave. That is what freedom means. It is precisely in the conception of ownership that man achieves mastery over his environment. Upon the institution of property depends the fulfilment of individual personality and the maintenance of individual liberty.

In a Socialist State, where ownership is the monopoly of the government, where everyone must rely on the State for his job, his roof, his livelihood, individual responsibility and individual liberty must wither and die. And so it is that we of the Conservative Party must maintain that the ownership of property is not a crime or a sin, but a reward, a right and a responsibility that must be shared as equitably as possible among all our citizens.

We believe, for example, that it is desirable to elaborate schemes whereby the private citizen and the returned soldier should be in a position not only to rent a house but to own one. We believe that the tenant farmer should be assisted and encouraged to become an owner-occupier. We would welcome schemes designed to enable the workers in industry to participate in its development and in the ownership of industry to a greater degree than they do at present.

How is this wider distribution of ownership to be achieved? There is one way in which it certainly cannot be achieved, and that is by mere redistribution of existing income. That field has already been pretty thoroughly ploughed over. The amount left, after deduction of tax, in the hands of all those earning £2,000 a year and over is equal to about one-fortieth part of the total gross national income. Therefore, "soaking the rich" is not going to benefit anybody. On the contrary, it may well be that we are reaching a state where excessive taxation of any section of the community will lead only to a reduction in the total amount of wealth produced. Incentive is necessary at all levels.

NATION-WIDE PROPERTY-OWNING DEMOCRACY

The fundamental condition for achieving a wider distribution of ownership is surely a great increase in the production of wealth in the country and in particular in the productivity of industry. The saving by an individual that leads to ownership can be achieved only where there is a sufficient margin of income over the requirements of day-to-day consumption. Recent developments in scientific methods of production and in the technique of industrial organization hold out possibilities of a very substantial increase in the rate of growth of our national income. But this will be achieved only by a united national effort. It does no service to this country to dwell as Socialists do, on the antagonisms between capital and labour, between individual enterprise and the function of Government. Rather we should concentrate on the essential unity of purpose between them that does exist and the harmony of operation that can be achieved.

It is becoming almost a commonplace to talk of Government, capital and labour as partners in industry. It is essential that we should make this conception a reality. It is no good Ministers appealing for a Dunkirk spirit in industry during the week and beating up the leaders of industry every week-end. I hope to have an opportunity to deal more fully with this aspect of our policy at Liverpool to-morrow night.

Our first concern then is with the national income. Our next is with the individual income. A national production drive will require extra effort from every citizen. The individual must therefore be satisfied that his increased efforts will bring him a commensurate reward and that a fair proportion of the money he receives will remain his to spend or to save. It must not be snatched away by a rapacious Chancellor or drained away by the burdens of ill health or unemployment. The feeling sedulously fostered for years past by Left Wing propaganda that increased effort brings no comparable reward to the worker is responsible for many of the difficulties that are facing us in industrial relations to-day. This myth must be dispelled.

The relation of individual effort to real earnings must be made clear. Essentially these are problems for industry itself, to be worked out through the traditional methods of voluntary negotiation. But this is not a matter that can be ignored by Government. It is for them to give the inspiration. At the same time I think we should do well to study the various schemes for co-partnership in industry, for employee participation in profits and so on, which have been attempted and many of which are at present in operation in this country.

There are many difficulties and possibly dangers inherent in some of these plans, but there are also, to my mind considerable possibilities that we must explore. Then in finance we should do well to recall Mr. Gladstone's injunction to allow money to fructify in the pockets of the people. This is the right policy for a free democracy, right so long as we can ensure that money fructifies in the pockets of all the people and that its distribution is allied as closely as possible to ability and effort. But it cannot be reconciled with excessive levels of taxation.

Finally there are the personal sufferings of unemployment and ill health which have so often led to the loss of hard-won savings. All parties hope that it will be possible in future to abolish mass unemployment. The Coalition Government produced a scheme for this purpose embodied in the White Paper of 1944. I believe that the methods set out in that Paper afford the best prospect we have known so far of countering the tragic effects of cyclical un-employment.

Similarly, the great schemes of National Insurance hammered out by the Coalition, which come as the culmination of the long development of contributory insurance in this country, provide every citizen with an income, as of right, to tide him over times of difficulty and interrupted earning. In the years to come, if we develop the comprehensive medical service, to which principle we as a party have given our support, if we can avoid mass unemploy-ment, if we can carry out these great schemes of national insurance, we shall have swept away many of the barriers to widespread saving and property owning which formerly existed.

There is to my mind no doubt that the present moment is one of the utmost significance for the future of the Conservative Party. The world in which we live has changed in the past few years to a degree which we cannot perhaps yet fully realize. The changes that are coming may be even greater and more radical. Now is the time to take stock and to readjust ourselves to the present and to the future so far as it can be foreseen.

The defeat that we sustained last year, grievous as it was, is in this respect a blessing, because it gives us an opportunity to re-define our faith and our political objectives, and to prepare our-selves for the long and crucial struggles of the succeeding years. We must not live in the past. As we walk forward into the age of atomic power and of increasingly rapid scientific development we must be prepared to adjust our ideas to the developing needs of the nation. Objectively, open-mindedly, we must draw guidance from the lessons of the past. That is one of the peculiar virtues of our Conservative Party. It was never more necessary than it is to-day.

There can be no doubt that we as a people have the power to achieve new standards of material prosperity that would have seemed unattainable barely a few years ago. By the full application of modern scientific methods of production and organization, developed not as a brake on, but in partnership with, the individual drive and initiative which has characterized our free enterprise system in the past, we can produce far more of all the things that are necessary and desirable for human existence. But, as this process develops, for develop it inevitably will, there is an increasing danger that we may find ourselves enmeshed in the cogs of our own economic machine. We may find that in achieving greater material prosperity we have lost far more in matters of the spirit. You cannot, to my mind, make a clear-cut division between a man's working life and his leisure time. If he is a slave at his work, he cannot be a free man away from it. We must have regard for the whole man. That is why I believe that the development of State Socialism will be fatal to individual liberty and responsibility.

But let us not, on the other hand, forget that the development of large-scale economic processes, of vast industrial units, will inevitably have just that effect, unless we take positive action to avoid it.

It is essential that the worker in industry should have the status of an individual and not of a mere cog in a soulless machine. To substitute the State for the private employer as boss won't give the worker that status. He will never have it under Socialism. Nor will he achieve it in the economy of the twentieth century under a system of free enterprise unless we are prepared to foster and encourage schemes for the distribution of capital ownership over a wide area, and for giving men and women a closer interest and share in the purpose and operation of the industry that employs them.

We cannot all be our own masters, doctors, lawyers, craftsmen, small-holders, shopkeepers. There has always been an important place in the economy of this country for those whom it is present-day jargon to describe as self-employed. May they continue to increase in numbers and to maintain their essential independence.

But let us not forget that in modern time the great majority of our people are employed either as wage or salary earners. Freedom for them in their employment cannot be the same as it is for the barrister or the costermonger, who is his own master, but it can be none the less real. The key to it, I believe, is knowledge. We must not be content that the work people in our industries should be mere units of labour. We must regard them as individuals who have a right to share in the knowledge of the common purpose of the industry in which they are working. If capital and labour are to be partners, they must be full partners, and labour is entitled to expect full information as to the achievements and the purposes of industry and the distribution of its fruits. Nothing less than this matches up to the needs of human personality.

I have been talking in broad general terms, but in the time at my disposal it has been impossible to do otherwise. It has been my purpose to describe what is the fundamental difference between the Conservative and the Socialist approach to the problems of this country, present and future.

We base ourselves upon the individual, upon the need to develop the individual personality. We recognize that the individual can develop only through membership of a living, united community. But unity is not mere uniformity; it can be created only out of diversity, only from harmonizing the desires, the aspirations and the efforts of the human beings who make a nation. Socialism says to a man: "You are a unit in the State. Work hard for the State, as the State thinks best, and the State will provide you with what it thinks you should have."

We say: 'You are an individual. Choose your own way in life and seek to develop to the full your own talents. If you do this, and if you are prepared to accept the obligations that are essential to life in an ordered community, then we regard it as the duty of Government to see that out of the fruits of your labour you can build a life of your own, for yourself and your family, and at the same time feel the satisfaction of sharing in the common purpose of a free society."

50

CONSERVATISM AND INDUSTRY

Parliament reassembled after the summer recess on October 12 to tidy up the loose ends of the session. The first session ended on November 6. During the last three weeks of the session the Atomic Energy Bill passed through the House of Commons, a full dress Debate took place on Foreign Affairs and the Government's plans for the Central Organization for Defence were discussed for two days. Mr. Eden spoke on the last debate but missed the Foreign Affairs Debate since he was away in Belgium leading a Parliamentary Delegation.

On Saturday, October 26, after returning from Belgium, he went to Plymouth and developed the theme of a property-owning democracy.

At the recent Conference at Blackpool I sought to outline the basis of our policy and to show how fundamentally it is opposed to Socialism. I would like to refer to that topic again this afternoon.

Our fundamental purpose is to achieve the fullest possible life for the individual. We seek to ensure for every citizen, irrespective of class, creed or political outlook, the fullest and freest life that can be lived within the context of an ordered society. Freedom does not grow of its own. It cannot grow unless the conditions in which it can flourish are established, and it can only survive as long as those conditions are maintained. The conditions are both material and spiritual. Unless a man can obtain the basic requirements of human life and unless he can be protected from the constant fear of want, he cannot be wholly free.

But, at the same time, it is quite possible for a man to live in conditions of assured comfort and enjoy no true freedom. This paradox is intensified by the development of the modern machinery of government. We are entitled to see in the potential organizing ability of government, and indeed in all the possibilities of modern large-scale organization, private as well as public, hopes of raising the standards of our people, and of freeing them from the ever-present fear of want arising from unemployment, ill health or the other accidents of economic life. But, at the same time, there is no doubt that an over-rapid or ill-thought-out development of all the powers of large-scale economic and social organization, public and private, can easily bring us to a point where, in achieving greater material prosperity, we shall have lost our spiritual freedom. The essential problem facing the modern world is to reconcile freedom and order. It is no new problem. It has been with mankind ever since civilization began. To each succeeding age it presents itself in a different form, and each generation must find its own solution. Wherever you may look you will see how in essence this problem, the reconciliation of freedom and order, underlies the struggles and the difficulties of statesmen and governments.

In the wide field of international relations it is the reconciliation of the claims of national sovereignty with the demands of international co-operation that sets the stage for all our discussions and deliberations. Similarly, in considering the domestic economy of this country, we find ourselves constantly faced with the problem of harmonizing the free play of competitive forces and of individual initiative with the organizing power of central government.

The two great political parties in the State, the Conservative Party and the Socialist Party, approach this problem from entirely different angles. Socialism lays its stress upon the material aspect and proceeds on the assumption that the solution of economic problems must automatically bring with it the solution of spiritual problems. The policy of the Socialists is already clearly declared. They believe in the nationalization of the means of production, distribution and exchange. This in practice, and it is the practice of governments rather than their theories that affects the lives of the common people, this in practice means nothing more nor less than State capitalism, the concentration in the hands of the Government and its satellite organizations of all the wealth of the community.

CONSERVATISM AND INDUSTRY

The Socialist claims that our problems can be solved by centring all ownership of property and productive power in the hands of the Government. Our view is diametrically opposed.

In a recent speech, Mr. Van Acker, lately Prime Minister of Belgium, said: ". . . in general the State is a bad industrialist, a bad salesman and a bad business-man."

Few who have had experience of Socialism would deny the truth of that. We believe that the policy of our Socialists is false on two grounds. First, the creation of a system of State monopolies is not the most efficient method of solving our economic difficulties. Secondly, this process would create spiritual problems and dangers even more harmful to our people in the long run than the economic difficulties that they seek to solve. Our ideal is not the concentration of ownership, but to spread over the widest possible field, and largest possible number of individuals. We believe that there are not too many capitalists, but too few. Our policy is based on achieving the widest and most equitable distribution of wealth into individual ownership.

I have defined our purpose to be to secure the fullest and freest possible life for the individual within an ordered community. To bring this about we must adopt two main lines of approach. First, what has been described as the establishment of a property-owning democracy. I believe that the existence of private property is essential to the maintenance of individual freedom. For man must be master of his environment, and it is precisely in the concept of ownership that he achieves this mastery. In a society in which every citizen depends for all his means of livelihood upon the Government, individual liberty, as we in this country cherish it, must wither and fade.

The second line of approach is this. Life must be taken as a whole. You cannot draw a clear line of distinction between man's working life and his leisure. If he is to have the status of a free individual, he must have it in his work just as much as in his leisure time. But the whole trend of the development of modern economy of itself militates against that individual status. The natural effect of the development of a machine economy is to depress the status of the workman in industry to that of a mere unit of production, It is for us to take the lead in finding the remedy for this otherwise inevitable process. I say take the lead advisedly, for this is not a matter which can be wholly solved by legislation, but on the other hand it will never be solved unless there is a lead from government. It is our duty to see that this lead is given.

CONSERVATISM AND INDUSTRY

There is one other issue that I must mention at this stage, for it is in effect a link between our two problems of the spread of ownership and the achievement of the status we want to see for the worker in industry. This is the question of productivity, or output, to give it a less pompous name. A substantial and steady increase in the output of industry and agriculture is a fundamental condition for achieving our purpose. A nation-wide property-owning democracy cannot be brought about by merely redistributing existing income.

That field has already been thoroughly ploughed over. The amount left, after deduction of tax, in the hands of all those earning £2,000 a year and over is equal to about one-fortieth part of the total gross national income. The truth is we have almost reached the stage where an excessive drag on individual incentive reduces the general standards of the whole community. A nation-wide property-owning democracy can only be achieved by a great increase in the production of wealth, and by ensuring that its distribution is closely related to ability and effort, and that savings, when won, are protected against the dissipating force of unemployment or ill health.

But, at the same time, the increased output that we need cannot be attained without the whole-hearted co-operation of all engaged in industry, in whatever capacity. I see that the Lord President of the Council recently admitted that "if production falls or stagnates, the cheques which the nation has already drawn on the future in form of increased wages and salaries, reduced hours, increased social services and a higher school-leaving age cannot be met".

That is undoubtedly true, but I must add: so do the Socialists reap what they have sown. All their plans depend upon output. But one of the main contributing factors to the present unsatisfactory level of output in industry is the persistent campaign Socialists have conducted for years past against extra effort and extra output. They have used every device to persuade workers in industry that increased effort does not bring increased reward, that extra toil benefits only the boss. Now they seek to make the people unlearn the lesson they have themselves taught them.

However keen the temptation, we cannot enjoy the spectacle of the Socialists "hoist by their own petard". For, if this problem of greater output is not solved, not only the Socialist Government will suffer, but the whole nation. It is the duty of every one of us at this time to make what contribution we can to raising the level of national output. It is the particular function of H.M. Opposition to criticize whatever is wrong with the Government's efforts. But also it is our duty to develop and propound our own alternative proposals. I will give you some of them.

The spirit of co-operation, which is the first requirement of success in solving our industrial problems, will not be achieved by the establishment of a rigid system of State capitalism. It will only be realized by developing a genuine spirit of partnership between Government, capital and labour.

Take, for example, the relations of Government and industry. The changed conditions of the present day make it necessary for the Government to play an increasing part in the economic life of the nation. Their duty is first to deal with some of the problems that would lie outside the scope of an unaided system of free enterprise.

Secondly, to assist in the task of obtaining the maximum benefits that can be won from the operation of such a system. The tasks of Government and industry are complementary. Their partnership should be based, in the words of a recent statement by the Federation of British Industries, "upon mutual confidence and forbearance, rather than upon domination and rigid control". The problems of full employment and of the distribution of industry, the achievement of balance and of steady expansion in our economy demands both the potential organizing power of Government and the thrust and drive of individual genius and initiative.

Then, there is the whole field of industrial relations in the narrow sense of relations between employers and workpeople. Here, too, our ideal must be partnership in the broad sense of the word, based upon mutual confidence and understanding, but also upon clear differentiation of function. The word co-partnership is much used to-day. But it is used from time to time in two different senses which may give rise to confusion. In the first place, co-partnership is sometimes used as a word to describe the broad concept of partnership between capital and labour in the common purpose of increasing production. But it is more often employed in a narrow sense with special reference to the various schemes for profit-sharing and workers' participation in profits that have been developed in this and other countries for some considerable time now.

To my mind, co-partnership in its narrow sense is, though important, only part of the whole broad problem of industrial relations to which I myself attach the broader term partnership in in-

CONSERVATISM AND INDUSTRY

dustry. The various co-partnership schemes that have been proposed and practised are worthy of our study.

But they are of less significance than the fundamental problem of capital-labour relations. The first essential of real partnership is mutual understanding. The key to an enhanced and more individual status for the workmen in industry is knowledge. We cannot build a satisfactory structure of industrial relations upon the present basis of suspicion engendered by misinformation.

All who are employed in industry are entitled to share in the knowledge of its operation and its purpose. All are entitled to be told how its resources are obtained and how its fruits are distributed. There has been during the war a great expansion of the practice of joint consultation between the two sides in industry.

It is of the first importance to strengthen and extend this consultation at all levels. There are, for example, gaps to be filled in. There are many examples of joint consultation machinery at factory level and at the national level, but as yet there is no adequate machinery for consultation at a level where similar problems affecting whole industries can be studied. This is a task to be undertaken. Moreover, machinery alone is not enough unless the will to operate it exists, and exists on both sides. Here the responsibility devolves upon management and upon the representatives of the workpeople, for it is they, and they alone, who can make joint consultation a success. The best devised schemes will not function if there is an atmosphere of mutual suspicion and hostility. This is not a matter, as I have said before, that can be determined by legislation; but, on the other hand, it is a matter on which we as a party must endeavour to give a definite lead.

It is no less important to ensure that, while partnership is based on mutual understanding, it is also based upon a clear differentiation of function. A team will not work unless there is a captain, and in modern industry it is essential to efficiency to maintain the authority of management. The purpose of joint consultation machinery is to ensure that management is fully aware of the point of view of the workers, and of how their interests are affected by managerial decisions, and on the other hand to make sure that the workpeople fully understand the motive and purpose of managerial decisions.

But it must be absolutely clear that the responsibility for taking those decisions and for carrying them through rests with management. Any blurring of this position can only militate against efficiency.

By these methods we can hope to realize a true partnership in industry between capital, management and worker. Meanwhile it is the duty of Government to strike that just balance between central planning and the free play of private initiative which will ensure to us the full benefits of both.

INDEX

(N.B. This index covers Mr. Eden's speeches only; it does not cover the introduction to his speeches.)

INDEX

INDEX

INDEX

Vichy Government of France, 104, 157

Vishinsky, M., 232

Wages, 376, 394

Wales, 149 ff.

War:
  threat of, 19, 20, 23, 34
  causes of, 64, 130
  world-wide, 154
  hatred of, 174
  effect on economic and social life, 48–9

War Cabinet, 137

Wavell, Field-Marshal Earl, 94, 126, 133

Welles, Mr. Sumner, 117, 138, 179

Western Europe, 388–90, 417

Wilson, Field-Marshal, 94, 274, 288

Winant, Mr. J. G., 117, 189

Yalta Agreement, 310 ff.; world press reactions, 322

Young Conservatives, 411–12

Youth, 16–17, 192, 351

Yugo-Slavia, 91 ff., 98, 133, 235–6, 318, 362; King of, 236

Zervas, General, 288